WHEN THE WOLF CAME

T0308782

The Civil War in the West

Series Editors: Anne J. Bailey and Daniel E. Sutherland

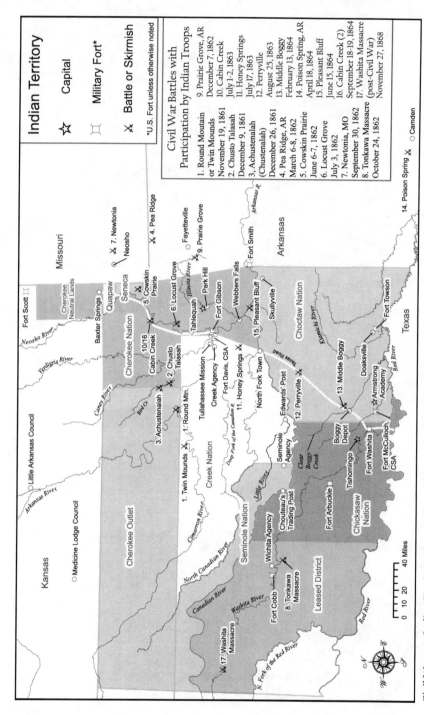

Civil War–era Indian Territory places and regional battle sites. *Map courtesy of Joseph Swain.*

When the Wolf Came

The Civil War and the Indian Territory

MARY JANE WARDE

The University of Arkansas Press
Fayetteville
2013

ISBN-13: 978-1-55728-642-0 (cloth)
ISBN: 978-1-68226-121-7 (paper)
eISBN: 978-1-61075-530-6

23 22 21 20 19   5 4 3 2 1

Designed by Liz Lester

♾ The paper used in this publication meets the minimum requirements
of the American National Standard for Permanence of Paper for
Printed Library Materials Z39.48–1984.

LIBRARY OF CONGRESS CONTROL NUMBER: 2013949293

CONTENTS

Series Editors' Preface

The Civil War in the West has a single goal: to promote historical writing about the war in the western states and territories. It focuses most particularly on the Trans-Mississippi theater, which consisted of Missouri, Arkansas, Texas, most of Louisiana (west of the Mississippi River), Indian Territory (modern-day Oklahoma), and Arizona Territory (two-fifths of modern-day Arizona and New Mexico) but encompasses adjacent states, such as Kansas, Tennessee, and Mississippi, that directly influenced the Trans-Mississippi war. It is a wide swath, to be sure, but one too often ignored by historians and, consequently, too little understood and appreciated.

Topically, the series embraces all aspects of the wartime story. Military history in its many guises, from the strategies of generals to the daily lives of common soldiers, forms an important part of that story, but so, too, do the numerous and complex political, economic, social, and diplomatic dimensions of the war. The series also provides a variety of perspectives on these topics. First, and most important, it offers the best in modern scholarship, with thoughtful, challenging monographs. Second, it presents new editions of important books that have gone out of print. And third, it premieres expertly edited correspondence, diaries, reminiscences, and other writings by participants in the war.

It is a formidable challenge, but by focusing on some of the least familiar dimensions of the conflict, *The Civil War in the West* significantly broadens our understanding of the nation's most pivotal and dramatic story.

Scholarly assessments of the roles played by American Indians in the Civil War have been mostly episodic. We know something of William Holland Thomas's raids in North Carolina and Tennessee. Mention of the massacre at Sand Creek often elicits a nod of recognition. The actions of one thousand Indian troops—mostly Cherokee—at Pea Ridge have received ample attention and comment. Nevertheless, most students of the war have only the vaguest idea of how that conflict unfolded in the Indian Territory or how it determined the fate of its people.

The classic study of the war in Indian Territory is *The American Indian as Participant in the Civil War,* published in 1919, by Annie Heloise Abel. Subsequent scholars have enhanced, amended, and expanded Abel's pioneering effort—most notably Laurence M. Hauptman, *Between Two Fires: American Indians in the Civil War* (1995)—but none has entirely supplanted it. And no wonder. It is a complex subject.

The peoples of Indian Territory found themselves in the midst of a war not of their choosing, squeezed between Union Kansas and Confederate Texas, with Confederate Arkansas as their eastern neighbor. They had no way to escape the conflict and no alternative but to suffer the consequences of the national upheaval.

Mary Jane Warde has devoted many years to researching and preserving the history of the old Indian Territory. Built on a solid foundation of published and unpublished sources, including such rich archival collections as the records of Cherokee, Choctaw, and Creek Nations, the present work demonstrates the impressive scope of her knowledge. From the removal acts of the 1830s to the post–Civil War readjustment of the western tribes, her sweeping narrative explores both the signal public events that marked that tumultuous era and the consequences for the territory's tens of thousands of native peoples. More than a story of the Indian Territory during the war, it is a strikingly new version of the standard story of the Civil War era, from the antebellum years through Reconstruction.

T. MICHAEL PARRISH
DANIEL E. SUTHERLAND

AUTHOR'S PREFACE

Even after 150 years we still live every day with the aftermath of the Civil War in the Indian Territory. Developments in neighboring states assured that the Indian Territory would be drawn into the Civil War, while what happened in the Indian Territory washed over into those states. The war in the Indian Territory also made possible the gathering of native peoples into this space now called "Oklahoma," which affected the national development of the United States. Consequently, at least ten states besides Oklahoma, from the Great Plains to the Pacific Coast, felt the impact of the Civil War in the Indian Territory.

As might be expected, this account describes politics, battles, leaders, and fighting men. It is also a personal history of the war in the Indian Territory. More than anywhere else, the Civil War directly involved red, black, and white people—men, women, and children—housewives, farmers, politicians, hunters, slaves, teachers, ministers, merchants, and doctors.

Fortunately, since 1934 the Oklahoma Historical Society Archives, now the Research Division, has been the guardian of much documentation of the Civil War and its impact on the Trans-Mississippi West. This includes Indian national and tribal records, the manuscript and historic map collections, the oral history collections, and the photograph and newspaper archives. The Friends of the Oklahoma Historical Society Archives, founded in 1996, understand the importance of not only maintaining that wealth of historical information but also of adding to it. We Friends also remember decades of service the staff has extended to scholars working on the next publication, genealogists tracking an ancestor, History Day students learning how to research a topic, and tribal people searching for recordings of old songs in danger of being lost forever.

This book, then, has been a collegial effort of the Friends, scholars, and Indian people who know, love, and value our history. We want to continue the work of collecting historical materials as they are discovered or generated today, preserving them, and making them accessible as technology changes. We hope this book will serve two purposes: educating those who want to know more about the causes, events, and long-term impact of the Civil War in the Indian Territory and generating supplemental funding to support the work the Oklahoma Historical Society Archives staff began more than seven decades ago.

Many, many people encouraged me in this project, and I will be forever grateful to them. The idea for this book was born in classes I taught for the Osher Lifelong Learning Institute. Special thanks go to William D. Welge, then director of the Oklahoma Historical Society Research Division; Chad Williams, his successor; and the Photo Archives staff. John Phillips and the staff at Edmon Low Library, Oklahoma State University, have been helpful as always. Those who supported the project on faith include the Friends Board of Directors and President Denise Dennison. Fellow Friends Roberta Clardy, *North Tulsa Magazine*; Sammie Dennison Harmon (Osage); and Dr. Alvin O. Turner read the manuscript with the professional eye of the editor, writer, and historian. Sammie, Roberta, and my son Chris Warde went along on road trips to Civil War sites. Louis F. Burns, or Hula Kiheka (1920–2012), a geographer, historian, and Osage elder whose grandfathers were Civil War veterans, also read the manuscript and gave it and me his special blessing.

Aho, mvto, wado—thank you, each and every one.

SPECIAL ACKNOWLEDGMENTS

Louis F. Burns (Osage)

Roberta Clardy, *North Tulsa Magazine*

Dr. Blue Clark (Muscogee Creek), Oklahoma City University

Dr. Bill Corbett, Northeastern Oklahoma University, Tahlequah

Dr. Clyde Ellis, Elon College, North Carolina

Sammie Dennison Harmon (Osage)

Dr. Patricia Loughlin, Central State University, Edmond, Oklahoma

Former Sac and Fox Nation chief Mary F. McCormick (Seminole-Sac and Fox)

Judith Michener, C.A.

Bob Rea, Oklahoma Historical Society

Dr. Myra Alexander Starr (Muscogee Creek)

Dr. Alvin O. Turner, Oklahoma Historians Hall of Fame

William D. Welge, C.A., Oklahoma Historical Society

Peace Chief Gordon Yellowman (Cheyenne), Cheyenne and Arapaho Tribes

WHEN THE WOLF CAME

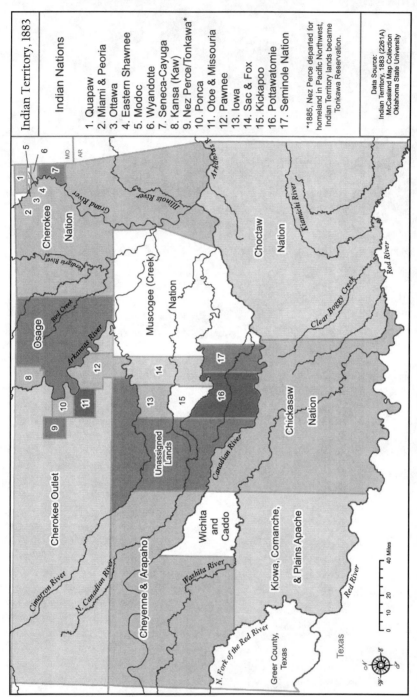

Indian Territory reservations and remaining homelands, 1883. *Map courtesy of Joseph Swain.*

CHAPTER ONE

Men and Things Are Changing Fast

On March 19, 1860, Israel Folsom, a Cumberland Presbyterian minister active in Choctaw politics, wrote to his friend Peter P. Pitchlynn, then representing the Choctaw Nation in Washington, D.C., "Rapidly do men of all classes seem to be losing confidence in each other. It seems men & things are changing fast." Noting that the white Christian missionaries were involving themselves in Choctaw Nation politics, he continued, "Surely as you say the whites will eat up & consume the Red Men where ever they come in contact with them."[1] This letter and his other writings suggest that Israel Folsom never forgot the injustices in past Indian-white relations, particularly the forced removal of his people from their old Mississippi homeland in the 1830s. Although his primary concern was Choctaw Nation affairs and current disagreements over its latest constitution, Folsom, along with many Indians who lived in the territory, kept a wary eye on developments in "the States," as the Indians called them. They knew the southern states were threatening secession if Abraham Lincoln was elected president in November and that trouble might then spill over onto their Indian neighbors.[2] Indeed, they were right. Within months the United States slid into civil war that engulfed the Indian nations, too.

Too often, histories of that Civil War either ignore or skim over events and conditions west of the Mississippi River between 1861 and 1865. That is somewhat understandable because the largest campaigns and battles took place hundreds of miles away in the eastern United States. The Indian Territory, along with its nearest neighbors—the frontier states of Kansas, Missouri, Arkansas, and Texas—are seen as a backwater of the conflict. However, for the people of the Indian Territory the war was a catastrophe. Indian peoples of the territory, as well as some that would be removed there in the following two decades, had to choose whether to remain loyal to their treaties with the United States or to ally themselves with the Confederacy. Their choices had less to do with the issues dividing the states than with their own leaders, history, conditions, and fears. One of their greatest fears was that the federal government would ignore its treaties with them and allow Anglo-Americans to overrun their lands and dispossess them again. As they struggled to find the right road, the Civil War engulfed the Indian Territory. It devastated their lives, homes, and communities, scattering them like leaves before a storm wind, as one territorial writer described it. When that storm was over, the Indian Territory would never be the same, and what had happened there would affect the rest of the United States.

What was the Indian Territory and how did its people become involved in the American Civil War? By 1860 the "Indian Territory" was roughly today's state of Oklahoma, minus the Panhandle and the far southwestern corner. Native peoples knew it well for its rich resources: animals good for fur, hide, utensils, and meat; plants for food and medicine; and useful minerals, wood, and stone. Alonzo Chalepah, an elder of the Apache Tribe of Oklahoma, recalled in 2003 that his ancestors lived comfortably in western Oklahoma for centuries. They hunted game and in season collected nuts, plums, prickly pear, and berries. "Those are some the things that we highly relied on to gather and eat," he said, "because nowadays we know they're highly nutritious."[3] Native peoples knew where those resources were located and the trails to reach them. Many tribes hunted in Oklahoma, including the Osages, who were based in Missouri and then Kansas in the 1700s and 1800s, respectively. Charles Whitehorn, an Osage, said in 1969 his ancestors "used to come hunting through here, in Oklahoma" on their way to "them places there was buffalo. Certain time they'd go there; then they kill them buffaloes . . . pack'em on the horses . . . . They'd travel through here. They'd see these trees and lots of game and good water, lots of good wood."[4] Caddoan peoples, too, such as the Wichitas, had lived in Oklahoma for hundreds of years, hunting and raising crops in the river valleys. In fact, by the early 1700s Wichita farmers, living in stockade-encircled villages along the Arkansas, Canadian, Washita, and Red Rivers and their tributaries, had used their surplus crops to base a flourishing trade network along those early trails. They profited by connecting nomadic Plains tribes such as the Comanches with French traders bringing European goods from the Mississippi Valley to exchange for furs, bison robes, horses, and slaves. However, the Wichita trade network had collapsed under Osage and then Spanish pressure by the late 1700s.[5]

In 1821 when Maj. Stephen H. Long followed the Canadian River eastward across a summer-scorched western Oklahoma, he reported it as sparsely populated although plenty of game trails marked its sandy soil. His report to the federal government included maps that labeled today's Texas Panhandle and western Oklahoma the "Great American Desert." The public took that to mean it was not suitable for white settlers interested in farming as they knew it then. During the two decades after Long's exploration, as Anglo-American settlers pushed the frontier westward across Arkansas, Texas, Missouri, Kansas, and other areas, the federal government referred generally to the lands still farther west as "Indian territory." By 1860 it had designated parcels of this vast space between the Mississippi River and the Rocky Mountains as reservations for Indian peoples who had been displaced by the settlers. The large area south of Kansas and north of Texas—part of the "Great American desert"—remained relatively open, and a number of Indian peoples were concentrated there by choice or federal action. Consequently, the "Indian Territory" shrank over time to the main body of the state of Oklahoma.[6]

Some population estimates suggest that by 1860 as many as 100,000 people may have been in "Indian Territory," that large rectangle of forested mountains and hills, fertile river valleys, and grass-rich prairies. It was hard to know for sure just how many there actually were. Some Caddos lived and hunted in western Oklahoma, and the Leavenworth Dragoon Expedition visited the Wichita villages in Devil's Canyon in 1834. Two years later Pawnee horse raiders struck a large Wichita village on the site of today's Fort Sill. In fact, Pawnee and Osage parties came through frequently to hunt, visit, and steal horses, while nomadic Plains peoples—particularly the Kiowas, Comanches, and Plains Apaches— considered western Oklahoma part of their range. Parties of Kickapoos, Shawnees, Delawares, Piankashaws, and other tribes sometimes set up camps while passing through this part of the frontier. According to the federal government, though, lands in the territory legally belonged to the Cherokee, Chickasaw, Choctaw, Muscogee (Creek), and Seminole Nations. A small area in the far northeastern corner had been carved out for the Quapaws and some of the Senecas and Shawnees. In the west-central part of the territory, by 1859, just before the Civil War, several tribes—including the Wichita and Caddo peoples—were forced out of Texas and resettled on lands leased from the Choctaw and Chickasaw Nations. A small population of non-Indians—soldiers, federal officials and employees, missionaries, traders, and other individuals licensed by the Indian governments—also lived among them. So, too, did their slaves and freedmen. Most were of African descent, but some had been captured in Mexico or other parts of the West. However, it was the five Indian nations not three decades removed from the southeastern United States who made up the majority of the Indian Territory population, and it was through them that the Indian Territory became so deeply embroiled in the Civil War.[7]

Although each Indian people had their own culture long before the arrival of the Europeans, these newcomers had been labeled "the Five Civilized Tribes" because of cultural changes that began in the late 1600s and early 1700s. Before that time, the Cherokees were the largest tribe in the southeast, with a population estimated at about thirty thousand. They lived mostly in today's North Carolina, South Carolina, Tennessee, and Georgia but also claimed parts of Virginia, West Virginia, Kentucky, and Alabama. Their neighbors included the Muscogees, later called by British colonists "Creeks," a confederacy of ceremonial towns with a population of about fifteen thousand in 1685.[8] They lived primarily in parts of Alabama, Georgia, and northern Florida, with a few in Tennessee. To the west of the Muscogees, the Choctaws lived in Mississippi, Alabama, and Louisiana. They were organized into three districts and had become the most populous of the southeastern tribes by about 1830. To their north were the Chickasaws, a related people, fewer in number and very independent. They lived mostly in northern Mississippi and northeastern Alabama, but they claimed West Tennessee and far-western Kentucky as their hunting ground and fiercely contested the Shawnees for it. The Seminoles, an offshoot of the Muscogee confederacy, were the smallest in number. While they had much in common with other Muscogees, they moved farther south into Florida in the 1700s, eventually becoming separated geographically and politically by about 1800.

The Cherokees were an Iroquoian people, but the other four were Muskogean, most speaking the Muskogee language or variations of it. What they all had in common was their way of life: They were sedentary peoples who lived communally in towns of thatch-roofed timber houses, often clustered around a council house and protected by a stockade. The men hunted, fished, and protected their people, while the women, who owned those houses, fed, clothed, and otherwise cared for their families. Farming was an important part of their economy, and the women raised crops of corn, beans, squash, and melons. These peoples had their own rich cultural heritage and strong spiritual life with ancient roots.[9]

Europeans entered what would be the southeastern United States in the early 1500s—first the Spanish, then the French, and later the British. As they did, warfare increased and epidemics such as smallpox swept the tribes, greatly reducing Indian populations. So did trade between Indians and Europeans. British/Indian commerce flourished when traders from the Carolina colony, founded in 1680, pushed deep into the southeastern Indian country. They offered European manufactured goods—firearms, brass kettles, knives, hatchets, beads, cloth, tools, and rum—in exchange for deerskins and slaves. Native people in the southeast became so dependent on the traders for these goods that over time they became commercial hunters, killing off herds of deer for their hides and competing with hunters from other tribes to pay growing debts to the traders. They also raided other tribes for captives that could be sold as slaves in New England markets or sent to West Indies plantations. In the early 1700s the southeastern tribes rebelled against abuses and conditions growing out of colonial trade but were unsuccessful in ending them. Surrounded by the British in Virginia, the Carolinas, and Georgia, by the Spanish in Florida, and by the French in Louisiana, the southeastern Indians struggled to maintain their independence.[10]

Another consequence of colonial/Indian trade was the appearance of mixed-blood children among the southeastern tribes. English, Scots, and Irish traders from the British colonies sometimes married or formed liaisons with Indian women. Their Anglo-Indian children would not have been welcome in the colonies. Among the southeastern Indians, however, a mother's children were accepted into her family, clan, town, and tribe. Anglo-Indian children often grew up learning the culture of both their parents, including English and their mother's language. Some learned to read and write and were exposed to Christianity. When they grew to adulthood, their skills in the English and Indian languages, literacy, and understanding of both cultures made them valuable to tribal leaders attempting to deal with Euro-Americans. Gradually some moved into leadership positions in their nation and increasingly influenced its affairs. By the early 1800s it was not unusual to encounter mixed-blood Cherokees named Vann, Rogers, or Adair; Chickasaws named Colbert, Cheadle, or Love; Choctaws named Folsom, McCurtain, or Harkins; and Muscogees named McIntosh, Kennard, or Carr. When Protestant Christian missionaries began working among the southeastern tribes about 1800, some mixed-blood Indians such as David Folsom, a Choctaw, supported their mission stations, which offered English education along with Christian teachings.[11]

Some mixed-bloods also led the economic change among the southeastern Indians in the late 1700s as the deer herds dwindled and the buckskin and slave trade declined. Farming had traditionally been an important part of their economies, and Indians expanded it to include raising cattle, horses, hogs, geese, and chickens, as well as European grains, peaches, apples, and cotton, which Indian women learned to weave into cloth about 1800. Unlike Anglo-Europeans, these southeastern tribes held land in common in the belief that it was not something that could be owned, bought, or sold. Rather, an individual could use as much land as he wanted as long as he did not intrude on land used by someone else. Now, though, some Indians, particularly the mixed-bloods, began taking up large tracts of land for farms and other enterprises. For example, James Vann, a Cherokee, had a large farm and operated a mill and a ferry on the Conasauga River in north Georgia by the early 1800s.[12]

Vann was also one of those southeastern Indians who acquired African slaves to work his farm and serve in his home. There are different theories about why and when the southeastern Indians adopted African slavery, but all five tribes eventually did, adding it to forms of slavery they had practiced for centuries. A census taken in 1832 found that the twenty-two thousand Muscogees enumerated owned more than nine hundred African slaves. By then African slavery had become one of the issues that led to the separation of the Seminoles from the Muscogees about 1800, and it continued to trouble their relationship after they arrived in the Indian Territory. The Seminoles were mainly of Muscogee origin but included other peoples, too. Boundaries drawn during the colonial period and the early years of the United States placed some of their towns and camps in the Spanish (briefly British, 1763–1783) colony of Florida. The Seminoles allowed runaway slaves from Anglo-American Georgia and South Carolina plantations to settle among them, not as Seminoles but as slaves under their protection. These runaways lived in their own camps and used their farming skills to raise crops and live-stock, a small part of which they paid their new Indian owners or patrons when required. The Seminoles resisted the demands of their slaves' former owners for their return and attempts by slave catchers to recapture them. Abraham and John Coheia (Cowiya, or Gopher John), two slaves who could speak English and knew Anglo-American ways, became valuable interpreters and negotiators for the Seminoles. Over time they and other skilled slaves achieved some status within the tribe. By about 1815 Euro-American colonial boundaries, internal politics, and the runaway slave issue had effectively separated the Seminoles from the rest of the Muscogee confederacy. However, some Muscogees who objected to developments among their own people in the early 1800s moved south and joined the Seminoles, further widening the gap between the two nations.[13]

In those early days of the American republic, the federal govern-ment was trying to find a way to deal with American Indians it viewed as blocking frontier settlement. It adopted the policy of establishing reservations for Indians, which would limit contact with non-Indians and, it was hoped, prevent conflict. Within these reservations the federal intent was to provide Indian children an English education that would help instill Anglo-American values, including Christianity, landown-ership, and individualism. The expectation was that Indian cultures would vanish within a short time as Indian young people acquired a higher (in the opinion of Anglo-Americans) level of civilization. This would lead to eventual U.S. citizenship and finally end the need for reservations. Consequently, Congress created the Indian Civilization Fund in 1819 to provide financial support for educating Indian children in agriculture and academics. In those days, the federal government was willing to cooperate with Protestant Christian missionary efforts to help accomplish its goals in Indian education. About the same time, a strong religious revival known as the Second Great Awakening was sweeping through the American population. Among other things, it spurred missionary activity directed at native peoples in the Pacific Northwest, Hawaii, and the southeastern Indian country.[14]

The first Protestant Christian missionaries to make lasting in-roads among the southeastern tribes represented the Society of United Brethren for the Southern States—the Moravians—who began work among the Cherokees at Springplace, Georgia, in 1801.[15] After them came Congregationalist, Presbyterian, Methodist, and Baptist missionaries who offered English education as well as Christianity. They generally taught reading, writing, and arithmetic in addition to Anglo-American homemaking skills for Indian girls and agriculture for the boys. By 1825 some young Indian men could attend Choctaw Academy, a Baptist school founded in Kentucky by Richard M. Johnson and supported financially by the Choctaw Nation. Literacy received a large boost among the Cherokees in 1821 when Sequoyah, or George Gist (Guess), developed a syllabary for the Cherokee language. It allowed a person who spoke Cherokee to become literate in that language within a very short time. By 1830 there were Cherokee, Chickasaw, Choctaw, and Muscogee Christian churches and schools in the southeast, although the Indian majority remained rather lukewarm toward them.[16]

By the 1830s, some southeastern Indian leaders realized that adopting aspects of Anglo-American civilization, particularly English education, was necessary if they were to survive constant pressure from the aggressively expanding United States. Although each of the southeastern tribes had ceded land to the new nation in various treaties, settlers still crowded their borders and remained hungry for more Indian land. Most southeastern Indians ignored the Shawnee Prophet's call in the early 1800s to reject Euro-American ways and goods and to return to their own traditions and culture. Nor did they support his brother Tecumseh's appeal for an intertribal alliance against Anglo-Americans.[17]

However, some conservative Muscogees, known as the "Red Sticks," did follow the Shawnee Prophet as well as one of their own, Hillis Harjo, or Josiah Francis. Their devastating attack on Fort Mims, Alabama, in 1813 galvanized the southern Anglo-American frontier. Gen. Andrew

Jackson then marched Tennessee militia south to subdue the Red Sticks, and contingents of Cherokee, Choctaw, Chickasaw, and "loyal" Muscogee warriors joined them. They helped him crush the Red Sticks at the Battle of Horse Shoe Bend (March 27, 1814). So many Muscogees died that day that the Tallapoosa River ran red with their blood, according to eyewitnesses. The Red Stick Rebellion then merged into the War of 1812 when Jackson led his army on to New Orleans later that year to stop a British invasion. Choctaws fought beside him in the victory that made him a national hero.[18] The southeastern Indians then witnessed Jackson's treatment of his Muscogee allies in forcing the Treaty of Fort Jackson on them. He punished all Muscogees for the actions of the Red Stick faction by taking, he proudly said, "20 million acres of the cream of the Creek Country, opening a communication from Georgia to Mobile."[19] In spite of their demonstrated loyalty to the United States, the southeastern Indians could only wonder what might happen to them in the future.

Older leaders, such as the Choctaw chief Pushmataha, were wary. So were young men on the rise, such as Cherokees John Ross, Charles Hicks, John Ridge, and Elias Boudinot. The last two were cousins who had attended a mission school at Cornwall, Connecticut, and each had married a young lady from that town. Boudinot began publishing a newspaper, the *Cherokee Phoenix*, in February 1828, using Sequoyah's syllabary. Its parallel columns in the Cherokee and English languages showcased Cherokee "progress" in adopting aspects of white culture while defending Cherokee sovereignty—the right to govern themselves by their own laws in their own territory.[20]

Some Indian leaders advocated changes in their governments toward the way their Anglo-American neighbors governed themselves. Each of the tribes already practiced a form of democracy, made decisions based on consensus, chose their chiefs from among men of experience and ability, and, among the Cherokee, allowed women a voice in their deliberations.[21] A visitor who witnessed Cherokee government in action in the early 1700s wrote, "The councils are attended by the whole nation, men, women, and children. The progress of deliberation is frequently impeded, in order to consult the assembled nation. A few dissenting voices will often destroy the most salutary measures."[22]

Major changes in southeastern Indian government occurred in the

1820s. The Choctaws had adopted a written code of laws even earlier and established a police force, called the lighthorse, to enforce them and punish offenders. In 1826 they wrote their first constitution. It recognized the existing three-part division of the nation with three districts, each headed by a district chief. The Choctaw Nation also had an elected council, a bill of rights, and a judicial system. The Cherokees reorganized their government between 1817 and 1827. The final version retained their principal chief as the executive but created a bicameral legislature. Their judicial branch included eight judicial districts, four circuit judges, a lighthorse police force, and a supreme court. The Chickasaws kept their traditional government, although the mixed-blood Chickasaws exerted much influence over its affairs. The Muscogees also retained their old confederacy governmental structure based on ceremonial towns. These towns were identified as part of either the upper or lower division, based mostly on whether they were located on the headwaters or lower reaches of Georgia and Alabama rivers. Outsiders considered the upper towns to be more traditional, while mixed-blood influence was stronger in the lower towns, particularly Coweta Town with Chief William McIntosh as its head. The National Council, made up of town representatives, met periodically to discuss national business. The Seminole, reinforced by some of the escaped Red Sticks and often embattled during the early 1800s, had neither time nor any wish to renovate their government.[23]

By the 1820s and 1830s white visitors to the southeastern Indian country of Tennessee, Georgia, Alabama, and Mississippi might see much that was familiar. Housing ranged from log cabins to substantial brick or timber mansions. There were farms with livestock, crops, and orchards sometimes worked by African slaves, general stores, cotton gins, blacksmith shops, ferries, toll roads, schools, and Christian churches. Indian women might have moccasins on their feet but were usually wearing cloth dresses much like those of non-Indian neighbor women, except they were neater, according to some observers. Those Indian women had probably carded the fiber and spun the thread they dyed and wove into the fabric they sewed for their clothing. Men might be wearing cloth shirts, trousers, and coats or be dressed in leather leggings and turbans. Because by this time the southeastern Indians had adopted so many aspects of white culture, non-Indians were beginning to call them the "Five Civilized Tribes."[24] In the mid-twentieth century,

Cherokee-Quapaw writer Louis W. Ballard discussed this ability of Indians to take what they find useful from other cultures. By using them, he concluded, they make them "Indian."[25]

However, not all the southeastern Indians accepted the new ways. For countless generations rituals such as the Green Corn Ceremony had united, revived, and renewed the southeastern Indian communities. At the urging of Christian missionaries, Indian converts abandoned ancient ways for new practices, activities, and attitudes. By doing so, according to traditionalists, they were severing ties and endangering their whole tribal community.[26] At the same time, mixedblood Indians, who tended to be more individualistic and materialistic than those who were full-blood, seemed to be straying from the old ways that valued generosity and sharing resources for the welfare of the entire community. One scholar has suggested that among the Cherokees at least, three categories of people developed: those whose goal was assimilation into the Anglo-American world, those who wanted to remain a separate people while adopting such things as literacy and Christianity; and those who wanted to maintain separation and traditional ways.[27] At any rate, these differences of opinion and worldview exacerbated decisions about the great issues that were forced on the southeastern peoples in the 1820s, 1830s, and 1840s and then again in 1861.

Indian removal had been an idea under discussion in the federal government at least since the days of Pres. Thomas Jefferson. By the time of Pres. James Monroe, it was becoming a federal policy. In the mid-1820s, about the same time Comanches and Kiowas were setting up their lodges in what would be western Oklahoma, federal officials were increasing pressure on the eastern Indians to move west of the Mississippi River. With Missouri and Arkansas already filling up with settlers, that destination shifted farther west into today's Oklahoma and Kansas. Some Choctaws and Chickasaws were familiar with the Arkansas and Red river valleys of today's Oklahoma because they had hunted, traded, and fought other tribes there from the mid-1700s into the early 1800s. A Cherokee faction, already settled in eastern Arkansas before 1800, increased as still more Cherokees left for the west under the increasing pressure from the federal government. A little later, these "Old Settlers" moved on into northwestern Arkansas and then after

1817 spilled over into today's northeastern Oklahoma as the federal government urged all eastern Indians to sign removal treaties and move west to an "Indian Territory."[28]

Differences of opinion over signing those treaties had a direct impact on the Civil War in the Indian Territory. It was a difficult choice for all five of the largest southeastern Indian nations, and it fractured tribal unity while it made internal divisions worse. Some leaders declared that they could not and would not leave what remained of their ancestral lands. Others, though, argued that their best course was to exchange their old homeland for new lands in the Indian Territory. Otherwise, they feared the United States might simply force them out and take their land anyway. Federal negotiators offered guarantees and cash incentives to the Indian governments, as well as to some Indian leaders, to persuade them to sign the treaties. Meanwhile, the new state governments of Georgia, Alabama, and Mississippi applied their own pressures on their Indian residents while ignoring white lawlessness against them. Grimly the Muscogee National Council renewed an 1811 law imposing the death penalty on anyone who signed a treaty selling tribal lands without its consent.[29]

Nevertheless, federal commissioners approached the Muscogee council at Broken Arrow Town in late 1824 about leaving their old country for new lands in the west. They hoped William McIntosh, principal chief of the Lower Towns and a progressive, could sway the council. Instead, the chiefs stated flatly, "We told you we had no land to sell . . . . General McIntosh knows our law. We have no lands to sell."[30] The following February, however, McIntosh and a few like-minded chiefs and ordinary citizens signed the Treaty of Indian Springs, ceding their remaining land in Georgia and some in Alabama in exchange for lands in the west. Opothle Yahola, of Tuckbatchee Town, sent by the council to observe that meeting, left immediately to report on the new treaty. The National Council quickly condemned McIntosh and the other signers and appointed Menawa, a well-known war leader and former Red Stick, to execute their death sentence. He and a party of one hundred men from Okfuskee Town surrounded McIntosh's home and ordered the white men to leave along with all the women and children. Chief McIntosh's son, Chilly, also a signer of the treaty, escaped unnoticed because of his light skin and carried out his little brother Daniel N. McIntosh. When only Chief William McIntosh and one other signer remained in the house, the executioners set fire to it and shot them down as they ran out the door.[31]

Because of these events President Monroe delayed promulgating the Treaty of Indian Springs. As civil war threatened in the Muscogee country in 1827 and 1828, members of the McIntosh faction gathered their belongings and slaves and left for the Arkansas River valley and the Three Forks vicinity, near today's Muskogee, Oklahoma. Still, the situation back in the old country worsened, with settlers flooding into the remaining Muscogee lands.[32] Almost a century later, Mary Hill, of Okfuskee Town in Oklahoma, related her grandmother Sallie Farney's oral history of those uncertain days:

> In every way we were abundantly blessed in our everyday life in the old country. We had our hunting grounds and all the things that are dear to the heart or interest of an Indian. A council meeting was mostly composed of men, but there were times when every member of a town was requested to attend the meetings. Many of the leaders, when unrest was felt in the homes, visited [them] and gave encouragement to believe that Alabama was to be the permanent home of the Muskogee tribe. But many different rumors of a removal to the far west was often heard.[33]

Finally, in 1832 the leaders of the Muscogee nation remaining in the east signed the Treaty of Washington ceding the last of their ancestral homeland in exchange for new lands in the Arkansas and Canadian river valleys in the Indian Territory. The treaty gave them a five-year grace period to remove, but white settler harassment provoked in 1836 a brief "Creek rebellion" put down by Gen. Winfield Scott. That was excuse enough to force the rest of the Muscogee people out of Alabama.[34] According to Sallie Farney,

> The command for a removal came unexpectedly upon most of us. There was the time that we noticed that several overloaded wagons were passing our home, yet we did not grasp the meaning. However, it was not long until we found out the reason. Wagons stopped at our homes and the men in charge commanded us to gather what few belongings could be crowded into the wagon. We were to be taken away and leave our homes never to return. This was just the beginning of much weeping and heartaches.

We were taken to a crudely built stockade and joined others of our tribe. We were kept penned up until everything was ready before we started on the march. Even here, there was the awful silence that showed the heartaches and sorrow at being taken from the homes and even separation from loved ones. Most of us had not foreseen such a move in this fashion or at this time. We were not prepared, but times became even more horrible after the real journey began.[35]

Another account of those days, told by Elsie Edwards of the Kechobadagee tribal town, came from an elderly woman named Sinecha, forced onto a boat bound for the Indian Territory:

When the events, with never no more to live in the east, had taken place, she, too, remembered that she had left her home and with shattered happiness she carried a small bundle of her few belongings, and reopening and retying her pitiful bundle she began a sad song which was later taken up by the others on board the ship at the time of the wreck and the words of her song was, "I have no more land, I am driven away from home, driven up the red waters, let us all go, let us all die together and somewhere upon the banks we will be there."[36]

Many did die along that road to the Indian Territory. According to Sallie Farney,

Many fell by the wayside, too faint with hunger or too weak to keep up with the rest. The aged, feeble, and sick were left to perish by the wayside. A crude bed was quickly prepared for these sick and weary people. Only a bowl of water was left within reach, thus they were left to suffer and die alone.

The little children cried day after day from weariness, hunger, and illness. Many of the men, women, and even the children were forced to walk . . . . .

The sick and the births required attention, yet there was no time or no one was prepared. Death stalked at all hours, but there was no time for proper burying or ceremonies. My grandfather died on this trip. A hastily cut piece of cotton wood contained his body . . . .

There were several men carrying reeds with eagle feathers attached to the end. These men continually circled around the wagon trains or during the night around the camps .... Their purpose was to encourage the Indians not to be heavy hearted nor to think of the homes that had been left.

Some of the older women sang songs that meant, "We are going to our home and land; there is One who is above and ever watches over us; He will care for us."

... Many a family was forced to abandon their few possessions and necessities when their horses died or were too weary to pull the heavy wagons any further.[37]

The forced removal of the Muscogee people who had remained in Alabama after the McIntosh faction left occurred during the bitter winter of 1836–1837. They arrived to find little or none of the supplies and tools promised in their treaty. They had no food, clothing, or shelter in this strange land. It is believed that almost all the infants, young children, and elders died on the way or shortly afterward, so that the total Muscogee population declined by about 40 percent in those early Indian Territory years. The McIntosh faction, who had brought their belongings and supplies with them in 1827–1828, had built new homes and established farms along the fertile Arkansas River valley. Those who survived the forced removal of the 1830s eventually settled farther south and west along the Canadian River and its North Fork and Deep Fork. The factions worked toward reconciliation, and eventually the hard feelings subsided while the Muscogee people rebuilt their nation in the West.[38]

The Cherokee people, too, experienced deep division over the issue of removal. Even though a series of treaties had recognized them as a nation with established boundaries, white settlers spilled into their country just has they had into Indian lands elsewhere. The situation became even worse when gold was discovered near Dahlonega in the Cherokee Nation in 1829. The Cherokees appealed for justice to the Anglo-American public through letters, speeches, and the press and to the U.S. federal court system in *Cherokee Nation v. Georgia*. So did Christian missionaries, when the State of Georgia punished some for not securing state licenses to preach in the Cherokee country. When they won their cases before the U.S. Supreme Court in the spring of 1832, Elias Boudinot wrote joyously to his brother Stand Watie, "It is a great triumph on the part of the Cherokees so far as the question of their rights were concerned."[39]

Still, Pres. Andrew Jackson, a supporter of Indian removal, refused to stop Georgia's encroachment. For one thing, he believed having an Indian nation within an American state was an intolerable condition. Furthermore, he insisted Indians must move elsewhere for their own good. From a political standpoint, too, removing Indians was advantageous. A large portion of the new Democratic Party he headed was composed of southern cotton farmers hungry for fertile Indian lands. During his first term, Congress passed the Indian Removal Act (1830). It formalized the federal policy of exchanging Indian lands in the east for new lands in the unorganized territory west of the Mississippi River, paying Indians for improvements on their eastern lands, and providing subsistence for one year after removal. Federal pressure mounted on all the southeastern Indians to move west. Cherokees remaining in Georgia, Tennessee, and North Carolina were urged to join the western Cherokees, or "Old Settlers," who by then made up about one-third of the tribe and lived mostly in today's northeast Oklahoma.[40]

By this time, John Ross had been principal chief of the Cherokee Nation under the Cherokee constitution since 1828. Although he was only one-eighth Cherokee, he firmly identified with the Cherokee people and had the support of the full-blood majority. Ross led their resistance to removal, stalling negotiations with the federal government by holding out for new lands elsewhere and demanding $20 million in compensation, which it could not pay.[41]

However, by the mid-1830s a faction developed that believed the Cherokee should agree quickly to a removal treaty rather than risk being driven out and having their lands taken without compensation. The leaders of this faction, the "Treaty Party," were Major Ridge, his son John Ridge, and John's cousins, Elias Boudinot and Stand Watie. The Ridge-Watie-Boudinot faction found allies among the "Old Settlers" living in today's northeastern Oklahoma. In 1832 John Ridge wrote to Stand Watie in reference to the Old Settlers, "their greatest hope is to cling fast to our friendship and reunite with us." Paraphrasing the Old Settler leaders, he assured Watie, "If the time ever should happen to come when we thought best to make a treaty, we should do so."[42] It was not unusual for the federal government to negotiate with a minority of an Indian tribe to achieve its goals. In late 1835, then, federal commissioners gave up

MEN AND THINGS ARE CHANGING FAST

dealing with Ross and negotiated the Treaty of New Echota with the Ridge-Watie-Boudinot faction. For $5 million, the Treaty Party exchanged the eastern Cherokee homeland for additional lands in northeastern Indian Territory, plus the cost of removal and subsistence for one year afterward. They moved west during the two years' grace period, but Ross and his followers repudiated the treaty and refused to emigrate. Out of patience, the federal government then sent federal troops to round up the remaining Cherokees and force them west, an event known as the "trail where they cried," or the "Trail of Tears."[43]

Although some of the soldiers took part in looting Cherokee homes, Pvt. John Burnett, a sympathetic army guard, wrote, "I saw helpless Cherokees arrested and dragged from their homes, and driven by bayonet into the stockades. And in the chill of a drizzling rain on an October morning I saw them loaded like cattle or sheep into six hundred and forty-five wagons and started toward the west."[44] Eventually thirteen emigrating parties set off, some taking different routes—all of them full of hardship—for the Indian Territory. Near Little Rock, Arkansas, Burnett stood vigil the winter night when Mrs. John Ross died of pneumonia. He helped bury her the next morning in a shallow grave. She was one of an estimated four thousand who died as eighteen thousand Cherokees were forced west.[45]

Although by 1839 the surviving Cherokee immigrants were settling into their new Indian Territory homeland, bitterness over the Treaty of New Echota remained strong. The Treaty Party, which had arrived about two years earlier, was on good terms with the Old Settler Cherokees and welcomed Chief Ross and his followers in 1838. However, conflict arose when Ross at once assumed authority over the whole nation to the chagrin of the Old Settlers, who already had their own government. Ross's supporters, who filled most posts in the new unified government, at the same time blamed the Ridges, Boudinot, and Watie for the agonies of the Trail of Tears and resented the Old Settlers for siding with them. That score was partially settled when on the morning of June 22, 1839, assassins killed Major Ridge, John Ridge, and Elias Boudinot. Only Stand Watie received enough warning to escape after viewing his brother's butchered body. The identity of the assassins was never revealed although there was strong suspicion in the Cherokee Nation and outside it that the murders occurred to benefit Ross. Later that summer the three factions officially reunited and wrote a new constitution that lasted until 1906. Ross won successive elections as principal chief, but he and Watie continued a private war until an 1846 peace agreement suppressed it. At any rate, hard feelings were still simmering when the Civil War fanned the coals back into flames.[46]

While the Chickasaws and Choctaws escaped the bloodshed over removal that occurred in the Muscogee and Cherokee Nations, the Choctaws barely avoided it. They had received land in western Arkansas and the eastern Indian Territory by the 1820 Treaty of Doak's Stand. Some had already moved to what is now LeFlore County, Oklahoma, when in the winter of 1829–1830 Mississippi tried to exert its authority over these nations. Laws passed in the state legislature provided for the future extension of state law over Choctaw and Chickasaw lands adjacent to organized counties. It made these Indians citizens of Mississippi, abolished their tribal governments, and decreed fines and imprisonment for any Indian official who exercised his duties as set by Indian law or custom. When the Choctaws and Chickasaws protested to Pres. Andrew Jackson, he replied that the federal government could not protect them from the State of Mississippi. Ironically, this occurred at the same time Jackson was threatening South Carolina with the full force of the federal government over that state's nullification of a federal tariff.[47]

As the Choctaws tried to decide what to do in the face of this threat, even the Christian missionaries among them became involved. Methodist missionaries supported district chief Greenwood LeFlore, a Methodist convert, who favored removal to the west. When the other two district chiefs resigned, he alone retained authority at that level. However, many full-blood Choctaws, who resented his actions, opposed removal and probably had the quiet support of the Presbyterian missionaries. When President Jackson arranged to meet with the Chickasaw and Choctaw representatives at Franklin, Tennessee, in 1830 to discuss removal, the Choctaw delegates stayed away to take part in their national election. LeFlore kept his office, but two full-blood candidates were elected to fill the two district chief vacancies. In July these chiefs used armed supporters to prevent Christian Choctaws from taking part in an annuity distribution. LeFlore, learning of this, marched his own followers, wearing war paint and carrying weapons, to the site. The confrontation ended peacefully when both sides had second thoughts about starting a Choctaw civil war and agreed to mediation. That trouble died down, but it was becoming clear the Choctaws had little choice except to agree to move west to the Indian Territory if they were to retain their sovereignty.[48]

Faced in 1830 with the Indian Removal Act and President Jackson's refusal to support them against Mississippi's aggression, the Choctaw leaders reluctantly agreed to leave their traditional homeland and resettle in the Indian Territory. They signed the Treaty of Dancing Rabbit Creek, placing their faith in the guarantee—reiterated in each of the five Indian nations' removal treaties—"no Territory of State shall ever have a right to pass laws for the government of the Choctaw Nation of Red People and their descendants; and . . . no part of the land granted them shall ever be embraced in any Territory or State."[49] With heavy hearts, the Choctaw people began preparing for their exodus from Mississippi. Summarizing these events, James Culberson, a Choctaw historian whose father experienced them, wrote bitterly, "No greater humiliation can be placed upon free people than to be ordered from their homes by a stranger. No greater forbearance can any people show than to give up these homes to be desecrated and destroyed by a stranger. Yet this is just what happened . . . and all because their head chiefs had asked them to do thus. Can you believe it?"[50]

Juanita Usray Lattimer, recounting her family's oral history in the Choctaw emigration of 1832, told how they sang a farewell to their old homeland as they crossed the Mississippi River. On the Arkansas side, they were loaded into hundreds of U.S. Government wagons. Latimer said, "The roads were almost impassable. It was raining and cold. Even for the well and strong, the journey was almost beyond human endurance. Many were weak and broken-hearted, and as night came there were new graves dug beside the way."[51] Pneumonia and cholera took many lives in that year's emigration, and the Choctaws who had removed in the winter of 1831–1832 experienced an epic blizzard as well. It is estimated that two thousand Choctaws died during their national removal.[52] No wonder Peter Pitchlynn, a Choctaw official, wrote, "The privations of a whole nation before setting out, their tur-moil and losses on the road, and settling their homes in a wild world, are all calculated to embitter the human heart."[53]

After the Choctaws agreed to removal, the Chickasaws refused repeatedly even after meeting personally with Pres. Andrew Jackson at Franklin, Tennessee, in 1830. According to Chickasaw historian Arrell Morgan Gibson, the tipping point for them was President Jackson's claim during that meeting that he could not control the aggressive behavior of the southern states toward the Indian nations. Still, the Chickasaw leaders delayed until 1837, when they finally agreed to remove and share the Choctaw country in the west.[54]

Gibson summarized the Chickasaw removal as the most peaceful and orderly of all the Five Civilized Tribes because they had a shorter distance to travel and their leaders managed the process better. The long delay meant that most families had time to collect and prepare their belongings, slaves, and livestock.[55] This included, according to A. M. M. Upshaw, the federal government's supervisor of the Chickasaw removal, four or five thousand specially bred, highly prized horses. "I have used all the influence that I had to get them to sell their horses," he wrote, "but they would about as soon part with their lives as to part with a horse."[56] Some Chickasaws emigrated by steamboat up the Arkansas River and others by wagon. Still, the trip was hard, particularly for those who traveled over the long, primitive, rutted road. Outbreaks of cholera, dysentery, and smallpox ravaged some of the emigrating parties during the trip and continued after their arrival in the Choctaw country between 1838 and about 1840. Corrupt con-tractors supplied such poor quality and short rations of corn, flour, and pork during the emigration and resettlement period that there was a federal investigation into their fraud and mismanagement.[57]

The Seminoles, like the Chickasaws, who resettled initially in the Choctaw country, agreed at first to live in another people's land. Back in Florida, by the 1820s settlers had pushed them into the middle of the peninsula but remained hostile, claiming the Seminoles stole their slaves and livestock. Meanwhile, displaced Seminoles endured hunger and hardship as they resettled farther south. A few chiefs were willing to con-sider removal and signed the Treaty of Payne's Landing in 1832, by which they agreed to visit the new Muscogee country in the west. If it pleased them, the Seminoles would remove there after three years and, according to federal expectations, reunite with the Muscogee people. However, Seminole dissatisfaction rose even though the visiting chiefs gave a good report from the trip. Some Seminoles believed they did not have to leave for twenty years. They also wanted their own country separate from the Muscogees, whom they distrusted and feared would take their slaves. The result was that while some Seminoles began emigrating, others prepared to fight removal from Florida. The young leader Osceola, who killed one of the treaty signers and remained defiantly antiremoval, was named the war chief as the Second Seminole War (1835–1842) erupted. Although he died in captivity in 1839, Seminole resistance continued for years under Wild Cat and Holata Mikko, or Billy Bowlegs. [58]

John Chupco led one of the last bands to emigrate to the Indian Territory. According to Mary F. McCormick, her great-great-grandfather Wadda was killed during the Seminole resistance. His wife, a sister of John Chupco, died on the journey west, and he took his orphaned nieces into his home. In the Indian Territory, those who followed John Chupco were known as the Hvteyievlke Band, meaning "just arrived."[59] By 1859 the Seminoles who could be captured and compelled to remove, including Holata Mikko, were in the Indian Territory.[60]

Neither the Chickasaws nor the Seminoles were happy sharing the country of another Indian nation. Both wanted their independence in their own lands. In 1855 the Chickasaws separated from the Choctaw Nation, purchasing the district they occupied. This was generally the middle third of the lands between the Canadian and Red Rivers in today's south-central Oklahoma. They retained an interest in the Choctaw resources and the lands to their west out to the Texas Panhandle. Because the federal government leased this western section for use by other tribes, it was known as the Leased District. The Seminoles initially settled in the Muscogee country with some in the Cherokee Nation. They were never truly content, and some even went as far as Mexico searching for a more satisfactory homeland. Finally in 1856 they received their own lands west of the Muscogee Nation and between the North Fork and the Canadian Rivers. This parcel stretched out all the way to the Texas Panhandle. Even then, some remained in the Muscogee and Cherokee lands.[61]

By their removal treaties, the Five Civilized Tribes had purchased their new homelands in the Indian Territory from the federal government in fee simple, the way Americans usually purchase land today. The price the federal government paid for the eastern homelands of these Indian peoples included their new western lands plus compensation for other considerations—all of which amounted to tens of thousands of dollars for each nation. Generally the federal government invested these funds on their behalf, and the proceeds were to be paid to the five Indian governments yearly as annuities. However, there were also special treaty-stipulated payments at other times. Each of the removal treaties also guaranteed that these new lands would be theirs forever, that no state would ever have the right to extend its laws over them, and that their new lands would never be part of any state or organized territory.

The federal government had also promised to protect their new lands, which they would be forced to share with other Indian peoples for the time being. As noted earlier, a small corner in the northeastern Indian Territory had been assigned to some Shawnees as well as the Seneca and Quapaw peoples uprooted from homelands farther east. They tried to live quietly on their own lands. While the federal government had been negotiating with the eastern Indian nations earlier in the removal process, it had also attempted to establish its authority in the region and over the various peoples that already lived, farmed, hunted, and traded there—including the Comanches, Kiowas, Plains Apaches, Wichitas, and Caddos. The government had negotiated a treaty with the Osages by which they ceded their claim to all the lands between the Canadian River and today's Kansas line. Even so, Osages and Pawnees from Nebraska, Kansas, and Missouri still came south to hunt, visit, trade, and raid other tribes' horse herds. Likewise, Kickapoo, Shawnee, Piankashaw, Delaware, Sac, and Fox hunters and traders frequently camped along the Cross Timbers. The federal government tried through intertribal meetings and negotiations to prevent or suppress conflict among these peoples and with the nations in eastern Indian Territory.[62]

It also built a series of military posts along the frontier, beginning in 1824 with Fort Gibson, established near today's Muskogee, Oklahoma, at the Three Forks—the junction of the Arkansas, Verdigris, and Grand Rivers. It remained in service until 1857. Fort Wayne, Fort Coffee, and Fort Towson were also established near the Arkansas border in that early time period. The responsibility of these garrisons was to protect the immigrating Indians, to keep out "intruders"—those prohibited by law from being in the Indian country—and to stop the illicit liquor trade. All three were abandoned well before 1860 as the U.S. Army built a second line of forts farther west to guard the frontier between the Plains tribes and the newly settled areas. In the Indian Territory, Fort Washita and Fort Arbuckle, part of this new defensive chain, were established on the lower Washita River in the Chickasaw Nation. Still, officials of the Five Civilized Tribes often complained of raids by those they called the "wild Indians" intent on stealing horses and cattle from their frontier farms and ranches. In 1859 Fort Cobb was built upstream on the Washita River in the vicinity of today's Anadarko. Its role was to protect Wichita Agency, established in the Leased District as a refuge for about 1,500 Wacos, Tonkawas, Anadarkos, Tawakonis, Ionis, Keechis, Delawares, and Caddos removed from the Brazos Reserve to prevent threatened extermination by the Texans.[63]

By that time, the people of the Five Civilized Tribes had made a remarkable recovery, even though the first years had been very difficult. Although those who had immigrated in the 1820s or earlier had usually arrived with the furnishings, tools, supplies, and other resources needed to reestablish themselves in the new country, those forced to remove later often arrived hungry, exhausted, sick, and destitute. They found that few of the supplies and tools promised in the removal treaties had been delivered in the amount, quantity, or good condition promised. Many newcomers fell ill and died, weakened by hardship and struck down by illnesses in a strange climate more extreme than they had known back east. Others despaired in this unfamiliar country, lost hope and energy, and sometimes turned for comfort to the truly terrible liquor smuggled into the territory, some of it brought from Texas by Seminoles, Caddos, Kickapoos, and Muscogees.[64] Siah Hicks, a Muscogee, speaking of some immigrants' yearning for their old homes in the east, said, "When they reached their new homes in the Indian Territory ... they said, 'We have started on the road that leads to our disappearance and we are facing the evening of our existence and are nearly at the end of the trail that we trod when we were forced to leave our homes in Alabama and Georgia.'"[65]

Other Indian immigrants, though, wasted little time on grief and despair. Elsie Beams Roebuck, according to her great-granddaughter, Josephine Usray Lattimer, lost her beloved husband to cholera during the Choctaw removal. She stayed behind with him when he became ill along the way, and she buried him in a grave she and her sons scratched into the ground with sticks and knives. Then, her descendant said, "Undaunted she took her paisley shawl and tied the baby onto her back and cautioning her boys to stay close to her," swam with them across a river and marched on down the road toward Fort Towson. There, relatives helped them resettle, but the Roebuck family remained independent. "They were never idle," Lattimer said, "there were days of hardship and toil . . . bitter trying days" the first year. Elsie and her boys "cultivated and harvested the crops and cared for the livestock, believing they were building a permanent home." Like most pioneers on the American frontier in their day, the Roebuck family lived in a log house they built themselves, made their own simple furniture, used a stump mortar to pound their corn into meal, cooked their food in a sod fireplace, and produced lye soap for washing. Elsie, Lattimer said, "dried wild plums, berries, and grapes. The boys killed wild hogs and game for their meat . . . They had pine torches for light at first and home-made candles. This little family was very industrious and later on with the small remuneration received from the Government, they saved enough to buy two slaves and they prospered."[66]

So generally did other immigrant Indians. Most chose to live in the eastern parts of their new lands, because they were more comfortable in a familiar green landscape of mountains, hills, and river valleys. A few of the more adventurous went out onto the plains to hunt, ransom captives—something of a frontier enterprise—or trade with the western tribes. Some of the more traditional Muscogee people kept their communities intact as they moved to the new homeland. They cleared and planted large common fields in the river valleys and reestablished their ceremonial grounds. Others chose to live on individual ranches and plantations. By the 1840s Indian farmers were raising crops of corn, beans, and squash along with peas, sweet and Irish potatoes, melons, peaches, apples, pears, plums, cherries, oats, rice, and cotton. Indian farmers raised turkeys, ducks, and geese and turned their hogs loose to multiply and graze on acorns in the eastern Indian Territory forests. Ranchers, though, sometimes resettled on the prairies to graze their cattle and horses on the abundant, head-high bluestem grass. Livestock, in fact, became the wealth of the Indian Territory by 1860 and was exported to neighboring states, even to the Ohio River valley. By the 1850s the southeastern Indian nations had entered what historian Arrell Morgan Gibson called the "Golden Years." The exception was the Seminole people whose protracted removal and resettlement period on Muscogee and Cherokee lands before they received their own kept them uncertain and often impoverished into the late 1850s.[67]

Although there were few towns in the Indian Territory as Anglo-Americans thought of them, there were small settlements scattered throughout the eastern portions. Several of the larger ones by Indian Territory standards lay along the Texas Road. This historic trail paralleled the Grand (Neosho) River as it entered northeastern Indian Territory from southeast Kansas, and it angled southwest all the way to Colbert's Ferry at the Red River crossing into Texas. In the 1700s the trail was called the Osage Trace, and Indian war parties as well as hunting parties used it to reach the Three Forks near today's Muskogee, Oklahoma, and points south. After Auguste Pierre Chouteau persuaded Big Foot, or Cashesegra, Tracks Far Away, to resettle his Osage band near his trading post at the Three Forks, packhorses carried loads of hides and furs over the trace to St. Louis markets. Union Mission, the first Christian mission in Oklahoma, and Fort Gibson, the first federal military post, were built near the trace in the 1820s. However, when settlers began streaming into Texas in the 1830s, wagons and herds of livestock widened it through use, and travelers renamed it the "Texas Road." It became the most important overland route through the Indian Territory.[68]

Several larger settlements—Cabin Creek in the Cherokee Nation, North Fork Town and Honey Springs in the Muscogee Nation, and Perryville and Boggy Depot in the Choctaw Nation—lay along the Texas Road. North Fork Town, like Perryville, was situated near the intersection of the Texas Road with the east-west California Road. In the 1830s Opothle Yahola and Oktarharsars Harjo (Sands) settled with their Muscogee followers near the junction of the Canadian River and its North Fork, which gave the town its name. The hamlet of scattered houses and farms that grew up there boasted three hundred residents by 1850. They thrived during the California Gold Rush in 1849–1851 as travelers stopped at the general stores for supplies, foodstuffs, corn, livestock, and news of the road ahead. By 1853 the post office was called "Micco," the Muscogee word for "chief."[69]

West of North Fork Town and Perryville on the California Road, 130 miles west of Fort Smith, lay the much smaller settlement of Edward's Trading Post, sometimes called "Edwards Store." Founded by James Edwards in the 1830s, it was located on the right bank of the Little River three miles above its junction with the Canadian River, near today's Holdenville, Oklahoma. Edwards, an intermarried white man licensed by the Muscogee Nation, set his log trading post near wood, fresh water, and the military road to Fort Gibson as well as a trail southward to Texas. Federal surveying parties, soldiers, freighters, and California-bound '49ers visited the post to resupply and repair wagons. Shawnees, Delawares, Keechis, Comanches, and Kickapoos also came to exchange furs, hides, mules, and captives for trade goods.[70]

Perhaps less colorful but more substantial was the Indian Territory town of Tahlequah, founded as the capital of the Cherokee Nation. Most Indian Territory towns consisted of a small commercial area surrounded by a scattering of homes and churches. There might be general stores, blacksmith shops, wheelwrights, lodgings for travelers, even a physician's office. Tahlequah was unusual in that it more closely resembled towns in neighboring states. It was incorporated in 1844, and streets and lots were laid out. By 1851 it boasted eight stores, a two-story brick hotel, two dentists, and an attorney in addition to the new log capitol building on the town square and the brick Cherokee Nation Supreme Court Building. Built in 1844, it housed the nation's Supreme Court as well as the press of the *Cherokee Advocate* newspaper. Tahlequah even had a two-story frame Masonic Lodge with a mostly Indian membership, a distinction it shared with North Fork Town.[71]

The Park Hill community, just a few miles from Tahlequah, served the Cherokee Nation as an educational, missionary, and printing center. There were, in fact, schools scattered throughout the Indian nations because many leaders had come to see literacy, whether in English or their native language, as a valuable tool. In 1841 the Cherokee government named Stephen Foreman, a Cherokee Presbyterian minister, the nation's first superintendent of public instruction. He directed the creation of a public school system that began operation in 1842 and offered a curriculum for students through the eighth grade. The Cherokee

Female Seminary and the Cherokee Male Seminary at Park Hill, the grandest buildings in the Indian Territory when they opened in the 1850s, educated advanced students. About the same time, the Choctaw Nation, which was also an enthusiastic supporter of English education, established a neighborhood school system as well as academies for older students. The Chickasaws shared the Choctaw school system until they became independent and then raised funds for their first academies about 1844. The Muscogee Nation and the Seminole Nation were a few years behind this surge of educational activity as Congregationalist, Presbyterian, Methodist, and Baptist missionaries helped establish and operate boarding schools in the Indian nations. Through the early 1840s there was anti-Christian sentiment among the later Muscogee immigrants, many of them traditionalists still bitter over their removal from the East. That moderated by the mid-1840s, and day schools and missionary institutions such as Tullahassee Boarding School in the Muscogee Nation opened there and in the Seminole Nation. These Indian school systems educated girls as well as boys, and some young men went on to institutions of higher education in "the States" or to Choctaw Academy in Kentucky.[72] For example, Stephen Foreman had attended Princeton Theological Seminary in New Jersey, and Dr. Thomas Jefferson Bond, a Choctaw, received his medical training at the forerunner of Johns Hopkins University in Baltimore, Maryland. It has been said that young people of the five southeastern Indian nations had better educational opportunities than those available in neighboring states at the time.[73]

Support and funding for these educational systems came from the federal government's Indian Civilization Fund, missionary organizations, and the federal annuities paid to the Indian national governments for their old homelands. In the Cherokee, Choctaw, and Chickasaw Nations, constitutions written after removal established new governments with executive, legislative, and judicial branches modeled on the federal and state governments. The Muscogee Nation, which traditionally had a national council of representatives from its ceremonial towns, remained divided into the Arkansas and Canadian Districts, each with a principal chief. In 1858 they wrote a constitution placing the generally conservative Upper Creeks and progressive Lower Creeks under one government, but it had not really gone into effect in 1861. Perhaps the traditional town chiefs were slow to give up their status and allow elected officials in a national government to control their national funds.[74] The Seminoles were somewhat behind in these changes. They did not become independent of the Muscogee Nation until 1856. They were still relatively poor, unsettled, and suffering the effects of a removal drawn out over two decades. Although Presbyterian and Baptist missionaries had converted some, they were just beginning to accept the white man's education, and they retained their traditional system of town chiefs and principal chiefs when the Civil War began.[75]

At least some members of these five nations were aware of rising political tensions in "the States" in the 1850s. Indian businessmen such as Robert M. Jones, a Choctaw who owned several plantations, many slaves, and riverboats, had contacts outside the Indian Territory. Peter Pitchlynn, a Choctaw educator and political figure, and George W. Stidham, a Muscogee merchant and rancher, were just two of the Indian diplomats sent to represent their nations at conferences with federal officials in Washington, D.C. Likewise, agents from the Office of Indian Affairs (today's Bureau of Indian Affairs) were stationed in the Indian nations in the territory. Although Indian newspapers published earlier in the territory had ceased publication by the late 1850s, "foreign" newspapers from surrounding states brought information on current events beyond its borders. News also spread through Indian missions and churches; personal, missionary, business, military, and federal correspondence; and word of mouth. Travelers brought news, too. In addition to the heavy traffic on the Texas Road and California Road, steamboats called at towns and plantation landings along the Red and Arkansas Rivers. Beginning in late 1858, the Butterfield Overland Mail stage followed a diagonal route from Fort Smith, Arkansas, through the Choctaw Nation to Colbert's Ferry on the Red River. Civilian and military travelers flowing through the Indian Territory in a constant stream to distant Santa Fe, Galveston, St. Louis, even California, brought the news with them.[76]

The talk in the 1850s was increasingly of African slavery, particularly its place in the westward expansion of the United States. Abolitionists, although still a minority voice, were loudly condemning the institution as evil and winning converts who could see no room for compromise on what they regarded as a moral issue. At the same time, it was a growing national political issue as settlers from the South took the institution into the western territories, squelching the antislavery moderates' hope that it would soon die out if left alone in the southern states. The 1854 proposal that the people who settled a territory should decide for themselves whether their future state would be slave or free had failed spectacularly just across the northern Indian Territory border. There violence between antislavery "jayhawkers" and proslavery settlers from the South had produced "bleeding Kansas."

Among the southeastern Indian nations, African slavery had been, of course, a fact of life for decades. Brought to the new Indian lands in the west, slaves cleared the land for farming and built housing for themselves as well as their owners.[77] The conditions for slaves varied from fairly benevolent to miserable even in the same nations. Mary Grayson was the daughter of a slave taken west from Alabama as a girl in the voluntary removal of the Muscogee McIntosh faction in 1827–1828. Mary, who belonged to Mose Perryman, considered herself a "native" of the Muscogee Nation. She said, "We slaves didn't have a hard time at all before the [Civil] War." Those she knew "always had plenty of clothes and lots to eat and we all lived in good log cabins we built." Each family "looked after a part of the fields and worked the crops like they belonged to us," Mary explained.[78] Henry Clay, who as a young man accompanied his master from North Carolina to Louisiana and then into the Muscogee Nation before the Civil War, lived on a plantation two miles from Honey Springs. He agreed, saying, "It seem like the slaves in the Creek country had a better time than most of the negroes in Louisiana."[79]

In the late 1930s some former slaves spoke well, even lovingly, of their owners. Polly Colbert belonged to Holmes and Betsy Love Colbert, from prominent Chickasaw families. After her mother's death when she was a small child, Polly said, "Master Holmes told us children not to cry, dat he and Miss Betsy would take good care of us. Dey did, too." They moved Polly and her sister and brother into their house "and look after us jest as good as dey could colored children. We slept in a little room close to them and she allus seen dat we was covered up before she went to bed." The Colberts raised hogs and cattle and had one hundred acres in production with more land waiting to be cleared. Slaves on other plantations recalled wearing rough clothing, having shoes only in the winter, and supplementing a sparse diet with what they could grow or animals they could catch when they had free time. The Colberts, though, seemed to have been unusually generous as well as practical in providing food, clothing, and medical care for their seven or eight slaves. Butter and milk were on the table daily, and during the winter they ate smoked meat, sausage, dried beans and peas, corn, potatoes, and turnips stored up for them. "Master Holmes allus say," Polly remembered, "'a hungry man caint work.'"[80]

Kiziah Love belonged to Benjamin Franklin Colbert, another Chickasaw, who operated a farm, Red River ferry, and stage stand on the Butterfield Overland Mail route. Colbert and his wife, Julie, Kiziah said, "was de best folks that ever lived." Occupied with his businesses, he left his slaves to do their work without an overseer because, according to Kiziah, they all "loved Master Frank and knowed just what he wanted done and they tried their best to do it, too." Unfortunately, his half-brother Buck was, Kiziah said, "the meanest man the sun ever shined on." Claiming to be a patroller, he harassed and whipped slaves he met on the road, even those with passes from their owners. He beat a slave woman to death because she could not stop his newborn infant from crying and then whipped the replacement nurse so badly that his wife left her bed to fetch his brother Frank to stop the beating.[81]

Frank and Holmes Colbert apparently were not unusual in giving their slaves a large degree of liberty. Nellie Johnson stated she was grateful that she and her family were the property of Roley McIntosh, principal chief of the Arkansas District in the Muscogee Nation, and did not belong to one of the Cherokee farmers just east of the boundary line. Chief McIntosh's slaves lived on scattered small plots near the prewar Coweta Town. They chose the locations for their small one-room log houses themselves and furnished and decorated them however they chose. In addition to his crops, they cultivated their own in their free time and on Saturdays and Sundays. "Old Chief," Nellie said, treated them as hired hands and "never bothered the slaves about anything." He checked on them occasionally and sometimes sent another slave to collect for market some of the chickens, turkeys, hogs, corn, and wheat they raised. She concluded, "I was a big girl before I knowed very much about belonging to him."[82]

The slaves of Jim Vann, a Cherokee of Webber's Falls, lived well, too, according to Lucinda Vann, born his slave about 1850. "Everybody was happy. Marster never whipped no one. No fusses, no bad words, no nuthin' like that," she said. Still, their lives were regimented to some degree, with a time to go to bed and a time to get up and receive instructions for the day. There was a hierarchy, too, according to Lucinda. The "first class" was made up of house slaves; then came those with special skills and responsibilities, including carpentry, caring for Vann's racehorses, and working on his steamboats. The field hands were the lowest class. All ate well from a commissary strictly managed by Lucinda's grandmother, housekeeper Clarinda Vann. It held "everything good to eat" and plenty of it. The owner of a stable of racehorses, Vann insisted his house slaves always ride horses rather than walk when they went out in public. The slave women never left the house in their cotton work clothes, or "common dress." To reflect well on him, Lucinda said, "We had fine satin dresses, great big combs for our hair, [a] great big gold locket, [and] double ear-rings . . . . We had bonnets that had long silk tassels for ties . . . . Everything was fine, Lord, have mercy on me, *yes*."[83] Vann's slaves had time to relax and to make small items they could sell for pocket money. They enjoyed music and dancing when the Vanns had guests, and there were presents for everyone at Christmas. Vann would even take them on excursions aboard his steamboat, tying up somewhere along the riverbank for a big fish fry.[84]

Other Indian slaves, though, lived in misery composed of hard work, privation, and fear. Charlotte Johnson White, born in 1850 in the hills east of Tahlequah, belonged to a Cherokee master. She spent her early childhood days alone in a small dark cabin, afraid of the shadowy corners and with only a baked sweet potato left for her midday meal. Her mother, a field hand, was chronically ill, but Charlotte said, "Dat didn't keep her out of de fields or the garden work." When her mother was unable to respond quickly enough to the work call one morning, her master beat her so severely that she died soon afterward. Charlotte said, "I guess the whippin's helped kill her, but she better off dead than just livin' for the whip." The same master pushed Charlotte headfirst into a pile of burning brush when as a twelve-year-old nursemaid she dropped one of his children. Pointing to her scarred face about 1937, she told her interviewer, "See this old drawn, scarred face?

Dat's what I got from de fire . . . and my back is scarred wid lashings dat'll be wid me when I meet my Jesus."[85]

Slaves were in some instances the first Christian converts and missionaries in the Indian nations.[86] Uncle Wallace and Aunt Minerva Willis, elderly slaves of Britt Willis, a Choctaw, earned a reputation for composing and singing spirituals. For their own protection just before the outbreak of the Civil War, Willis hired them out to work at Spencer Academy near Fort Towson. Reverend Alexander Reid, the staunch antislavery superintendent assigned to the Choctaw school by the Presbyterian Mission Board, opposed renting slaves for field and house work. However, Uncle Wallace and Aunt Minerva entertained the staff, their families, and visitors in the evenings by singing songs Uncle Wallace composed as he worked in the fields. Among them were "Steal Away to Jesus," "I'm A'Rolling, I'm A'Rolling," and "Swing Low, Sweet Chariot."[87]

Although some owners did not permit their slaves to hold Christian church services, others such as Isaac Love, a Chickasaw who was not Christian, did. His former slave Matilda Poe said, "My, we'd have happy times singing an' shouting. They'd have church when they had a preacher and prayer meeting when dey didn't."[88] "Young Joe" Vann, a Cherokee living at Webber's Falls, who, like his father "Rich Joe" Vann, owned many slaves, also allowed his people to have hymn singings and be baptized, according to former slave Betty Robertson.[89] Henry Clay, who lived on a plantation near Honey Springs in the Muscogee Nation, recalled that the slaves "went to a place where the colored preacher was Reverend Seymour Perry, and we used to baptize in the Elk [Creek]."[90]

Education was another matter. Betty Robertson, the former Vann slave, said, "We couldn't learn to read or have a book, and the Cherokee folks was afraid to tell us about the letters and figgers." Cherokee law prohibited teaching a slave to read, and "there was a big fine if you show a slave about the letters."[91] Phoebe Banks, a slave of the prominent Muscogee Perryman family, recalled that most Indian slave owners did not want literate slaves. However, she said, the Perrymans "even helped the younger slaves with that stuff."[92]

Some slaves were able to use their knowledge of farming and stock-raising or special skills, plus the sometimes-lenient attitude of their owners, particularly the Muscogees and Seminoles, to earn enough money to buy their freedom. "Free blacks" became farmers, ranchers, merchants, hotel proprietors, freighters, blacksmiths, stone-masons, and carpenters. Historian Gary Zellar pointed out that both slave and free blacks in the Indian Territory had more independence and opportunities to improve their condition than those in neighboring states, but they still lived with a degree of risk. Slaves could be sold away from their families and communities, and slave hunters could steal them, re-enslave the freedman, or cheat legitimate Indian owners out of their slave property. Then, too, the more-relaxed Indian slave codes began to tighten toward 1860.[93]

Although some slaves may not have realized it, by the late 1850s, their condition was one of several issues troubling the Indian nations. Some traditional Indian people, for example, Opothle Yahola in the Muscogee Nation, owned several slaves. However, slave ownership was more common among the mixed-blood Indians who had adopted some Anglo-American ways. During the previous three or four decades their control over their nations' affairs had grown. This included replacing traditional government by consensus with a republican form of government based on a written constitution. Full-blood Cherokees, who were the majority in their nation, increasingly resented minority mixed-blood domination of their government. According to historian William G. McLoughlin, as slavery grew more divisive in the United States in the 1850s, Principal Chief John Ross, who was himself a slaveholder, tried to guide his nation along a neutral course. That, however, alienated Cherokee slaveholders, who believed that an alliance with the American southern states, by then loudly defending slaveholding as their right, was the better course. Generally those pro-Southern Cherokee slaveholders were also affiliated with the old Ridge-Watie-Boudinot Treaty Party from the bitter removal period.[94]

Missionaries working in the Indian nations were also caught up in the slavery question, as church organizations in the United States split into northern and southern factions. It was not unusual for missions to rent slaves to perform necessary labor. However, as some of their supporting organizations back east adopted the antislavery position in the 1840s, they were pressured to preach against slaveholding. In the Cherokee Nation the most active Christian organizations were the Southern Baptists and the Northern Baptists, with most slaveholders being Southern Methodists. In 1855 the Southern Baptist Convention voted to send proslavery missionaries to the Cherokee, Choctaw, and Muscogee Nations.[95] The first to reach the Cherokee Nation two years later was James Anderson Slover, a Tennessean. Often questioned as to what he preached about slavery and whether he shared the views of Baptist missionary Evan Jones, an abolitionist, he replied he "did not preach politics nor make stump speeches upon political subjects ... [only] the same gospel alike to the rich, the poor, the bond, and the free."[96] Even then questions and suspicions about him continued. Such division among Christian missionaries was not limited to the Cherokee Nation, as Choctaw minister Israel Folsom noted in March 1860, when he wrote that men and things were changing fast. It contributed to the growing tension in the Indian Territory, particularly in the Cherokee Nation.

That nation was the post assigned to Evan Jones, an Anglo-American who spoke and wrote Cherokee. He had been a Baptist missionary among the Cherokee people since well before their removal. Along with several other missionaries, he went with them to the Indian Territory in the late 1830s. He and his son John Buttrick Jones, now Northern Baptists and abolitionists, worked mostly among the full-blood majority that strongly supported Principal Chief John Ross. Originally not much concerned about slavery, this majority came to oppose it along with pro-Southern Cherokee slave owners.[97] In the 1850s the Joneses joined full-blood Cherokee leaders in organizing the Keetoowah Society. It was based on an ancient Cherokee society that represented and preserved Cherokee values, ideals, and rituals. Even though the leaders of the 1850s organization were Christians, they incorporated into the reinvigorated traditional society important elements that were compatible with being Cherokee. The Keetoowah Society, as described by McLoughlin, "defined a 'true Cherokee patriot' as a full-blood, true to traditional values, national unity, and Cherokee self-determination through consensus."[98]

Much to Chief John Ross's dismay, in 1855 a proslavery secret society known as the Knights of the Golden Circle spread into the Cherokee Nation from adjacent southern states and established chapters there. Rumors circulated that they were headed by his old enemy, Stand Watie. Several influential Watie party members joined the organization, hoping to counteract the Cherokee Light Horse controlled then by Cah-skeh-new Mankiller, a Keetoowah.[99]

The Keetoowah became convinced the Knights of the Golden Circle and Cherokee slaveholders were leading the nation into trouble by supporting the Anglo-American South.[100] Some time before 1860, Keetoowah Society members began wearing two crossed straight pins under the lapel of their coat so they could recognize fellow members. This practice led to their nickname, "Pin Indians." Within a couple of years of their founding, they outnumbered the Knights of the Golden Circle and dominated both houses of the Cherokee legislature. Meanwhile, they staunchly supported Chief Ross in his position of neutrality with regard to sectional hostility in the United States. These developments helped set the stage for Cherokee-on-Cherokee violence even before the first shots of the Civil War were fired.[101]

By the spring of 1857, external conflict over slavery had arrived on the doorstep of the Cherokee Nation. Some Cherokee farmers— among them the Hursts, Rogerses, McGhees, and Walkers—had settled along the Neosho River in the Cherokee Neutral Lands. This 800,000-acre rectangle was adjacent and belonged to the Cherokee Nation but lay mostly in southeastern Kansas along the Missouri border. White settlers had also moved illegally into the Neutral Lands, and the new Territory of Kansas created two counties there in 1855. Some of the white squatters even joined raids led by partisans such as William C. Quantrill and James H. Lane. Raiders, claiming to either support or oppose slavery, crossed the Missouri, Arkansas, and Indian Territory boundaries to steal slaves and livestock. There was little opposition from federal authorities, even though they were bound by the removal treaties to protect the Indian nations from intruders. Not until 1860 did fifty troopers led by Capt. Samuel D. Sturgis begin to remove the squatters. Still, the violence that had plagued Kansas the last few years and now spilled across the border into Cherokee country heightened the tension between the factions.[102]

Meanwhile, the Indian nations watched anxiously as the United States presidential election of 1860 drew near. The Northern Baptists, who had missionaries in the Indian Territory, had given their support to the new Republican Party. Indians who were aware of the situation in "the states" had heard that the Republican candidate, Abraham

Lincoln, opposed the spread of slavery to the territories. It was rumored he might free the slaves, and they knew some of the southern states were threatening to secede if he was elected.[103]

At the same time, there was an additional concern for them as citizens of Indian nations. Even though their removal treaties permanently guaranteed them their new Indian Territory homelands, they knew some federal officials already coveted those lands. Elias Rector, a senior official of the Office of Indian Affairs, had enthusiastically praised the development potential of the Indian Territory in his 1858 annual report. He described its "rich alluvial valleys . . . vast extents of the most beautiful and fertile limestone prairies; incalculable wealth of coal, limestone, and marble; salt springs, water power; everything in short that is needed to make a great and flourishing State." It was true, he conceded, that the five Indian nations held this land in fee simple, but that *really* (his emphasis) meant little to the average tribal citizen. Soon, he predicted, the supreme law of nations must compel the federal government to allot that land to individual Indians, allow them to sell or lease their allotments to non-Indians, and make them U.S. citizens. Rector concluded, "how insignificant their petty nationalities and half independencies, and quasi-ownership of the soil which they cannot alienate!"[104] What this senior federal official was saying publicly was that the federal government could ignore notions of Indian nationhood and sovereignty, the Indian citizens' deep loyalties to their nations, and its own treaty guarantees regarding their lands.

The federal government had already approached the Muscogee Nation in 1859 about allowing their lands to be surveyed and allotted in homesteads to individual citizens. Surplus lands could then be opened to non-Indians.[105] However, Principal Chief Motey Kennard of the Arkansas District and Principal Chief Echo Harjo of the Canadian District replied firmly that they had tried "sectionalization," their term for dividing land into allotments, in their old Alabama homeland in 1832 at the federal government's insistence. The results, the chiefs said, had been "evils and evils continually" as non-Indians flooded their country even before the process was complete. They drove Indians out of their homes and swindled Muscogee people unfamiliar with Anglo-American land surveys, deeds, and leases. The chiefs stated flatly that result "is still fresh on our minds. Hence there is no consideration that can induce us to try the experiment again."[106] Undeterred, commissioner of Indian affairs A. B. Greenwood made the same proposal to Principal Chief John Ross in late 1860.[107]

While these proposals came from federal officials whose sympathies were proslavery, the issue of Indian land tenure also surfaced in the 1860 presidential campaign of Abraham Lincoln of Illinois. Anglo-Americans interested in settling new land and pushing the frontier on through Kansas, Texas, and beyond generally viewed Indian reservations as a hindrance and Indian people as undesirable neighbors. The relatively large and undeveloped Indian Territory, set apart for the five large southeastern Indian nations and a few smaller reservations seemed to impede development in surrounding territories and states. Republican campaigner William H. Seward was addressing this concern when he declared in a well-publicized Chicago speech, "The Indian Territory . . . south of Kansas must be vacated by the Indians."[108] According to historian Lawrence M. Hauptman, this speech ushered in a new era of violence against Indians in Kansas.[109] Indian leaders in the territory found Seward's statement ominous. The federal government had guaranteed the Choctaw Nation their new homeland "while they shall exist as a nation and live on it."[110] Choctaw, Muscogee, Cherokee, Chickasaw, and Seminole adults remembered only too well the removals of the 1830s. If Lincoln won the election, would the federal government force them to remove again? And where might they be sent this time?

So as the year 1860 edged from fall into winter, the attention of the Indian nations as well as the American states focused on the presidential election and its consequences. Abraham Lincoln emerged the winner, and before Christmas the State of South Carolina seceded from the Union rather than endure continued northern attacks against slavery and a president believed hostile to that institution.

From a thousand miles west of South Carolina, the leaders of the Indian nations paid close attention to these events. They remembered their own experiences with the federal government, and they questioned whether they could trust that government to uphold its treaties with them, especially if Abraham Lincoln presided over it. Would his administration continue to guarantee their lands and sovereignty? Would it keep out intruders and protect their property, including their

slaves? Could they trust Anglo-Americans, who, as Choctaws Israel
Folsom and Peter Pitchlynn believed from past experience, would "eat
up & consume the Red Men where ever they come in contact with
them?"[111] When they looked at their own national affairs—particularly
the Muscogees, Seminoles, and Cherokees—they thought about the
old enmities, new alliances, and barely healed scars. They realized that
1861 would usher in a very dangerous time.

CHAPTER TWO

Now the Wolf Has Come

I n early winter of 1862–1863, Thomas Pegg, acting chief of the
Cherokee Nation, reflected on what had happened to his people
in a little more than a year's time. Pegg, or Ayuñadegi, was about
sixty, an Old Settler, and had been active in his nation's affairs for
decades. At various times he had represented Saline District in the
Cherokee legislature and served as an associate Supreme Court justice.
He had even been a Cherokee "delegate" in Washington, D.C., one of
those Indian diplomats sent by their nations to the Anglo-American
capital to try to influence the federal government's handling of Indian
affairs. Clearly he was a man respected and trusted by other Cherokees.
Yet since midsummer 1861, he had served first as a major in a
Cherokee military unit allied with the Confederacy and then switched
his support to the Unionist faction—actions that could be interpreted
as dishonorable. How had that happened?[1]

Pegg's behavior mirrored the conduct of the Cherokee national
government long headed by Principal Chief John Ross, now in federal
custody. His government had signed a treaty with the Confederacy and
then swung to the Union side in a few months' time, reflecting the con-
flicting loyalties among Cherokee citizens. Looking back over the year
1861, Pegg explained, "our Government has been paralyzed by the
incursion of an overwhelming force from the army of the Confederate
States . . . . Our legitimate protection, the Government of the United
States was far away. And every channel of communication cut off.
Every Military Post in our vicinity was abandoned or occupied by the
Enemy. We were perplexed and Embarassed. Our wisest men knew not
what to do." The choice, Pegg wrote, was "suffering the ravage and ruin
of our country" or aligning with the Confederacy and winning a
breathing space until "deliverance might come from our friends the
Government of the United States."[2]

Whether or not Pegg made a convincing explanation for the apparent inconstancy of the Cherokee Nation, those who lived through the uncertain days in the Indian Territory in late 1860 and early 1861 shared his perspective. Bordered on three sides by states aligning with the Union or the Confederacy, the Indian nations witnessed political developments in the United States with alarm. In late December 1860 South Carolina seceded from the Union in response to the election of Abraham Lincoln. Then the southern states, including neighboring Arkansas and Texas, called up their militias and seized federal arsenals within their boundaries. In March Pres. Abraham Lincoln was inaugurated, and the southern states that had seceded to date created the Confederate States of America. By early April hostilities in the Civil War had begun with South Carolina's bombardment of Fort Sumter. Envoys had already approached the Indian nations on behalf of the Confederacy, but the federal government, with its eyes turned east, seemed to have forgotten them. By summer the Civil War was lapping over into the Indian Territory, and this "white man's war" was turning even members of the same Indian nation against one another. Each person, family, community, and nation looked for the best option.

Confederate and Union interest in the Indian Territory was understandable, but in the end the Union valued it less. Both the heavily traveled Texas Road and the California Road crossed the Indian Territory, connecting the eastern states to the western territories, the Gulf of Mexico, and the Pacific Coast. It could be a buffer zone or an invasion route for Unionist Kansas, Confederate Arkansas and Texas, or the border state of Missouri, already torn by disputed loyalties. As historian Arrell Morgan Gibson pointed out, the Indian nations were rich in resources for war. There was very little hard currency in the Indian Territory, but it was wealthy in livestock—horses, hogs, and cattle routinely marketed back east. Hogs and cattle would provide meat for troops, while leather from cow and horse hides would be turned into shoes, boots, saddles, harnesses, holsters, and many other items. Horses would be used as cavalry mounts, move artillery, and, along with mules and oxen, pull supply wagons. Indian Territory grain—mostly corn, wheat, and rice—would feed troops. Northeastern Indian Territory had rich deposits of lead for bullets and weaponry, and salt harvested from Indian Territory springs would preserve meat for the armies.[3]

The territory could also provide manpower, including experienced fighters and scouts. Although the long, bloody Cherokee-Osage War had concluded in the early 1830s, sporadic raids by the Osages, Pawnees, Comanches, Kiowas, Wichitas, and Caddos on frontier farms and ranches were common through the 1850s. According to James Roane Gregory, a Muscogee judge and writer who grew up on that frontier, in earlier days, "Creek blood splashed the wild prairie flowers by Pawnee arrows and lance far and near."[4] He described how as late as 1859 Euchee hunters Tiger Bone, Long Tiger, and their brother fought off a Comanche-Wichita war party on Tiger Creek in today's Seminole County, Oklahoma. Recently, the last emigration party of Seminoles, so long at war with the United States, had settled west of the Muscogee country. Their fighting skills had become legendary throughout the United States. Then, of course, there were men such as Delaware scout Black Beaver and Jesse Chisholm, a Cherokee trader, who knew the frontier, its trails, the many tribes that lived there, and their languages. They could prove invaluable during this coming war, which would likely spread to the Trans-Mississippi West. The people of Arkansas, convinced that there were as many as 25,000 fighting men in the Indian Territory, were particularly concerned about which side the Indians would support.[5]

The side that won over the Indian nations would have useful allies, and federal Indian agents and some Protestant missionaries serving among them had recognized that earlier. Democrats had held the presidency through much of the 1850s and routinely appointed fellow Democrats to federal posts. In the Indian Territory as Lincoln took office were Creek Agent William H. Garrett of Alabama, a strong secessionist; former Cherokee Agent Robert J. Cowart of Georgia, accused of proslavery agitation; and Seminole Agent Samuel Rutherford, a Virginia-born, former Arkansas legislator. Jefferson Davis had recommended Choctaw and Chickasaw Agent Douglas H. Cooper, a Mississippian, for his post. He was so popular for his integrity, honesty, and fairness that the Chickasaw legislature adopted him as a Chickasaw citizen. Within the federal Office of Indian Affairs hierarchy, these men reported to Superintendent Elias Rector, brother of Arkansas governor Henry M. Rector, a strong proslavery man. These officials influenced and supported the pro-Southern, proslavery factions in the Indian nations.[6]

Missionaries, too, influenced their Indian congregations, as Evan and John Jones had many Cherokees. Joseph S. Murrow, a young Baptist missionary from Georgia, built a growing congregation that supported adopting white ways and included Heniha Mikko, or John Jumper, who favored the Southern cause. However, his rival for Seminole leadership, Assistant Principal Chief John Chupco, was a convert of James R. Ramsey, a Presbyterian abolitionist.[7]

There were several additional factors that probably predisposed the Indian nations to favor the South more than the North. Although the Cherokees, Chickasaws, Choctaws, Muscogees, and Seminoles had suffered harsh treatment by the people of the Southern states, their old homelands lay in those states. Many Indians still yearned for them. Some still had relatives there who had chosen to give up their tribal identity rather than remove, and some had non-Indian family there, too. Economic ties between the Indian nations and the South were strong, but there were also cultural ties. Many members of the southeastern Indian nations and Southern non-Indians shared religious affiliations, educational ties, and the agricultural way of life and economy, which included slaveholding. Indians who owned slaves feared they would lose them if, as they expected, President Lincoln moved to abolish slavery. Their governments were understandably concerned, too, about their national wealth. Large sums of money they received from the federal government for their old homelands had been invested in state bonds, most issued by Southern states. Counteracting that factor somewhat was the knowledge that, since they did not collect taxes, the annuities they depended on to support their governments and school systems came from the federal government. But, as some writers have suggested, perhaps they blamed the federal government more than the Southern states for the agonies and injustices they had suffered during the removals and so would not support the Union.[8]

All these factors probably came into play in early 1861 as the Civil War began and the five Indian national governments tackled the problem of what they should do in this crisis. On January 5, the Chickasaw legislature resolved that the five nations form a union aimed at protecting their interests with regard to the federal government. The Muscogee Nation responded by inviting delegates to meet at North Fork Town on February 17. Although Principal Chief John Ross sent a delegation, he urged harmony among the Indian nations and warned them against a hasty reaction to the "family misunderstanding" in the states.[9] Apparently the Chickasaws and Choctaws took his warning seriously because they did not join the Cherokees, Muscogees, and Seminoles at the meeting.[10] Both the Choctaw Nation and the Muscogee Nation had tightened their slave laws, the latter passing legislation that required all free blacks in their nation to dispose of their property and choose an owner before March 10, 1861, or be sold for twelve months to the highest bidder.[11]

Meanwhile, there was increasing outside pressure on these five Indian nations stemming from their proximity to pro-Confederate Arkansas and Texas. According to historian Alvin O. Turner, "frontier issues were paramount in Texas in 1860." When the Republic of Texas had agreed to annexation to the United States, it expected federal troops would guarantee peace by suppressing the Indian menace on its frontiers. When that did not happen, Texans such as politician and newspaperman John S. "Rip" Ford and John Baylor argued that federal failure to deal with the Indian problem gave Texas reason enough to secede from the Union. In February 1861 they sent commissioners to the Indian nations to advocate alignment with the secessionist Southern states. While Texans held their own secession convention, they planned invasions of New Mexico and the Indian Territory and considered seizing Fort Washita, charging it was garrisoned by a "foreign government." Pressuring the Indian nations to join the secession movement, Turner charged, was "a clear demonstration of hostile intent if not an act of war."[12]

The pressure from Texas was especially disturbing in the Choctaw Nation, which was in the final phase of negotiating a large payment from the federal government dating back to the removal era. One of the primary negotiators was Peter P. Pitchlynn, a Choctaw political figure who expected to receive a commission on the payment. Believing the Choctaw Nation should side with the Union to protect its (and his) interests, Pitchlynn persuaded George Hudson, the new governor, to agree. However, a party of Texans crossed into Choctaw territory, came to Pitchlynn's house, and threatened him if he continued to support the Union. When the Choctaw legislature met, Robert M. Jones, a full-blood Choctaw planter said to own five large plantations and five hundred slaves, gave a fiery address threatening anyone who opposed Southern secession. Confederate supporters from Arkansas and Texas even intruded into the Choctaw legislative session to lobby for their cause. Under all this pressure, Choctaw governor Hudson switched his support to a Choctaw-Confederate alliance.[13] On June 14 Hudson proclaimed that the Choctaw Nation general council four days earlier had resolved that it was "independent, and free to enter into alliance with other governments." This step was justified, they reasoned, because the United States was dissolved with the secession of eleven states, there was a war between the states, and the federal government had failed to meet its treaty obligations.[14]

Proximity to secessionist Texas also affected the Leased District tribes and the federal troops stationed on the western frontier to protect them and their Indian Territory neighbors. That frontier was a restless, sometimes dangerous place with Kiowa, Comanche, and other Plains tribes raiding the eastern Indians' ranches, farms, and settlements—an activity significant to their way of life. They also made frequent forays south of the Red River, infuriating Texans. By the early 1800s, when Anglo-Americans were colonizing Texas, several tribes and tribal divisions had also migrated or been pushed into the same area. This included the Caddos and Anadarkos; some Shawnees, Delawares, and Kickapoos; along with Wichita peoples such as the Taovayas, Wacos, Ionis, Keechis, and Tawakonis. In 1854 they were assigned to the Brazos Reserve in Texas, along with the Tonkawas, a Southern Plains tribe generally friendly to Anglo-Americans. In fact, in May 1858, the Tonkawas and other Reserve Indians made up half of a Texas Ranger expedition led by John S. Ford that struck the Comanches in far-western Indian Territory. Then in late September, 135 Wacos, Delawares, Caddos, and Tonkawas joined Maj. Earl Van Dorn and the 2nd Cavalry on an expedition to the vicinity of today's Rush Springs, Oklahoma. There they struck a Comanche camp set up near a Wichita village, dealing the Comanches a hard blow, killing several Wichitas, and damaging the Wichitas' crops and livestock. On both of these expeditions, which took away the Comanches' sense of safety in the Indian Territory, Placido, or Hashukana (Can't Kill Him), the Tonkawa chief (1826–1862), was in the forefront of the fight. Nevertheless, by 1858 Texans newly settled near the Brazos Reserve were threatening to annihilate all the Indians if they were not removed immediately. Escalating violence against them gave that threat credibility. Maj. Robert S. Neighbors headed the emergency exodus of about 1,500 Brazos Reserve Indians, minus most of their belongings and livestock, out of Texas in the sweltering heat of August 1859. They resettled in the Washita River valley near the new Wichita Agency, and the town of Anadarko grew up nearby. Among those who settled close by was Black Beaver, the Delaware scout, along with traders William and John Shirley.[15]

Because these newest Indian immigrants would now be living close to the Comanches and Kiowas, the federal government established Fort Cobb at a site chosen by Maj. (later Lt. Col.) William H. Emory just up the Washita River from the new agency.[16] A severe drought devastated Kansas and the Indian Territory during 1860, and there was often skirmishing between the Texas Indian immigrants and the Plains tribes in the vicinity. Emory, who commanded Fort Cobb and the 1st Cavalry, with contingents downstream at Fort Arbuckle and Fort Washita in the Chickasaw Nation, tried to keep peace in the Leased District. Meanwhile, his officers and men watched political developments back east with concern. One of them identified only as "Rover" wrote regular letters from Fort Washita that were published in the *Daily Times* of Leavenworth, Kansas Territory. He noted the occasional visits of secessionists to the Indian Territory settlements and forts that summer. In the fall he wrote, probably tongue in cheek, "The election of Lincoln is hailed here with much joy. The most ignorant suppose that it will lead to a disbanding if the army, and thus they [the Indians] be set at liberty."[17]

But by January 1861, when the secession of the Southern states had become a real threat to the federal government, alarm replaced humor. Rover reported there was "quite a panic" when troops at Fort Arbuckle heard from the army paymaster that there was no money to pay them and no word when any funds would be available.[18] However, five wagons of supplies for the troops at Fort Washita had just arrived. "If rumor can be credited, Forts Cobb, Arbuckle, and Washita, are at present in danger of being attacked by a Texan mob, to get possession of the arms, horses, mules, and stores, belonging to Uncle Sam," Rover wrote. He continued, "Should such be the case, the Texans will find it rather hot work to carry their threats into execution. There are sufficient troops at each of the forts above mentioned, to protect all Government property."[19] Meanwhile, some soldiers were already making the difficult choice between serving the United States or their home states. In March, Rover noted soberly that 1st Lt. Alfred Iverson, a fellow officer in the 1st Cavalry, had resigned his commission. The son of a former Georgia senator, Iverson had accepted a captaincy in the "Georgia army."[20]

In late March and early April, with war between the Confederacy and the United States ever more likely, the U.S. Army command back east was deciding how to allocate its limited resources. This decision included what should be done about four forts highly important to the Indian Territory and which also guarded the northern approaches to the Texas frontier. Fort Gibson across the Arkansas River from today's Muskogee, Oklahoma, had been abandoned since 1857 and its campus handed back to the Cherokee Nation. Downstream and just across the border in Confederate Arkansas, federal troops still precariously occupied Fort Smith. The report suggested its garrison should march west to Frozen Rock, in today's southeast Muskogee, Oklahoma, fifteen miles downstream from Fort Gibson. Fort Arbuckle in the western Chickasaw Nation had been closed briefly during 1858 and was rated militarily unimportant, so its current two companies were to be broken up and reassigned elsewhere. However, Fort Washita in the eastern Chickasaw Nation was in good repair and located near major transportation routes and the Texas border. Because it had high military value, Lieutenant Colonel Emory was ordered to transfer his headquarters there.[21]

That left the fate of his former station, Fort Cobb, the westernmost fort and the one most responsible for the peace and security of the Leased District tribes, in question. Weighing against it were its exposure on the western frontier, its location relatively near Confederate Texas, and the difficulty of keeping it supplied. Balancing the safety of its garrison against the security of the Wichita Agency Indians, the army's decision was to pull the troops out and abandon Fort Cobb. The question remaining was what to do about the poorly armed and vulnerable Indians under its protection. They could not accompany the withdrawing troops because the Choctaws and Chickasaws did not want them camped around Fort Washita. In the end the federal government left them to the care of their agent, Matthew Leeper.[22]

By then it was becoming clear that the Choctaw and Chickasaw Nations were leaning toward alliances with the Southern states, with whom, according to a resolution of the Choctaw General Council, they shared, "natural affections, the educations, institutions and interests of our property."[23] On March 19 rumors of an attack from Texas on Fort Arbuckle led Capt. William E. Prince to move Company E, 1st Infantry, from there to greater safety at Fort Washita. Meanwhile, Rover noted in a letter dated March 31, "A few sympathizers with the Southern rabble, have deserted, taking with them horses, pistols, carbines, and everything they could lay hands upon."[24]

But by mid-April 1861, Lieutenant Colonel Emory, who had received fairly broad discretionary powers, knew even Fort Washita, now the headquarters of the 1st Cavalry, was too vulnerable. He explained to the assistant adjutant general of the army that because his supplies came through Arkansas and Texas, he was planning a retreat north up the Texas Road toward Fort Scott, Kansas. Emory knew they would need to wait for the arrival of Capt. Samuel D. Sturgis and Companies A and B of the 1st Cavalry. They had evacuated Fort Smith, Arkansas, during the night of April 23 about an hour before Arkansas secessionists moved in behind them. They were headed west to join forces with the Indian Territory troops.[25]

Rover wrote six days later that the garrison at Fort Washita was packing up to move out while keeping a wary eye on rebels edging ever closer. "Our horses have, for the last four nights been tied to a picket rope fastened around the quarters," he said. Clearly they meant to leave little behind for the rebels. Rover wrote, "Ox wagons, and teams of all kinds, have been employed to carry provisions, ordnance, Quartermaster's property, and stores . . . . The families of the soldiers were all sent off yesterday. They are to proceed to Fort Arbuckle, and there await our coming." Rover continued, "There is great reluctance on the part of the troops, that they are to abandon the Fort without making the traitors smell powder." Rover shared the men's opinion, stating, "I can't see into the policy of the Administration. The evacuation of the forts will certainly give the traitors more territory, as well as increase the numbers of adherents to [Confederate president] Davis' creed. If the Government does not put a stop to these rebellious scoundrels, they will soon have the upper hand."[26]

Captain Sturgis and his command arrived on April 30. Companies A and B with twenty wagons had completed the 160-mile journey from Fort Smith, Arkansas, in seven days. Next morning the combined Fort Smith–Fort Washita contingents moved out, heading north up the Washita River. One Louisiana newspaper reported, it is not known how accurately, that Captain Mayberry's Dead Shot Rangers from Jefferson, Texas, closed in immediately, capturing fourteen wagons abandoned by the federals. Emory was also said to have thrown guns, ammunition, and stores into the river and abandoned clothing, provisions, and field pieces. Emory, though, wrote he had abandoned nothing useful and described an orderly withdrawal.[27]

On the road to Fort Arbuckle, 2nd Lt. William W. Averell, Regiment of Mounted Riflemen, caught up with the column. A West Point graduate, Averell had been severely wounded while serving on the New Mexico frontier in 1858 and had reported to the War Department for duty from two years' sick leave just after South Carolinians fired on Fort Sumter. From Washington, D.C., he traveled in disguise for sixteen days through hostile country by train, stagecoach, and horseback—although he had not ridden a horse for two years. He delivered new orders to Lieutenant Colonel Emory to evacuate all federal troops from the Indian nations and march to Fort Leavenworth, Kansas. On the road along the east side of the Washita River about five miles from Fort Arbuckle, they met its two companies, just paroled by the large force of Texans that had overrun their post. The combined train moved on to Fort Cobb on May 3. It was good that they had left quickly and moved fast, because the 11th Texas Cavalry moved in right behind them to occupy the abandoned Indian Territory posts.[28]

Emory's train took the road "which lies on the open prairie to the north of the Washita River, so as to render the cavalry available" in case of an attack. He wrote, "On the 9th, I found the command from Cobb (two companies of foot) thirty-five miles northeast of that post, and on the same day I took the most direct course to Leavenworth that the nature of the ground would permit."[29] Apparently he also acquired the services of Delaware scouts Possum and Black Beaver. The latter had a farm along the river just east of Anadarko.[30]

Their route north lay generally along the ancient path some called Black Beaver's road or by the later 1860s the Chisholm Trail, roughly today's U.S. Highway 81.[31] It skirted the Cross Timbers and connected good springs, timber, grazing, and fords. They crossed the Arkansas River ten days later, likely close to today's Wichita, Kansas. Emory, much relieved, wrote, "I am now in Kansas, on the north side of the Arkansas River, with the whole command—eleven companies, 750 fighting men, 150 women, children, teamsters, and other non-combatants."[32] Twelve days later, his mile-long train rolled through Leavenworth, Kansas, to the cheers of people on the street. There were "Several ambulances, containing officers' wives, and about eighty wagons containing army stores, with about six hundred horses and mules attached, followed by the soldiers." The *Leavenworth Times* reported, "The men looked weary and jaded after their long and tedious march, but many of them seemed to be full of vigor and animation."[33] Emory wrote with satisfaction they were "in good condition, not a man, an animal, an arm, or wagon ... lost except two deserters."[34]

Most of the federal troops and officers in the withdrawal from the Indian Territory forts went on to serve the Union cause during the Civil War, and some, Samuel D. Sturgis among them, achieved high rank. However, Lt. Oliver H. Fish, Company B, 1st Cavalry, and Lt. Seth M. Barton, Company F, 1st Infantry, having fulfilled their duty to the United States Army, then resigned and left to join the Confederate states.[35]

Although the decision to abandon the Indian Territory posts was rational by military standards, the Indian nations saw it as a serious breach of faith and violation of their removal treaties. Troops from Arkansas and Texas were now entering their lands unopposed, while Indian frontier farms and settlements were left exposed to raiders. On May 25, 1861, the Chickasaw legislature declared its independence from the United States. In part it justified that action by stating "the Lincoln Government ... has shown its course towards us, in withdrawing from our country the protection of Federal troops." They punctuated their declaration of independence by "calling upon the Chickasaw warriors to form themselves into volunteer companies ... and hold themselves, with the best arms and ammunition together with a reasonable supply of provisions, in readiness at a minute's warning to turn out ... for the defense of their country."[36]

Soon afterward, on June 10, the Choctaw Nation, echoing the words of Thomas Jefferson in the Declaration of Independence, also separated itself from the United States. Concerned for the safety of the Choctaw Nation, four days later Gov. George Hudson issued a proclamation ordering the creation of volunteer and reserve militia as well as a Home Guard. "Our position now requires," he concluded, "that every effort be used to defend the country and repress all disorderly and unlawful acts."[37] Peter Pitchlynn, perhaps positioning his people for better treatment in defeat, argued in 1865 that the Choctaw Nation had no alternatives during the secession crisis once the United States withdrew its forces. They must choose between a Confederate alliance "or an invasion by forces from the States of Arkansas and Texas to which they could offer no resistance."[38]

The withdrawal of federal forces from the Indian Territory also had an impact on the Muscogee Nation. According to Georgianna "Annie" Stidham Grayson, a young girl at the time who probably drew her information from her father, George W. Stidham, and future husband, George Washington Grayson, "the very atmosphere seemed charged with excitement and rumors of war, rendering the wisest heads unsteady, and at a loss to know the course best to pursue." Muscogee leaders, including her father, had not received from Washington any statement of policy, plan, or advice about what to do in this crisis.[39] Nor had the federal government paid the treaty-guaranteed annuities for 1860. Because the Indian nations did not collect taxes, they needed these annuities to support their governments and school systems.[40] "On the other hand," Annie Grayson wrote, the Muscogee leaders "had what appeared to them to be clearly convincing evidence that the Indian allies of the Government were being left to shift ... for themselves. This evidence consisted in the withdrawal of U.S. troops which, in compliance with treaty stipulations, had long been stationed at strategic points on the borders of the Indian Territory to prevent hostile incursions of the nomads of the western prairies."[41]

Into this fog of uncertainty and alarm stepped Albert Pike of Arkansas—teacher, newspaper editor, attorney, poet, 32nd degree Mason, and newly appointed Confederate commissioner to the Indian Territory nations. Many Indians knew Pike, who had been employed by the Choctaw, Chickasaw, and Muscogee Nations to work on their claims against the federal government. Others, members of the North Fork Town and Tahlequah lodges, knew him as a brother Mason. In the summer of 1861, when he came to the Indian Territory as a representative of the Confederacy, the Choctaws and Chickasaws, already well disposed to the Confederacy and influenced by their agent, Douglas H. Cooper, gave Pike a warm reception.[42]

However, in the Muscogee Nation there was much more disagreement about the best thing to do. Many who had adopted views similar to Anglo-Americans on such things as English education, Christianity, constitutional government, and private property, including African slaves, thought their best course was to sign a Confederate alliance. However, more traditional Muscogees, including some substantial slaveholders, favored neutrality. According to Annie Grayson, the sticking point was their earlier treaties with the United States. "In the minds of the old Creeks," she wrote, "the thought of a tribe going back on its word given in good faith in a treaty such as they had with the United States was for a time not to be entertained."[43]

Complicating the question were the smoldering hostilities from the removal period. Chilly and Daniel N. McIntosh, sons of William McIntosh, who had been executed in 1825 for signing a land cession treaty, favored a Confederate alliance. Current Lower Creek chief Motey Kennard, George W. Stidham, Benjamin Marshall, the Herrods, and "the old full-blood patriarch Tuckabatchee Micco" agreed with them. Leading the opposition, though, was "the grand old man," Opothle Yahola, a bitter political opponent of the McIntoshes since before the Removal, along with Oktarharsars Harjo, or Sands.[44] Pike had once met Opothle Yahola while involved in a per capita payment to his nation. Pike remembered, "He was a tall, large man, with [a] large head and features," reminding him of Senator Daniel Webster. Opothle Yahola's face while business was being conducted was "inscrutable in its massiveness and melancholy gloom." But when it was concluded and he had made his point to Pike, he suddenly smiled. "I never saw a human face so changed in my life," Pike wrote. "It lighted up all over."[45]

In early July 1861 Confederate commissioner Albert Pike went to North Fork Town to meet with representatives of the Muscogee, Choctaw, and Chickasaw Nations. With him was Brig. Gen. Ben McCulloch, recently assigned military responsibility for the Indian Territory and lands west of Arkansas. McCulloch was a rather odd choice for negotiations designed to recruit Indian allies for the Confederacy. He was, among other things, a Texas Ranger who had helped break the power of the Comanches in central Texas.⁴⁶ Diarist Mary Chestnut, acquainted with him during his stays in the East, commented, "How he hated Indians!"⁴⁷

During their tour of eastern Indian Territory, Pike presented similar treaties with the same guarantees to each of the five southeastern nations: (1) The annexation of the territory to the Confederate States of America but with the Indian nations retaining their land titles; (2) the right of the Confederacy to construct and garrison military posts, build roads, reserve rights of way for telegraph and railroad lines, and establish a postal system; (3) guaranteed protection for slavery; (4) Indian representation in the Confederate Congress; (5) Confederate protection of the Indian nations from invasion; and (6) assumption of the federal government's obligations for the annuities owed them. In return, each Indian nation would raise troops which the Confederacy would arm, equip, and pay but which would not serve outside the territory without their government's permission. The Muscogees and Seminoles would raise one regiment; the Choctaws and Chickasaws, one; and the Cherokees, one.⁴⁸

Chief Motey Kennard of the Muscogee Arkansas District had called a national council to hear Pike's message. About a thousand people attended the council and camped in fine summer weather on the well-watered, grassy prairie near North Fork Town (or just west of today's Eufaula, Oklahoma). Local merchants supplied free groceries, and rancher Watt Grayson had his slave cowhands drive in a herd of cattle to provide meat. The debate held in a large brush arbor on Baptizing Creek was unusually intense and acrimonious. Opothle Yahola argued eloquently and stubbornly for honoring their last treaty with the United States; Sands, Locha Harjo, and Cotchochee backed him up. When he saw after two or three days' debate that he could not persuade the pro-Confederate faction to his position, he and his supporters withdrew from the council ground and went to the Antelope Hills on the far-western edge of the Muscogee Nation for a council with representatives of the western tribes—the Kickapoos, Delawares, Caddos, Anadarkos, Ionies, Wichitas, Keechis, Tawakonis, Tonkawas, and Comanches—as well as some Cherokees and Seminoles. The McIntoshes, Chief Kennard, and G. W. Stidham then led the signing of Pike's treaty committing the Muscogee Nation to a Confederate alliance. Someone also added the names of men who had gone west with Opothle Yahola. Two days later, the Choctaw and Chickasaw Nations signed similar treaties.[49]

The division of the Muscogee Nation at the North Fork Town council preceded a similar division among the Seminoles. Their representatives had attended the March meeting of the intertribal council at North Fork Town. However, influenced by Chief Billy Bowlegs, or Sonaki Mikko, and John Chupco, a comparatively recent arrival from Florida and convert of abolitionist minister James R. Ramsey, they spoke against a Confederate alliance. Nor did they send a delegate to meet Pike at North Fork Town in July. They were suffering from the prolonged drought and destitute.[50] Making matters worse, in 1861 the federal government refused to pay the Indian nations their annuities, citing fear it would fall into the hands of "armed rebels and banditti"[51] in transit. That meant they could expect no relief that year.

John Jumper, or Heniha Mikko, John Chupco's political rival, went with a party of Seminoles to the Fort Scott, Kansas, vicinity to meet with U.S. commissioner E. H. Carruth. They gave him the impression the Seminoles would remain loyal. Later, though, Jumper met secretly and unofficially with Pike, who told him the other Indian nations had signed alliances with the Confederacy. Pike also said the "cold people" from the north would take the Seminoles' land. In the end Jumper secretly recruited forty-six men on the promise that six hundred Rangers would come from Fort Cobb to suppress Seminoles loyal to the Union. They never arrived, but, according to a federal official at the time, the Union failed to exert the small amount of effort needed then to keep the Seminole Nation loyal to the United States.[52] However, tribal factionalism also played a role. By late summer about half the Seminole people saw following John Jumper into a Confederate alliance as the best course, while the other half tried to uphold their treaty with the United States and remain neutral.[53]

Within the Cherokee Nation, Principal Chief John Ross still hoped to maintain neutrality. The commissioners from Texas had visited him in March, and he "received [them] with courtesy but not cordiality."[54] They reported that Ross believed the same as President Lincoln, that the Union was not broken and the Confederacy should be ignored. However, they reminded him that the Cherokee Nation was already fracturing, with the slaveholding elite on one side and the common Indians, much influenced by abolitionist missionaries John and Evan Jones, on the other. That spring Confederate Arkansas was exerting pressure on the Cherokee Nation, and in May the Confederate government had plans in place to formalize a relationship with the Indian nations and incorporate the territory into its military organization. Before Albert Pike and Brigadier General McCulloch could deliver this message to the Cherokees in early June, a pro-Confederate delegation met them at the border. It included Stand Watie, his brother-in-law John Bell, his nephew Elias C. Boudinot, and William Penn Adair. With or without the agreement of their principal chief, these "Southern Cherokee" leaders meant to support the Confederacy. Ross held his neutral position through Pike and McCulloch's visit to the Cherokee Nation after the July meeting at North Fork Town. Watie, though, risked violent conflict with the Pins by accepting a commission as a Confederate colonel and arms for three hundred Confederate-allied Cherokee soldiers.[55]

Word of these developments filtered even into the scattered communities of the Cherokee Nation. In the Cherokee Neutral Lands, Cherokee settlers were primarily mixed-bloods who accepted slavery and favored the Cherokee-Confederate alliance. Among them was Tahlakitehi, or George Washington Walker. As a young boy he had survived the Cherokee removal from Tennessee, which he never forgot or allowed his children to forget. In 1861, with his wife, Rachel Rogers Walker, he farmed on the west bank of the Neosho River near the village of Chetopa. On June 4, 1861, he and his neighbors held a "secession meeting" and created a pro-Confederate Cherokee home guard unit. Most of the twenty-five enlistees were Cherokees and intermarried white men, but there were also some white Kansans and even two Osages. George Walker signed up to protect his neighbors from pro-Unionists in the area. However, Stand Watie quickly absorbed the unit into the 1st Cherokee Regiment and ordered it south into the Cooweescoowee District to guard the northern Cherokee Nation boundary.[56]

About that time, Blackbird Doublehead, then about twelve years old, lived on his father's farm in the rural Cherry Tree community (near today's Stillwell, Oklahoma). He told an interviewer in 1937 how rumors of war circulated through the community for several months as representatives of the North and South visited throughout the nation. Finally a man named Dirteater called a community meeting close to Candy Mink Springs, a Keetoowah area. Blackbird accompanied his father to this meeting, at which the speaker was Cyclone from along Greasy Creek. They discussed what business they had in this war, Blackbird told his interviewer, because some claimed they would be forced sooner or later to choose a side and fight. The Old Settlers, more sympathetic to the Watie faction, had mostly moved on years ago when Trail of Tears survivors such as the Doublehead family moved into the area. With no one left to dissent in 1861, the conservative Cherry Tree community agreed to support the North.[57]

It is not known exactly when this local meeting took place, but Pike and McCulloch laid the same argument before Principal Chief Ross during their June visit to Tahlequah, the Cherokee capital, and to Ross's home at nearby Park Hill: in spite of Ross's efforts to hold the Cherokee Nation neutral during the secession crisis, he could not do it much longer. Still, Ross refused their treaty offers. Summing up that visit, Pike reported that internal Cherokee politics was complicating his mission. He had discovered that, in spite of what the "Southern Cherokees" told him about the situation, they had their own agenda. They said the missionary Joneses had organized full-blood Cherokee abolitionists to block their support of the Confederacy. Instead, he had learned, the Pins' purpose was "depriving the half-breeds of all political power . . . and [that party] was organized and in *full* [his italics] operation long before Secession was thought of."[58]

With no success in the Cherokee Nation, Pike and McCulloch moved on to other Indian tribes. Accompanied by contingents of Confederate-allied Seminoles and Muscogees, Pike went west to the Leased District in August. At Shirley's Trading Post he met with the Wichitas, Caddos, Tonkawas, and Delawares living near the Wichita Agency as well as some of the Comanches. During the negotiations he supplied the trade goods, rations, and gifts that were customary in plains diplomacy. In response, some tribal leaders signed Confederate treaties. Tosawa (Toshaway) signed for the Penateka Comanches, and Showetat, or George Washington, signed for the Caddos. Pike promised them weapons and supplies, and they promised him they would confine their raids to Unionist Kansas. Pike reasoned, "To go on the warpath somewhere else is the best way to keep them from troubling Texas."[59] With pressure relieved on the Texas frontier, its manpower could be sent east of the Mississippi River toward the primary war front.[60]

While Pike was still in the Leased District recruiting Indian allies, events back east raised hope substantially for Southern independence. In late July after some small-scale engagements, Confederate troops won the first major Civil War battle, which occurred at Manassas, or Bull Run, near Washington, D.C. Meanwhile, events in neighboring Missouri culminated in the first major battle in the Trans-Mississippi West. Most Missourians favored neutrality, but a strong pro-Confederate faction, which included the governor, had armed and raised troops. It had not so far secured Missouri's secession, and Capt. Nathaniel Lyon of the U.S. Army had kept St. Louis and the nearby federal arsenal out of its hands. He had also captured one of their main camps, secured the state capital, and forced pro-Confederate forces to retreat toward Springfield in southwest Missouri. In mid-July, Lyon, promoted to brigadier general, followed them and occupied Springfield, a railroad center for the region. On August 10 federal troops battled Missouri state and Confederate forces at Wilson's Creek just south of Springfield. Lyon was killed in the day-long fight, and Maj. Samuel Sturgis—lately of Forts Smith and Washita—safely extracted the federal troops from the field, leaving the Confederates to claim victory.[61]

Among them was eighteen-year-old George Bent, the half-Cheyenne son of Indian trader William Bent. With several other mixed-blood Indian boys attending Webster College for Boys near St. Louis, he had enlisted in Col. Martin E. Green's cavalry unit in the Missouri State Guard. Bent recalled that they charged into battle that day giving Indian war cries, adding to the intimidating din. A small contingent of pro-Confederate Cherokees led by Joel B. Mayes and including Stand Watie's nephew Elias C. Boudinot were said to have been in that fight, too.[62]

The impact on the Cherokee Nation was strong. Principal Chief John Ross reconsidered his position of neutrality and moved toward a Confederate alliance. Historian William G. McLoughlin noted that no one involved left specific reasons for the shift of the Cherokee government toward the Confederacy other than it was for the common good. However, there had already been incidents of factional violence —including murders—in the nation. Recent friction between the pro-

Southern slaveholders at Webber's Falls and the Pins could easily have turned violent. The Ross government wanted to prevent further division among the Cherokees. Besides, there had been no support from the federal government and no annuity payment for 1861. Ross's old enemy Stand Watie was becoming more troublesome, leading his Confederate-allied Cherokee troops on raids into Kansas. The few that participated in the Battle of Wilson's Creek won applause from the Arkansas press and some Cherokees, who admired warriors. Watie's influence was growing, while Ross seemed to lack solutions to the burgeoning problems of the Cherokee Nation.[63] Another theory offered for his political shift was that a Confederate victory over the Union would place a neutral Cherokee Nation at a disadvantage. Worse perhaps from Ross's point of view, the Confederacy might then help Stand Watie depose and replace Ross as principal chief.[64]

Whatever his motivations, Ross called a public council in Tahlequah on August 20 and 21, 1861. After a day of speech making, some of the audience left believing Cherokee neutrality would continue, while others went home expecting to become Confederate allies. The second day, though, Ross's task was to unify the Cherokee people around their government. He explained that, given the present situation, they must make the same choice their Indian and white neighbors had—to support the Confederacy. Speaking to his Keetoowah supporters, he urged them to hold to their ancient traditions, particularly unity. As Cherokees first, he said, they must suppress their dislike of slavery for the good of the nation. They must also stand firm against Watie and the progressive mixed-blood faction because that would strengthen Ross as their principal chief. McLoughlin concluded not one in ten people who attended the public meeting truly understood that Ross was allying the Cherokee Nation with the Confederacy. Watie's Southern-allied Cherokees did understand, but they were frustrated even though they got what they wanted in that new alliance. They realized that Ross's political conversion strengthened his control over their government.[65]

A few days later William Penn Adair and James M. Bell fumed in a letter to Watie, "[the public council] in reality tied up our hands & shut our mouths & put the destiny & everything connected with the Nation . . . in the hands of the Executive." They added, "The Pins already have more power ... than we can bear." If they were to become the treaty-making power, too, Adair and Bell concluded, "you know our destiny will be inalterably sealed."[66] Clearly even with some unity on a Cherokee-Confederate alliance, their nation's well-being was still perilously fragile.

The new Confederate treaties the Indian nations signed that summer obligated them to organize regiments that would defend the Indian Territory, using weaponry, supplies, and funds from the Confederate government. The Choctaw and Chickasaw governments had already called on their citizens to gather arms and supplies and to be ready to defend their nations at a minute's notice. They jointly raised the 1st Regiment of Choctaw and Chickasaw Mounted Rifles. Lt. Col. Tandy Walker, a former governor of the Choctaw Nation, was named commander. Daniel N. McIntosh, a planter, pro-Southern legislator, and son of Chief William McIntosh, organized and commanded the 1st Regiment of Creek Mounted Volunteers. The Seminoles raised the 1st Battalion of Seminole Mounted Rifles, commanded by Maj. John Jumper, or Heniha Mikko. The six-foot, four-inch, two-hundred-pound Jumper was an experienced fighter. He took part in the 1835 Dade Massacre during the Second Seminole War against the United States and came as a prisoner to the Indian Territory.[67]

In the Cherokee Nation, this process was more complicated. Principal Chief John Ross in early summer had denied Confederate brigadier general Ben McCulloch's request to allow Cherokee volunteers, including Stand Watie, to serve in the Confederate army. Ross feared that might lead to actual warfare between Confederate-allied Cherokee troops and the Pins. Watie, covered by the Confederate army, might even try to overthrow Ross and his administration. However, McCulloch ignored Ross, commissioned Watie, and armed his three hundred volunteers. Ross countered this in August by creating the 1st Cherokee Mounted Rifles and named as its colonel John Drew, a sixty-five-year-old trader and respected legislator married to Ross's niece. Drew's officers included Lt. Col. William Potter Ross and Maj. Thomas Pegg. As might be expected, full-blood Cherokees who supported Ross filled the ranks of this Cherokee regiment.[68]

Eventually, all these new Confederate Indian units were placed under the command of Col. Douglas H. Cooper, who during the

Mexican War had fought at Buena Vista and Monterey with the 1st Mississippi Rifles, commanded by Col. Jefferson Davis. As the Confederate military expanded and organized, he was named second-in-command to Brig. Gen. Albert Pike, commander of the Provisional Army of the Department of Indian Territory.[69]

Not surprisingly, the Indian regiments were mounted. Historian Stephen B. Oates explained that the two or three decades of Indian fighting on the American frontier before the war had raised the value of cavalry beyond performing reconnaissance, escorting supply trains, screening and supporting the infantry—still viewed as the backbone of an army—and covering a retreat. The Civil War on the western frontier further enhanced the value of cavalry units as they were dispatched on strategic raids, sometimes accompanied by horse artillery and supply trains, to strike the enemy and damage his ability to make war. Beyond military theory, though, there was the simple fact that Indians in the region, including prodigious runners such as the Pawnees and Osages, loved and valued their horses. Chickasaws had even bred their own horses for running, working, and hunting. These first Indian units were mounted, but later units theoretically raised as infantry also insisted on riding their ponies to war.[70]

All the martial activity that summer of 1861 helped spread the news about the war in "the states" and territorial people's involvement in it. Civilians reacted with alarm and began thinking about what preparations they should make if war actually came to the Indian Territory. For most adults, memories of the removals and the accompanying violence and loss were all too fresh and bitter. To make things worse, the past year had been extremely hard because of the punishing drought across the Plains. In neighboring Kansas less than an inch of rain and no snow fell from September 1859 through October 1860.[71] In early January 1861 Baptist missionary Henry F. Buckner described already hard times in the Muscogee Nation, where shortages made prices high. Corn, their staple crop, had failed, so there was not enough meal for bread. Buckner told a friend, "not one family in ten can get bread enough to eat. Many are subsisting on wild winter greens and such."[72] If war came they might have to deal with even worse conditions.

Well-to-do Indians were in a better position to protect their families and property. Some sent their children east to boarding schools in the belief they might be safer in Arkansas, Georgia, or Alabama.[73] Some sold off their slaves or livestock for cash, which was easier to transport and manage. Morris Sheppard, a slave of Joe Sheppard, a Cherokee farmer who lived near Webber's Falls, was about nine in 1861. Morris recalled that night-riding Pins living up the Illinois River frequently raided Cherokee farms in the Webber's Falls area. "Dey would come in de night and hamstring de horses and maybe set fire to de barn," he said. Among them were "Joab Scarrel and Tom Starr [who] killed my pappy one night just before de War broke out." Joe Sheppard sold off most of his slaves then, keeping Morris and his family for the time being.[74]

Other well-to-do Indians moved their slaves and herds of horses and cattle to Texas, where they expected them to be out of harm's way. Judge George W. Stidham, who had four stores in the Muscogee Nation as well as farms and ranches, took thirty of his male slaves—considered the most valuable—to east Texas, paid cash for land, and put them to work cultivating it. Muscogee chief Motey Kennard rounded up his best horses, drove them south into Texas, and then returned to the North Fork Town area to await events. His national treasurer, Benjamin Marshall, had a large farm near today's Muskogee, Oklahoma. About one hundred slaves raised corn, oats, and wheat, which he shipped, along with wood and pecans, down the Arkansas River from his own landing. Taking his family and thirty slaves, he moved farther south hoping to avoid trouble. Each night on the road, Marshall had his slaves bury the national funds in coffee pots and gallon jugs for safekeeping, according to his grandson in the traveling party.[75] This was generally an orderly exodus because people had time to make decisions, gather their belongings, and travel at a comfortable pace. However, it was only the first phase of a mass exodus from and within the Indian Territory set off by the Civil War.

Non-Indian residents of the Indian nations also thought it might be time to leave for safer areas. Among them were federal employees, millers, blacksmiths, teachers, physicians, merchants, and missionaries. Once the millers left, flour and meal became even scarcer and more expensive, so Indian women got out their old hand mills to grind their own. Suspicion of outsiders, even old friends, flourished. Dr. Ward Howard Bailey, originally from New York City, had practiced medicine in North Fork Town since 1850 and had many white and Indian friends. But when war seemed likely he received threatening letters because "he was a Northern man in a Southern country," according to his grandson. After a family conference, Dr. Bailey took his younger children and wife to Fort Smith in her home state of Arkansas and went back alone to New York. On her own, Mrs. Bailey supported her family by taking in boarders. Their older son Benjamin Hawley Bailey, however, returned to the Muscogee Nation as soon as he was of age and enlisted in Company A, 2nd Creek Mounted Volunteers, with his Confederate-allied Indian friends.[76]

Missionaries were also told to leave the Muscogee Nation. Among them were Dr. William Schenk Robertson and his wife, Ann Eliza Worcester Robertson. Her father, Samuel Austin Worcester, had been imprisoned in Georgia for supporting Cherokee sovereignty, and she had come as a child to the Indian Territory with the Cherokees during their removal. The Robertsons were teachers and translators at Tullahassee Mission and took no sides in Muscogee politics or the slavery issue. In 1861, however, their northern roots made them suspect. With their children, an elderly retired lady missionary, and a few belongings— including the first sewing machine in the Indian Territory— they left for Ann Eliza's family home at Park Hill Mission in the Cherokee Nation. There they expected to join her brother and sisters.[77]

Once they reached Park Hill, though, they found tensions just as high and planned to go on north out of the Indian Territory. The youngest Robertson daughter, Mary Alice, who was seven, still remembered years later, "Sitting in the gloaming on the stone steps, I watched my young aunt stitching many gold pieces into a canvas belt. She took from me a most solemn promise never to tell about this belt of gold." They left behind every unnecessary item, as well as Ann Eliza's sister Hannah, a missionary and printer who had married Abijah Hicks, a bilingual Cherokee assistant at the mission. He was to escort them safely out of the Cherokee Nation. Their driver, Peter Passen, was a full-blood Cherokee Christian and a Pin. They prepared the wagon with a cover, cushioning, food, and minimal cooking gear—things they would need along "the terrible rocky trails of the Ozarks." Then, Alice remembered, "When night came we told them good bye, and out into the darkness [we] went through trails that Peter Passen knew" into Arkansas, where "passports," or safe conduct letters, allowed them to travel on toward the North.[78]

As the summer months passed, tensions increased in the Indian Territory. By August the focus was shifting to the western Muscogee Nation. Opothle Yahola's home lay just southwest of today's Checotah, Oklahoma, near the bend of the Deep Fork of the Canadian River. One of the wealthiest men in the Muscogee Nation, he had been a partner in a trading post and now had a large prairie-land farm worked by his many slaves. Muscogees who shared his views of the Confederate treaty began to gather around him.[79]

On August 5 these "Loyal Creeks" deposed chiefs Motey Kennard and Echo Harjo on the grounds they had violated council procedure by signing the Confederate treaty. They agreed with Sands, or Oktarharsars Harjo, a leading full-blood chief, who said he "thought the old U.S. was alive yet and the [old] Treaty was good. Wont [sic] go against the U.S. himself."[80] Col. Douglas H. Cooper made one more attempt to win Opothle Yahola over in a meeting at the council ground near High Spring (north of today's Hitchita, Oklahoma). He found Opothle Yahola still adamantly opposed to the Confederate-Muscogee alliance supported by the McIntosh faction, as well as a magnet for those of a like mind.[81]

His antipathy to the McIntoshes aside, Opothle Yahola intended to remain neutral for two reasons according to some accounts: First, he had given his allegiance to the United States in 1814 after the Red Stick defeat at Horseshoe Bend, Alabama, and he would not break his word. Second, he was trying to communicate directly with Pres. Abraham Lincoln. On August 15 the old speaker and Sands sent a letter to the president, reminding the Indians' symbolic Great Father that when they were removed to the Indian Territory,

> you said that in our new homes we should be defended from all interference . . . and that no white people . . . should ever molest us . . . but the land should be ours as long as grass grew or waters run, and should we be injured by anybody you would come with your soldiers & punish them, but now the wolf has come, men who are strangers tread our soil, our children are frightened & the mothers cannot sleep for fear.

Sands and Opothle Yahola, who had headed the 1832 delegation to Washington, D.C., to negotiate the Muscogee removal treaty, reminded Lincoln,

> I was at Washington when you treated with us, and now White People are trying take our people away to fight against us and you. I am alive. I well remember the treaty. My ears are open & my memory is good.[82]

In this letter Opothle Yahola and Sands were addressing current concerns among their people. Confederate agitators were circulating among the Indian Territory tribes, warning that the federal government meant to dispossess them again and claiming the Confederacy was their only friend. What the Muscogees and other tribes needed from the federal government right then—and what Opothle Yahola and Sands were asking for—was protection from those intruders and reassurance their people would not be driven out of their homes again.[83]

The letter was still on its way to Lincoln when Micco Hutke, Bob Deer, and Joe Ellis set out in September for Washington by way of Kansas with a second letter updating the Indian Territory situation as they understood it. By then some of the Loyal Creeks had withdrawn up the Little River, and Micco Hutke reported that this group had called a council of the territorial tribes. Muscogees, Cherokees, Chickasaws, Seminoles, Caddos, Shawnees, Senecas, Quapaws, Kickapoos, Delawares, Weas, Piankeshaws, Wichitas, and Comanches had attended. (Some of these tribes had divided historically, and some factions had already signed Pike's Confederate treaties or soon would.) Only the Choctaws, almost wholly committed to the Confederacy, had not come. The consensus of this council, according to Micco Hutke, favored neutrality and loyalty to the federal government. Working against that was the infestation of the territory with Confederate agents, who were spreading lies, distrust of the Union, and general uneasiness. This letter requested that a federal agent come, reassure people, and tell them what they should do. They made tentative plans for a meeting somewhere in Kansas north up Black Beaver's road, but it never happened. Micco Hutke and his party met briefly with federal officials, who sent them on to Washington.[84]

At some point, Pres. Abraham Lincoln responded to Opothle Yahola and Sands. By then their adherents had moved upstream on the North Canadian River to a site near today's Boley, Oklahoma, where the elderly dissident camped with about three thousand followers. When Lincoln's answer finally came, Opothle Yahola called Samuel W. Brown, a young Euchee, to read and translate the letter, its paper now worn and soiled from handling, to the gathering of Loyal Creeks. Lincoln's reply was simply that the conflict between the federal government and the Confederacy did not concern the Indians or their interests and that they should remain neutral. What it did not do was offer the reassurance they needed, nor did it promise them help, a federal agent to serve as their liaison with the government, or troops for protection. The loyal Muscogees and like-minded members of other tribes were on their own. It was not until November that Sands, Micco Hutke, and a few Seminoles and Chickasaws reached Leroy, Kansas, by way of Black Beaver's road. They learned there that Maj. George A. Cutler was their new agent, and they were sent on to Washington to see for themselves how the Union was fighting the war.[85]

As summer turned into fall, the number of people who wanted no part of the war and left home to join Opothle Yahola continued to grow. He had sent word to the free blacks and slave settlements in his own and the Seminole nations, offering them freedom if they joined him. Many did, along with some of their owners. Later Sands reported that twenty-seven Muscogee tribal towns, or *tvlwv*, mostly in the western part of the nation, had by November chosen to follow Opothle Yahola. There were so many people they could not all camp together, so they settled into sub-camps at several locations. Runners kept them in constant contact.[86]

These "loyal" Indians included more than just the Muscogees and Seminoles. The Quapaws were one of several tribes already divided by choice or circumstance during the 1700s and 1800s. In their case, one group of the Quapaws had lived on a small reservation northeast of the Cherokee Nation in today's Ottawa County since 1834. However, another part of the "downstream people," as they had been known since prehistory, had chosen a more traditional way of life in Texas and later in the Muscogee Nation on lands along the Canadian River. In

1861 they joined Opothle Yahola and stayed with the Union, while the reservation Quapaws became Confederate allies.[87]

In another instance, the once-powerful Osages, their population down to about 3,500 people by the 1850s, occupied a large reservation in southeastern Kansas. That meant they were precariously situated near the troubled Kansas-Missouri border. Father John Schonmakers, a Jesuit missionary dear to them, had warned them to stay neutral with regard to the white people's disputes. However, Andrew J. Dorn, their agent, had also proved himself to be their friend in the 1850s. At the outbreak of the Civil War he became the Osage agent for the Confederate Indian service and drew them toward the Confederacy. In the fall of 1861 while Schonmakers was absent from Osage Mission for several months, Dorn and Augustus Captain, a mixed-blood Osage, persuaded them to attend a meeting with Albert Pike at Tahlequah in the Cherokee Nation.[88]

Principal Chief John Ross hosted this meeting in early October. It included representatives of the Quapaw, Shawnee, and Seneca tribes as well as the Osages. Like the Quapaws, the Senecas and part of the Shawnees had small reservations in the northeastern part of the Indian Territory, while divisions of their people lived elsewhere. According to Osage elder and geographer Louis F. Burns, the ratio of Osages who favored the Union over the Confederacy at this time was probably about five to one. However, the Lincoln administration did nothing to hold their support. Furthermore, the Osage leaders mistakenly believed Ross supported the Confederacy, and because they respected him, they were willing to listen to Pike. The Senecas, Shawnees, and Quapaws signed Confederate treaties at nearby Park Hill, but the Osages divided on the matter. In the end, the representatives of the Big Osage division signed, but Hard Rope, who could be contrary, and Little Bear, both representing the Little Osage division, refused.[89]

Once these tribes had signed their Confederate treaties, Chief Ross, Joseph Verner, William Potter Ross, Richard Fields, and Thomas Pegg put their signatures on a Confederate treaty for the Cherokee Nation. Even though the Cherokee people appeared reconciled for the moment, tensions were still high between the Ross and Watie parties, with armed men on the streets. Pike tried to work with both factions and maintain the fragile peace. Within a very short time, though, Ross realized his mistake in siding with the Confederacy. It became clear that its war for independence was not going to end in a quick victory, nor was it giving the Indian nations the attention and benefits it had promised.[90]

To make things worse, the trouble in the Muscogee Nation was spreading outside its borders. That nation no longer had a stable government and its population was in turmoil. Included in its population, of course, were African slaves. Some slave families had already been torn apart in the first exodus from the nation. When Judge George W. Stidham took his thirty most valuable slaves to Texas, he included Tom, his blacksmith from his ranch near Honey Springs, but he left Flora, Tom's wife, behind. At the time they had a teen-aged son and twin daughters. Their youngest child, Jim, was about five. With Tom and Judge Stidham gone, Flora and her children were left with less protection in a deteriorating situation. Their teen-aged son took the opportunity to run away toward Kansas and freedom.[91]

Other slaves did the same. Phoebe Banks, a slave of Mose Perryman, who had a large farm in the Choska Bottoms near today's Muskogee, Oklahoma, related how her father, William McIntosh, and uncle, Jacob Perryman, were "fixers" who helped slaves run away. Phoebe explained that some of the slave owners had already had runaways and were taking their slaves to Texas to prevent more escapes. The Perryman slaves now believed their best chance lay with Opothle Yahola and the Loyal Creeks. Phoebe explained, "That's the ones my daddy and uncle was fixing to join, for they was afraid their masters would take up and move to Texas before they could get away."[92]

That Opothle Yahola and the Loyal Creek camps were attracting runaway slaves escalated the unease in the Muscogee Nation and the neighboring Cherokee Nation. On September 11 from the High Spring council ground, Muscogee colonel Daniel N. McIntosh wrote to Cherokee colonel John Drew news of "alarming character." Opothle Yahola, he said, had made allies of the "wild tribes" and now publicly opposed the South. Moreover, slaves were "fleeing to him from all quarters—not less than 150 have left within the last three days," McIntosh wrote. He warned, "This state of things cannot long exist here without seriously affecting your country."[93]

However, Drew and Colonel Douglas H. Cooper of the Choctaw-

Chickasaw regiment seemed less concerned at first and looked on Opothle Yahola's defection as being a Muscogee problem—not theirs.[94] Chief John Ross shared their attitude, calling this "the Creek feud," an affair that could have been handled peacefully with more political skill.[95] By November 10, Cooper was more alarmed because Opothle Yahola was now said to be planning an attack on his Confederate camp. It was rumored he might even bring along one thousand Kansas Jayhawkers said to be up near the Arkansas River.[96] By then the old speaker's own followers were estimated to number seven or eight thousand. What might happen if they joined forces with Gen. John C. Fremont's federal troops in Missouri and swept down on the Arkansas River valley farms, ranches, and settlements in the Indian Territory?[97]

About the first of November those who sided with Opothle Yahola received the order to gather and move toward the junction of the Cimarron and Arkansas Rivers.[98] Malucy Bear, who was a young Muscogee girl living near Okemah then, compared those days to what she had been told about her family's removal from Alabama. No one had time to harvest crops that had been planted that year, so sweet potatoes had not been dug from the ground, and mature corn was left standing in the fields. When the call came, the people took just what they could carry and left the rest behind. With their neighbors gone to join Opothle Yahola, Malucy remembered the sadness of abandoned farmsteads. "We would see some lone cow that had been left," she said. "The roosters would continually crow at some deserted home. The dogs would bark and howl. Those days were lonesome to me, as young as I was, for I knew that most of our old acquaintances were gone."[99]

Some who chose to go had gathered at Hilliby Creek, north of today's Paden and Boley, Oklahoma. James Scott, a Muscogee boy of nine or ten at the time, sensed the uneasiness without understanding just why his family had joined Opothle Yahola. When runners brought word to prepare to leave, though, he was old enough to help round up the livestock. He recalled, "I wondered at the vast amount of cattle being killed and the meat being dried, the pork being cooked down, and all the numerous preparations." The Scotts—James; his father, Artuss Yahola; mother, Lizzie Scott; and sister Lizzie—were part of a small group, which joined a larger group, which joined still larger groups moving out when the order was given. This included the

Muscogees that had first gathered around Opothle Yahola near the Deep Fork-North Fork junction. Even James recognized "the grand old man who had led them only a few years before . . . from their homes on the Coosa and Tallapoosa [Rivers] in Alabama."[100] Included in the mustering were more runaway slaves. Phoebe Banks, an infant then, learned of the exodus later from her family. "All our family join up with him . . . when they made a break for the North" riding horses stolen from the owners.[101]

Up to this point, the Confederate Indian allies had kept their distance while messengers took "solemn pledges" of peaceful intentions to Opothle Yahola's camps, along with recommendations that his followers go home. There was no response from the Indians.[102] Principal Chief John Ross had even sent Joseph Vann and a Cherokee delegation to see him in early October, advising that "all the red brethren was to be united and friendly among themselves."[103]

Meanwhile, Col. Douglas H. Cooper had sent for reinforcements. The 9th (4th) Texas Cavalry had recently arrived in North Fork Town, and some five hundred men commanded by Lt. Col. William Quayle answered Cooper's call. Orderly Sgt. George L. Griscom of the 9th Texas explained in his diary, "the Tory half of the Creek Indians" had refused to accept Pike's treaty and "were becoming very troublesome," forcing Cooper to retreat until reinforced. After a hard ride, the Texans reached his camp on November 12. Their welcome from the Choctaw, Chickasaw, Muscogee, and Seminole troops included firing off weapons and an all-night war dance, which the Texans joined.[104] On November 15 Cooper moved toward the main Loyal Creek camp with some 1,400 Indian troops and the Texans. Over a trail wide enough for a stagecoach, they rode toward Sell's Store on the Deep Fork and on to Brown's Creek. They had plenty of meat but little corn, and there was no grazing for their horses because the Indians they followed had burned off the grass. After three days they reached Opothle Yahola's camp but found it deserted, although there were signs women and children had been camped there.[105]

Ten days earlier, Opothle Yahola had given the order to leave. By then his followers included about half the Muscogee people, freedmen, and two or three hundred slaves, along with members of other tribes. Some estimated there were as many as nine thousand people. Only about two thousand were fighting men. These included veterans of the Seminole wars—Billy Bowlegs (Sonaki Mikko), John Chupco, Halleck Tastanaki, Fos Harjo, and Pascofar. Opothle Yahola knew less about the men from other tribes, their skill, and dependability in battle. Under the circumstances, moving on ahead of the approaching enemy was wise.[106]

The Confederate allies picked up a few stragglers who told them that the main body was headed toward the Red Fork of the Arkansas River, also called the Cimarron River. That was evident from the wide trail left by many horses, livestock herds, wagons, and those on foot. The Confederate allies immediately set off in pursuit, crossing the Cimarron River on November 19.[107]

There has been much speculation and argument about the route that eventually took Opothle Yahola's people into Kansas. Existing documentation is somewhat unclear, and oral history, while it should not be dismissed, was mostly collected in the 1930s from people who were children at the time. They may have had a limited view or understanding of conditions and events, and sometimes they received their information second-hand.[108]

Likewise, the location of the first battle of the Civil War in the Indian Territory, which occurred shortly after the hostile forces crossed the Cimarron River, has been in dispute for decades. In the 1940s Muriel H. Wright of the Oklahoma Historical Society proposed a site near today's Keystone Lake west of Tulsa. This lake covers the convergence of the Cimarron (Red Fork of the Arkansas) River and the Arkansas River, and there were ancient trails along the valleys. However, based on additional research by amateur historian John Melton and professional historians Berlin B. Chapman and Angie Debo of Oklahoma A and M College (today's Oklahoma State University), the Payne County Historical Society marked a site east of Yale, Oklahoma, near the Twin Mounds as the first battleground. A conference with National Park Service historians in 1993 failed to reach consensus. Research on the location continues today, and so does the controversy.[109]

What is clear is that the fugitive column moved as quickly as possible. They knew from scouts' reports that Cooper's troops were behind them and not hampered by herds of livestock, wagons, carriages, buggies, and people on foot. The pursuers were closing fast.[110]

James Scott remembered a McIntosh slave brought the first command to stop, perhaps from Cooper. "He rode the length of the wagon train issuing these orders. Many of our men answered, 'We are not going to stop; we are on our way.'"[111]

According to James Roane Gregory, a Muscogee teenager then who lived among the Loyal Creeks, some of Opothle Yahola's people had gone on ahead. The rest, aiming to join them, swung in a quarter circle to the northeast around Cooper's right flank.[112] A statement made in 1868 by Daniel N. McIntosh, James M. C. Smith, and Timothy Barnett—all in the Muscogee Confederate-allied regiments—said the oncoming troops followed the broad trail until November 19. That day there was constant skirmishing with the rearguard of Muscogees, Seminoles, Euchees, and Kickapoos commanded by Euchee chief Little Captain.[113]

According to Gregory, Cooper caught up with them at the Cimarron near dusk, followed them across the river, and made camp about two miles north. Cooper reported that Opothle Yahola's retreating rearguard drew them toward a Loyal Creek camp "a few miles North of Red Fork near a place called 'Round Mountains' in the Cherokee Country."[114]

The Confederate-allied troops consisted of six companies of the 1st Choctaw and Chickasaw Mounted Rifles; the 1st Creek Regiment, commanded by Col. Daniel N. McIntosh; the Creek and Seminole Battalion, commanded by Lt. Col. Chilly McIntosh and Maj. John Jumper; and Quayle's detachment of Texas cavalry.[115] If a fight indeed developed, Indians would be fighting other Indians in what had been called a "white man's war." Worse, it could be Seminoles against Seminoles, Chickasaws against Chickasaws, and Muscogees against Muscogees. Opothle Yahola's men were wearing yellow corn shuck badges. That would distinguish them from the "Southern" Muscogees.[116]

Sergeant Griscom wrote in his diary on November 19 that the Texans set off early that morning to "cross the Red fork of the Ark river." They killed some cattle for a "hearty dinner" before turning downstream. Soon they came across enemy pickets and sent back for Lieutenant Colonel Quayle. After the rest of the regiment came up and deployed, Griscom wrote, they charged about five miles but found the Indians gone. Still, they kept on "at a furious rate 3 miles to Round Mountain Creek" where they found the Indians "posted in a horseshoe of Timber the prairie forming a neck into which Capt. B[rinson] & his squadron charged & came *into line* [Griscom's italics] in fine style."[117]

The Texans soon learned a lesson about fighting the Loyal Indians. Opothle Yahola did not lead his fighting men in battle; he trusted that to his Seminole war chiefs. Again, the noncombatants went ahead to another camp, leaving the pursuers facing a strong and determined rear guard. It was already dark, but the Texans charged the camp, not realizing it was abandoned. They ran into tough resistance as the Loyal Indians set fire to the prairie. Griscom wrote that evening, "Still the enemy tried to turn our left flank in heavy force."[118] To defend themselves, the Texans formed a hollow square. Griscom continued, "Col Cooper with his Choctaws Coming up about this time . . . met them & a bloody fight of 15 minutes turned them back."[119]

That attack in the smoke and confusion of the burning prairie cost the Confederate allies several killed, wounded, and captured. The next morning they entered the Loyal Indians' abandoned camp, finding the bodies of the allies' wounded or prisoners from the previous night. They speculated the women had used their hominy pestles to bash in the prisoners' heads.[120] There was reason to believe the Indians had lost seventy-nine dead and more wounded, but by now they were too far ahead for the pursuit to continue. As tired and hungry as their horses, the Texans, Griscom wrote on November 20, took time "to bury our dead about 3 [miles] from there on a pretty spot near the Red fork of Ark in a grove of bl[ac]k Jacks firing the usual salute over their graves & feeling for the 1st time as one does when leaving comrades slain on the field." Griscom also noted, "our Creeks taking some scalps the 1st I ever saw."[121]

Of that first battle of the Civil War in the Indian Territory, Muscogee writer James Roane Gregory commented, "A small band of Creeks had taught Gen. Cooper on the Cimmaron [*sic*] what they could do in a night fight, causing him to retreat."[122] However, that fight had cost the fugitive Indians valuable supplies—flour, sugar, coffee, and salt—as well as twelve wagons, a buggy, many cattle, and horses captured by their pursuers.[123]

Both sides enjoyed a short respite then. Cooper, hearing that Union general John C. Fremont was about to invade Arkansas from the Springfield, Missouri, area, returned to his base at Concharty near today's Haskell, Oklahoma. Once there he learned that the planned Union expedition had been abandoned and that Brig. Gen. Ben McCulloch did not need the Indian Territory troops for defense after all. Cooper turned his attention back to Opothle Yahola, but by then his troop numbers had dropped from about 1,400 to about 780. However, Col. William B. Sims of the 9th (4th) Texas Cavalry was near Tulsey Town, and Col. John Drew of the 1st Cherokee Mounted Rifles, made up mostly of full-bloods, had been posted near Coody's Bluff. They were available to reinforce Cooper.[124]

Meanwhile, the Indian noncombatants aimed toward "Skiatooka's place." This 1850s Cherokee settlement lay on the Arkansas River near today's Cleveland, Oklahoma. From there they could follow one of the Osage trails into Kansas. Their route took them by way of the Coody settlement on Bird Creek. It was known as Caving (or Cave-in) Banks, or Chusto-Talasah, near today's Sperry, Oklahoma. This was the far-southwest corner of the Cherokee Nation proper, almost in the Cherokee Outlet. Cherokees who lived in the settlement included the Van (Vann), McDaniel, Coody, Melton, and Parker families. There were many full-blood Indians in the area, and Opothle Yahola knew they sympathized with his neutral but anti-Confederate treaty stance. Farms and homes lay along the winding creek and on the prairies on either side of it. Its margins, though, were heavily timbered with thick undergrowth. The creek bed was as deep as thirty feet in places, and the banks were steep. It could be forded, but outsiders generally did not know the few crossing points. The noncombatants moved on northwest under escort following Hominy Creek toward the safety of Achustenalah. Their fighting men stayed behind to cut trees to fortify Horseshoe Bend, a large east-looping curve of Bird Creek. A house and outbuildings occupied the bend, while a long rail fence stretching onto the prairie and the shelving creek banks made natural fortifications and firing steps.[125] The site recalled Tohopeka in Alabama where Red Stick Muscogees had fortified and defended another "Horse-shoe Bend" in 1814.

While the fugitives rested, regrouped, and prepared their defenses, still others came to join them. Some were the people of Tulsey Lochapoka, mostly full-blood Muscogees who had migrated as a community to the Indian Territory and settled along the north side of the Arkansas River about where Tulsa (then called Tulsey Town) stands today. In early winter 1861 they left their homes again with everything they could carry to march northwest to the Coody settlement. According to Joseph Bruner, whose mother Lucy was among them, it was like another Trail of Tears when they went to join Opothle Yahola and the Loyal Creeks.[126]

The calm lasted until early December. Then Brigadier General Cooper moved toward them again on reports that they were destroying stock and menacing Cherokees who did not side with them. There was also a rumor that Opothle Yahola was conniving with the Plains Indians and threatening an attack on Tulsey Town. Cooper expected to meet Colonel Sims and the 9th Texas Cavalry and Col. John Drew with the 1st Cherokee Mounted Rifles in the Bird Creek vicinity. However, Cooper reached the area on December 8 without connecting with them. He did locate Drew's camp, set up within shouting distance of the Loyal Creeks' lines. There was also a message from Opothle Yahola saying he wanted peace. Cooper responded by sending Maj. Thomas Pegg and three others over with a reply that he, too, wished to avoid shedding Indian blood and asking what terms the old speaker wanted. However, they returned later that night to report that Opothle Yahola's warriors had painted themselves for war and were prepared for an attack likely to start at any moment. Pegg said their diplomatic party had been allowed to leave only on the excuse they needed to escort some women and children to safety.[127]

Meanwhile, there was a drastic development in Drew's camp while he was waiting with Cooper for Pegg's report. In the twenty-four hours the 1st Cherokee Mounted Rifles had been camped near the Loyal Creek outposts, they had come to a "good understanding" with them.[128] Those conversations had caused the regiment to begin disintegrating, its morale weakened by the possibility of shedding the blood of Indian neighbors with whom they sympathized, even of fellow Keetoowahs. They had no quarrel with the Loyal Creeks; nor did they feel the Confederate cause had much to do with them.[129] Then, Pegg and his party returned with the news that the fight they did not want could start any minute. That completed the disintegration. Four companies of Drew's regiment crossed over the lines to join the Loyal Creeks, while others simply left for home. Major Pegg, with some other officers and a few privates, started back toward Fort Gibson, leaving the Cherokee regiment's wagons and tents where they stood. Cooper received this "astounding news" from Drew and about thirty-five Cherokee officers and men who had stood fast.[130] The next morning Cooper retrieved what supplies and equipment he could from Drew's camp, but he knew the fugitives now had an even greater advantage of numbers.[131]

No attack occurred that night, so the next morning, December 9, Cooper went on the offensive, moving his troops into position to attack the fugitives' fortified position in the loop of Bird Creek. The fight, a kaleidoscope of fierce, ragged combat, often hand-to-hand, began about eleven o'clock and continued through the day. There was a series of attacks, charges, and ambushes on the prairies, across the creek, and along timber-choked ravines. According to Col. Daniel N. McIntosh, commanding the 1st Creek Regiment, Opothle Yahola's war chiefs had planned this battle well. His post-analysis said,

> 1st. From all appearances it was a premeditated affair by them. They had placed their forces in a large creek, knowing by marching across the prairie that he [the Confederate allies] would be likely to pass in reach of the place.
> 2nd. The grounds they had selected were extremely difficult to pass, and in fact most of the banks on the creek were bluff and deep waters, so that no forces could pass across only at some particular points, which were only known to them.
> 3d. This place was fortified also with large timber on the side they occupied, and on our side [the] prairie extended to the creek, where the enemies were bedded, lying in wait for our approach.[132]

McIntosh continued, "Having completed the above plan, they sent out to us a small portion of their forces to make the attack, in order to draw us down to their desired and selected place, which was done on our rear guard, and immediately we marched on to our enemies."[133]

This highly fluid fight bore little resemblance to the battlefield organization and tactics then standard among military commanders from the eastern United States. There were no lines of uniformed soldiers marching in ranks across open ground. The battle at Chusto-Talasah was frontier-style warfare, fought by Texas horsemen and Indians from eastern, prairie, and plains tribes who prepared for battle and fought in traditional ways. Many of them were veterans used to fighting as individuals or in small groups, taking advantage of the cover, and making quick adjustments to the situation and enemy. Movements that December day might start off as a cavalry charge or advance on foot by twos, but they quickly dissolved and reformed to fit the circumstances. Capt. William B. Pitchlynn of the 1st Choctaw and Chickasaw Mounted Regiment later commented, "The mode of warfare adopted by the enemy compelled us . . . to abandon strict military discipline and make use of somewhat similar movements in order to be successful."[134]

Men on both sides at Chusto-Talasah fought fiercely and with determination. Most wore no uniforms that early in the war, and it was sometimes difficult to tell one's ally from the enemy. At one point, Colonel Sims of the 9th Texas Cavalry ordered Lieutenant Colonel Quayle to take a mixed detachment of about one hundred men toward Bird Creek to support Choctaw troops who would be on their right. Sims wrote,

> He advanced with his command on to the creek, to the left of the Choctaw regiment. Not finding the enemy there, he returned and charged a ravine on the right of the Choctaws, which he succeeded in taking, under a heavy fire from the enemy. Driving them from their position, he marched on and charged another ravine still farther on the right, but when he got into the ravine the Indians, who had possession of its mouth, opened a raking fire upon his men. He ordered them to charge down the ravine, which they did, and put the enemy to rout. A party of Indians still kept up a heavy fire upon them from the right, who were at first supposed to be Choctaws, as they were wearing our badges, but they were deserted Cherokees and Creeks. In the last charge with Colonel Quayle there were about 20 Choctaws, who acted with the greatest bravery.[135]

Similarly impressed, Orderly Sgt. George L. Griscom observed in his diary that night, "The Indians here showed marked bravery, one half breed Perryman (& and there were 6 Brothers in our ranks) killed a foe from behind a tree took the captured gun & killed a second scalped the 2 took both guns & brought one pony out himself escaped unhurt." Griscom also commented on "the Gallant Col Cooper who was ever present when the bullets flew the thickest hat off[,] encouraging his men."[136]

The nature of the conflict at Chusto-Talasah probably made it inevitable that the combatants would find themselves facing men of the same Indian nation, sometimes even men they knew, who were now the enemy. Maj. John Jumper, former Seminole principal chief, led the Muscogee-Seminole column on the left in the initial Confederate-allied attack. Some of the warriors he faced, of course, were Seminoles and commanded by Opothle Yahola's Seminole war chiefs.[137] Likewise, Col. Daniel N. McIntosh reported late that afternoon, "finally the Creek regiment, under my command, charged upon the enemy [including the Loyal Creeks] and chased them out from their strong fortified place and took the creek from them."[138]

Opothle Yahola's warriors knew what their purpose was that day. As Joseph Bruner, the son of a Loyal Creek woman, explained in 1937, "To comprehend it you must bear in mind that Opuithli-Yahola was taking all of his followers with him, women, children and even the aged and sick.... The women and children fled in advance under orders, the soldiers were to follow."[139] Before those Indian soldiers could follow, they must hold off and discourage their enemies until their women, children, and elders got safely away. That was what they did at Chusto-Talasah, and their noncombatants reached the vicinity of Hominy Falls about twenty miles west near today's Skiatook, Oklahoma. So as the sun was setting on that short winter afternoon, Opothle Yahola's warriors, their task done, simply disengaged, disappeared from the battlefield, and left it to the Confederate allies.[140]

After the battle at Chusto-Talasah, Cooper pulled back to his own camps and claimed victory, with about fifteen of his troops dead to more than four hundred of the fugitives reported killed. He believed that he had shaken their confidence by demonstrating, he said in his report, "whenever we could find them we could defeat them."[141]

However, Opothle Yahola's people believed they had discouraged their pursuers. According to Muscogee oral history, the people of the Nuyaka and Autusse tribal towns felt confident enough from the outcome of the battle that they returned to their homes on the North Fork and Deep Fork Rivers. The rest, though, were still in condition to make an organized exodus toward some safe place and intent on doing so. That was no longer the Cherokee Nation, so it would have to be farther north toward Kansas. Moreover, they were still gaining reinforcements.

The night of the battle about one hundred Cherokees passed through Vann's place on their way to join them. Still, the fugitive column had lost valuable supplies and ammunition they had no way to replace.[142]

Cooper was also short of ammunition and supplies, there were the dead to bury, and there was the issue of the deserters from Col. John Drew's 1st Cherokee Mounted Rifles to be resolved. Worried the Cherokee defections might spread to men of the other Indian nations, he was nervous about continuing to pursue Opothle Yahola until more white troops bolstered his command. About 150 of the 420 who deserted Drew's regiment had stayed with Opothle Yahola, while many others had simply gone home. The Confederate-allied forces withdrew to Choska in the Muscogee Nation, and Cooper rode with a small escort to Fort Gibson to confer with Principal Chief John Ross, resupply, and try to stop the seepage of dissident Cherokees to Opothle Yahola. Cooper also sent a request for reinforcements to Col. James McIntosh (no relation of the Muscogee McIntoshes) at Van Buren, Arkansas.[143]

At Fort Gibson Ross and Cooper discussed the deserter "situation" in a general council, while a measles epidemic swept the camps. Orderly Sergeant Griscom wrote in his diary, "The Indians [are] having sham fights & war Dances &c to infuse a war spirit into the lukewarm bosoms of the runaway Cherokees (*The Pin Party*, [his italics], now Returned)."[144] Cooper wanted to court-martial them, and Stand Watie believed they deserved execution. According to Griscom, though, "Ross . . . who some have accused of Union sentiments" made a conciliatory speech in which he "entreats them to keep in good faith the treaty made by Albert Pike."[145] Ross reconstituted the regiment and pardoned those who rejoined it. Given the current Cherokee political picture, he needed them as a counterweight to Watie. Cooper decided to let the matter drop. Opothle Yahola was the primary problem, and Indians from several tribes were moving across the Indian Territory to join him.[146]

Meanwhile, Colonel McIntosh moved quickly to join the pursuit of Opothle Yahola. At Fort Gibson, he and Cooper sketched out a plan. Cooper, reinforced by Maj. J. W. Whitfield's battalion and with Drew's reconstituted 1st Cherokee Mounted Rifles along, would move up the Arkansas River to the Big Bend, locate one of the tributaries of the Verdigris River, and follow it around behind the refugee Indians' camp at Achustenalah. By getting north of them, he could cut off any escape toward Kansas. McIntosh, with four companies of his own 2nd Arkansas Mounted Riflemen, five companies of the South Kansas-Texas Regiment, part of the 6th Texas Cavalry, seven companies of the 3rd (11th) Texas Cavalry, and one additional company of Texans, totaling 1,380 men, would go north up the Verdigris River. Opposite the refugee Indian camp he would look for a tributary from the west and follow it toward the camp. According to McIntosh, because forage for the horses was scarce this time of year, he and Cooper agreed the one who located the refugee camp first would attack it.[147]

As it turned out, McIntosh set out across a snowy landscape on December 22. Cooper was already concerned about keeping up with his pace on another winter expedition because his horses were less fit than those of the other column. Then the desertion of his teamsters caused further delay, and he sent McIntosh a message to proceed without him. However, he also sent Col. Stand Watie and the 2nd Cherokee Mounted Rifles north up the Verdigris River to support McIntosh. Neither Cooper nor Watie caught up with him in time. On Christmas night, while the Arkansas column was camped about twelve miles from Achustenalah, a party of refugee warriors suddenly appeared. McIntosh sent troops to check them out but soon decided this was just an attempt to taunt the Confederates into a "fruitless chase." McIntosh recalled his "impatient men" but made preparations to attack the next day without waiting for either Cooper or Watie.[148]

The next morning, December 26, it was so cold the Texas cavalrymen walked beside their horses to maintain blood circulation.[149] The column searched westward about twelve miles, finding the refugee Indian camp near Achustenalah. The noncombatants had taken refuge in a small valley sheltered by three rugged hills west of today's Skiatook, Oklahoma, and Quapaw Creek. The smoke from their campfires was plainly visible.[150] It was, according to Maj. Elias C. Boudinot of the 2nd Cherokee Mounted Rifles, "the roughest country I ever saw."[151]

Between the noncombatants and the approaching Confederate allies, about 1,700 Loyal Indian warriors were stationed on a steep hillside west of Battle Creek. They were a daunting sight and sound to the approaching men from Arkansas and Texas. While the Confederates built fires and warmed up a quarter mile away, the warriors shot off their guns, screamed and howled like panthers and dogs, and taunted them with turkey gobbles, daring them to attack. At the base of that hill, the Seminoles commanded by Halleck Tustunuggee had taken positions behind rocks and trees. Behind the Seminoles the Loyal Creeks and Indians from other tribes sat astride their ponies. More Loyal Creeks lined the crest of the hill. When the Confederate advance guard moved slowly forward, it soon came under fire, and McIntosh ordered his other units across the creek in support. He also sent the 6th Texas Cavalry over toward an open space that might allow them to flank the fugitive Indians.[152]

According to an interview Opothle Yahola and Halleck Tustunuggee gave in January 1862, they had believed the way to Kansas was open after the battle at Chusto-Talasah. "Our men were greatly scattered having gone out to kill game, hunt for food and select camping grounds. Only a few of us could fight. Opothleyaholo led us in this fight."[153]

The steep slope bristled with small oak trees and exposed rock layers, and it seemed to McIntosh there was an Indian rifleman or bowman behind every one. An 1849 West Point graduate, McIntosh had served on the frontier and developed a reputation as being "impulsive, reckless, and courageous to a fault," a man who "liked nothing better than plunging headlong into a fight."[154] In something of an understatement, he wrote afterward, "It seemed a desperate undertaking to charge a position which appeared almost inaccessible." But at noon he gave the order, the Confederate troops gave "one wild yell . . . and the living mass hurled itself upon the foe."[155] Every fifth man in Companies A and B of the 3rd Texas had been left behind to hold the horses. One of them, Pvt. Henry Miller, just eighteen, burst into tears as he watched the others charge without him.[156] For Pvt. James H. Kearly, who had enlisted in the 6th Texas in September, "Tustanola" was his first battle with these Indians. He recalled, "As we went up the mountain after them, they slapped their sides and gobbled like turkeys."[157]

At the top of the hill, a rock ledge made a natural breastwork, which the Indians used as a shield. At first the Confederates could only get around the ends of it, but the fighting was hand-to-hand as the 3rd Texas Cavalrymen led the scramble over the top. The 2nd Arkansas pushed into a thicket to drive out Indians that had taken cover there, while the 6th Texas Cavalry succeeded in flanking them on the right.

With their ammunition running out, the fugitive Indians soon began breaking off from the fight and hurrying away.[158] Some refused to run, though. One of the 3rd Texas cavalrymen remembered, "some of those Indians were very brave and daring and would not leave . . . . One big feathered cap fellow stood out from the trees and continued shooting until he fell. I had shot both barrels of my gun and one of my holster pistols at him before he fell."[159]

Others ran toward their camps and regrouped there.[160] According to Muscogee oral history, Conchate Emathla and twenty-five men of the Muscogee Wewoka Town made a stand near Opothle Yahola's camp. They fought off Colonel Young's Texans until they ran out of ammunition. Then they reversed their rifles and fought on, using them as clubs, until only one man was left on his feet. He killed Lieutenant McQuirk, grabbed the bridle of his horse, and sprang into the saddle. Luckily, there was a pair of pistols with the saddle, and this man used them to fight his way out and escape.[161] Other Loyal Indians fled in ones, twos, and small groups. "The enemy by this time were much scattered and had retreated to the rocky gorges amid the deep recesses of the mountain," McIntosh reported, "where they were pursued by our victorious troops and routed in every instance with great loss."[162] Later Capt. John J. Good of Dallas mused to his wife, "how blunted are our sensibilities amid the perils of war . . . . Men ride over the Battlefield and laugh at what would once shock them." Another man said later, "I took the scalp of two Indians that day; that was all that I had time to fool with."[163]

By four o'clock the battle was over, and McIntosh and his troops occupied Opothle Yahola's camp. Unlike the battle at Chusto-Talasah, this time they had struck a devastating blow to the fugitive column. "We captured 160 women and children, 20 negroes, 30 wagons, 70 yoke of oxen, about 500 Indian horses, several hundred head of cattle, 100 sheep, and a great quantity of property of much value to the enemy," McIntosh wrote. "The stronghold of Hopoeithleyohola was completely broken up, and his force scattered in every direction, destitute of the simplest elements of subsistence."[164]

The fugitives that escaped from Achustenalah were now truly desperate. In a story passed to Joseph Bruner by his mother, Lucy, who was widowed that day, Spocogee, an elder of the Muscogee Kahsita

Town, had entrusted a woman, Mary Hutpa, with a bag of gold. "Knowing that Mary was in the advance flight while he had to stay and fight, old Spocogee thought she would be able to save his bag of gold," Bruner explained. "The flight was sudden. In their fright the women threw away everything but their most prized possessions; their haste could not be encumbered with anything that seemed unnecessary." As it happened, Mary was a shell-shaker. She helped set the rhythm for her town's social and ceremonial dances by shaking bands of pebble-filled turtle shells tied around her lower legs. Bruner continued, "So Mary threw away the bag of gold and kept her precious turtle shells . . . . When Spocogee found he had lost his gold, they said he tried to swear in white men's words, his anger was so great."[165]

For most of those in what Bruner called the "mad flight north," possessions mattered less than escape.[166] One Seminole warrior who survived said later that "we were whipped and our people cut to pieces badly." He continued, "our men were killed and women and children were not spared. Those that escaped death did not escape without some wound being inflicted on them and all our horses and provisions were captured."[167] The black McIntosh family was caught up in the panic as the Confederate soldiers moved toward the main camp. They knew that as runaway slaves they could expect harsh treatment, a return to slavery, or even death. To make matters worse, Col. Stand Watie had arrived with the 2nd Cherokee Mounted Rifles, too late for the fight but not for hunting the fleeing. Oral history handed down within the McIntosh family and retold by Phoebe McIntosh Banks, an infant at the time, provided a snapshot of events. Although it lacked specificity, it probably referred to the aftermath of the battle at Achustenalah:

> Then long before the morning lighten the sky, the men hurry and sling the camp kettles across the pack horses, tie the littlest children to the horses' backs and get on the move farther into the mountains. They kept moving fast as they could, but the wagons made it mighty slow in the brush and the lowland swamps, so just about the time they ready to ford another creek the Indian soldiers catch up and the fighting begin all over again.[168]

By dawn McIntosh and Watie were on their heels. McIntosh pursued one group twenty-five miles before he captured them and burned two wagons. Not far away, Watie was chasing another group through hills and gorges too rough for their horses. Major Boudinot, also with the 2nd Cherokee Mounted Rifles, charged into a ravine, flushing out fifteen men, who were killed, and capturing several women and children. Reports came in of fugitives killed or captured in numerous small fights. Watie intercepted a group of fifty to sixty armed Cherokees making their way north toward Kansas and killed one of them in the arrest.[169]

Phoebe McIntosh Banks, too small to remember, described what her elders saw:

> Dead all over the hills when we get away; some of the Negroes shot and wounded so bad the blood run down the saddle skirts, and some fall off their horses miles from the battle ground, and lay still on the ground. Daddy and Uncle Jacob keep our family together somehow and head across the line into Kansas.[170]

Panicked people scattered in all directions, trying to escape the Confederate allies. James Scott, a boy of nine or ten, could not forget one image even in his old age. "One time we saw a little baby sitting on its little blanket in the rocks. Everyone was running because an attack was expected but no one had the time to stop and pick up the child," James said. "As it saw the people running by, the little child began to wave its little hands. The child had no knowledge that he had been deserted," James concluded sadly.[171]

Pvt. James H. Kearly remembered that his fellow soldiers in the 6th Texas Cavalry captured a number of women and children, along with fine beef cattle and camp equipment. They turned the women and children over to Colonel Cooper. The next day they came across an old woman, lying on a buffalo robe. Kearly said, "She was so old she looked like a pile of wrinkles. We tried to feed her, but she shut her eyes and would not look at us."[172]

It was not only the soldiers the fugitives feared. The weather was worsening. There had been sleet during the night, and they had lost what they needed to survive a winter journey of about a hundred miles. Their routes toward safety in Kansas are still disputed. Some may have taken the Osage trail northwestward along Bird Creek or gone even farther west to follow the Arkansas River or Black Beaver's road. Still others could have gone eastward to intercept the Osage trails north along the Caney or Verdigris Rivers.[173] Whatever their route, oral history depicted a common experience. James Scott summarized,

> We faced many hardships; we were often without food, the children cried from weariness and the cold, we fled and left our wagons with much needed provisions, clothing, and other necessities. Many of our friends, [and] loved ones perished from sickness, and we all suffered from the cold as it was during the winter that we were on our flight to a neutral country. When our provisions went low, some of the members of the tribe turned to eating horse flesh.[174]

Making matters worse, a ferocious winter storm blew in across the Plains, bringing harsh winds, frigid temperatures, and snow. Some fugitives had been captured and sent back to their home countries. The others, many now barefoot, trudged on toward the Kansas line, hoping to find protection, shelter, and relief. Some froze to death on the way. Their bodies, left where they fell by people who lacked the means, energy, and time to bury them, fed hungry wolves.[175]

By this time, the Confederate allies were also suffering from the weather and short supplies. Pvt. P. G. Beauchamp, a twenty-year-old Texan, wrote years later, "We were on this raid two months—December and January—and came near freezing several times. [We] were without anything to eat eight days at one time except two Indian ponies and some buffalo hides. We all looked like we had been through a spell of sickness, but with plenty to eat we were soon all right again."[176]

Under the circumstances, the Confederate allies did not pursue the fugitives all the way to Kansas. However, the Muscogees and Cherokees wanted to make sure Opothle Yahola and his followers were really leaving the Indian Territory. A three-day scout launched four days after the battle brought no results because some fugitives had burned the prairie behind them. This hid their tracks and destroyed forage for the pursuers' horses. The Confederate allies soon gave up and returned toward Tulsey Town and their bases. Along the way, they encountered and turned back parties of Muscogees, Cherokees, and Seminoles going the opposite direction in hopes of escaping trouble. There were also civilians from other tribes moving north. The Confederates released the Osages they met, but Cooper was acquainted with the Delawares they came across on the road. They were relatives of Black Beaver and had hunted and scouted for the former agent when he visited Fort Cobb. He gave them tents and provisions and sent them toward home.[177]

As the year 1861 closed in the Indian Territory, it appeared that the major source of trouble—Opothle Yahola and his dissidents—was unlikely to cause any more. The Confederate authorities claimed three victories against him, and they could also exhibit evidence of his collusion with the Union and demonstrate its perfidy. The federal government had finally tried to open communication with the Indian Territory tribes. Letters collected from the refugee camp at Achustenalah promised to right old wrongs against the Indian nations and send support from a president and government in Washington that was not dead after all. The Union was even courting the Plains tribes, promising them the support and supplies needed to make war on frontier settlements. This was illustrated by a letter to Wichita chief Tusaquach:

> FRIEND AND BROTHER: It is the wish of the commissioner of the United States Government that you either come to Kansas with your friends the Seminoles or send two or three of your best braves. We also want the Keechies, Ionies, Cadoes [sic], and the Comanches to send some of their men to meet and have a talk with the commissioners of your Great Father at Washington. His soldiers are as swift as the antelope and brave as the mountain bear, and they are your friends and brothers. They will give you powder and lead. They will fight by your sides. Your friend Black Beaver will meet you here, and we will drive away the bad men who entered your company last spring. The Texans have killed the Wichitas; we will punish the Texans.[178]

At the same time, though, Cooper and Watie were irritated with Col. James McIntosh, who claimed victory at Achustenalah. They believed his failure to wait for them to get into position and haste in attacking the Loyal Indians had cost them their chance to capture Opothle Yahola and safely disperse his followers. Instead, the old troublemaker was now in Kansas beyond their reach, along with perhaps five hundred of his followers, while bodies of the fugitives littered the hills and prairies of the western Cherokee country. Cooper's official report that refugees they captured had been treated humanely and sent home to the care of their families could not cancel that fact.[179]

They were right to be uneasy. Opothle Yahola was beyond their reach in Kansas, and he was still a threat. The old man was sick and weakened from the journey, but the events of the last six months had stoked his old enmity toward the McIntoshes and any Muscogees who would follow their lead. The ordeal of these neutral people had just begun, because they would find little relief from cold, hunger, and homelessness in Kansas. Months later, a federal official asked Opothle Yahola how Union forces should treat the "Southern" Indian women and children they encountered. The old man replied vindictively that the best way to wipe out a bad breed of dogs was to kill the bitch.[180]

The Civil War in the United States had barely begun when these events occurred in the Indian Territory. Seminoles had spilled the blood of Seminoles; Muscogees, of Muscogees; and Cherokees, of Cherokees. In early 1863, when Acting Principal Chief—formerly Major—Thomas Pegg tried to explain what happened and why individuals and the Indian governments made the decisions they did in 1861, his rationalization was as convoluted as those times. One had only to examine his personal decisions—first to be a Confederate officer and then to side with the Unionist Pins—to sense the quandary so many Indian Territory people faced. For the moment, as the year 1862 began, the Indian nations seemed to have a breathing space, although several of them were already divided and bleeding. The Cherokee Nation was still united, but that unity cobbled together by Principal Chief John Ross was perilously fragile.

Truly, the wolf had come.

CHAPTER THREE

Squally Times in This Territory

In January 1862 Joseph S. Murrow wrote letters describing conditions in the Indian Territory to his friends and colleagues. Originally from Georgia, Murrow was only twenty-six but had already spent four years as a Baptist missionary to the Muscogee and Seminole peoples. When the Civil War began, he had moved his young family to Texas and then returned to the territory.[1] Recently he had accompanied the Texas Confederate troops serving with Col. Douglas H. Cooper on what Murrow called their four-week "scout" in pursuit of Opothle Yahola. Murrow depicted him as "an old chief, an enemy all his life to Christianity and improvement." Describing the campaign, with its fights on the Red Fork near Tulsey Town, Chusto-Talasah, and Achustenalah to "Brother Jones" at the Choctaw Agency, Murrow said:

> We suffered very severely—were three days without food except horseflesh, and our horses were six days without food—we had no tents, no wagons—were exposed to very hard weather, rain, sleet, snow, and cold strong winds. Yet, God preserved us in a remarkable manner. Many of the horses died, and the men were compelled to return on foot over rocky mountains—no roads, and frozen streams. Such are our sufferings out here. Yet we endure them cheerfully for the sake of Christ and our country.[2]

Murrow had written a similar letter describing the pursuit of "Old Posey" or "Holy Poko," as some white troops called him, to another colleague. It gave a sobering assessment of conditions:

> The western portions of this Indian Territory are all ruined and laid waste. All improvements are burned, stock all driven off or killed, and the entire western settlements are deserted. 'Tis sad, and made my heart ache as I beheld settlements and farms, where a few months ago families lived in plenty and pleasure, now

deserted and ruined—nothing but the rock chimnies [*sic*] left. It seems as if the good and wise God is purposing to destroy this Indian race entirely.[3]

Murrow was quite concerned about what would happen in the spring. In those days before paved all-weather roads allowed armies to move easily and maintain a constant stream of food and supplies, they rarely campaigned or fought during the winter months. The difficulties the Confederate allies had experienced in the pursuit of Opothle Yahola illustrated why. Troops usually went into "winter camps," returned to their barracks, or were furloughed during the cold, wet months. Commanders usually waited until spring when the roads dried up and the grass grew high enough to feed their livestock before they began a new campaign season.

The young missionary was thinking along those lines as he wrote his letters. While he acknowledged that Col. James McIntosh had succeeded in driving Opothle Yahola's Loyal Indians into Kansas, the young missionary agreed with those who believed if he had waited for Colonel Cooper to arrive with reinforcements, "we could have bagged them all." There was unlikely to be any more trouble this winter because the fugitives that had reached Kansas in December were in no condition to strike back immediately. "Next spring, however," Murrow predicted, "there will be squally times in this territory again, unless there is a considerable force of Confederate troops on the Kansas border to oppose 'Old Posy' and his wild Indians and wilder Jayhawkers."[4]

Another minister also commented on the situation in the territory. Stephen Foreman, a generation older and a Cherokee Presbyterian, had been assistant editor of the *Cherokee Phoenix*, the nation's first superintendent of public instruction, clerk of the Senate, and an associate chief justice in the Cherokee government. In the 1830s he had supported John Ross in opposing removal but was now a staunch follower of Stand Watie.[5] On January 3, 1862, he wrote in his diary,

> Quite a number of soldiers passed along the road on their way to their winter quarters . . . . They are just from Opothleaholah's camp, whither they went to give him, as they said, a brushing. They whipped such of his men as they found, but did not find the old man himself. It is estimated that they killed about two

hundred prisoners, including some women and children. They captured a large number of wagons, horses and cattle and provisions. As a thing, of course, they lost several men, about 14, they report, killed and a number wounded. How many did not learn.[6]

Whether they killed prisoners and, if so, how many was in question, but Foreman clearly had little sympathy for Opothle Yahola and his followers.

Still, the recent campaign to deal with him and the neutral Indians continued to trouble the Cherokee Nation. Although Principal Chief John Ross had papered a pardon over the matter of the mass desertion from Col. John Drew's regiment, pro-Confederate Cherokees such as Foreman and Col. Stand Watie neither forgave nor forgot. In Tahlequah in late December, the murder and scalping of Chunestotie, believed to be a Keetoowah, or Pin, agitator, illustrated the continuing division in the Cherokee Nation. He had deserted from Drew's regiment, fought with the neutral Indians at Chusto-Talasah, and then returned home unpunished. His killer was believed to be Charles Webber. Watie downplayed the killing, saying the young man was drunk at the time. Because it was a military matter, Ross complained to Col. Douglas H. Cooper and then to Brig. Gen. Albert Pike, but their investigations brought him no satisfaction. Nor did the Confederate commanders admonish Watie's troops, then patrolling the northern Cherokee-Kansas border, whom Ross accused of harassing innocent (perhaps meaning "pro-Union") Cherokees.[7]

The nation remained tense, and Stephen Foreman was one of those who believed Ross was secretly pro-Union at heart despite agreeing to the Cherokee-Confederate alliance. When Ross had Drew's regiment stationed near Rose Cottage, his home at Park Hill, the missionary, who lived nearby, saw it as evidence of Ross's fear and guilt. Foreman wrote in his diary, "His regiment showed their hand and his hand too at the Bird Creek [Chusto-Talasah] fight when they fought against our men. Mr. Ross showed his hand also in pardoning all those men without even a trial. Mr. Ross also showed his hand harboring the leaders of those traitors of their country . . . in his own house."[8]

Perhaps to escape this building tension, Cherokees continued to migrate across the Kansas line, joining Opothle Yahola's survivors and other Indian refugees. They must have been shocked at the conditions they found. The federal Interior Department and its Office of Indian Affairs were responsible for the Indian tribes on reservations in eastern Kansas—such as the Osages, Sacs and Foxes, and Potawatomies. Their employees were not prepared for the sudden flood of refugees from the Indian Territory in December 1861.

George A. Cutler, an Indian Office official in Kansas, marveled that the refugees had completed a round-about journey of nearly three hundred miles, fighting three battles on the way. The last had cost them most of their supplies, bedding, and ponies. Families had been separated in the wild confusion, but the main body of refugees, many of them thinly clad and barefoot, had held together and trudged on. He wrote, "their suffering was beyond description . . . . The weather was intensely cold, with a bitter northwest wind in their faces, and over the snow-covered roads, they travelled all night and the next day, without halting to rest." The survivors at last crossed over into Kansas, but, Cutler wrote, the Muscogees, who had probably suffered the most in his opinion, had "lost everything but what they had on their backs. Families who in their country had been wealthy, and who could count their cattle by the thousands and horses by hundreds, and owned large numbers of slaves, and who at home lived at ease and comfort, were without even the necessities of life."[9]

Indian Office personnel in Kansas scrambled to deal with a refugee problem that grew so large so quickly and kept growing. On their way north, Opothle Yahola's people had at some point encountered hunters from the band of Sacs and Foxes of the Mississippi, whose reservation was in Osage County, Kansas. These hunters had taken the news of the exodus back to federal officials in Kansas who began preparations for their arrival. The Muscogees temporarily settled along the Cottonwood, Fall, and Walnut Rivers—tributaries of the Verdigris River—in southeastern Kansas. These were lands on the western edge of white settlement that had been assigned to the New York Indians but remained mostly vacant. Opothle Yahola's people, though, were just the first large wave of refugees. Eventually Indian Territory refugee camps were scattered for two hundred miles across southern Kansas from the Neosho River to the Arkansas. At the extreme end of western supply lines and subject to a federal bureaucracy struggling through a national crisis and too much corruption, the refugees' situation was about to become even worse.[10]

In late January A. B. Campbell, an army surgeon, visited and reported on their camps. Campbell met with the leaders of the Muscogee, Seminole, and Chickasaw refugees. He also consulted the recent census of the refugees. It showed 3,168 Muscogees with fifty-three slaves and thirty-eight freedmen, 777 Seminoles, 136 Quapaws, fifty-nine Cherokees, thirty-one Chickasaws, and members of a few other tribes. The total was about 4,500, but that number continued to grow as more arrived—from twenty to sixty per day.[11]

Campbell wrote, "It is impossible for me to depict the wretchedness of their condition. Their only protection from the snow upon which they lie is prairie grass, and from the wind and weather scraps and rags stretched upon switches; some of them had some personal clothing; most had but shreds and rags, which did not conceal their nakedness, and I saw seven, ranging in age from three to fifteen years without one thread upon their bodies."[12] Opothle Yahola was sick with a fever. Campbell wrote indignantly that it was past time the government provided the old man with warm blankets. Instead, this once wealthy man lay in a shelter made of one small blanket stretched over a flimsy ridge-pole but too short to reach the ground by a foot. Most of the shelters put up in the timber along the river were even worse than his.[13]

Campbell had brought donation boxes from Chicago. They contained thirty-five comforters or quilts only thirty inches wide. There were forty pairs of socks, three pairs of pants, seven undershirts, a few shirts, and four pairs of drawers. Distributing them to these desperate people was difficult for the sympathetic surgeon. Campbell said,

> I had the wagon driven round the margin of the woods. I walked through the woods, and selected the nakedest of the naked, to whom I doled out the few articles I had, and when all was gone, I found myself surrounded by hundreds of anxious faces, disappointed to find that nothing remained for them. The pillow cases were the most essential articles next to the food, for they were the only means that families had to receive their portion of meal or flour furnished to them.[14]

The refugees' health was deteriorating because of their destitution. With no axes or hatchets it was hard to cut firewood for warmth. Without cooking utensils they had to eat whatever provisions they received raw. Many had frostbite and foot injuries—cuts from stepping on shards of ice or sharp sticks under the snow—because they had no shoes or moccasins. Eventually more than one hundred frozen fingers, toes, and limbs would have to be amputated. Many of the refugees were sick with inflammatory diseases affecting their chests, noses, and eyes, and these quickly spread to new arrivals. Some two thousand Indian ponies starved that winter, so dead horses lay throughout the camp and along the river. Campbell recommended they be removed and burned as soon as possible, because the first warm spell would cause them to putrefy and breed still more diseases.[15] Campbell indignantly concluded his report, "Why officers of the Indian department are not doing something for [the refugees] I cannot understand; common humanity demands that more should be done, and done at once, to save them from total destruction."[16]

Something was done eventually. The U.S. Army supplied provisions as long as it could. When a new source had to be found, Congress, which usually dealt with Indian appropriations in its spring session, in February 1862 finally approved tapping the annuity money due these tribes. Congress had held the funds back during the secession crisis in early 1861 to prevent its falling into the hands of "armed rebels and banditti."[17] That, of course, had been a primary reason why the Indian nations joined the Confederacy. Now their annuity funds paid for refugee provisions and firewood. The latter became an issue after the Indian Office officials moved the Muscogee refugees thirty miles east to the Neosho River valley near Leroy, Kansas. The Sac and Fox peoples had hospitably offered the refugees space on their reservation about twenty-five miles farther north. However, the Muscogee refugees, anxious to return to their homes in the Indian Territory as soon as possible, preferred to stay closer to it. Their new camp was on private property, and they did not understand that the white landowners considered the timber growing on it to be private property, too. Apparently once Agent George A. Cutler paid them for it, the landowners tolerated the Muscogee refugees as their neighbors.[18]

Cutler also took a new refugee census. About 240 Muscogee

refugees had died in their former camp; now the number of dead had climbed to 400, which may have included people of other tribes. The October 1862 census reported 3,619 Muscogees, 919 Seminoles, 165 Chickasaws, 400 Kickapoos, 89 Delawares, 19 Ionies, and 53 Keechis. There were 223 Cherokees with another 2,000 who had lately arrived at Fort Scott, Kansas. By age and gender, the largest groups were 2,040 women and 2,583 children. There were only 864 men in the camps.[19]

The lower number of men and the sharp increase in Cherokee refugees stemmed from events that occurred in the Cherokee Nation once the spring of 1862 arrived—that spring Baptist missionary and Confederate soldier Joseph S. Murrow had dreaded. The first development was the Battle of Pea Ridge, or Elkhorn Tavern, in northwest Arkansas. At the end of 1861 the Confederate military had undergone some reorganization. The Trans-Mississippi District, which included northern Louisiana, Arkansas, Missouri, and the Indian Territory, was created with Maj. Gen. Earl Van Dorn placed in command. Brig. Gen. Albert Pike, commanding the "Department of Indian Territory," remained in this new organization, but Pike and Van Dorn detested each other. Pike had written the War Department a letter of protest over the Indians killed in Van Dorn's raid on the Wichita Village in western Indian Territory in 1858. Now Pike began constructing Cantonment Davis across the Arkansas River from Fort Gibson. The latter had been abandoned since 1857 and was badly run down. Most people referred to the new fortification as "Fort Davis," and Pike intended it to be the Confederate headquarters in the Indian Territory. The collection of log buildings sat atop a prehistoric Indian mound on top of a hill, providing a good view of Fort Gibson. The surrounding timber made fine cover for scouts and sharpshooters.[20]

Van Dorn took little interest in the place, territory, or Confederate-allied Indian units, but he sent for them as an emergency developed in early 1862. In February Brig. Gen. Samuel R. Curtis set out to secure Missouri for the Union by driving Maj. Gen. Sterling Price and Confederate forces out of Springfield and the southwest corner of the state. Knowing he could not hold that territory, Price withdrew to northwest Arkansas. About the same time, Van Dorn decided to move into Missouri to free it from the Union grip, hoping to capture St. Louis and perhaps even launch an invasion of the Ohio River valley.

Van Dorn ordered Brig. Gen. Ben McCulloch to bring his troops from Fort Smith and sent word to Pike to bring the Indian regiments to Elm Springs in northwestern Arkansas by March 5 to help stop the federal advance. He was not concerned that the Indian-Confederate treaties prohibited using the Indian troops outside the Indian Territory without their governments' consent. Pike, whose true interest was serving Arkansas and the Confederacy, protested but sent for them anyway.[21]

Unfortunately, he could not get the Indian regiments started with the speed Van Dorn ordered. Although the Confederate treaties had promised to arm, supply, and pay the Indian regiments, very little had arrived by early spring 1862. That being the case they were not inclined to get moving quickly. Missionary Joseph Murrow, by then serving with the Confederate-allied Indian regiments, reckoned that the number of volunteers from the Indian nations was proportionally higher than those from the Southern states. "Yet," he concluded, "less has been done for the Indian department than for any other in the Confederacy. Indian soldiers have been worse armed, worse fed, and worse paid than any others, and until recently haven't even been allowed the services of a chaplain. Most of the native preachers are in the army."[22]

The recent improvement Murrow alluded to was probably due to Pike's initiative once Van Dorn called for the Indian regiments. He had money in hand, so Pike began distributing it, a three-day process which he hoped to have completed by the time Van Dorn really needed them in northwest Arkansas about a hundred miles away. He finally got on the road with two companies of Texas troops. Col. Stand Watie and Col. John Drew joined him on the way with their Cherokee regiments as did Col. Daniel N. McIntosh's 1st Creek Mounted Volunteers. The Choctaw and Chickasaw units, though, living farther away, were still somewhere behind them. As a result, the Confederate Indian allies missed the opening skirmish at Bentonville, Arkansas, between the Confederate advance units under Maj. Gen. Sterling Price and Union troops late on March 6.[23]

Pea Ridge in northwest Arkansas is a sloping plateau near the Missouri line. The most prominent building in the farming community around it in 1862 was Elkhorn Tavern on the Telegraph (Wire) Road connecting Springfield, Missouri, and Van Buren, Arkansas. It was also at the intersection of routes connecting Bentonville and tiny Leetown to the west and Huntsville to the southeast. As milder weather broke and bitter winter returned, Curtis arrived in the vicinity with the Army of the Southwest, about 10,500 men. They encamped near Elkhorn Tavern with the bulk of Big Mountain at their back to the north. Meanwhile, short supplies and bad weather hampered Confederate general McCulloch's men, so that they reached northwestern Arkansas hungry and exhausted after their trek over the Boston Mountains. The arrival of Pike, the two Cherokee regiments, and the Texans—about nine hundred men—brought the total to some sixteen thousand and encouraged Van Dorn. Still, he was frustrated he had not yet been able to engage Curtis in battle.[24]

The Confederate commander wanted to attack as soon as possible, but getting his troops into striking position before dawn on March 7 proved impossible. There was no bridge over Little Sugar Creek along the base of the mountain, and that caused congestion and slowed their crossing. All were exhausted, and some were not fit for battle. The Indian troops, who were in better condition, did not even get across until sunrise.[25] To save time, although McCulloch and Price opposed the idea, Van Dorn divided his army, expecting to reunite the two parts by noon. He and Price took the Bentonville Detour around the north side of Big Mountain toward the Telegraph Road intending to cut Curtis and his army off from reinforcements and supplies. They succeeded in driving out the federals and occupying Elkhorn Tavern by sunset. The "fatal flaw" in this plan, Pea Ridge historians William L. Shea and Earl J. Hess pointed out, was that no reunion occurred, leaving them now outnumbered and cut off by the federal army.[26]

McCulloch, meanwhile, reversed his half of Van Dorn's army, swung back south around Big Mountain toward Leetown but turned east along Ford Road parallel to its base. Recently arrived brigadier general Albert Pike and the 1st and 2nd Cherokee Regiments, as ordered, fell in behind Texas cavalrymen. White troops gaped at them as they straggled into line that morning in clothing ranging from regular suits to blankets, breech clouts, buckskin leggings, and moccasins. Some sported bells and tinklers and wore feathers in their hair and paint on their faces.[27]

By then the federals were alert to Confederate forces moving along both sides of Big Mountain and turned to face them. Near noon the

Texas and Cherokee cavalry units were suddenly ordered off the dirt road and into the woods lining one side of it. About three hundred yards across a fenced field and small prairie on the Foster farm, a federal battery of three cannon and five companies of cavalry opened fire on the column's right rear. A Texas artillery unit wheeled to fire back, but Brigadier General McIntosh led the Texans in a spectacular "Napoleonic charge" at the federal guns. Brigadier General Pike could see nothing through the brush, so he ordered the 2nd Cherokee to dismount and advance a little way past the fence line. Contrary to legend, according to historians Shea and Hess, the Cherokees did not join the Texans' spectacular charge. However, they did join the excited Texans celebrating around the captured federal guns and generally gawking at the scene.[28]

Pike gave a different account, which some historians discounted:

> The enemy opened fire into the woods where we were, the fence in front of us was thrown down, and the Indians (Watie's regiment on foot and Drew's on horseback), with [the Texans], charged full in front through the woods and into the open ground with loud yells, routed the cavalry, took the battery, fired upon and pursued the enemy, retreating through the fenced field on our right, and held the battery, which I afterwards had drawn by the Cherokees into the woods. Four of the horses of the battery alone remained on the ground, the others running off with the caissons, and for want of horses and harness we were unable to send the guns to the rear.[29]

Pike had lost only three men killed, he said, when Colonel Watie told him there was another Union battery nearby with a heavy force of infantry. Pike stated, "Colonel Drew's regiment was in the field on our right, and around the taken battery was a mass of Indians and others in the utmost confusion, all talking, riding this way and that, and listening to no orders from any one." While Pike was trying to get the guns reversed and ready for action, two shells dropped nearby. He wrote, "The Indians retreated hurriedly into the woods out of which they had made the charge. Well aware that they would not face shells in the open ground, I directed them to dismount, take their horses to the rear, and each take to [hide behind] a tree, and this was done by both regiments, the men thus awaiting patiently and coolly the expected advance of the enemy." It never came. More than two hours later, that day's action at Pea Ridge ended. Pike summarized the Indian troops' conduct as cool while shot and shell fell into the woods and credited them with keeping the captured battery from being used by the enemy.[30] So did Baptist missionary Joseph S. Murrow, who was with them throughout the expedition to Arkansas. In a letter ten days later to the *Baptist Banner,* Murrow wrote, "I was in the battle throughout .... Our Indians fought well, taking one battery of four guns, brass pieces, and held them until ordered off the field. We then burned the wheels and spiked the guns as well as we were able."[31]

Although Pike presented the Cherokees' behavior as understandable from their experience, harsher critics concluded the federal artillery fire so demoralized them they were "of little use to the Confederate cause for the rest of the battle."[32] There were reports that afternoon they were shooting at anyone in a blue coat, including some Confederates. There would be worse criticism to come.[33]

At midafternoon Pike learned that the deaths of McCulloch and McIntosh in separate incidents and the capture of Col. Louis Hebert made him the ranking officer on the Leetown battlefield. Besides being an amateur, he lacked information about Van Dorn's plans. He was unable to gain command and heard some seven thousand Union troops were coming his way. Pike decided the best course was to withdraw toward the Confederate headquarters, but failure to get that word to all his troops created more confusion. That evening Col. Douglas H. Cooper and the Choctaw-Chickasaw regiment finally caught up with him as did Col. Daniel N. McIntosh with two hundred Muscogees. It was too late to do any good.[34]

That same evening Van Dorn discovered that his troops were running out of ammunition. His ordnance wagons had disappeared, and his men could not get back around the Union lines to reach their supplies. Nevertheless, he made plans to continue the battle the next morning, with the main venue shifting to Confederate-held Elkhorn Tavern. Van Dorn stationed the 2nd Cherokee along the top of Big Mountain as a cavalry screen, "a task for which the Indians were reasonably well-suited," according to Shea and Hess.[35]

Next morning Curtis counterattacked with a two-hour artillery barrage near Elkhorn Tavern that created havoc in the main Confederate infantry lines and artillery stations. A general Confederate withdrawal began by midmorning. Pike and the Indian regiments joined it and helped protect the supply train from Pea Ridge to Elm Springs about thirty miles southwest. Once they were back in the Indian Territory, Watie's regiment went to Cowskin Prairie near today's Grove, Oklahoma. Drew's moved south to Webber's Falls, and the rest returned to Boggy Depot.[36]

The Confederate loss at the Battle of Pea Ridge, the largest engagement west of the Mississippi River during the Civil War, was a damaging blow to the Confederacy in the West. It reinforced federal control of Missouri and gained a new foothold in Arkansas, making possible eventual control of the Arkansas River valley. Maintaining supply lines and contact with the Confederate armies in the West and Indian Territory's allied nations would become more difficult. Joseph Murrow noted on March 22, "I fear greatly that communication between Georgia and the West is cut on the Memphis and Charleston Road. The fall of [Fort] Donelson, Bowling Green, Columbus, and Nashville has considerable [sic] embarrassed our operations out here. I think it was those reverses that has occasioned the proposed withdrawal of our forces from these Western borders and their removal farther south."[37]

Murrow believed a Confederate withdrawal from the Indian Territory would be devastating. He wrote, "The fate of the Territory is now hanging in the balance. Van Dorn is threatening to withdraw his forces from Fort Smith to Pocahontas in eastern Arkansas. Pike proposes to withdraw to Red River on the Texas border. If these movements are effected, and Price is compelled to relinquish southwestern Missouri, then we are left to the mercy of the Jayhawkers. There will be no protection for us. Anarchy prevails here now."[38]

Van Dorn did receive orders soon after the Battle of Pea Ridge to move his forces east across the Mississippi River to defend Tennessee, leaving the Confederate military in the West needing reorganization and chronically lacking supplies. As Murrow surmised, the loss at Pea Ridge demonstrated that the Confederacy could not protect the Indian Territory and left it vulnerable to a Union invasion, which fortunately did not occur then. The Indian nations' confidence in the Confederacy and hopes of benefiting from alliances with the new nation were shaken, yet they had burned their bridges with the Union. Cherokee principal chief John Ross commented, "This state of affairs naturally begets apprehension and anxiety."[39]

Another problem developed as well. Some Missouri troops had enlisted in Confederate units to defend their state. According to Wiley Britton, a Union veteran and historian of the Civil War in the border area, some were secessionists. Others were not and had no interest in going east with Van Dorn to defend the other Confederate states. Many of these Union men made it back home and enlisted in the Union army. But some, caught in the Confederate retreat from the Pea Ridge battlefield, scattered or simply deserted. They could not get back to Missouri because federal forces now lay between them and home. These "bushwhackers" sometimes banded together, plaguing secessionists in the border area, and paying no attention to law or the boundaries separating the states and Indian Territory.[40] Others, according to later historians, were partisans who preferred to fight their own war nearer home in their own way and for their own reasons. Some were even sanctioned by the Confederate command.[41] However, people trying to survive near the borders applied the term "bushwhacker" to raiders whatever their politics. "Jayhawking" also became a verb with a meaning beyond Kansas politics.

But for now, it was the Indian soldiers' conduct in the battle at Pea Ridge under scrutiny. Within a week Union general Samuel R. Curtis sent a stiff letter to Confederate general Van Dorn stating that the Indian soldiers were said to have used not only rifles but also bows and arrows and tomahawks during the battle. Moreover, they had scalped and mutilated the dead.[42] Ignoring the slaughter and maiming done by muskets and artillery during the battle, Van Dorn responded that he was pained to hear it. He hoped the report was a mistake because these Indians had "for many years been regarded as a 'civilized' people."[43] Curtis's staff, however, collected several affidavits, most from the 3rd Iowa Cavalry, affirming that at least eight bodies, some exhumed for a second look, had, indeed, been scalped. Curtis wrote to the chairman of the Committee on the Conduct of the Present War, "large forces of Indian savages were engaged against this army at the battle of Pea Ridge, and . . . the warfare was conducted by said savages with all the barbarity their merciless and cowardly natures are capable of."[44] Cherokee historian Robert J. Conley commented that scalping "seemed to offend the whites more than did the killings."[45]

The United States had, of course, used Indian auxiliaries in the American Revolution, the Red Stick War, and the War of 1812. In the last conflict that included men from the same Indian peoples now being condemned. It would continue to use Indian auxiliaries for another twenty years after the Civil War in subduing other Indian nations. However, there was frequently some Anglo-American uneasiness about allowing them to fight in their traditional ways, and they were usually limited to scouting or action against other Indians. The conduct of the Indian Territory troops at Pea Ridge also influenced questions federal officials were considering at the time: whether and how to make use of the able-bodied Indian men in the refugee camps in southern Kansas. Senator James H. Lane, a Kansas Republican and an ardent abolitionist, supported allowing them to serve as soldiers. Secretary of War Edwin Stanton and senior staff in the War Department opposed it, believing Indians did not make disciplined, reliable soldiers. There was also concern about their behavior in time of war, which the Battle of Pea Ridge seemed to exemplify. That stain proved to be indelible, clinging to Brig. Gen. Albert Pike, too.[46] Capt. Eugene Payne of the 37th Illinois Infantry wrote home two months after Pea Ridge, "These Indians are blood thirsty and savage. We know when we fight them that we have to fight on a different principle than we would white men. We must be constantly on our guard as if we were fighting wildcats."[47] Another soldier predicted, "There will be no quarter shown them after this, that is certain."[48]

However, on March 19, about the same time Curtis was complaining to Van Dorn, the War Department agreed to allow the Indian refugees to enlist. They were limited, though, to fighting against other Indians and in defense of their own homes and territory. The refugee men were willing to join. They longed for their homes, and they had scores to settle. Federal officials placed them initially in two irregular "home guard" regiments intended to protect their own people and support a planned expedition to recover their country. The 1st Indian Home Guard Regiment had eight companies of Muscogees and Euchees and two of Seminoles. The 2nd included Cherokees, Osages,

Delawares, Quapaws, and Shawnees. Both regiments also enlisted run-away slaves and free blacks who had followed Opothle Yahola to Kansas. The federal government agreed to provide their weapons and supplies. Opothle Yahola even wanted them to have "wagons that shoot," or artillery. Some men had their own guns, but they lacked powder horns, shot bags, and other necessary equipment. What they received were "Indian rifles," antiquated long-barreled rifles that used a percussion cap to fire round shot. Some of these weapons would not even work, and no uniforms arrived. Although these troops were sup-posed to be infantry, most had their own horses and chose to ride them. As eager as they were to get back to their own country, they still wanted reassurance that white troops would go with them.[49]

Recovering control of the Indian Territory, getting the refugees safely back to their own homes, and relieving federal authorities of responsibility for their subsistence and safety was a priority for federal officials and military officers in Kansas. A Union expedition into northeastern Indian Territory, they hoped, would demonstrate the continuing power of the federal government and perhaps win even more recruits for the Indian Home Guard regiments.[50]

It could also help suppress secessionist guerrillas. After Pea Ridge, Major General Van Dorn sent Pike and the Confederate-allied Indian regiments back to the Indian Territory. He did not expect them to do more than harass any invading Union force by damaging bridges, blocking roads, and destroying supplies and fodder for their livestock. With recent criticism in mind, his orders concluded, "you will please endeavor to restrain them from committing any barbarities upon the wounded, prisoners, or dead who may fall into their hands."[51] Col. Stand Watie soon proved very good at this type of guerrilla warfare. Using Spavinaw Creek and Cowskin Prairie in the Cherokee Nation as his base, he made frequent forays into southwestern Missouri. There Union families, unable to evacuate to the safety of Union-held Springfield, were easy prey for guerrillas and Confederate regulars. Missouri State Guard colonel James J. Clarkson, an ardent proslavery man with plans for interrupting the federal military supply line between Fort Leavenworth and the Colorado-New Mexico area, fre-quently joined forces with Watie. Even though Union troops skir-mished with these Indian and white secessionists several times near

Neosho, Missouri, none stayed to protect it. Neosho was not that far from Cowskin Prairie.[52]

The arrival of six companies of the 24th Missouri Infantry and a company of the 10th Illinois Cavalry at Neosho in late May 1862 illustrated the effectiveness of Watie and the Confederate raiders. Locals assured the Union officers that Watie's regiment and Col. John T. Coffee's cavalry were at least forty miles away. Reconnaissance eight miles out from the Union campsite just north of town found no sign of them. On the night of May 30–31, a false alarm that the surrounding woods were full of horses caused a brief disturbance, but afterward the nervous white troops spent a quiet night, unaware the enemy was nearby. Early the next morning gunfire and war whoops erupted from the surrounding timber, and panicked Union soldiers bolted from the camp. An embarrassed officer reported,

> Within ten minutes from the time of the first shot the camp ... was clear of men, all the camp equipage and train being abandoned. No adequate reason can be assigned for this precipitate flight ... The enemy undoubtedly was in superior force, but not so much so as to [negate] all chances of success; and whatever the superiority may have been, it had not at that time been demonstrated. The screaming and whooping of the Indians is said by the officers of the command to have rendered their untrained horses nearly unmanageable. They further remark that quite a number of refugees had accompanied the command to Neosho in the hope of being reinstated in their homes, and that they fled en masse at the first shot, tending to confuse and alarm the troops.[53]

Watie was not present, having sent only part of his regiment to Neosho with Capt. R. C. Parks in command. Writing from his headquarters at Elk Mills, Missouri, though, he reported that the Union troops fled on foot, with Coffee's cavalry on their heels for miles.[54]

So with several reasons for a Union expedition into the Indian Territory, planning got underway with the full support of the controversial Kansas abolitionist, Senator James H. Lane. Command of the "Indian Expedition" was assigned to Col. William Weer (or "Weir"), who proved to be an unfortunate substitute for Brig. Gen. James G. Blunt, called to other duties at Fort Leavenworth. Weer's forces—five white regiments, two artillery batteries, and the two new Indian Home

Guard regiments—gathered at Baxter Springs, Kansas, in early June 1862. Their families, anxious to get back to their homes, came over from the refugee camps to follow along. The plan generally was to move south along the Texas Road connecting Fort Scott in Kansas with Fort Gibson.[55]

Before they could leave Baxter Springs, though, scouts brought word that white and Indian troops were camped at Round Grove on Cowskin Prairie in today's Delaware County, Oklahoma. Hoping to surprise Watie and the white Confederate troops, Col. Charles Doubleday, without waiting for Weer's approval, led units of infantry, cavalry, and artillery to that location. He ordered a bombardment the evening of June 6, and the Confederate allies scattered under artillery fire that lasted until after midnight. Although Watie and most of his regiment (about a thousand men) escaped, they left behind more than five hundred head of livestock.[56]

Getting the rest of the expedition moving took more time. This concerned Colonel Weer because reports indicated Watie might be gathering a force to destroy the Indian Expedition.[57] The Indian Home Guard regiments were slowing things down, too. Some of their men were absent, and the second regiment was still mustering with Osage men coming in to enlist. They all needed outfitting with uniforms and gear. Weer hoped to move them to Fort Scott, where they would have the good example of white troops and be away from the influence of their families and chiefs. Weer's relationship with the Indians was uncomfortable. He did not understand them, and they seemed fearful of him with a "thousand excuses" for not doing what he wanted and questions about their future he could not answer. Then there were the customs he found strange but which were important to them. On June 13 he wrote of his Indian troops, "They ... have gone into camp, separate from their families, preparatory to a final start. Tonight they have a grand 'war dance.' They have all taken their medicine and consider themselves bullet proof."[58]

Otherwise, Weer had good reports of conditions among the Indians of the territory, which made him optimistic. He told Capt. Thomas Moonlight, the adjutant general, that twenty lodges of secessionist Osages had recently come north to join the Union faction of their tribe. He believed there was still strong loyal sentiment among the Indians, so he had sent runners into the Indian Territory to spread the word that the Indian Expedition was coming. He had learned,

> They have a secret society of Union Indians called Ke-too-wah. One Salmon sends me word to notify him confidentially of my approach and begs that we will not abandon them. The messenger [describes] a sad state of oppression of Union men, and [says] that we will be hailed as deliverers from a state of most tedious tyranny. He thinks Colonel Doubleday's routing of Stand Watie will cause renewed violence against the Union men. John Ross is undoubtedly with us, and will come out openly when we reach there. I am in receipt of information that large bodies of Union Indians exist among all these people clear to Fort Cobb, and that they await our advance in order to take the field in behalf of the Government. I am satisfied that the Indians here will fight when I reach their own country!

Weer urged Moonlight to send weapons, powder, and lead to arm the Indians who were sure to turn out to meet them as the Indian Expedition advanced into the territory.[59]

Colonel Weer was correct in some of his assumptions, but things did not turn out quite that way. The two Indian regiments finally got outfitted at Humboldt, Kansas, west of Fort Scott. Superintendent of Indian Affairs William G. Coffin wrote that they

> left for the Indian Territory in good stile and in fine spirits . . . with their new uniforms and small Military caps on their Hug[e] Heads of Hair made rather a Comecal Ludecrous appearance[.] [T]hey marched off in columns of 4 a breast singing the war song all joining in the chourse and a more animated seen is not often witnessed. The officers in command of the Indian Regements have labored incessantly and the improvement the Indians have made in drilling is much greater than I supposed them capabell of.

He had high hopes that they would surprise everyone and "be the most efecient troops in the Expedition."[60]

The first section of the expedition included units from Ohio, Wisconsin, Kansas, and Indiana as well as the Indian Home Guard, freedmen, and escaped slaves. It finally left Baxter Springs, Kansas, on June 28; the second section left a day later. Indian civilians followed along behind. While the main column paused on the Grand River to wait for the supply train, a detachment crossed over to the east bank of the Spring River to scout as far as the Missouri line about five miles away. This whole area was known to be infested with dangerous irregulars and raiders such as Watie, Clarkson, and Coffee. They could not afford to let the Union gain a foothold there and expect to hold the Indian nations for the Confederacy. Nor could they allow a backdoor into Arkansas and Texas.[61]

Watie's troops snapped at the advance guard of the column near Spavinaw Creek, but Weer struck the Confederate allies a more damaging blow. After receiving word that Colonel Clarkson was near Locust Grove in today's Mayes County, Oklahoma, he took about three hundred men from the 9th and 10th Kansas, the 1st Indian regiment, and a section of artillery on a hard night march some twenty miles south. Just about dawn on July 3 their battery opened fire on the sleeping camp, while the 1st Indian, commanded by Lt. Col. Stephen H. Wattles, and the 9th Kansas attacked.[62] Weer wrote later that the dense brush throughout the campsite meant each man was virtually fighting alone because he could not see the rest of his unit. Clarkson's men were too confused and demoralized to put up much resistance, and the timber was too thick for them to form an effective firing line. In gunfire that continued most of the day, the federals killed about thirty of the enemy and captured Clarkson along with some one hundred men who could not escape into the brush. Weer captured all sixty wagons of a supply train just arrived from Fort Smith, as well as the draft horses, mules, harness, and baggage. The victory lacked only the capture of Col. Stand Watie, who had left the camp not long before the fight began. Still the Indian Expedition had reason to celebrate July 4. The captured military supplies restocked the Union regiments, while the Indian soldiers received the gunpowder they needed for their antiquated rifles. The Indian refugee civilians encamped near the mouth of Cabin Creek happily accepted several bales of citizen clothing, which the soldiers could not use.[63]

Although Colonel Weer officially credited all his troops for the victory, the account that reached the commissioner of Indian affairs was apparently quite different. In his annual report for 1862 he stated, "The Creek Indians were first in the fight . . . . We do not hear that any white man fired a gun unless it was to kill the surgeon of the 1st Indian regiment . . . . In reality, it was a victory gained by the 1st Indian regiment; and while the other forces would, no doubt, have acted well, it is the height of injustice to claim this victory for the whites."[64] The commissioner did not mention that the 1st Indian included escaped slaves and freedmen, who also contributed to the victory.[65]

Although relatively small, that skirmish at Locust Grove was significant to the Cherokee Nation. Clarkson's men who escaped through the woods straggled into Tahlequah about thirty miles away and spread the news of the Union attack. Many Cherokees who were still uneasy with their nation's Confederate alliance and biding their time came out then for the Union side. Cherokee missionary Stephen Foreman, a Watie supporter, noted in his diary in late June there was great restlessness and dissatisfaction in Col. John Drew's regiment. He believed some were in constant communication with the Cherokees who had followed Opothle Yahola to Kansas or had since become Unionists. When Drew's men deserted again, Foreman believed Drew, William Potter Ross, and their officers knew of the plot but did nothing to stop it. So many of them made their way north to the Indian Expedition column that they filled the remaining vacancies in the 2nd Indian Home Guard Regiment or became the first members of the 3rd. Among those who joined the 3rd Indian were John Ross's older sons James, Allen, Silas, and George. Union emissaries, including missionaries Evan and John B. Jones, had accompanied the expedition. They rode to Park Hill to try to persuade Principal Chief John Ross to repudiate his nation's alliance with the Confederacy. Although the Cherokee pendulum was swinging back toward the Union, Ross was still being very careful. He declined to override the decision and authority of the Cherokee people expressed in the vote favoring a Confederate alliance. At the same time, he did not comply with Brig. Gen. Douglas H. Cooper's emergency order to draft all Cherokee men between the ages of eighteen and thirty-five for Confederate service.[66]

While the Indian Expedition camped on the prairie on the west side of the Grand River near Flat Rock Creek, Colonel Weer learned that Confederate-allied troops were gathering at Fort Davis to repel the Union invasion. He sent Maj. William T. Campbell and part of the 6th Kansas Cavalry to scout it out. Campbell found some Confederates occupying the abandoned buildings at Fort Gibson, but they escaped. He discovered that the main body of Confederate troops was just across the Arkansas River at Fort Davis. Campbell ran up the Stars and Stripes, notified Weer, and then waited for orders.[67]

Meanwhile, Capt. Harris S. Greeno took another company of the 6th Kansas Cavalry toward Tahlequah. He expected some resistance but found few men in the town and went on to nearby Park Hill. There he found Chief Ross still mulling over his best course. Federal troops were actually in the Cherokee Nation in force now, and Union victories were accumulating in the east. In the end, Greeno made his decision for him. He placed Ross under house arrest as a prisoner of war, relieving him of blame when in early August Ross allowed himself, his family, and the Cherokee Nation records to be removed to Kansas.[68]

Mary E. Hudson James, then about six, remembered the coming of the Indian Expedition because it completely changed their family circumstances. Sarah and Thomas Joshua Buffington Hudson had survived Cherokee removal from Georgia and rebuilt their lives on a farm along Hudson Creek northeast of today's Fairland, Oklahoma. Well-to-do according to some standards, they regarded themselves as being an "average Cherokee family in this new country, adding little by little each year to our houses, increasing the acreage around us and life each year . . . becoming more comfortable." They lived in a "big double log house with side rooms and tall chimneys, big barns full of grain, and good stock." Outbuildings included slave quarters, but their slaves had already left with a federal wagon train at the beginning of the war.[69]

However, when the Indian Expedition came through, federal troops found the Hudson farm. Mary said,

> The first raid through here the Federals took all of our stock, except one gray horse. They killed mother's chickens and turkeys . . . between three and four hundred. They raided our smoke house and took our bacon and meat and set the cans of lard out in the yard and greased their guns with the lard and destroyed what was not used. Stand Watie, our friend, came up through the country and left with us a horse . . . . Father hitched this horse with our gray one to a hack and loaded his wife and children into this with what few things we could carry.

They went north to the Sac and Fox Agency, where her father got work in a sawmill until he could move the family on to Lawrence, Kansas, for the duration of the war.[70]

Life also changed drastically for some slaves in the Cherokee Nation, according to Moses Lonian, born a slave in Saline District in 1857. The soldiers with the Indian Expedition, sweeping down the Grand River in 1862, he said, had been told to free every slave they could find. Moses and his family belonged to Louis Ross, who had not been a kind master. His slaves were afraid to leave when it was time to go, as were other Cherokee slaves. "They were afraid the northern soldiers could not protect them and get them out of the country as they said they would," Moses explained. "They were afraid of beatings if their masters came after them, but the soldiers told them to load up their master's belongings and made them leave." He recalled,

> The soldiers told the slaves they had earned everything their masters had many times over and told them now was the time to get it. They made us load everything we could find, including all of Louis Ross's fine furniture and looking glasses . . . . Every wagon and team and ox on the place was rounded up, and hitched to the wagons . . . . Every hog, cow, and horse on the plantation was rounded up and driven off that could be found . . . . After all the slaves and stock that could be found on the east side of the river were gotten together, we crossed the river at Salina and hit the Old Military Trail.[71]

They followed it past Baxter Springs, Kansas. When they were five miles beyond the state line, "which the soldiers called 'the Mason Dixon Line,'" Moses remembered, "they bade us farewell and told us to 'now skedaddle, and you better not let them Indians catch up with you.'" The soldiers gave them plenty of rations and about five hundred head of stock, but the slaves were so afraid of being followed and caught with the stolen goods, "they turned loose about five hundred head of cattle and broke up all the fine furniture and looking glasses as soon as the soldiers got out of their sight." Moses concluded, "If we had kept all the cattle . . . we would have fared well but as it was we nearly starved to death before the war was over."[72]

In spite of some successes, the Indian Expedition was floundering by mid-July 1862. There had been no rain after the column entered the

Indian Territory, and the prairie grass, which should have been green and tall around the main camp near Flat Rock Creek, was instead dry enough to burn. In the regiments from the northern states men unused to the Southern Plains heat and humidity were suffering. The horses, too, were not properly shod for the area's rough, flinty ground, and they were worn out. Although the commissary rarely ran out of fresh beef—plenty of good Indian cattle were all around them—other foodstuffs were running out. At the same time, Colonel Weer seemed to have lost the focus of this expedition with too many side-ventures. Enemies surrounded them, but he had not heeded repeated warnings not to get too far from Fort Scott and their supply source. The grumbling spread and increased, until on July 18 the officers rebelled. Col. Frederick Salomon, citing Weer's rashness, failure to observe and enforce proper military conduct, abusive treatment of his officers, and well-known drunkenness, arrested him and took command. The colonel ordered a withdrawal from the Indian Territory, and the Indian Expedition trekked back toward Fort Scott. For Indian Expedition soldiers such as Wiley Britton, it was a sad, sour ending to a noble undertaking.[73]

Moreover, the aborted expedition had major ramifications for the peoples of the Indian Territory. News of its coming had caused another wave of pro-Southern Cherokees and Muscogees to leave their country for the safety of the Red River valley. As the expedition withdrew, Cherokees who had publicly declared for the Union during the brief occupation of their nation realized they were now at risk of reprisal from the pro-Southern faction. So, too, were the families of the men who had deserted Col. John Drew's 1st Cherokee Mounted Rifles to join the Indian Home Guard. They knew they would be targets of retaliation when Col. Stand Watie and the other pro-Southern troops flooded back into their nation. There seemed no other option for them now but to leave the Cherokee Nation, their homes, and the crops they had planted that spring. Trailing the retreating expedition back to Fort Scott, they joined the disappointed refugees who had hoped the expedition was their chance to go home. Like them, this new wave would have to depend on others for food, shelter, and necessities.[74]

The violence that wracked the Cherokee Nation in those days seemed to grow ever worse, sparing not even the most harmless and helpless. Among them was the Hicks family of Park Hill. Hannah

Worcester Hicks was the daughter of Samuel Austin Worcester, the Vermont missionary who had been imprisoned in Georgia in the 1830s for defending Cherokee sovereignty. She had come as a child to the Indian Territory during the Cherokee removal, and the Cherokee Nation was her home. In 1852 she had married Abijah Hicks, a young Cherokee farmer, merchant, and missionary's assistant. It was Abijah who had helped Hannah's sister Ann Eliza Robertson and her family, suspected of sympathizing with the North, to escape from Tullahassee Mission in the Muscogee Nation through the Cherokee hills to Missouri. On Independence Day, while the Indian Expedition troops and refugees were celebrating the victory at Locust Grove, Abijah left for Van Buren, Arkansas, to buy stock for his store. Along the way bushwhackers stopped him and demanded he join their gang. When he refused and drove on, they shot him in the back and left him dead in the road.[75]

Not long afterward, Hanna wrote in her diary,

> Oh, what a year to remember, will this year ever be to me, and to us all. We thought we had some trouble last year, but how happy was that compared with this. On the 4th of July, my beloved husband was murdered, killed away from home, and I could not even see him; so far from it—he had been buried twenty-four hours, before I even heard of it; buried without a coffin, all alone, forty miles from home.[76]

A few weeks later, she noted, "This is the ninth Sabbath that I have been a widow; two sad weary months. How many times in days past have I wondered what my future would be . . . left a widow at twenty-eight, with five children growing up around me, and Oh! Most dreadful of all, my dear husband murdered." Then Hannah learned something even more disturbing. "I begin to hear now," she wrote, "that my poor husband was killed by the 'Pins' but through a mistake—they intended to kill another man."[77]

Even in her deep grief and distress, Hannah behaved with courage and charity toward her neighbor, minister Stephen Foreman. In spite of his pro-Southern politics he sympathized with her loss. On Sunday, June 6, Foreman learned of Abijah's death and noted, "he was an inoffensive man and if killed, it was either for his abolition sentiments or his property, for no one who has a good horse or any good property is safe, though I have heard of no one being killed yet for his sentiments, still I should not be surprised if it came to that."[78]

Ten days later Pins came looking for Stephen Foreman. He hid out first in his cornfield and then in his attic before Hannah Hicks hid him in her house. While lying low, he had time to think about the situation and concluded that the Pins were after him not because he was Southern in principle but because he was a Watie partisan. These incidents deepened his distrust and bitter dislike of John Ross, whom the Pins supported. In late July Foreman learned Cherokees were complaining to Chief Ross that Watie's men were robbing and killing women and children. Foreman wrote in his diary that if that were so, Watie's men were taking only half as much as the Pins.[79] Things did not improve for him even after the Indian Expedition began its withdrawal from the Cherokee Nation. On August 5 a Union escort evacuated Ross, his family, and the Cherokee Nation records from Rose Cottage, beginning his wartime exile in the United States. The same day and just a little distance away, the Pins, "their faces all painted," came looking for Foreman again.[80] He endured the worsening conditions until mid-September, when he moved his children and some belongings over to the Muscogee Nation. For now that seemed a safer place than the Cherokee Nation.[81]

Conditions continued to deteriorate that summer for the Cherokees. On August 1, less than a month after Abijah Hicks was killed, Hannah's house was burned. It was, she wrote, the "first great trial" she had had to face without him although less a trial than losing him. Her neighbor Stephen Foreman had found safety at the now-vacant North Fork Town home of his son's Muscogee father-in-law, George W. Stidham. Hannah and her children, though, had little choice but to stay in the Cherokee Nation. She wrote, "This weary weary time of War! Will the time of suspense never end? I know not what is to become of us: famine and pestilence seem to await us!"[82]

On September 10 Hannah visited the office and bindery of the Park Hill Mission Press, part of the mission station founded and nurtured by her father. Established in 1836, the press had printed almost 14 million pages of Scripture, hymns, almanacs, pamphlets, and textbooks in the Cherokee, Choctaw, Muscogee, and English languages. It ended production in 1861.[83] Hannah had learned the printer's trade from her father and worked there until she married Abijah. After going through the two-story press building and bindery, she wrote, "I did not know before *how completely it had been cleaned out; the Press, types, papers &c. all carried off or destroyed* [her emphasis]." Such destruction was becoming epidemic. Hannah also noted, "We hear today that the 'Pins' are committing outrages on Hungry Mountain and in Flint [District], robbing, destroying property and killing . . . . [A]las, alas for this miserable people; destroying each other, as fast as they can." Men from families she knew were at risk of abduction or murder or both. James Ward, a missionary for many years at New Springplace, had been murdered, and William Spears, another minister, had disappeared. Hannah recorded, "William Spears was killed some weeks ago: his wife has been searching for him until yesterday she succeeded in finding a part of his bones and the remanents [*sic*] of his clothing. It is said that they told him to Pray and that he did so, and was kneeling in prayer a second time when he was shot."[84]

This was only the beginning of a war in which civilians, caught between warring forces, fell victim to both sides. Fall brought the Hicks family new misery. Hannah described what happened on November 17:

> Today we have had experience in being robbed. As soon as it was light they came and began: They took many valuable things and overhauled every closet, trunk, box and drawer they could find. The most valuable things are gone for good and all. So many things the robbers took that I would regret so much if I felt that the loss of anything short of life itself, was worth regretting now. They took about three barrels of sugar, *all* [her emphasis] my blankets, most of my quilts, sheets, pillow cases, towels, table cloths, my teaspoons, all but one, and oh, that large pretty white bed spread that Mrs. Ross had given me; so many little things that I most highly prized; ribbons, sewing silk, pins, needles, thread, buttons, boxes of letters, my mantilla, calicoes, woolen stuffs, white cloth I was saving to make up, part of my underclothes and stockings, with the childrens new shoes, their little shawls, &c.; from Mother they took some blankets, one shawl, her shears, mine also, her best shoes and all, some other things, the linen sheet and table cloth of my mother's weaving. If the officers had not made them return some things, I and my children would

have been left utterly destitute, for they bundled up all our clothing of every kind; (my knives, forks and large spoons were
returned) they opened and overhauled the letter box which was
under my bed, took some letters and some little things of Mrs.
Vann's that I had put in to save. They tore the trimming off Susie's
bonnet, broke open a chest which was locked, and took what they
pleased. They drove off nearly all our cattle, but most of them
got away and came back.[85]

With winter closing in, Hannah and her family were desperate. They
still had some of their livestock, but their horses had been stolen. While
Hannah did not identify the men who stripped her home of almost
everything of any value, she noted it was troops commanded by
Confederate brigadier general John Sappington Marmaduke of
Missouri that came later and took the wheat and grain she had hauled
and stored in her corncrib.[86]

While most of the plundering and violence against civilians
seemed to be limited to the Cherokee Nation for the time being, it also
occurred in the Muscogee Nation. James Roane Gregory, the son of a
white father and a Muscogee mother, was about twenty when his
neighbors in the western part of the nation near today's Bristow,
Oklahoma, left to follow Opothle Yahola. Some months later he helped
drive cattle to a ranch on Pryor Creek in the Cherokee Nation. He was
at Concharty on his way home when some "Creek Confederates"
arrested him. They had also arrested his father who had come to meet
him. The Gregory family never knew why unless it was to settle some
old grudge. The elder Gregory was sixty-six and, held captive away
from his home, died from cold and exposure in the winter of 1861–
1862. James made his way to Kansas when he could. He said later, "We
had not taken sides, but were trying to care for our property. Every act
of concession to gain the good will of our captors being unavailing,
the results were that the writer now has a military record . . . for service
rendered in the [Union] Ninth Kansas Cavalry."[87]

Men such as James Roane Gregory who became soldiers in Union,
Union Indian, or Confederate-allied regiments entered a new life. For
the young men, especially, soldiering may have been at first a welcome
change from farming, ranching, store-keeping, or school, as much an
adventure, perhaps, as the war seemed for young white men in the

beginning. This generation of Indian men grew up on stories of famous warriors and how their grandfathers, fathers, and uncles had fought at Horse Shoe Bend or New Orleans and might even have battled the Comanches, Caddos, Pawnees, or Osages. Most probably had not had the opportunity to take the second step in the traditional cycle of an Indian man's life. During that summertime of his life, the young Indian man was expected to provide for and defend his people as a warrior and to earn his war name. Now that opportunity had come for them. For older men with families, though, there was concern whether their wives, children, and elders could look after their farms, businesses, and slaves if they had any, or, perhaps just survive in a refugee camp.[88]

One of those young men was George Washington ("Wash") Grayson, a mixed-blood Muscogee who grew up near North Fork Town, attended the national schools, and even studied at Arkansas College in Fayetteville for two years before the war forced it to close. About nineteen years old in 1862, Wash yearned to join the 1st Creek Mounted Regiment commanded by his kinsman, Col. Daniel N. McIntosh, or the newer regiment, commanded by Chilly McIntosh. Unfortunately, Wash was responsible for his widowed mother, Jennie, and younger brothers and sister. While he clerked in a North Fork Town store to support them and helped with the family farm, he was acutely aware others thought he lacked the courage to fight. It is not clear how long that galling situation lasted, perhaps through 1862, but by spring 1863 he was finally able to join the 2nd Creek Mounted Regiment. He served among neighbors and members of his family, the Tiger clan, and his ceremonial town, Coweta. He also left an unusual extensive memoir of those years.[89]

As lieutenant of Company K, he knew the promises of the Confederate treaties with regard to outfitting, arming, and paying the Indian soldiers were rarely kept. Historian Robert L. Kerby, looking at conditions in the Trans-Mississippi West by 1863, summarized, "the Confederacy was an eighteenth-century country trying to support a nineteenth-century army in an effort to win the first twentieth-century war." It lacked the resources, industry, and transportation to succeed in the East, let alone in the undeveloped West.[90] The Indian Territory troops were at the extreme end of a long supply line stretching from the beleaguered Confederate states. Supplies meant for them, Brig. Gen.

Albert Pike complained, were usually siphoned off somewhere along the way for use by white troops. Only a fraction of his orders for tents, shoes, shirts, pants, drawers, and small arms ever arrived in the Indian Territory. On one occasion his officers even tracked down and retrieved medicines and percussion caps meant for his troops but boxed up and already loaded for shipment to white soldiers elsewhere. In May 1862 Pike complained to his superiors, "Hardly a box comes here that has not been opened and part of the contents abstracted." Even the mules that drew his baggage train, he fumed, were "scarecrows . . . [but] considered good enough for the Indian service."[91]

Consequently, his Indian troops, according to Pike, wore their regular clothes, rode their own ponies, and were "armed very indifferently with common rifles and ordinary shot-guns."[92] Young Lieutenant Grayson agreed. Reminiscing in about 1912, he reflected that the men in his company "presented a very motley appearance" and "were never very presentable."[93] There were times when the lack of clothing, let alone uniforms, became critical. His men "yamped," or appropriated, whatever they could use from people they regarded as enemies. They routinely stripped prisoners of clothing and exchanged it for their own.[94]

That custom provided him with one of his favorite memories of the war years. About the only uniform piece of clothing the Confederate Indian troops received was a hat. It was standard Confederate issue and made of unbleached (and from the smell, unwashed) sheep's wool. Once it got wet, it returned to its basic cone shape. The Indian soldiers liked to add their personal decorations to their hats. Wash's cousin and best friend, Valentine McAnally, had shaved the shaft of a hawk's feather thin and attached it to the crown of his hat so that it swayed and bobbed with every movement of his head. When Valentine captured a prisoner, a tall gangling white man, he took the man's hat and gave him his own in exchange. The memory of that man's woe-begone face, topped off by Valentine's Indian hat and bobbing feather, still made Wash laugh more than fifty years later.[95]

The lack of uniform clothing was a problem the Confederate Muscogees had in common with fellow Creeks in the Indian Home Guard regiments. Wiley Britton wrote of the Muscogees, Cherokees, and Seminoles he served with in the Union Indian Brigade, "Care was not taken to see to it that the clothing issued to the Indian soldiers fitted them properly. The pants legs were frequently too short or too long, and the coat rarely ever fitted . . . giving the Indian soldiers a comical appearance, mounted on their ponies with badly fitted clothing, and wearing 'Hancock Hats,' with their long black hair falling over their shoulders, and legs astride their mounts coming down near the ground."[96] Britton added though, there was nothing comical about their ability to fight. Screened from the enemy in the brush and timber and able to rest their long-barreled rifles to take careful aim, they "were in their element" and deadly.[97]

The same was true of the pro-Southern Indians, something Brig. Gen. Albert Pike appreciated even as he recognized their shortcomings. He noted that their Confederate treaties, "invariably stipulated that they should be allowed to fight in their own fashion." As they had demonstrated at Pea Ridge, he explained, "They will not face artillery and steady infantry on open ground, and are only used . . . as skirmishers when cover can be obtained." He held the common view on both sides that in battle out in the open they needed stability and support from white officers and troops.[98] Second Lt. William P. Bumpass of the 5th Texas Partisan Rangers, who fought beside the Confederate-allied Indians in Arkansas and the Indian Territory, agreed. He stated the Indian soldier made "a good scout, but we never succeeded in holding them in line in an open field and fighting to our plan except once and then the line of battle was along the foot of a mountain range and was amongst underbrush and great boulders . . . and in passing that part of the line after the battle, it was easy to discover the effects of their deadly aim, secreted as they were among the rocks and bushes."[99]

Wash Grayson agreed with Pike and Bumpass on some of these points. There were times his Muscogee troops frustrated him, too. Having served as adjutant of the 2nd Creek Mounted Volunteers and then as lieutenant, later captain, of Company K, he knew Indian officers had little interest in paperwork and writing reports even if they were literate or could speak English. That was the common language in an army with men from several nations speaking at least four different languages. Most white men only spoke and wrote in English. The Indian troops did not see the need for drilling or any benefits from fighting in formation. Nor were they inclined to hang around camp when there was no activity or fighting to be done. That they often simply went home without leave bothered their Indian officers far less than it did their white officers. Lieutenant Grayson, always conscious that most white officers looked down on Indian troops, himself included, understood the Indian soldier's ways but tried to make his company conform to white expectations. The men usually came back when they were needed. Moreover, their independence, knowledge of Indian Territory geography and terrain, and traditional fighting skills made them very good at the kind of war being fought in the Indian Territory.[100]

The white soldiers in the Indian regiments were often another matter. They were not usually citizens of the Indian nations, intermarried, or even residents of the Indian Territory. Dallas and Granville Bowman from Panola County, Texas, were so eager to enlist in the 1st Choctaw and Chickasaw Mounted Rifles that seventeen-year-old Dallas pretended to be eighteen.[101] According to Capt. B. W. Marston, who inspected Colonel Cooper's command in late 1864, white enlistees with few exceptions "saught [sic] service in the Indian Rgts to get out of service" elsewhere. "I don't think there are less than a thousand white men in the Indian Division," Marston wrote. Some whole companies were filled with them. In his opinion, these white men were "one of the greatest evils" afflicting the Indian regiments and a demoralizing influence because of their lack of discipline and soldiering skills. Yet they expected the same prerogatives as the Indian soldiers. Marston believed transferring them to some white division elsewhere would remove a major hindrance to improving Indian troops' discipline and skills.[102]

Although many of the Indian soldiers were Christians, others were not and still observed centuries-old traditions associated with making war. Sgt. Jackson Lewis was listed on the roster of Company K, 2nd Creek Mounted Volunteers, as the medical officer. A full-blood Muscogee-Hichita, Lewis, a survivor of the removal, had been trained in traditional medicine and was widely known for his skill and power as a healer. He was also a Baptist deacon and Mason. When Company K prepared for battle, Lewis painted the men's cheeks and chests red for war and black for death. Then he made the sign of the cross over them. Once the fight was over, he had them cleanse body and spirit by washing in a creek, drinking water, and vomiting it. Jackson Lewis, whose war name was Lahta Yahola, had been promoted to second lieutenant by the war's end. While he was a traditional healer, Dr. Thomas Jefferson Bond, a

Choctaw, also served the Confederate Indian forces as a medical officer. He was a surgeon who had trained in Baltimore, Maryland, at the forerunner of Johns Hopkins University.[103]

By autumn 1862, the Civil War had engulfed the Indian Territory, with many men already in military units and a Union campaign to recover the territory launched. Still, some tribes remained uncommitted, not knowing what was best to do. Among them were the Absentee Shawnees, who had been expelled from Texas just before the war. In 1862 they were living near the Delaware, Piankashaw, and Kickapoo peoples in the western Muscogee Nation close to Tullahassee ceremonial town. According to Thomas Wildcat Alford, an Absentee Shawnee born in 1860, when these tribes met in council together in 1861 to discuss the coming war, they agreed it was the white man's fight, not theirs. But they had friends, other Indians on both sides, especially in the Muscogee Nation, who constantly urged them to join one side or the other. By 1862 their chances of remaining neutral were dwindling.[104]

About then John Rogers led a party of Shawnees south to invite the Absentee band to join them on their Kansas reservation. At the time, according to oral history passed to Alford, "Our people did not want to leave their homes. They had crops growing; some had cattle and hogs. But there was no way to keep out of trouble where they were." To avoid prying eyes, the tribes being solicited to declare allegiance in the war agreed secretly to gather at Council Grove, a well-known meeting place on the frontier between the Plains and Eastern tribes. It lay in a bend of the North Canadian River and was known for its fine spring, good timber, abundant water, and grass for livestock. Today little remains to mark that place in the western Oklahoma City suburb of Bethany. One result of the 1862 meeting was that the Shawnees, still hoping to stay neutral, agreed on a plan: Each Shawnee family would leave its home in the Muscogee Nation separately as if going on a routine hunting trip to the western plains. Although these "hunting parties" would take separate routes, they would rendezvous later at Council Grove. Thomas Wildcat Alford, just a toddler then, related how his family left their small farm and most of their belongings, including his father's farming equipment, their hogs and cattle, and that year's young corn crop. His mother could take only a few of her herd of fifty horses, a gift from her mother.[105]

Once they all reached Council Grove, the Absentee Shawnees found people from other tribes already camped. There was even a band of runaway slaves hiding out from their masters and slave catchers. Their descriptions of slavery and determination to avoid recapture influenced the Shawnees' decision not to join the Confederate-allied Muscogees. Instead, they decided to go on to Kansas and avoid the war. They held firm to that decision even when a band of Confederate soldiers, most of them Muscogees, appeared and demanded the Shawnees go back east with them. Outnumbered, the soldiers left Council Grove, but the Shawnees realized they had better start north before the men returned with reinforcements. The trip across the treeless prairie was long and slow, but the Shawnees hunted bison for meat and hides along the way. They finally reached their kinsmen near Belmont, Kansas, in early 1863.[106]

While the war divided other tribes, according to Alford, it provided the opportunity to improve relations between the Absentee Shawnees and the Black Bob Shawnee band, divided geographically and by historical events for more than fifty years. Able to visit, tell stories, and share their common culture, they reestablished a good relationship. Although the Absentee Shawnees had avoided being drawn into the conflict on the Confederate side, in Kansas many of the men, including Alford's father, gave in to pressure to enlist in Company M, 15th Kansas Cavalry, in the Union army. Alford reflected, "Perhaps the younger men relished the thought of a real fight, having heard so many interesting stories of warfare in earlier days."[107] His favorite memory of those days, though, was of the army uniform overcoat his father sent home. Alford's mother cut up the heavy blue wool garment to make clothing for her three children. She used the sleeves to make leggings for little Thomas, who wore them proudly with his shirt and moccasins, earning his first English nickname, "Soldier."[108]

Other tribes in the Indian Territory were also leery of becoming involved in the white man's war. Albert Pike had contacted some of the Comanches and Kiowas on his visit to Wichita Agency in 1861. However, these nomadic tribes were composed of independent bands that lived apart and generally only gathered for special occasions such as the Sun Dance. No single chief could sign a treaty that would bind the whole tribe. The Peneteka Comanches had signed a Confederate treaty Albert Pike offered at Wichita Agency, but the other Comanche bands and the Kiowas, Plains Apaches, Cheyennes, and Arapahos—all part of a loose alliance formed in 1840—mostly stayed northwest of the Indian Territory in Kansas and Colorado Territory the first two years of the war.

Some Kiowas, though, took the opportunity to even scores with the Leased District Indians once federal troops had withdrawn from Forts Cobb, Arbuckle, and Washita. In 1860 Plains Indian attacks along the Santa Fe Trail through the Smoky Hill River area of western Kansas had grown so bothersome that federal cavalry units, guided by Caddo, Tonkawa, and Wichita auxiliaries, had struck back. Among the casualties was T'ene-badai, or Bird-Appearing, a prominent and handsome young Kiowa man killed by a Caddo. The next winter his brother Gaabohonte, or Crow Bonnet, led a revenge raid against the Caddo camp on Sugar Creek a few miles north of Anadarko. They killed and scalped one Caddo. Smallpox struck the Kiowa camps during the winter of 1861–1862, but the next year Tone-tsain, or Stray Horse, inspired by Crow Bonnet's success, got up his own war party—six Kiowas and four Plains Apaches—for the summer of 1863.[109]

Unfortunately, Tone-tsain set off with his raiding party during the Sun Dance, which was strictly forbidden. They traveled all the way from the Arkansas River to the Washita River before coming across a lone Caddo out hunting on foot. Unable to escape, he talked his way out of trouble by inviting them back to his camp to eat. Hoping to find more victims, they followed him to the junction of Cache and Chandler Creeks just north of the Wichita Mountains. Too late, they realized they were entering a large camp of Peneteka Comanches, Caddos, and Confederate soldiers who had come west from Fort Arbuckle to hunt buffalo. The Kiowa war party brazened it out for a while. They turned their horses loose to graze and pretended to relax until they noticed a stir running through the camp. They bolted for their horses then but could not get to them all. Some of the Kiowas were forced to ride double, so the Indians and white soldiers soon caught up with them. Tone-tsain escaped the charge of one Confederate soldier, but a Caddo shot him in the back of the head. The rest of the Kiowa war party then ran on west along Chandler Creek; but only two of them, one a young warrior on his first raid, escaped. The next spring, yet another Kiowa war party came into Caddo country to avenge Tone-tsain's death. Near the Keechi Hills in today's Caddo County, Oklahoma, they ran into a large party of Caddos, who tracked them with hounds west beyond Rainy Mountain Creek. The pursuers and the Kiowas kept going on foot until the Caddos got within rifle range. These expert marksmen then killed four Kiowas, but the rest of the war party escaped. This ended the series of Kiowa raids but fed long-term enmity between the Kiowas and Caddos. Kiowa historians recorded all these events by painting "calendar histories," a series of pictographs noting each year's significant events, on tanned hides.[110]

Otherwise in the Leased District, the general uneasiness that had begun with the withdrawal of federal troops from the frontier forts grew during the summer and fall of 1862. No sooner had they left in May 1861 than Confederate colonel William C. Young and a small contingent of Texas state troops occupied Fort Cobb, built to protect and support Wichita Agency. Matthew Leeper retained his position as Indian agent under the Confederate Indian Department. Even after Albert Pike negotiated Confederate treaties with the Leased District tribes in July, there was fear and friction among the two thousand resident Indians and between some of them and the agency staff. While Peneteka Comanche chiefs Tosawa and Isahabbit were generally friendly toward white people, Buffalo Hump, another Peneteka chief, could be hostile, arrogant, and demanding. He came up against Agent Leeper, a cantankerous man who could not even get along with his own staff and superiors. Another persistent problem was that the other agency Indians disliked the Tonkawas, who shared the reserve with them. Men of that tribe had often scouted for the Texans and U.S. Cavalry during earlier Indian campaigns. Most recently they had followed Chief Placido on the 1858 expeditions against the Comanches and their Wichita allies. Moreover, the Tonkawas' neighbors believed they practiced cannibalism, a custom repugnant to other Indians.[111]

By August 1862 it was clear the Confederacy was not keeping its promises to support and protect the Leased District Indians, particularly after the Confederate troops, too, abandoned Fort Cobb. The poorly armed Indians were left vulnerable, while rumors circulated that Texans were planning some hostile action toward them. Meanwhile, relations between Buffalo Hump and Leeper continued to deteriorate. The result was that about half of the agency Indians—among them some of the Wichita peoples, Caddos, and Delawares—slipped away to Kansas hoping to find refuge there. They set up camps along the Arkansas River near today's Wichita, Kansas, and spent the rest of the war there. As conditions worsened at the agency during the summer, Matthew Leeper, who had just returned from a business trip to Texas, left again, this time to escort his family back to Texas. He placed interpreter Horace P. Jones, who usually got along with the Indians, in charge of the agency in his absence.[112]

This volatile situation reached a flashpoint on October 23 when a Union scouting party filtered into the Wichita Agency. Confederate Indian Territory superintendent of Indian affairs S. S. Scott later reported it included some Shawnees and Delawares, as well as Kickapoos, Seminoles, Cherokees, and Osages—about one hundred men in all—some of whom had only recently left Wichita Agency for Kansas. Led by Ben Simon, a Delaware, they circulated among the agency Indians, prodding them to attack the remaining Confederate staff. About the same time, word spread that the Tonkawas had recently killed a Caddo boy and were planning to eat his body during a feast. The return of the unpopular agent Matthew Leeper seemed to trigger the violence that exploded that night. Two hours after dark raiders struck the agency, killing four employees in the first rush and burning down the building with their bodies inside. Barking dogs alerted interpreter Horace C. Jones in time to escape out a rear window of his cabin and spread the alarm. Agent Leeper also escaped in his nightshirt through a window and hid in the woods. Comanche Chief Tosawa found him there the next morning and gave him a horse to ride back to Texas. Jones, the agency doctor, scout Phil McCusker, and the Shirley brothers, who ran a trading post near the agency, escaped to Texas together.[113]

The Tonkawas were not so fortunate. They lived along the Washita River south of the agency, and the noise and fire woke them that night. Alarmed, they fled across the river west of today's Anadarko, Oklahoma, and then east along the Washita valley. Near dawn they stopped to rest in a ravine about two miles from the agency. That was where the other Indians, who held old grudges against them and believed the stories about Tonkawa cannibalism, caught up with them. Superintendent Scott, who received his information from the Tonkawa survivors, reported, "they attacked the Ton-ca-wes . . . killing their chief, Placido, a good man, twenty-three of their warriors, and about a hundred of their women and children. The Ton-ca-wes, although armed with only bows and arrows, while their assailants had weapons of the latest and best pattern furnished them by the North, inflicted upon the latter, it was said, a loss of twenty-seven men in killed and wounded."[114] About forty Tonkawa men and fewer than a hundred women and children survived and fled, leaving the bodies of their dead unburied in the ravine. A few days after the attack, they straggled into Fort Arbuckle on foot or riding the few ponies they were able to save. Scott arranged with the Chickasaw Nation for them to camp along Rocky Creek, but he noted, "They were in a most miserable and destitute condition."[115]

Word of the Tonkawa Massacre circulated through the refugee camps in the Indian Territory and Kansas, but most people had their own troubles. Among them was Confederate brigadier general Albert Pike. Although Col. Frederick Salomon had turned the Indian Expedition around and started back toward Kansas on July 19, the three Union Indian Home Guard regiments stayed behind. They were combined into the "Indian Brigade," and their assignment was to observe the activities of the Confederates and their Indian allies along the Grand and Verdigris Rivers. Almost from the first, though, their morale plummeted, and many members of the second regiment deserted. Meanwhile, Colonel Salomon set up camp on the Quapaw lands in today's Ottawa County, Oklahoma, justifying that position militarily as commanding the valleys of the Neosho—Grand River in Oklahoma—and Spring River as well as Shoal Creek. Salomon was not called to account for his mutiny against Colonel Weer. Brig. Gen. James G. Blunt, commanding the Department of Kansas and concerned about the abandonment of the Indian Territory, accepted his rationale for it and sent him supplies and a section of artillery.[116]

Pike was fortunate that Salomon withdrew the Indian Expedition because he did not have the means to oppose the Union force. Just before the expedition set off for the Indian Territory, Gen. Thomas C. Hindman, now in charge of the Confederate Trans-Mississippi District, ordered Pike to send his white troops and artillery to Little Rock, Arkansas. His view was that Arkansas took priority because it was nearer the major war activity and in more danger. Pike, however, was loath to dismember a troop force he had put together and supplied the best he could, even paying several thousand dollars out of his own pocket when necessary. He had made promises of protection and support to the Indian nations on behalf of the Confederacy, promises that the Confederate authorities had not to date been able or willing to fulfill. At the same time, he was aware that his critics, such as Maj. Gen. Earl Van Dorn, ignored his accomplishments, condemned the behavior of his Indian troops at Pea Ridge, and sneered because he had constructed and set up his headquarters at Fort McCulloch on the Blue River one hundred fifty miles south of the fighting in the beleaguered Cherokee Nation.[117]

Pike had actually been busy, as had his troops. He reasoned that the location of Fort McCulloch allowed him to observe and control major transportation routes with his limited troop numbers better than Fort Davis near the Cherokee-Muscogee border. As for using his troops, his assistant adjutant reported as of June 9 that Col. Stand Watie and the two Cherokee regiments were still patrolling the Kansas line. The 1st Creek Regiment under Col. Daniel N. McIntosh was on its way north along the Verdigris River and headed ultimately toward the Santa Fe Trail. The 2nd Creek Regiment under Lt. Col. Chilly McIntosh was moving toward the Great Salt Plains, Walnut Creek in Kansas (where so many refugee Indians were camped), and possibly as far west as Fort Wise in Colorado Territory. Along with Lt. Col. John Jumper's Seminole Battalion and Lt. Col. J. D. Harris's Chickasaw Battalion, they were to intercept Santa Fe–bound traffic and so hinder Union war activity in the West. There is no record that they actually reached their goals. Maj. Simpson N. Folsom's Choctaw Battalion was to march to Camp McIntosh seventeen miles east of Fort Cobb, join forces with Hart's Spies, and scout toward the Wichita Mountains to prevent trouble along the Texas frontier.[118]

General Hindman became impatient, though, when he did not receive what he considered a timely reply from Pike or the white troops and artillery he had ordered sent to Arkansas. He repeated his orders to Pike in mid-June. In addition, he told him to move back north to Fort Gibson across the Arkansas River from Fort Davis. He ordered Col. Douglas H. Cooper, Pike's subordinate, to move north of the Canadian River to take command of all the Indian troops except Colonel Jumper's Seminoles.[119]

Relations between Pike and Hindman deteriorated rapidly through June and July, partly because they had different views on how the war should be conducted. On July 27 Col. Stand Watie suffered a defeat at Bayou Menard a few miles east of Fort Gibson when Union colonel William A. Phillips and the 3rd Indian Home Guard probed deeper into the Cherokee Nation. Watie lost several men killed and captured. Pike did not approve of Watie's aggressiveness generally, especially in that locale, which he thought would not support an army. He also believed the Indian troops should be used primarily for defense, as did Principal Chief Ross, not in support of Confederate actions in neighboring states. Hindman's demands that Pike strip the Indian Territory of men, equipment, and resources for the war else-where exacerbated their relationship further. Meanwhile, malicious rumors about Pike were spreading in Texas. Finally, Pike, bitter over the "incredible villainy of a slander so monstrous, and so without even any ground for suspicion," wrote a farewell address to the Indian nations. He urged them to remain true to the Confederacy for their own self-preservation. Facing specious but serious charges that he had mishandled Confederate funds, he resigned and slipped out of the Indian Territory for good.[120]

Pike's departure occurred about the same time other major changes and events took place in the territory. With Pike gone, Col. Douglas H. Cooper was in position to be named commander of the Indian Territory troops. He also aspired to be superintendent of Indian affairs in the Confederate Arkansas and Red River Superintendency, but that position went to S. S. Scott. About the same time, the Confederacy finally made good on its treaty guarantee to allow the Indian nations representation in its Congress. Elias C. Boudinot became the Cherokee delegate, while the Choctaw and Chickasaw nations selected Robert M. Jones to repre-sent them. The Muscogee and Seminole Nations were unable take advantage of this opportunity. Meanwhile, after Union troops removed Principal Chief John Ross from the Cherokee Nation in August, there was a leadership vacuum. Chaos and vengeance between the Watie and pro-Union factions ruled. The Watie faction took advantage of the situation then to call a convention and elect Stand Watie principal chief. However, things did not calm down until Gen. Thomas Hindman, who had recently transferred to Fort Smith, Arkansas, came to Tahlequah himself and took charge. He suppressed guerrilla activity and maraud-ing, at least for the time being.[121]

In late September 1862 Confederate forces again advanced into northwest Arkansas and southwest Missouri. South of Joplin, Missouri, lead production at Granby and gristmills around Newtonia produced items the Confederate allies needed. Approximately four thousand men—Col. Joseph Shelby's Missouri cavalry, Texas cavalry, and Indian troops commanded by Brig. Gen. Douglas H. Cooper—occupied the area around Newtonia. To prevent them from establishing that foothold in southwestern Missouri, Brig. Gen. Frederick Salomon launched an expedition from Fort Scott, Kansas. It included the newly formed 3rd Indian Home Guard, composed mostly of Pin Cherokees who had emerged during the recent Indian Expedition. Early on September 30 some of the oncoming federal troops launched a premature cavalry, infantry, and artillery attack on Texans occupying the town. They sheltered behind Newtonia's sturdy stone walls and buildings while they waited for help from Confederate allies camped nearby. The federals were gaining the upper hand when the Missouri and Texas cavalry struck them hard from the rear. Meanwhile, Cooper and Col. Tandy Walker led the Choctaw-Chickasaw regiment straight through Newtonia and into the fight.[122] According to Cooper, they "entered the town at full gallop, passed through without halting, singing their war-songs and giving the war-whoop."[123] The double blow forced the federals to retreat.

A lull in the fighting from noon to midafternoon ended with a federal artillery bombardment that pushed the Confederate allies back. The 3rd Indian Home Guard used stone fences and brush along the hollow below the town gristmill for cover to pour a damaging fire into the Confederate right flank. The Choctaws and Chickasaws checked that by working their way through a cornfield to flank them. Cooper reported, "The booming of the cannon, the bursting of shells, the air filled with missiles of every description, the rattling crash of small-arms, the cheering of our men, and the war-whoop of our Indian allies, all combined to render the scene both grand and terrific."[124] It was too much for the federals. They abandoned the field and hot-footed it into the next county with the Choctaw and Chickasaw soldiers on their heels. As at Pea Ridge, reports said some of the dead were scalped without naming the guilty suspects.[125]

Even so, federal agent E. H. Carruth wrote later that the Union Indian soldiers had proved "not only their loyalty but their ability to fight" and that "they will do good service in our border warfare."[126]

Once Union reinforcements arrived in the area in early October, the Confederates were forced to withdraw to Arkansas and the Indian Territory, taking with them, according to Union veteran Wiley Britton, "nearly all the guerrilla bands of western Missouri."[127]

Newtonia marked the last time Confederate forces were a real threat to southwestern Missouri and southeastern Kansas. Less than three weeks later, Brig. Gen. James G. Blunt followed Cooper's army out of northwest Arkansas and into the Cherokee Nation. He caught up on Beattie's Prairie near Old Fort Wayne. The current site was just inside the Cherokee Nation in today's Delaware County, Oklahoma. It had been abandoned since 1842, and Colonel Watie had used its remaining buildings as a base to organize his Cherokee regiment early in the war. In October 1862 Union commanders became convinced Cooper was planning a raid into southern Kansas. Actually he lacked the men and resources for it. His Texas troops, except Howell's Battery, had already left for home, and he was having difficulty keeping his Choctaw and Chickasaw troops in camp so far from their own country. Winter was approaching, but many of his men, he reported, were nearly barefoot and naked. It had been so long since they had received promised shoes and clothing they were beginning to believe the Confederacy had abandoned them. Blunt's Union troops, including the 1st and 3rd Indian Home Guard, struck them at 5:00 A.M. on October 22. Half an hour was enough to capture the Texas battery and break the hastily organized Confederate defense. Abandoning most of their supplies and the artillery, Cooper's troops scrambled for the safety of Fort Davis, with Watie's regiment covering their retreat. They were no threat for the rest of 1862. Once again, Union forces controlled the area north of the Arkansas River both in Arkansas and the Indian Territory.[128]

Union victories at Cane Hill, Arkansas, on November 28 and at Prairie Grove on December 7 emphasized that fact. In both battles the soldiers of the 1st and 3rd Indian Home Guard performed well. At Prairie Grove the 1st Indian fought dismounted, taking their place left of the center of the line between men from Kansas and Iowa. There was a "five minute panic" when the Iowa troops, new to battle, fired a volley past them, but they rallied, reformed, and moved on up through a cornfield to support Captain Allen's battery. In his report, Lt. Col. Stephen Wattles, commander of the 1st Indian, complimented his officers and noted, "Of the Indian officers, Captain Jon-neh, of the Uches, and Captain Billy Bowlegs, of the Seminoles, and Captain Tus-te-nup-chup-ko, of Company A (Creek), are deserving of the highest praise. Our loss was 2 killed and 4 wounded, as far as reported, but the Indians entertain a prejudice against speaking of dangerous occurrences in battle, and report no wounds but such as the necessities of the case demand."[129]

About the same time, pro-Confederate Cherokees in the Neutral Lands of southeast Kansas received the latest of several hard blows from Union forces. In September 1861 Colonel Watie had set out to destroy anything in the Neutral Lands that might aid the Union, while irregulars attacked pro-Union white settlers. A raid on unprotected Humboldt, Kansas, in early September led to the attempted arrest of Chetopa's entire male population. Most pro-Confederate Cherokees such as George Walker escaped the round-up. Frustrated, Lt. Col. James G. Blunt ordered their property destroyed. The result was a second pro-Confederate Cherokee raid on Humboldt in October. Blunt then declared the Chetopa vicinity enemy country, and some Cherokee civilians were forcibly removed from the town and interned near Leroy, Kansas, among Unionist Indian Territory refugees. The pro-Confederate Cherokees in Chetopa held out while the Indian Expedition advanced into and then retreated from the Cherokee Nation during the summer of 1862. The next year, though, brought disaster. The frustrated Union commander in southeast Kansas sent Col. Charles Willetts and the 14th Kansas Cavalry to drive them out in November 1863. Among those exiled were Rachel Walker and her five small children. With his home and farm buildings destroyed, his livestock confiscated, and his family taken away, her husband, George Walker, chose to ride with the pro-Confederate Cherokees for the rest of the war.[130]

While these events were unfolding at the juncture of the Indian Territory, Kansas, Missouri, and Arkansas, important national developments were taking place east of the Mississippi River. With the war now more than a year old, reality had eroded optimism on both sides, particularly the notion that the war would be quickly over and fairly bloodless. Casualties and costs in manpower and money were mounting. There had even been discussion in the remaining United States of emancipating the slaves and using them in the war effort in order to damage the Confederacy. At the beginning of the war, some free blacks had tried to enlist as a unit and serve as Union soldiers, but they had been rejected. In the summer of 1862, though, a new militia act allowed the enlistment of slaves in the Union army for whatever purpose they were needed. Some abolitionists and black leaders such as Frederick Douglass also supported enlistment of black troops along with ending slavery. Following the Union victory at Antietam in September, Pres. Abraham Lincoln moved toward emancipating slaves in areas in rebellion, but his Emancipation Proclamation did not go into effect until January 1, 1863. It allowed emancipated slaves and "contrabands," a term for runaway slaves, to enlist and serve as U.S. soldiers. The belief was that their role would be limited. They would garrison forts and hold occupied places, but they would not fight on the front lines. White officers in the black regiments, though, were often abolitionists who used the army to train their soldiers for citizenship. The military experience of black soldiers became an important part of their transition from slavery to freedom.[131]

Kansas, with its abolitionist component, had become a haven for "contrabands" even before the war. A few Kansans began advocating the enlistment of black soldiers quite early. Among them was Senator James H. Lane, the notorious, dynamic free-state partisan. Lane had raised state troops for the Union and currently commanded "Lane's Brigade" of Kansas volunteers. In August 1862 he set in motion the organization of the 1st Kansas Colored Volunteer Infantry Regiment by Capt. James M. Williams, a fellow abolitionist.[132] This occurred over the opposition of some Kansans who believed slaves were incapable of being soldiers. Other Kansans, though, recognized there were simply not enough white troops available to suppress the Confederate regulars or the rampaging guerrillas in the border region they shared with Missouri and Arkansas.[133]

The men of the 1st Kansas began proving the doubters wrong when they were among the first black Americans to go into battle in the uniform of the United States Army. Company I included Indian Territory runaway slaves and free blacks, some recruited from the refugee camps at Sac and Fox Agency in Kansas. On October 28, 1862, 225 men of the 1st Kansas faced, repelled, and defeated about 500 Confederates who attacked their camp at Island Mound, Missouri. They acquitted themselves well, with ten of them killed and twelve wounded. "Island Mound" was the first name on their battle flag, but it would not be the last. Other ribbons would commemorate their future actions in the Indian Territory and Arkansas.[134] The 1st Kansas Colored Volunteer Infantry Regiment, until then a state unit, was formally mustered into the United States Army on January 13, 1863, the fourth black unit of many to come and well ahead of more famous units such as the 54th Massachusetts Infantry, which would not be authorized to begin recruiting for another two weeks.[135]

A number of former slaves, of course, were already serving as Union soldiers in the 1st Indian Home Guard Regiment even before the 1st Kansas was organized. These were men such as Jacob Perryman, the slave of the Muscogee Perryman family and "fixer" who had helped other slaves escape before he followed Opothle Yahola to Kansas. His regiment had been organized at Leroy, Kansas, in May 1862 and had already been in numerous fights large and small. The Indian Home Guard regiments made no real distinction between the Indian and black soldiers, although some companies in the 1st Indian were primarily Muscogee, Seminole, or Yuchi. Indians served as sergeants and corporals, but the higher-ranking officers of these regiments were white. English-speaking former slaves were particularly useful because they could often serve as interpreters between white officers and soldiers who only spoke native languages.[136]

Black soldiers, whether they were in a Home Guard company or with the 1st (and later 2nd) Kansas Colored, faced additional dangers wherever they engaged Confederate troops or their allies. The idea of black men in the uniform of the United States appalled southerners, including the Confederate-allied Indians, and upset their view of the right order of the world. Black soldiers learned not to expect mercy if they were captured. Among the most notorious incidents of the killing of black prisoners was Fort Pillow, Tennessee, in April 1864. However, another, which involved the 1st Kansas Colored Volunteer Infantry, took place on May 18, 1863, when Maj. T. R. Livingston, a guerrilla leader from Missouri, surprised a foraging party near Baxter Springs, Kansas, on the border with Indian Territory. The guerrillas captured several black soldiers and shot one of their white prisoners. Captain Williams of the 1st Kansas Colored had a prisoner shot in retaliation. He wrote that he visited the scene the next morning and found that the dead and wounded had had their brains beaten out and their bodies mutilated.[137] Unfortunately, there would be other incidents of the killing of black soldiers in the Indian Territory and surrounding states in the years ahead.

Unlike the runaway slaves who served with the 1st Indian Home Guard or the 1st Kansas Colored Volunteer Infantry Regiment, some slaves of the Indians found themselves serving with the armies in the Indian Territory with no say in the matter. Henry Clay, a slave who had been brought to the Muscogee Nation as a young man, became a teamster for the Confederate-allied Indians. In the late 1930s he said,

> War come along and Master go with the south side, and I went along to drive a wagon, but I got separated from Master the first thing and never seen him but once or twice in the War.
>
> When they was going to strike a battle somewhere they would come and get us and our wagons and we would haul stuff for several days and nights to some place where they could get it. Then we would go off away from there before they had the battle so they wouldn't get us captured.
>
> I've hauled like that all around Webbers Falls and Fort Gibson and Fort Davis and all over these rocky hills sometimes when we had to take an axe and cut a road at night, but I never seen but one battle and that was just the smoke.[138]

Some other Indian Territory inhabitants were just as helpless to control their circumstances as Henry Clay when 1862 was drawing to a close. The Choctaw and Chickasaw Nations were still relatively undisturbed. Likewise, once Opothle Yahola's followers left, things became fairly quiet again in the settled parts of the Muscogee and Seminole Nations. However, the Cherokee Nation had been in constant turmoil for more than a year.

The Cowart family lived about a mile west of today's Stillwell, Oklahoma, in the Flint District of the Cherokee Nation. By late 1862 they believed it was no longer safe there for them because the father of the family was a Confederate soldier. According to his son, William L. Cowart, born in October 1862, "the trouble was not caused by the regular forces of the Union Army but by the 'Bushwhackers' among the Cherokee. They took out their spite on the helpless non-combatants and robbed and burned and committed crimes, as there were no civil officers and no law in the Cherokee Nation at that time, and the Bushwhackers operated unmolested, when and where they pleased." In 1862 the Cowart family moved east into Arkansas, believing they would be more secure there.[139]

Cowart's father came home on furlough in January 1863. His son explained,

> Our home in Arkansas was out in the open some distance from the timber. On the day my father was to return to the army, he looked out and saw a bunch of men in the edge of the timber and thinking they were after him, he took his rifle and blankets and some provisions and slipped out of the cabin opposite these men. He had been gone long enough to be safely away, my mother thought, when he returned. My mother said she never knew why he returned, but just as he reached the house, a bunch of Bushwhackers closed in from the other side of the house, unseen by my parents, and captured my father.
> Before the Bushwhackers left the community, they had taken seven men, either Confederate soldiers or sympathizers. These men, of whom my father was one, were lined up and shot. These bandits were not regular Union soldiers but were Cherokee Indians who favored the Union . . . . These men knew my father and knew where he moved to and why he came to Arkansas.[140]

The experiences of the Cowart family, widowed Hannah Hicks and her children, and minister Stephen Foreman were becoming much too common in the Cherokee Nation by the end of 1862. No one was safe as new offenses were heaped on long-standing grudges, and neighbor turned on neighbor. Nor did the resulting misery stop at the Cherokee borders as the Tonkawas knew. The wind was gusting across the Indian Territory and buffeting people who had only the dimmest information about the political and social hurricane taking place in the eastern United States. As missionary Joseph S. Murrow had feared back in January, squally times had indeed come to the territory. There was little people could do now except keep their heads down and hold on until the storm passed.

CHAPTER FOUR

An Enemy's Country

A lthough it was only a lull in the storm of war, the coming of winter in 1862 brought the Indian Territory both relief and fear. Drought and crop failure had affected the whole area the preceding summer, but the Cherokee Nation was in a particularly desperate condition due as much to man as nature. On January 19, 1863, Union colonel William A. Phillips charged that the Confederates had burned what crops had survived in order to discourage federal incursions, concluding, "The Nation is little short of a desert."[1] Dr. Daniel Dwight Hitchcock, a missionary as well as a surgeon at the federal brigade hospital at Camp John Ross near Scott's Mill, Missouri, echoed that description. Writing to a friend about the possibility of returning the Cherokee refugees to their own country that spring, he asked rhetorically, "But where are the supplies to come from for the people? Farms are ruined—corn and meat eaten up. I do not think the people can raise enough for themselves. You have no conception of the desolation the different armies have caused." Speaking of the Union troops, he summarized, "And wherever we go is an enemy's country; you may well believe nothing is spared."[2]

Winter came late that year. The Choctaw and Chickasaw troops went back to their own countries, leaving the Cherokee, Muscogee, and Seminole troops to guard northern Indian Territory. Cherokee minister Stephen Foreman, now a refugee in the Muscogee Nation, visited the Indian regimental camps near Fort Gibson on Christmas Day 1862. He was appalled at the goings-on he saw there. Close to the fort near the junction of the Arkansas and Verdigris Rivers, there had been for some years a spot local folks called "Sodom" because, whenever crowds gathered around the nearby Creek Agency, gambling, cockfights, and horse races flourished. The oval racetrack they used belonged to Muscogee colonel Daniel N. McIntosh.[3]

Foreman was scandalized and in his diary exclaimed that he witnessed dancing and whiskey drinking at "twenty dollars a bottle!" Horse races, he fumed, were "the besetting sins of the officers and soldiers of this regiment. All go to horse races, as far as I know, without any exception, Baptists, Methodists, and Presbyterians. Colonel McIntosh, once a Baptist preacher, is the leader in horseracing now." Foreman sniffed, "Had the Federals come today many a one of the Regiment would have been killed or taken prisoner, and it would have been well enough, for it seems to me that this Regiment needs some heavy affliction to teach them their duty in guarding against the approaches of the enemy."[4]

The apparent laxness of the Muscogee troops concerned other Cherokees, too. Foreman noted that 150 of Col. Stand Watie's men had been there earlier in the day but left for their own camps "because Col. McIntosh would not take any active measures in guarding against the approach of the enemy."[5] The following day McIntosh did take sixty men out on a scout, but Union troops were already in the area. In fact, federal representatives came in under a flag of truce to ask for terms under which Opothle Yahola's followers might return to their homes. Colonel Phillips was in the Cherokee Nation to destroy any Confederate troops he could find, but the winter rains had set in, flooding the streams, leaving the roads churned to mud, and making it impossible to accomplish much. On December 27, though, Phillips's troops burned Fort Davis, leaving its wood buildings in ruins atop the stone foundations. That done, the Union troops went back into Arkansas.[6]

Stephen Foreman had been staying with his children at Muscogee judge George W. Stidham's house, very near the ruins of Fort Davis. This new trouble made him believe the Muscogee Nation was getting as dangerous for him as his own country, especially since he was Cherokee national treasurer under the Watie government. About the beginning of January, he left the Stidham place and moved to within five miles of Colonel Watie's winter camp at Briartown on the lower Canadian River. After visiting the camp on January 10, he commented, "So far as I could see, the soldiers appeared to be quite comfortable and contented. They were rather short of bread stuffs, but have beef a plenty. In some instances they are destitute of shoes and clothing." As he visited with a number of Cherokee acquaintances, he heard their views on their situation. "So far as I could learn the majority of the officers and soldiers," he wrote in his diary, "are opposed to going any further south, and yet they cannot go back into the Nation, because they have not the force to maintain their ground." Foreman urged them to fall back to the Arkansas River, fortify themselves, and wait for the Confederacy to send the help it had promised.[7]

Within a few days, a stretch of relatively mild weather broke. On January 14 rain turned to snow, piling up four to five inches. Foreman, who was still in Watie's camp, commented, "The soldiers must suffer a great deal in weather such as this, because it is impossible to keep the feet dry for the snow and slop around the fire. They nearly all have good tents to screen them from the snow and rain overhead, but cannot protect their feet." The next day a cold wind brought ten more inches of snow. Twenty horses, already suffering from lack of fodder, died of starvation.[8] Across the territory line in western Arkansas, Union troops also suffered from the bitterly cold weather. Colonel Phillips noted on January 19 the temperature had dipped to four degrees below zero, while so much rain had fallen, "the country here is saturated with water."[9]

The winter weather did not, however, prevent the Ross Cherokees from countering the Watie party's government with one of their own. The two mostly Cherokee Indian Home Guard regiments were spending the winter in Missouri near their nation's border. In mid-February they crossed over into their own country to hold a council on Cowskin Prairie. Assembled there with some other Ross Cherokees, they repudiated the Watie government and declared themselves the legitimate Cherokee government, with Maj. Thomas Pegg as their acting principal chief. Lt. Col. Lewis Downing became president-pro tem of the upper house of their legislature with Spring Frog as speaker of the lower house. They affirmed their loyalty to the United States and deposed any Confederate sympathizer holding a government post, which, of course, included Watie and his followers. They also emancipated the slaves of the Cherokees and repealed laws denying them literacy and possession of firearms, among other things. Still, they did not make their freedmen citizens and allowed them to remain in the nation only as contract labor. As was the case with the federal government's Emancipation Proclamation aimed at slaves in areas in rebellion, most Cherokee slaves were unaffected just then because they were physically beyond "loyal"

Cherokee control at the time, either outside the nation's borders or still held by Watie's pro-Confederate followers.[10]

Meanwhile, Colonel Phillips kept a close eye on the territory and maintained communication with Loyal Cherokees and some Muscogees, including indirectly Col. Daniel N. McIntosh. He knew there was growing disaffection among some Cherokees and Muscogees who had earlier supported the Confederate alliances. On February 6 he reported that Captain Christy of the 3rd Indian Regiment had scouted along the Arkansas River as far as Fort Smith. He had discovered about three hundred mixed-blood Cherokees and whites, former Watie supporters, lying low in the cane breaks in the big bend of the river. They did not want to fight, but, Phillips thought, were likely "afraid of the old feud between them and the full bloods of the Nation." He concluded, "I think the case is one requiring rather delicate handling but from which good results may follow." Furthermore, he had also learned that a "long line of persons, many on foot, are straggling up this way through the snow from the direction of the Creek Nation. They wear on their hats a white badge of cloth, on the right side, the sign agreed upon with McIntosh's men as the one to wear when they come within our camp as friends." Even though the Indian nations were still in the Confederate sphere for the moment, Phillips believed they could be won over. So little organized resistance remained that he could take and hold the Indian Territory come spring, preferably in time to get the spring planting done.[11]

Cherokee and other "loyal" refugees, marking time in their camps, hoped for the same thing. By the beginning of 1863 federal officials had a better grasp of the problem that had so taken them by surprise the year before with horrendous consequences. Refugee camps were scattered from southwest Kansas to southwest Missouri. In January 1863 twenty-six men representing groups of loyal Caddos, Ionies, Shawnees, and Comanches visited Indian agent S. G. Colley at Fort Larned far out west on the Santa Fe Trail. They asked permission to settle temporarily in his area of southwest Kansas. They told Colley that they were from Wichita Agency and had good homes and farms there. However, when their agent, Matthew Leeper, joined the Southern army last year and tried to force them to join as well, about a thousand of them took what belongings they could carry and started north. They had been surviving by hunting buffalo along the Arkansas River tributaries. They were farmers as much as hunters, they told him, and needed a place to live and land to cultivate. Colley was sympathetic and soon got permission from the commissioner of Indian affairs to settle them nearby and supply the provisions and clothing they needed.[12]

Other refugee Indians from the Indian Territory were allowed to live on vacant tribal lands or share other tribes' reservations in eastern Kansas. The Union faction of the Osages remained on their own large reservation in southeast Kansas, while the Senecas, eastern Shawnees, and Quapaws were accommodated on the Ottawa reservation. The loyal Seminoles and Muscogees were at Neosho Falls, Kansas. The handful of loyal Choctaws and Chickasaws were with the Sacs and Foxes on their reservation in Osage County, Kansas. Agent Isaac Coleman looked after them as well as Kickapoos, Euchees, and some Cherokee refugees. There were Shawnees, Delawares, Cherokees, Comanches, Wichitas, Keechis, Tawakonies, Ionies, and other members of the Wichita Agency affiliated tribes—about two thousand people—near Belmont in Woodson County, Kansas. Word that some of the Tonkawas had survived the October 1862 massacre had apparently not reached the upper levels of federal Indian administration in Kansas yet. According to Superintendent W. G. Coffin of the Office of Indian affairs' Southern Superintendency, the Tonkawas were believed to have been annihilated. He had been told that a Tonkawa woman was the only survivor of the massacre of her people at Wichita Agency.[13]

Then, of course, there were the rest of the Union Cherokees, pining as they all did for their old lives and Indian Territory homes. In addition to Cherokee refugees already in Kansas, about nineteen hundred more had left the Cherokee Nation proper for the Cherokee Neutral Lands in Kansas to be near the protection of Fort Scott. This occurred after the Indian Expedition advanced into and then withdrew from their nation, stirring the stew of Cherokee factionalism. In October the military had abruptly moved about nine hundred of them over to Neosho, Missouri. This action by Maj. Gen. James G. Blunt, commander of the Army of the Frontier, came about for several reasons. First, Blunt felt responsible for them because he commanded their men in the Indian Brigade. When they had returned from the first Indian Expedition, they found their families hungry, sick, and unhappy. He meant to improve their conditions, and he also suspected Superintendent Coffin and other members of the Indian Service of filling their pockets at the expense of the Indians.[14]

However, Blunt's transfer of the Cherokees to Neosho dumb-founded Superintendent Coffin, who had not been consulted. Neosho, he believed, was "one of the worst, if not the very worst, secession strongholds in Missouri." Supplying refugees there would be difficult and expensive, requiring heavy protection from federal troops. Some did at least get to spend the winter in homes vacated by local white secessionists. By March, though, Col. William A. Phillips, commander of the Indian Brigade, apparently also recognized the inherent flaws in the move and was urging Superintendent Coffin to get the Cherokees ready to go back to their own country as soon as possible.[15]

In his annual report, the commissioner of Indian affairs, William P. Dole, recognized his duty toward those he called "ignorant savages." He admitted federal negligence and abandonment of the Indian Territory had contributed strongly to the defection of so many Indians to the Confederacy. He particularly sympathized, though, with the prosperous and progressive Cherokees, Muscogees, and Seminoles who had seen their farms and homes pillaged and destroyed and their vast herds of horses, mules, and cattle stolen or slaughtered "in the most wasteful and extravagant manner" to feed the refugees. The goal of most federal officials dealing with the refugee problem was to get them back in their own country as soon as possible so they could feed and care for themselves. Providing for them was terribly expensive. Speaking of the Cherokees, Coffin reported, "Their trust fund interest is exhausted, and they are now being subsisted from funds belonging to the Seminoles, Choctaws, Creeks, and Chickasaws."[16]

Apparently the federal Indian officials did not see a problem in using the other nations' funds to support the Cherokees, and conditions were marginally better for the refugees in early 1863. Opothle Yahola's followers had been forced to live in make-shift shelters last winter. At least in September 1863 the Choctaws and Chickasaws lived in army tents that had been condemned as unfit for use by the military and provided inadequate protection from the winter weather.[17] There was also more food, but Dr. A. V. Coffin, directing physician for the Refugee Indians, blamed it for the gastric or gastro-enteric diseases he identified as the most common type of sickness among the refugees. He explained,

> flour made from damaged grain is issued; it contains but little nutriment. The Indian is accustomed to [meat]. Now to satisfy the demands of his system he must consume a large quantity; undue distention of the stomach is the result, and a great irritation, if not severe inflammation . . . . Or lean, inferior beef is issued. The proportion of bone is so great that seven-day rations are consumed in four, if not three, days, and the remainder of the seven days must be passed without animal food. Excessive hunger is the result, and, when the sufferer receives his next supply, he gorges to satisfy, and a severe, if not fatal, attack of gastritis or gastro-enteritis is sure to follow.[18]

Otherwise, the Indian refugees suffered the same complaints, conditions, and illnesses—fevers, agues, and rheumatism—that afflicted lower-class Anglo-Americans. Still, Dr. Coffin, who was not particularly sympathetic toward the "superlatively wretched beings" who were his patients, could understand their poor health in the refugee camps. He summarized,

> Deprived of comfortable houses, of their accustomed food, forced to use the same diet for months without change, compelled to take the earth for a bed, with but a miserable excuse for a roof above them, their social relations rudely broken up—in short, subject to a combination of mental and physical causes sufficient to crush an iron constitution, it is no cause of surprise . . . if we find them falling victims of maladies that otherwise would not be regarded.[19]

Diet and shelter could be improved, Dr. Coffin concluded, but the best remedy for their chronic homesickness would be getting them safely back in their old homes.[20]

Even though the loyal Indian refugees were sharing common experiences and conditions, old and new antagonisms sometimes flared, setting individuals, factions, and tribes against one another. The federal officials admired and respected Opothle Yahola. He was still a force to be reckoned with up to his last days in late March 1863. He had enormous influence over the loyal Muscogees and that sometimes extended to the other tribes, too. Even on his deathbed, his mind was as sharp as ever, and he was actively engaged in Muscogee politics and negotiations that he believed would benefit his people. George A. Cutler, who served as federal agent to the loyal Muscogees in Kansas, described him as "probably the greatest Indian that ever has lived."[21] Southern superintendent Coffin also wrote that "he was no ordinary man."[22] Yet, Coffin reminded Commissioner Dole that Opothle Yahola flatly rejected Dole's recommendation that, when the loyal Muscogees returned victoriously to their own country, mercy should be shown to those who had opposed him politically, particularly their women and children. Opothle Yahola's response had been "when a man has a bad breed of dogs, the best way to get rid of them is to kill the bitch." Coffin noted, "The feeling between the loyal and disloyal Creeks is of the most unrelenting and deadly character, and in my opinion can never be removed." Opothle Yahola's vindictive and unforgiving attitude exemplified it and would have been a barrier when the day came for Muscogee national reconciliation.[23]

Intertribal trouble erupted periodically, some of it related to jayhawking, which had come to mean general thievery as much as attacking people because of their politics. Early in February 1863 word reached Superintendent Coffin that a band of Keechis and Tawakonies—refugees from Wichita Agency—had recently made a raid into the Muscogee and Cherokee country, hoping to find something worth stealing and selling. It was not an uncommon activity for the "wild tribes of Indians" now living in the Fall and Verdigris river camps to rustle their Indian neighbors' livestock. In fact, Superintendent Coffin reported a recent incident in which "they sold some [stolen Indian] cattle to a white man, he sold them to the contractor, and they [were] fed to the Indians." But this time, in Cherokee country, they "murdered a good Union man there, captured two young women, [one] a mother, and two children, one twelve and the other two years old." On the return trip, "they dropped the mother's body, telling the others she froze to death. The little boy, two years old, they slung as far as they could into the brush. His older brother ...attempted to go to him, but they drew their bows and arrows at him, and he had to leave him." The raiders then stripped the older boy and surviving young woman of their footwear and most of their clothing, so that they were nearly naked in the very cold weather. The raiders delivered them to the agent in Kansas, who took in the prisoners but apparently did not punish their abductors.[24]

Furious when he heard the story first-hand from the surviving Cherokee boy and girl, Superintendent Coffin talked to Jim Ned, a Delaware who was part black and "a kind of a king with all the wild tribes." They agreed to hold a council to discuss the jayhawking, but twelve inches of snow followed by unusually intense cold that affected the whole region in February 1863 prevented it.[25] Meanwhile, Coffin learned that Jim Ned's "wild Delawares" had also angered the Osages by rustling some of their ponies. This time, though, the Osages struck back and killed two of the Delawares. Fed up with the thievery, the Osages were preparing to make war on the Delawares. This alarmed white settlers in the area who complained to Coffin.[26] To make matters worse, the Shawnees were angry because an Osage had killed a Shawnee out on the plains. Coffin did his best to cool tempers. In spite of the awful weather he met with the Delawares and Shawnees, promising to deal with their concerns. Although Coffin was not able to arrange a full council of all parties concerned until April, Jim Ned and the other chiefs of the prairie tribes called their young men in and told them the jayhawking expeditions must stop.[27] At the same time, Coffin did his best to soothe their victims, noting "considerable bad feeling exists on the part of the Cherokees" because of the latest raid by the "wild tribes," which resulted in an unusually large loss of cattle, horses, and mules. He could only promise that if the livestock were found, his officers would check for brands, try to identify the owners, and return their property to them.[28]

The number of depredations in the Cherokee Nation was not a good sign for federal military and Indian Service officers who wanted to move Indian refugees back into their own country as soon as possible. Superintendent William G. Coffin, who shared the ongoing mutual antipathy and mistrust between the U.S. military and Indian Service personnel, was skeptical that the army could provide adequate protection for the refugees. In mid-March guerrillas had killed Judge Hildebrand and wounded Dr. Palmer, both leaders of the loyal Cherokees then staying at Neosho, Missouri. The incident confirmed Coffin's conviction that it was too early and too dangerous to move them back home. Besides, word was that Confederate brigadier general Sterling Price would soon try to retake Arkansas and Missouri. If that happened, Coffin believed the military would be too busy thwarting him to protect Indian refugees. He wrote to Commissioner Dole,

> I am as anxious as any man can be for an early return of the Indians to their homes, as I am most heartily tired and sick of the surroundings here in Kansas; but until I am satisfied that it can be done with some degree of safety, and without having them all butchered, I take not the responsibility of recommending their removal, notwithstanding the croaking and charging of the cormorants infesting the army, who so greatly desire the return of the refugees, that they may make fortunes out of furnishing them supplies.[29]

Nevertheless, Cherokee agent Justin Harlan and Colonel Phillips began preparation for the six-day wagon trip that would see the Cherokee refugees back into their own country. Colonel Phillips was genuinely concerned about the welfare of the families of the men under his command. He knew meat could be procured for them along the way, but he recommended the priority supply list include cornmeal and flour, seed corn, potatoes, vegetable seeds, and the tools and harness they would need to cultivate the land.[30]

Timing the departure of the return expedition was critical as late winter dragged into early spring. Given the desolation of the Cherokee Nation, the expedition could not move south until the grass had grown enough to feed their livestock. At the same time, they could not delay leaving so long that the refugees would be too late getting their crops planted. Finally the first week in April Colonel Phillips led the Indian Brigade into the Cherokee Nation from Arkansas. On April 9, the refugee train, which was about a mile long and made up of a variety of vehicles, delivered about one thousand people to Park Hill. There was a joyful reunion as soldiers and families that had experienced so much apart during the last months met again. In the next few days many scattered to their homes in the Cherokee and Muscogee Nations with what seed was available to plant crops on their own ground.[31]

For the moment there was not much opposition from the Confederate allies. They had had little success in regrouping and reorganizing their regiments after the demoralizing loss at Fort Wayne in

October 1862. Then Brig. Gen. William Steele, instead of Col. Douglas H. Cooper, became Confederate commander of the Indian Territory in January 1863. It was not a good development as far as the Indian nations were concerned. They did not like being considered simply an appendage of Confederate Arkansas and wanted the Indian Territory to be a separate military division, reflecting its status as Indian domain, their sovereignty, and the importance they believed they had to the Confederacy. Steele, though, kept his headquarters in Fort Smith and gave Arkansas and Texas priority. He had little respect for Indian troops or officers, except perhaps Watie, and no use for "Indianized white men" such as Cooper. When Steele took command, he ordered the troops in the territory back toward the Red River to improve his chances of sub-sisting, recruiting, and equipping them. However, he still intended to hold the Arkansas River line and set up depots there for a spring offen-sive before Union troops could come back down from Missouri.[32]

So, when part of the Union 3rd Indian Regiment scouted as far south as Webber's Falls and the ford there across the Arkansas River, they fought only one skirmish and brought three hundred head of cattle back to Kansas. For the moment, it seemed the Union Indian Brigade and the loyal refugees were relatively secure. Still, Colonel Phillips was very conscious, first, of Confederate troops in Arkansas, and, second, that his supply line stretched all the way back to Fort Scott, Kansas.[33]

Although getting the Indian refugees out of the camps and back in their homes was an important part of the Union return to the Cherokee Nation, the military goal was retaking, repairing, and hold-ing Fort Gibson. It could then serve as the base for reestablishing fed-eral control of the territory. On April 13, the Indian Brigade and many of the refugees arrived at the fort. Repairs to the long-abandoned buildings and construction of new buildings and earthworks soon began. Colonel Phillips renamed it "Fort Blunt" in honor of his com-manding officer, but the historic name "Fort Gibson" still stuck. Among the additions were the new brick bake ovens that allowed pro-duction of better quality bread. The ovens, according to Wiley Britton, and the fresh bread they produced were a symbol of the improved well-being and comfort of the men. However, the missionaries at Tullahassee Mission a few miles west noted when they returned to the

Muscogee Nation that the bricks used to build the ovens were torn out of the walls of their kitchen.[34]

The reoccupation of Fort Gibson and its repairs and expansion raised morale among the pro-Union Cherokees and Muscogees in the vicinity. Before long, a brisk commerce developed as neighboring folks brought in items to sell or trade, including produce from their spring gardens. Wiley Britton recalled, "It was not an unusual sight that spring to see in the camps of the soldiers Indian women with little sacks of wortleberries brought in on their ponies from a distance of thirty to forty miles, for exchange for some part of the regular food ration."[35] Word of this trade opportunity and Colonel Phillips's considerate treatment of the refugees spread, encouraging local Indians to come to Fort Gibson and declare themselves back on the side of the Union. Muscogees and Seminoles, with their families along, arrived to fill the vacancies in the Indian Brigade.[36]

It was about this time that the Cherokee family of Blackbird Doublehead, now a young boy, came to Fort Gibson from their home in the Flint District near today's Stillwell, Oklahoma. They had been through extremely dangerous times, with bushwhackers and Confederate raiders "pillaging homes and farms and carrying away everything. Then the Cherokee women and children were forced to go to the woods for protection," Doublehead explained in the 1930s. For example, raiders caught Mrs. Tony Leach, whose husband had enlisted in the Union army with Doublehead's father, and her two young sons gathering corn in their garden. Unable to get away, both boys were shot—one dead and the other wounded—and the raiders took the corn they had gathered as well as their wagon and team. When word of the raid reached Fort Gibson, a contingent of the Home Guard went hunting the raiders but could not find them. According to Doublehead, incidents such as this caused some men to lie low near home rather than enlist. "These men were not slackers as we call men now who would not go into the army," he explained. "They were hiding around to protect the homes of some of the men who were fighting."[37]

After this incident and a subsequent fight nearby, the Cherokees in the neighborhood decided it was becoming too dangerous to stay in their homes. Besides, they had heard rations were being handed out to Indian women and children at Fort Gibson. So the Doublehead family and the other women in their community moved there and set up camps about a mile and a half to the east.[38]

Ironically, about the same time some Cherokee families who supported Principal Chief Stand Watie and the Confederate alliance came to the same conclusion: life in their nation was becoming too precarious. Twice in April Colonel Phillips led raids into Webber's Falls, a community of well-to-do, slaveholding planters on the Arkansas River. Watie had recently chosen it for a council meeting site. Unfortunately during one raid Confederate-allied Indians deliberately killed Dr. Rufus Gillpatrick, a white Unionist physician and go-between, who had been called to attend a wounded Confederate Indian soldier. Thereafter, Phillips had little sympathy for the Cherokees at Webber's Falls.[39]

Among them was the family of John Salaule Vann: his wife, children, and stepdaughter from Mrs. Vann's first marriage to William Shorey Coodey, a prominent Cherokee Treaty Party leader and diplomat. When she had lived at the Coodey home at Frozen Rock near today's Muskogee, Oklahoma, Mrs. Vann had often entertained army officers from Fort Gibson, and two of her brothers-in-law were currently Union generals. Mrs. Vann's daughter, Ella Coodey, was sixteen that spring and had grown up in Vann's richly furnished fourteen-room house on the ridge north of the Arkansas River at Webber's Falls. Pin Indians sometimes pilfered from them, but so far they had escaped the worst of the war.[40] That April, though, life changed for the family when Phillips's troops came through the area several times "and burned and robbed as they went," according to Ella. She recalled that when they came to her home the first time all the adults were away in the army, on business, or, in the case of her pregnant mother, checking on the welfare of her eldest son, reported to have been taken prisoner. Ella said,

> I was left alone with the little children when a detachment of negro soldiers from Colonel Phillips's division [swept] down and took possession of the house. The big insolent negro men went through the house, taking everything they wanted and destroying the things they couldn't take. They ripped open the feather beds and let the feathers blow away. The men would try to put on my mother's dresses and would tear them to pieces. They took all the groceries and food in the house and left us with nothing. The little children were so frightened that they clung to me in terror

but didn't say a word. I was no less frightened myself . . . . When Mother returned, she was panic stricken but there was no place to go or anything to do. Late that evening another detachment of Union soldiers came with Colonel Phillips himself in charge and set fire to the house and burned it to the ground. They went through and kindled a fire in every room. Mother pleaded with him to allow her to remove a few prized pieces of furniture (her bed was one). He refused and said, "Madam, it's entirely too fine." Mother replied, "Well, it's mine and paid for." They went through the house with an axe and broke every mirror and marble slab on the furniture. Mr. Allen [the overseer] was there and in the confusion managed to get two or three mattresses, a few quilts, and one or two pieces of furniture out.[41]

The slaves were too frightened to help, and some ran away. Ella and her mother moved what little had been saved into an empty slave cabin. Late that night they cooked some food the overseer brought from Webber's Falls. It was their first meal in thirty-six hours. Ella's stepfather heard the news and came home briefly to move them into a small vacant house nearby. "Some of our neighbors who had not been burned out gave us a few things," Ella said, "but in a few days Union troops set fire to the little village and burned the whole place out." Everyone left Webber's Falls, trying to find a safe place, and many headed to Texas. Ella said, "We did not have very much to move after having been robbed and burned out."[42]

The arrival of the Indian Brigade in the Cherokee Nation and the reoccupation of Fort Gibson sent a wave of alarm through the adjacent Confederate-allied Indian nations. The word went out for men who had been furloughed for the winter (or had simply gone home) to return to duty. They congregated about ten miles north of North Fork Town in the Muscogee Nation at the settlement of Honey Springs (near today's Rentiesville, Oklahoma). There was abundant grazing and good water from the springs at this well-known stopping point for travelers on the Texas Road, so it was a good place to set up a military supply depot. On April 22 the Confederate-allied Cherokee, Muscogee, and Texas troops in the vicinity listened to addresses from their commanders. Chief Motey Kennard addressed the Muscogee troops in their language, calling on them to defend their nation with honor and dedication. Col. Daniel N. McIntosh interpreted for him as he thanked the Texas troops for their aid. After he spoke, Captain Spears of Col. Stand Watie's regiment spoke "with a lot of pathos" to the Cherokee troops in their language with Stephen Foreman translating his message into English for the others.[43]

Among them was the young Muscogee, George Washington Grayson. At some point in the last months, Grayson had finally enlisted in the 2nd Creek Mounted Volunteers, a regiment commanded by Col. Chilly McIntosh, his relative and a fellow member of Coweta tribal town. As a Muscogee writer said of him years later, this son of Chief William McIntosh "was an old man, but bravely took up the work of leading his men in the military service of the Confederacy .... He was a person of fairly good education and a Baptist preacher."[44] In addition to Chilly McIntosh, Grayson was among other relatives and friends. However, he mused later that he probably decided to enlist in the regiment at this time because as a soldier (and likely an officer because of his English education) he could expect pay and perhaps a share of any captured goods. Both would help support his widowed mother and five younger siblings now that inflation was adding to wartime troubles even in areas relatively unscathed by the war.[45]

Everyone was feeling the pinch as goods became scarce on store shelves and prices rose accordingly. This was especially true for "imported" items—those manufactured or processed outside the territory. Stephen Foreman worried about it as he tried to provide for his motherless children with the help of his oldest daughter Susie. On January 26, he had written,

> It is truly astonishing to see what high prices are asked for the most common articles of clothing, tobacco and shoes, and still people will buy for many of them are compelled to have some of the articles. For example, some plain jeans [cloth] sold for seven dollars per yard today, suit jeans before the war sold for fifty cents per yard. Brown domestic sold for 2 ½ per yard, bleached domestic the same. Common shirts and drawers, nine dollars apiece, common tobacco $5 a plug; the lowest quality of home made shoes, $12 per pair.[46]

Flour and cornmeal had almost disappeared off the store shelves once the millers left the Indian Territory at the beginning of the war. With the recent drought, what was left was too expensive for most people. Meat and vegetables were still available, but who knew what the weather and raiders would leave come spring? So sometime in early 1863 Wash Grayson took his horse and cap and ball pistol and went off to war.[47]

So did other Indian men, among them the Osages. Although their numbers and once-great power on the prairies had been greatly reduced by the end of the eighteenth century, they occupied a reservation in southeastern Kansas that was a buffer zone between the white settlements in Kansas and secessionist areas to the south and east. With the assistance of Father John Schonmakers of the Osage Mission, federal representatives had held almost all of the Osages except the Black Dog band and a few others neutral or loyal to the United States. A company of Osages had enlisted in the 2nd Indian Home Guard, but Osages also kept watch over the prairies. They were instructed to arrest and disarm intruders on their reservation, particularly roving bands of thieves, rebels, bushwhackers, and potential troublemakers.[48]

That was just what they did on May 23, 1863. The day before, about twenty men, all Confederate officers commanded by Col. Charles Harrison and Col. Warner Lewis, had left the vicinity of Joplin, Missouri. They headed west, perhaps toward New Mexico and Colorado. The previous November Lewis had planned but not participated in a joint attack with Capt. William C. Quantrill on the Union post at Lamar, Missouri. This May mission, according to papers recovered later from their baggage, was to incite Indians in Colorado and Dakota territories to attack white settlements on the northern frontier. Lewis, the only one to survive the war, gave a more palatable explanation later. He said they were ordered to locate and recruit Confederate sympathizers who had left Missouri and Union states to avoid being drafted into the Union army. His men were supposed to collect and deliver recruits to the Confederate army in Texas.[49]

Whatever their mission, they crossed the western Missouri state line on the first day of their journey and followed Cedar Creek into eastern Kansas. On the second day they entered the Osage reservation. A party of ten Big Hill Osages led by Hard Rope, or Wehesaki, a seasoned warrior and counselor, came across their trail, which they were making no effort to hide, and followed them. When the Osages caught up with and questioned the intruders, the Confederates claimed to be irregulars from the federal post at Humboldt, Kansas. However, federal officers there had made sure the Osages knew all their men, and they did not recognize any of these travelers. Not fooled, the Big Hills told the strangers to come back to the post for identification. They resisted; in the scuffle one of the white men killed an Osage, and they rode on. The Big Hills picked up their companion's body and raced back to their village for reinforcements.[50]

Apparently unconcerned, the Confederate officers were just re-saddling after a midday rest when Hard Rope and perhaps two hundred angry Osages caught up with them. Colonel Lewis later gave his version of what happened:

> To avoid a conflict we moved off at a brisk walk, and they followed us. We had not gone far until some of them fired and killed one of our men . . . . We then charged them vigorously and drove them back for some distance. My horse was killed in this charge and I was severely wounded in the shoulder with an arrow. I mounted a mule from which [another man] was killed. The Indians kept gathering strength from others coming up. We had a running fight for eight or ten miles, frequently hurling back their advances . . . . Our horses were becoming exhausted, so we concluded to halt in the bed of a small stream . . . to give them rest. The Indians here got all around us at gunshot range, and kept up an incessant fire. We had only side arms, and pistols and were out of range . . . . I dismounted from the mule and mounted [a dead companion's] horse. This incident was the saving of my life. . . . When our horses were rested we made a dash for liberty.[51]

One by one the Confederates were killed, wounded, or captured as they raced for the Verdigris River about two miles away. Unable to get down its steep banks and across to the other side on horseback, the survivors hid in the timber, which the Osages used as cover to close in on them. Lewis and one other man made their way down the bank and then turned upstream on foot, but their companions who managed to reach the water were driven onto an exposed gravel bar. There they were easy targets for the Osages, who ignored their white flag of surrender. Only Lewis and his companion, both wounded and on foot, escaped the Osages, but they had no food and only one pair of shoes between them. Ultimately they lost those, too. They walked back to Jasper County, Missouri, in about three days.[52]

When the news reached the federal post at Humboldt, the commander sent out a scouting party, which found the bodies "shot, tomahawked, scalped, and decapitated."[53] Beheading was the age-old Osage punishment for intrusion into their territory and a chilling warning to other offenders. A search of the victims' baggage by the federal troops who buried them turned up documents that revealed the identity of the dead as Confederate officers and their mission in Colorado and New Mexico. Hard Rope and the Osage war party were relieved they had indeed killed rebels and not Union people, something they tried very hard to avoid during the war so as not to provoke the United States Government.[54]

With satisfaction Superintendent Coffin reported, "Had this party of rebels reached the wild tribes of Indians on the plains, restless and warlike as they are, and organized and led them, a vast amount of damage would have resulted to the emigration and supply trains destined for the military posts in New Mexico, Colorado, and Dakota, and might have cost the government millions of dollars to have them crushed out."[55] Coffin was so pleased he invited the Osages to a council and distributed two or three thousand dollars' worth of clothing and shoes to show his appreciation. As for the Osages, he reported a month later they "were still feeling decidedly fine over their success."[56] Word of their coup was also on its way to the Confederate-allied Osage faction via a representative present at the council. Both factions wanted reconciliation, and Coffin promised the dissidents protection if they would come back and guard the frontier against bushwhackers and rebels.[57]

Things generally seemed more positive among the federal Indian officials in Kansas by late spring. The process of getting some of the refugees off their hands by returning them to the Indian Territory had begun. There was also progress in persuading the tribes to cede some of their lands to the United States. Federal treaties with Indians always promised that the lands set aside for their latest reservation would be theirs forever. However, pressure for the tribe to give up part or all of their land later was as sure as the changing seasons. That was especially true of the large Osage reservation in southern Kansas, but other tribes holding lands adjacent to the Kansas-Missouri border felt similar pressure and uncertainty. The outbreak of the Civil War and the defection of the Indian Territory nations to the Confederacy brought new opportunities frontier expansionists, businessmen, and politicians such as Kansas senator James H. Lane were quick to seize. If they could use the disloyalty of the Indian nations as an excuse to appropriate their lands in the Indian Territory, there would be a new place to relocate the Kansas tribes and another lever to force the move.[58]

In fact, at the time of his death that March, Opothle Yahola had been negotiating for recognition of the pro-Union faction of his people as "the Creek nation." Superintendent Coffin recommended that the treaty he finalized with these "Loyal Creeks" in late summer should be "a model for all that are to follow with the broken and greatly reduced and fragmented tribes in the Indian Territory . . . especially in view of the removal of the Indians from Kansas and Nebraska, as contemplated by a recent act of Congress."[59] For $200,000 the Loyal Creek faction agreed to cede an irregular wedge of land roughly twenty-five by forty miles on the eastern edge of the Muscogee Nation. It lay along the north side of the Arkansas River from today's Muskogee, Oklahoma, to Tulsa. Opothle Yahola's followers may have taken some satisfaction in ceding this land their agent, George A. Cutler, described as "the finest portion of the Creek country." It was the area inhabited by the mixed-blood rebels, he said, so it contained "many fine residences, extensive farms, and large orchards of peaches and apples. The bottom lands are said to be equal to any in the west, and the country is well watered with running streams, besides having vast numbers of excellent springs." He concluded, "taken altogether, it is a country well calculated to make a pleasant home for either the white or red man."[60]

The federal government was not alone in its readiness to use Indian land for its own purposes. That summer of 1863, as the tide began to turn against the Confederacy, Elias C. Boudinot, Cherokee delegate to the Confederate Congress, forwarded a proposal that infuriated the Cherokee government headed by Stand Watie. It proposed the Cherokee Nation award land grants and Cherokee citizens' rights to white men to induce them to enlist in the Confederate army. The council fired back a reply that vibrated with indignation over this assault on Cherokee sovereignty. Noting that the Cherokee-Confederate Treaty guaranteed them protection and their rights in their own country forever, they pointed to the hardships Cherokee people had endured and the blood they had shed the last two years as allies of the Confederacy. Yet now they were being asked to give land and Cherokee citizenship to foreigners. "Two things above all others we hold most dear," they declared, "our nationality and the welfare of our people." They replied, "We . . . in justice to ourselves and our people, cannot agree to give a part of our domain as an inducement to citizens of another government to fight their own battles and for their own country."[61]

This exasperating development occurred about the same time hopes diminished that the loyal Cherokees could safely return to their homes. The Union occupation of Fort Gibson had begun on April 13, but by mid-May it was clear the troops could not protect them unless they remained in its shadow. Judge Justin Harlan, their agent, wrote he had reluctantly agreed to their return because the military assured him Gen. James G. Blunt and Col. William A. Phillips would each lead an army through the nation, sweeping out the bushwhackers and keeping the Confederates south of the Arkansas River. However, Blunt's force was diverted elsewhere, and now Phillips and the Union Indian Brigade were pinned down at Fort Gibson. Brig. Gen. Douglas H. Cooper kept troops hovering around Fort Gibson for just that purpose. The heights later known as Agency Hill, directly across the river, made a fine place for soldiers such as young Ben Bailey, now in Company A of Col. Chilly McIntosh's 2nd Creek Mounted Regiment, to spy on the fort. From this spot, he had a bird's-eye view of the whole area. He could watch not only the troops and their maneuvers but also their livestock, which they herded away from the fort to graze. The Confederate allies constantly preyed on them for beef as well as draft animals. There were sorties from the fort to dislodge the Confederate allies, but these had limited effect.[62]

In addition to the nuisance attacks, twice in the spring of 1863 when the roads dried out the Confederates made larger assaults on Fort Gibson. The first time Cooper sent two regiments of Texas cavalry, the Confederate Indian regiments, three small howitzers, and a prairie gun. The movement failed, according to Confederate Indian Territory commander Steele, due, "in my judgment to the command of the expedition devolving upon an Indian officer deficient in energy and capacity, and who did not enjoy the confidence of the white troops under his command."[63] The second time Col. Stand Watie attempted to take Fort Gibson from the rear, but supporting troops under Gen. William L. Cabell failed to get there in time and join the assault.[64]

However, the Confederates constantly threatened the supply line from Fort Scott.

Meanwhile, the Cherokee refugees had been so eager to get home, Agent Harlan wrote, "No advice of mine could restrain them from scattering, and they scattered." Once beyond the protection of the fort, they were easy prey. The whole country, he reported, was now infested with bushwhackers and rebels who stripped the Cherokee families of anything they wanted or could use. "If any resistance is made, or one known to be a soldier is found, they murder without mercy. There are but few men in the country; almost all are in the army, away from home, and, women and children alone at home, the rebels have their own way."[65]

Harlan blamed himself for agreeing to their premature return, now that "every promise has failed." He estimated there were nearly six thousand destitute and hungry Cherokees in the nation. "Rebel beef" was still plentiful and easily available, as was salt they could boil down themselves from the nation's many saline springs. Flour, though, was in short supply and desperately needed. What there was could be distributed to the people living closest to the fort, but, robbed of their livestock, Cherokees living at a distance could not get there to collect the supplies available. Stores of coffee, sugar, and tobacco were also exhausted. "They can do without them," Harlan wrote, "but they grumble at me as if I was the only cause of their privations." Lastly, the people were in dire need of clothing and shoes.[66]

Under these circumstances, everyone looked forward to the arrival of supply trains from Fort Scott, Kansas. They needed a heavy escort, and the 1st Kansas Colored Volunteer Infantry Regiment had recently been assigned that duty. It was not front-line fighting, but it had its dangers, particularly from Confederate raiders. According to veteran and historian Wiley Britton, a black soldier with the Indian regiments took the opportunity to build their image among the Confederates lurking around Fort Gibson. Captured while herding stock, he claimed to be merely an officer's servant. Under questioning, he provided a seemingly frank and positive description of the fortifications and garrison. At the time, there was a lot of concern in the Indian Territory about these new black Union troops. Would they fight? What could Indian slave owners expect from runaway slaves now armed and wearing Union uniforms?

Their hope was that the white officers said to be in charge of them would keep them under control.[67]

The "servant's" captors were particularly curious about the ones said to be stationed at Baxter Springs, Kansas, only a few miles north of the Indian Territory boundary, on the Texas Road. According to Britton, the servant claimed to have seen the 1st Kansas Colored on dress parade, their ranks stretching in a line half a mile long. He described them as wearing sharp new dark blue coats and light blue trousers with polished shoes. Their muskets and bayonets gleamed with polish, too, he said, and they were so well drilled their gun butts hit the ground with a single thud when they received the command to "order arms." The prisoner described them as "mostly colored men from Missouri, healthy, husky looking fellows . . . intelligent as the average white man" and well paid and well treated by their white officers. This glowing description was not meant to encourage the "servant's" ragged and worn captors.[68]

The Confederate allies were, indeed, planning to strike the supply train that entered the territory near the end of June. They were well aware of federal plans through their scouts keeping watch near Baxter Springs. A section of the train, escorted by seven or eight hundred Indian soldiers, had already arrived at Fort Gibson to reinforce its garrison, but the main body was still some distance north on the Texas Road. Scouting reports said Confederate general William L. Cabell had left Fort Smith with about two thousand men and artillery. He was headed west through the Cherokee Nation. They suspected he intended to join Confederate forces in an attack on the main supply train at the ford across Cabin Creek just upstream from its junction with the Grand River, near today's Pensacola, Oklahoma.[69]

On June 26 Col. James M. Williams, commanding the 1st Kansas Colored Volunteers, received orders to catch up with the train and did later in the day.[70] According to Wiley Britton, they were "eager for a fight . . . . They knew that there was prejudice among the white soldiers against them on account of their color." If they got into a fight, "they determined . . . their performance should be creditable to any military organization."[71]

The supply train, which consisted of a miscellaneous collection of two hundred wagons, moved on, accompanied by Maj. John A.

Foreman and the 1st, 2nd, and 3rd Indian Home Guard, towing their mountain howitzer. There were three companies of the 2nd Colorado Infantry [Cavalry]; Company B, 3rd Wisconsin Cavalry; Company C, 9th Kansas Cavalry; and Company B, 14th Kansas Cavalry, along with one section of the 2nd Kansas Battery. All together, about nine hundred Union troops were escorting the supply train to Fort Gibson. The long drought had broken, and recent rains had swollen the eastern Indian Territory streams. High water, though, also interrupted General William L. Cabell's march from Arkansas. Eventually it forced him to turn back rather than join the Confederate allies planning to ambush the supply train at the Cabin Creek crossing.[72]

When the train arrived at the ford about noon on July 1, Confederate troops already held the crossing, using the thickets and fallen timber along both sides of the creek for cover. Colonel Williams, the senior federal officer, did not know at the time he was facing Col. Stand Watie. He just realized there was a substantial body of enemy troops along the creek. Later, a prisoner revealed they included the 1st Cherokee, 1st Creek, part of DeMorse's 29th Texas Cavalry, and the 5th Texas Partisan Rangers, totaling more than sixteen hundred men. They had established a strong position with observers up in the taller trees and on a high ridge at their backs. After initial skirmishing between their pickets and Foreman's Indian troops, Colonel Williams ordered up the mountain howitzer and one of the twelve-pounders. The two guns used shells and canister to drive the Confederate pickets back across the creek to the west side. While this was going on, soundings of the creek showed the water was too deep to drive the wagons across for the time being.[73]

Colonel Williams's first responsibility was the supply train, so he had it driven back a couple of miles northeast along the Texas Road and parked under guard on the prairie for the night. He also pulled his troops back to camp. The black troops knew their chances of surviving if the coming battle went against them. The word was that the Confederates would take no black prisoners. After meeting with his officers that evening, Colonel Williams decided to attack before Cabell could arrive with Confederate reinforcements. His plan called for Major Foreman to lead the attack with one company of the Indian Home Guard, followed by the 1st Kansas Colored Volunteers, then the

2nd Colorado Infantry with three cavalry companies behind them. The rest of the Indian Home Guard would watch the fords above and below the battle site. Early the next morning he left a strong guard around the train and marched the rest of his troops toward Cabin Creek, which had receded somewhat during the night.[74]

At eight o'clock the federal artillery began a forty-minute cannonade from about two hundred yards away, throwing shell and canister into the Confederate lines. When it ended on the assumption it had suppressed the Confederates along the opposite creek bank, Major Foreman led his Indian soldiers down into the deep streambed. He was mounted, but they waded into the still-high waters, holding their weapons and powder above their heads. The Union companies quickly learned the enemy was still hunkered down in the timber when they loosed heavy fire on them. Several musket balls struck Major Foreman and his horse, throwing him into the water. He was forced to retreat toward the bank, and his men pulled back in confusion, too. The artillery bombardment resumed for twenty minutes more. Meanwhile, as planned, the 1st Kansas Colored Volunteers and the 2nd Colorado Infantry hurried up to take their places. When the bombardment stopped again, some provided covering fire while others waded into water still up to their armpits. This time they scrambled up the steep bank on the far side and reformed their ranks. They opened fire, but then the center of the 1st Kansas drew back. This allowed the two companies of Union cavalry to ride through. One split right and one left to reform a long single line facing the Confederates. On command they drew their sabers and charged. Under this fresh assault, the Confederate allies became disorganized and began to fall back. As they retreated from the battlefield, the federals pursued them for about five miles until recalled. Then they gave up the chase, reassembled, and returned to the supply train, which was soon rolling on toward Fort Gibson.[75]

Colonel Watie left the battlefield discouraged but not defeated. On July 12, he wrote a hasty reassuring note to his wife, Sarah Caroline Bell Watie ("Sallie" or "Sally"), "I had a hard trip of it . . . one of the serviest [sic] fights that has been fought in the country on the bank of the Cabbin Creek fought two days, the Feds forced and drove our men away from the ford, the second day by a severe cannonade . . . . I lost but few men. I am safe you must not be uneasy about me I will take care of myself."[76]

Still, the loss was a blow for the Confederate allies. A second note explained why he believed the Union force prevailed. Watie's own cannon had not arrived, placing the Confederate allies at a disadvantage. "I fought them about six hours at the crossing of Cabbin Creek at Joe Martin's place if the Creek [troops] had stood I could have fought them longer but they wont do it." He summarized, "I am proud of my men, they stood cannonading as well and better than any souldiers [*sic*] could have done." He placed his loss at no more than fifteen but guessed, based on the number of dead federal horses left on the battle-field, "many a man killed."[77]

William J. Candler was twenty-seven and a Confederate soldier in Company F, 5th Texas Partisan Rangers, when they were engaged in the fight at Cabin Creek. One of his fellow soldiers wrote later,

> Bill Candler was not a talker, but . . . when volunteers were called for, he stepped to the front without a word and was ready for duty. He was the only man killed in the Cabin Creek fight. He was wounded in the bowels and we put him on a litter and started to carry him off the field. We had gone but a short distance when he said he was dying and was soon gone. We dug his grave as best we could with our big knives, and as his blanket was bloody, I wrapped him in my own. He was buried near where he fell. Such was the fate of many a good man. May the good Spirits keep watch over his lonely resting place.[78]

Word that something significant was happening at Cabin Creek reached Fort Gibson long before the supply train did. Up near the junction of the creek and the Grand River, some Cherokee women heard the commotion and saw the smoke. They rode for the fort, arriving two days ahead of the supply train, and gave the news. Confirmation of the victory and the arrival of supplies and reinforcements raised morale among the Union troops and Indian civilians still camped nearby, mostly loyal Seminoles and Muscogees who dared not go home. There was great satisfaction that the troops had defeated and dispersed the strongest Confederate force yet assembled in the Indian Territory. Although the Cabin Creek engagement had been hard fought, the losses were relatively small. Colonel Williams reported one killed and twenty wounded among his troops. They guessed there were perhaps fifty killed among the Confederate allies. Another encouraging outcome was that the black troops had demonstrated at Cabin Creek that they had the will and skill to fight for the Union. Some have said it was the first time white, black, and Indian troops had fought together in Union uniforms.[79]

Pro-Confederate Indians were alarmed. There was already a great deal of uneasiness as Union agitators circulated through the Cherokee Nation ostensibly preaching to the slaves. Ella Coodey of Webber's Falls said they were actually "inciting them to all kinds of meanness and deviltry. [The slaves] tried to be faithful to their owners and at the same time were bewildered by what was being told them by these men. The [Cherokee] women stayed at home and tried to keep things together and care for their families but . . . they never knew what a day would bring forth."[80] That the reinforcements at Fort Gibson included black soldiers in Union uniforms was even more frightening to slave owners.

Although the supply train arrived soon after the attack at Cabin Creek, more Union reinforcements were almost on its heels. Maj. Gen. James G. Blunt, commander of the Army of the Frontier, had learned from his scouts that General Cabell and his force were on the Arkansas–Cherokee Nation border, possibly headed west to join other Confederate troops in the area. A sailor, physician, abolitionist, and now an amateur general, Blunt was courageous and known for taking the offensive. He decided to strike first. He moved rapidly south from Fort Scott over the Texas Road with about six hundred men, including a battalion of the 6th Kansas Cavalry and another of the 3rd Wisconsin Cavalry, two twelve-pound howitzers, and two sections of the 2nd Kansas Battery. They covered 120 miles in three days, arriving unexpectedly at Fort Gibson (or "Fort Blunt") on July 11.[81]

Col. William A. Phillips immediately organized a reception for them. In a public address Blunt announced three significant pieces of news: the Union victory at Gettysburg, Pennsylvania; the surrender of the Confederate fortress at Vicksburg, Mississippi; and the failure of a large-scale Confederate attack on Helena, Arkansas—all within the last two weeks. That could mean many more federal troops, freed from duties elsewhere, would be available soon to help retake the southwestern region of the Confederacy. However, Blunt did not mean to wait for them. He intended to move against Brig. Gen. Douglas H. Cooper as soon as possible. The Union was no longer on the defensive in the Indian Territory; it was taking the offensive.[82]

Meanwhile, Col. Stand Watie and the Confederate allies that had fought at Cabin Creek had returned to their camps in the Honey Springs vicinity. They, too, had heard of the recent Confederate losses in the east and the incorporation of black troops into the Union army. They were concerned, but they decided in council they should send for General Cabell to join them and make a stand along Elk Creek just north of Honey Springs. They believed they had a short breathing space because the rivers were still too deep to ford.[83]

Blunt, though, was also thinking about Cabell. He knew time was running out to attack Cooper, whom he believed already outnumbered him two to one, before Cabell brought reinforcements. The Arkansas River was still too high to ford below the mouth of the Verdigris River, and Confederate pickets were stationed in rifle pits at every ford along its banks. Blunt planned to ferry about three thousand men plus artillery and horses across, so he ordered rafts constructed. On the evening of July 15, though, Union scouts reported that the water level was dropping along the Verdigris, making it possible to cross upstream northwest of Fort Gibson. Blunt, who had recently lost thirty pounds and been in bed the day before with a high fever from encephalitis, did not let that stop him.[84] He said later, "I took 250 cavalry and four pieces of light artillery, and marched up the Arkansas about 13 miles, drove in their pickets from the opposite bank, and forded the river, taking the ammunition chests over in a flat-boat." He swung back down the south side of the Arkansas hoping to capture the Confederate pickets at the mouth of the Grand River and prevent them from warning Cooper.[85]

It was too late. That same morning the officer in charge of the Confederate pickets had reported to headquarters that the water level in the rivers was falling and federal officers had been checking the fords. Two Confederate spies, Clark and Lane, had been hanging around Fort Gibson and delivered the same information. Confirmation came when lookouts reported Blunt's cavalry and artillery moving toward Nevin's and Rabbit Fords near Frozen Rock, just north and east of today's Muskogee, Oklahoma. Alerted about daylight, the pickets slipped away and rode south to the main Confederate outpost about five miles north of Elk Creek. Cooper ordered them to concentrate on Coodey's Creek, about a mile south of today's Muskogee, Oklahoma, but to watch the other crossings, too.[86]

Undeterred, Blunt spent the rest of July 16 ferrying his troops across the Arkansas River at the mouth of the Grand River. Taking men, horses, and mules across on open-sided ferries was a slow, dangerous process even though the water level had fallen. Henry Sepping, a teamster for the 1st Kansas Colored Infantry, drowned attempting to ferry his wagon and mules across. Privates Huston Mayfield, Key Dougherty, and Tocahlegeskie, all of Company F, 2nd Regiment, Indian Home Guard, died while swimming the dark river about eleven o'clock that night. Those who had crossed earlier rested as they much as they could, but many were already marching south along the Texas Road by ten o'clock that evening. The veterans knew what to expect, but the 1st Kansas Battery had never been under fire before.[87]

Dawn broke cloudy, warm, and humid. Col. Tandy Walker, who commanded the 1st Choctaw and Chickasaw Mounted Rifles, and Capt. L. E. Gillett of the Texas Cavalry Battalion had received orders to move north to the vicinity of Chimney Mountain, just northwest of today's Summit, Oklahoma. This spot was near the intersection of the Texas Road and the road to Creek Agency. About daylight Company F of the 6th Kansas Cavalry, leading the Union advance south along the Texas Road, approached the little rise on which Walker and Gillett had stationed their Choctaw, Chickasaw, and Texas troops. Capt. William Gordon formed up Company F and attacked but quickly found himself outmatched. He fell back, but by then the other three companies of the 6th Kansas had come up. Together, without much trouble, they drove the Confederate allies back south toward Elk Creek.[88]

Later, Walker's Chickasaws and Choctaws complained their gunpowder refused to ignite, which was why they pulled out of the fight. Brigadier General Cooper, too, blamed the humid morning. He explained, "many of the guns [failed] to fire in consequence of the very inferior quality of the powder, the cartridges becoming worthless even upon exposure to damp atmosphere. Soon after the Federals had been driven back, it commenced raining heavily, which rendered their arms wholly useless."[89] Cooper said that his men pulled back slowly and in good order, hoping to resupply at their camp. Some, though, stayed about three miles north of Elk Creek hoping to give the impression a much larger force awaited Blunt's army. The federals did pause, Cooper reported, which gave the Confederate allies time to prepare for battle and deploy.[90]

Blunt knew his men were hungry and tired after more than twenty-four hours on the move. He had personally made a reconnaissance toward Elk Creek and found the Confederate allies concealed in the brush lining the north side and ready for battle. Returning to his column, he had his troops halt behind a little ridge about half a mile from where he knew the enemy waited. He gave them two hours then, time to rest and to eat the rations they had packed in their haversacks at Fort Gibson. They were thirsty, too, so they filled their canteens from the puddles in the road, full from that morning's downpour. They also checked their cartridge boxes to be sure their ammunition was dry and ready.[91]

With time to look around, they could see scattered low hills, small areas of prairie, and, off to the southeast, the bulk of Pumpkin Ridge at the north end of the Rattlesnake Mountains. The landscape was green with blackberry thickets, prairie grasses, and hardwood forests dominated by a mixture of small tough native oaks. There were a few scattered farmhouses, mostly log buildings on stone foundations, along with small barns, sheds, smokehouses, and corncribs. Yards were swept clean around Indian homes to keep away snakes and spirits, but brush arbors for a cool place to work or rest during warm weather were common. Rail fences protected garden plots and cornfields from deer and livestock. The scene did not look much different from rural areas elsewhere on the frontier. Although the Union troops were only about three miles from the Honey Springs community, it was simply a scattering of farmsteads with a few businesses that catered to travelers on the Texas Road. Its strategic importance in July 1863 lay in the depot for the supplies the Confederate allies had stockpiled there.

As for the Texas Road, it was not so much a "road" as an unpaved trail of variable width, depending on the ground it crossed. During wet weather travelers would swing wide of mud holes; during dry weather they would try to avoid dried ruts by edging farther out. Herders driving livestock along the road might let them drift out a way toward grass that had not already been cropped short. The result was that the Texas Road could be quite wide in some places and narrow where natural features constrained its boundaries. It was only a few feet wide where it dropped down into the relatively deep valley carved by Elk Creek (also called Durdy or Dirty Creek). There was only one bridge, placed in the large oxbow curve the creek made near the north end of Pumpkin Ridge. It would be valuable to troops in a hurry or moving artillery and supply wagons near Honey Springs. There were also fords above the bridge that would have to be defended or captured, but the water level was still high from recent rains.

Brig. Gen. Douglas S. Cooper had those crossings in mind when he planned the defense of Honey Springs that morning. He ordered Col. Daniel N. McIntosh to take the 1st and 2nd Creek Regiments to the fords above the bridge, forming his left wing. The 1st and 2nd Cherokee Regiments were on his right, with Col. Tandy Walker and the Choctaw-Chickasaw troops in reserve near Honey Springs, along with Scanland's and Gillett's squadrons of Texas cavalry. The rest of the Texans—the 20th and 29th Cavalry and the 5th Partisan Rangers— would form his center, dismounted and posted in the brush along the bluff north of the bridge. There they would support Capt. Roswell W. Lee's light battery of four howitzers. That was Cooper's plan, but things went awry from the beginning. Colonel Walker was out of position, having misunderstood Cooper's order to send *some,* not all, of his men to scout the nearby roads. Also, Colonel Watie, on an assignment elsewhere, was not there to command his Cherokees. His lieutenants, Maj. Joseph F. Thompson and Lt. Col. James M. Bell, were thought to lack his high degree of military skill.[92]

Until the last few hours, folks living near Honey Springs had no idea something major was about to happen. Lucinda Davis, a slave of Tuskaya Hiniha, was about thirteen then and lived on his farm near the Texas Road between Elk Creek and Honey Springs. Most of the men slaves had run off to Kansas, leaving only the women to work the farm. Just before sunrise on July 17, Lucinda, a nursemaid, was outside in the arbor with the baby she cared for when a horseman came galloping across the little prairie near the house. Lucinda remembered,

> he was coming a-kiting and a-laying flat out on his hoss. When he see de house he begin to give de war whoop, "Eya-a-a-a-he-hah!" When he git close to de house he holler to git out de way 'cause dey gwine to be a big fight, and old Master start rap-

ping wid his cane and yelling to git some grub and blankets in de wagon right now!

We jest leave everything setting right war it is, 'cepting putting out de fire and grabbing all de pots and kettles. Some de ... women run to git de mules and de wagon and some start gitting meat and corn out of de place whar we done hid it to keep de scouters from finding it befo' now. All de time we gitting ready to travel we hear dat boy on dat horse going on down de big Texas road hollering, "Eya-a-a-he-he hah!"

Den jest as we starting to leave, here come something across dat little prairie sho' nuff. We know dey is Indians de way dey is riding, and de way dey is all strung out. Dey had a flag, and it was all red and had a big criss-cross on it dat look lak a saw horse. De man carry it and rear back on it when de wind whip it, but it flap all 'roun de horse's ear and de horse pitch and rear lak he know something going to happen, sho!

'Bout dat time it turn kind of dark and begin to rain a little, and we git out to de big road and de rain come down hard. It rain so hard for a little while dat we jest have to stop de wagon and set dar, and den long come more soldiers dan I ever see befo'. Dey all white men, I think, and dey have on dat brown clothes dyed wid walnut and butternut, and old Master say dey de Confederate soldiers. Dey dragging some big guns on wheels and most de men slopping 'long in de rain on foot.[93]

These were some of the Texans hurrying to their place in the battle lines. W. K. Makemson of Georgetown, Texas, unlike most of them, had opposed secession and supported the Union. But when Texas seceded, Makemson, then about twenty-five years old and with political ambitions, "answered the call of his State and did his duty as a Confederate soldier."[94] He had enlisted in Company A, 5th Texas Partisan Rangers, and served in the Missouri, Kansas, and Indian Territory border area. He wrote later of that day, "Our line of battle was formed in the edge of the bottom of Elk Creek about 7 o'clock in the morning of the 17th of July, 1863 .... We remained there in line of battle and waited for the enemy until 9 or 10 o'clock."[95]

Meanwhile, General Blunt was deploying his Union troops across a wide, gentle slope ragged with prairie grass and bisected by the Texas

Road. He knew the Confederates facing him were in a line that stretched about a mile and a half and was centered on the road. He realized they outnumbered him, but he had twelve artillery pieces to their four. About ten o'clock he ordered his troops into two columns, one on either side of the Texas Road, compacted to conceal their true numbers.[96]

In the column on the right (or west), Col. James M. Williams spoke to the 1st Kansas Colored Volunteers while they waited for the command to advance. He ordered them to attention and then, according to Wiley Britton, said, "This is the day we have been patiently waiting for; the enemy at Cabin Creek [gave] you [the] opportunity of showing them what men can do fighting for their natural rights and for their recently acquired freedom and the freedom of their children and their children's children." He told them he was proud of them as soldiers he had trained and of leading them. He continued,

> We are engaged in a holy war . . . soldiers never fought for a holier cause . . . the preservation of the Union and the equal rights and freedom of all men. You know what the soldiers of the Southern armies are fighting for . . . the continued existence and extension of slavery on this continent, and if they are successful, to take you and your wives and children back into slavery. You know it is a common report that the Confederate troops and their officers boast that they will not give quarter to colored troops and their officers . . . . Show the enemy this day that you are not asking for quarter, and that you know how and are eager to fight for your freedom . . . finally keep cool and do not fire until you receive the order, and then aim deliberately below the waist belt. The people of the whole country will read the reports of your conduct in this engagement; let it be that of brave, disciplined men.[97]

About the same time Colonel Williams was addressing the 1st Kansas, Col. Chilly McIntosh was reminding the 2nd Creek Mounted Volunteers in the Confederate line what they were fighting for. Perhaps because this was his first engagement, twenty-year-old Wash Grayson, waiting with the rest of his company in the wet brush of the Elk Creek bottom, considered his words particularly striking, the best war talk he ever heard. The Muscogee elder said, "When you first saw the light, it was said of you, 'a man child is born.' You must prove today whether or not this saying of you was true. The sun that hangs over our heads has no death, no end of days. It will continue indefinitely to rise and to set; but with you it is different. Man must die sometime, and since he must die, he can find no nobler death than that which overtakes him while fighting for his home, his fires, and his country."[98]

Blunt wasted no time moving his troops onto the battlefield. They included the 1st, 2nd, and 3rd Indian Home Guard, the 1st Kansas Colored Volunteer Infantry, detachments of the 2nd Colorado Infantry, 6th Kansas Cavalry, and 3rd Wisconsin Cavalry, as well as the artillery. He reported later, "I moved up rapidly to within one-fourth of a mile of their line, when both columns were suddenly deployed right and left, and in less than five minutes my whole force was in line of battle, covering the enemy's entire front. Without halting, I moved them forward in line of battle, throwing out skirmishers in advance, and soon drew their fire, which revealed the location of their artillery."[99]

The Union artillery replied, and that duel opened the battle. In the center of the Confederate allies' line, Capt. Roswell W. Lee's four pieces—3 twelve-pound mountain howitzers and a rare experimental mountain rifle—supported the two dismounted Texas cavalry regiments. They were about three hundred yards from the federal line and mostly hidden in the timber that cloaked the edge of the bluff above Elk Creek. Directly opposite them were 4 twelve-pound Napoleon guns near the 1st Kansas Colored Volunteer Infantry. Four Union artillery pieces backed the 2nd Colorado Infantry. Two each were assigned to the 3rd Wisconsin on the far right and to the dismounted 6th Kansas Cavalry on the far left. For the next hour and a quarter, the Confederate artillery threw "shot, shell, and canister" at them, mortally wounding Sgt. Daniel Sayer, whose leg was blown off above the knee, and killing a private and four horses belonging to Capt. Henry Hopkins's Kansas battery. The federal gunners concentrated the fire of four of their Napoleons on one of the Confederate pieces they had spotted in the timber and put it out of action quickly. Captain Lee, though, used the little mountain howitzer to target and pick off some of Blunt's officers.[100]

Although the artillery went into action first, General Blunt reported, "the entire force was engaged. My men steadily advanced into the edge of the timber, and the fighting was unremitting and terrific for two hours."[101] The 3rd Wisconsin, dismounted and stationed on the right, battled the Confederate allies that had taken shelter behind a rail fence at the edge of a cornfield.[102] The men of the 6th Kansas Cavalry were posted on the extreme left, but Lt. Col. William T. Campbell realized very quickly that the Confederate Cherokees were filtering through the timber in an attempt to flank them. He dismounted his men and sent them into the woods where they had "sharp work" for an hour and a half. They were very glad when the 1st Indian Home Guard rushed past them and drove the Cherokees back, giving the Kansans a chance to catch their breath and regroup.[103]

Early in the action when the cannonading was constant, General Blunt went to Colonel Williams and said, according to Col. John Bowles of the 1st Kansas, "'I want you to move your regiment to the front and support this battery . . . keep an eye on those guns [artillery] of the enemy, and take them at the point of the bayonet, if an opportunity offers.'" Williams told his men they had work to do then and to fix bayonets. Bowles wrote later, "We then moved to the front and center." The brush was so thick they could only make out the location of the Confederate cannon from the smoke of the constant firing, but the 1st Kansas never faltered. Bowles said,

> [W]hen our gallant colonel gave the command "forward," . . . every man stepped promptly and firmly in his place, advancing in good order until within 40 paces of the concealed foe, when we halted on the right of the Second Colorado. Colonel Williams then gave the command, "Ready, aim, fire," and immediately there went forth two long lines of smoke and flame, the one from the enemy putting forth at the same instant, as if mistaking the command as intended for themselves, or as a willingness to meet us promptly.[104]

Colonel Williams was wounded in three places and fell along with his horse, but thick brush hid him from Colonel Bowles's view. It was too late when Bowles realized he was now in command, so he never gave the order for the bayonet charge.[105]

About four hours into the battle the outcome was still undecided. Lieutenant Colonel Bowles had taken command of the 1st Kansas when he finally realized Colonel Williams was down. He ordered the men to lie prone on the ground and keep shooting from that position.[106] Firing all along the lines continued without pause until Bowles noticed a lull on the extreme right. There, he saw,

> some of our Indians had ridden in the brush between us and the enemy. I immediately ordered them to fall back, and to the right. The enemy . . . the Twenty-ninth Texas Regiment, commanded by Colonel De Morse in person, who was badly wounded in the right arm, supposed from the command that we were giving way in front, and, like true soldiers, commenced to press, as they supposed, a retreating foe. They advanced to within 25 paces, when they were met by a volley of musketry that sent them back in great confusion and disorder. Their color-bearer fell, but the colors were immediately raised, and again promptly shot down. A second time they were raised, and again I caused a volley to be fired upon them, when they were left by the enemy as a trophy to our well-directed musketry.[107]

The 1st Kansas pushed the Texans—actually the 29th and some of the 20th Texas—back through a cornfield as they retreated in confusion. Bowles did not try to pursue them but got his men reorganized and back in line. About that time the 2nd Indian Home Guard passed in front of the 1st Kansas and picked up the colors the 29th Texas had dropped. Angrily some of the men of the 1st Kansas yelled at them and wanted to go take back the colors they had won, but Bowles refused them permission for the time being.[108]

The rush of the Texans into the volley from the 1st Kansas when they thought the Union line was retreating tipped the battle in the federals' favor. The Confederate allies began falling back in small groups. Dallas W. Bowman, the nineteen-year-old Texan in Company K, 1st Regiment of the Choctaw and Chickasaw Mounted Rifles, wrote to his mother, "[W]e were badly disappointed we all were too sure of whipping them but no, we fought over 3 hours under a heavy fire all the time but at last their firing began to get too heavy for us at the same time dismounting one of our pieces of canon [sic] we were compelled to fall back, and our men began to scater [sic] which caused confusion and we had a general stampede."[109]

Even then, according to General Blunt, although his troops "pushed them vigorously," some of the Confederate allies turned to make "determined stands, especially at the bridge over Elk Creek."[110] Because of the recent rains, the water level was shoulder deep, too deep for the Confederate artillery teams to use the fords to get their three movable guns away from the battlefield. The bridge was their best option, and the Texans defended it fiercely, using their muskets as clubs when their faulty ammunition failed or gave out. Their determination to hold the bridge allowed the three remaining Confederate guns to cross and move up onto the prairie beyond the timber south of the creek.[111] Between their losses north of Elk Creek and down near the bridge, the battle took a heavy toll on the Texas troops. Pvt. James Johnson, with Company C of the 20th Texas Cavalry, commanded by Col. Thomas Coke Bass, received only a slight head wound. However, of the 365 men who went into the Battle of Honey Springs, only 105 came out.[112]

As the Confederate line began pulling back south, the 1st Indian Home Guard, positioned at the east end of the Union line, followed them down the bluff into the creek bottom. According to their commander, Captains Nokosolochee and Sonukmikko led the Union Muscogees and Seminoles as they "advanced under a destructive fire from the enemy, after hard fighting gained a position in the timber, and finally drove them across the stream, on the left of the bridge, the enemy forming several times, and desperately contesting every foot of ground." Lt. Col. George Dole was one of the first to cross Elk Creek and did it "under a most galling fire."[113] However, Lt. Col. Frederick W. Schuarte of the 2nd Indian Home Guards claimed his Cherokees "were the first who charged through Elk Creek and took position in the farther edge of the timber opposite to where the enemy had massed the first time."[114] Given the distance between their assigned positions in the Union line, thick undergrowth, and smoke hanging over the battleground in the humid air, each commander was honest in claiming his men were first across the creek.

Although the Confederate allies were retreating, for now they were doing it in good order, and the battle was not yet over. Lt. Col. William T. Campbell of the 6th Kansas Cavalry reported, "Shortly after crossing the creek, I charged into a large body of rebels, whom I took to be Stand Watie's Indians and Texans. They retreated to the woods, where they made a stand. My men dismounted and opened a vigorous fire, which, together with a section of Hopkins's battery and the mountain howitzers soon put them to flight."[115]

When he saw his troops beginning to pull back, Cooper had decided to make a stand on the prairie south of Elk Creek to protect the Honey Springs supply depot and allow his wagon train to get away. Captain Lee's remaining three cannon turned to face north, and some of the Texas cavalry units were ordered to support him. However, Union captain Henry Hopkins had been ordered to move the available guns of the Kansas Battery forward at the double-quick, and he took a new position at the edge of the timber north of the prairie. One section opened fire on the Texans, dispersing them and sending them on south along the Texas Road.[116]

Cooper tried to collect his scattered units and concentrate them at Honey Springs, which lay about two miles south of Elk Creek. Among them were the 1st and 2nd Creek Mounted Volunteers, still waiting in the Elk Creek bottom for their chance to get into the fight. By then Col. Tandy Walker had arrived with his Choctaw and Chickasaw troops. Cooper took personal command of them and led them in one of their standard charges. "With their usual intrepidity," he wrote, "the Choctaws went at them, giving the war-whoop, and succeeded in checking the advance of the enemy until their force could be concentrated and brought up."[117] Young Dallas Bowman took part in that charge and described it to his mother, saying merely "the enemy followed us out to a prairie (about a half mile from the battle ground) at whitch [sic] time our battalion charged on them and held them in check until the train could get out of the way."[118] Cooper commented, "Colonel Walker and his Choctaws behaved bravely, as they always do."[119]

The Union troops followed, intent on capturing the depot at Honey Springs. Lt. Col. Thomas Moonlight, General Blunt's chief of staff, accompanied the 1st Kansas Colored Volunteers as they maintained their ranks for a march of about three more miles. Along the way they fended off skirmishers on the west slope of Pumpkin Ridge or scattered over the prairie ahead.[120]

By then Cooper had come up with a plan, he explained later, to deceive and alarm Blunt enough to make him withdraw to Fort Gibson. Cooper would send his troops east, rather than south through North Fork Town to their camps along the Canadian River. He hoped that would make Blunt think they were finally linking up with General Cabell, who arrived along with Colonel Watie late that afternoon but too late to affect the battle. Blunt, Cooper hoped, would think he had been reinforced and fear a counterattack or even a threat to his base. The problem, Cooper explained later to his Confederate superiors, was that getting his train of supply wagons moving east toward Briartown meant he could not evacuate the supplies from the Honey Springs depot.[121]

To keep them out of Blunt's hands, he ordered them burned. That job was assigned to a few Texas troops, among them W. K. Makemson. He recalled that his unit, the 5th Texas Partisan Rangers, and Captain Scanland's Texas cavalry squadron were the last Confederate troops to leave the battlefield once "our lines were broken and the entire force utterly routed." In fact, he said, they "were the only commands that left the field in formation." Makemson and a detail were sent ahead to burn the supplies, but it was still a close call. He remembered, "The Federals were within 200 yards of myself and detail while we were setting fire to the commissary and quartermasters stores at the Springs."[122] They were so close, in fact, that the fire did not have time to destroy the supplies before Union troops put it out, saving much of the stored bacon, flour, and preserved beef. The weary but victorious Union soldiers ate well that night.[123]

It was another story for the Confederate allies. Nursemaid Lucinda Davis and the Tuskaya Hiniha household were caught in the stream of troops hurrying to and then away from the battle. Stuck in their wagon along the muddy Texas Road between Elk Creek and Honey Springs early that morning, they were close enough to hear "de guns sound lak hosses loping 'cross a plank bridge way off somewhar." Once the cannonade started, there was a new urgency among the Confederate troops streaming north past them. "De head men start hollering and some de hosses start rearing and de soldiers start trotting faster up de road," Lucinda remembered. Unable to get through the crowd, they drove their wagon across the prairie to a deep creek bed with a rocky overhang about half a mile from Honey Springs. Lucinda said, "We hear de guns going all day, and along in de evening here come de South side making for a getaway. Dey come riding and running by whar we is, and it don't make no difference how much de head men hollers at 'em dey can't make dat bunch slow up and stop. After while here comes de Yankees, right after 'em, and dey goes on into Honey Springs and pretty soon we see de blaze whar dey is burning de wagon depot and de houses." At nightfall the household went home to find everything much as they left it. "Dem soldiers going so fast dey didn't have no time to stop and take nothing," Lucinda reckoned. "Den long comes lots of de Yankee soldiers going back to de North, and dey looks wore out, but dey is laughing and joshing and going on."[124]

W. K. Makemson agreed with Lucinda Davis about the officers' inability to stop the flight of Cooper's army after the Battle of Honey Springs. He recalled, "After we had set fire to the commissary and quartermasters stores, I was ordered by General Cooper to assist in herding up the straglers [sic] and turn them down in a southeasterly direction. No herd of Texas cattle was ever more thoroughly scattered or demoralized by a stampede than were [our] Indian forces. Every Indian was running his dead level best. They were all finally rounded up in camp at a place called Briartown down on the Canadian [River]."[125]

The defeat of the Confederate allies and their flight from the battlefield was an embarrassment that caused particular chagrin among the Muscogee soldiers. Wash Grayson wrote later he always believed the day was lost to "bad management . . . for our Gen. Cooper did not even get all his men out on the firing line . . . before he ordered his forces to retire." The 2nd Creek Mounted Volunteers were ordered to stay under cover in the dense undergrowth of the Elk Creek bottom until ordered into the fight. Grayson wrote, "Here we remained listening breathlessly at the rattle of small arms and an occasional exulting whoop . . . anxious to take a hand in the affray, but [we] could do nothing without orders. The morale of our men was the best, and they could and would have made things alarmingly unpleasant for [the enemy] . . . . While awaiting orders for a forward move, here came orders for us to fall back and retire in good order, which reluctantly our men did." Grayson finished sarcastically, "The good order of our men was perfect since there was no enemy or other thing in sight to cause disorder."[126]

By evening, most of the federal units had been recalled to rest and eat before they began the return march to Fort Gibson. Some, though, scouted through the Honey Springs area burning buildings and rounding up slaves they would take to Fort Gibson and freedom. Some soldiers came to the home of George W. Stidham. The wealthy Muscogee rancher and merchant had taken his more valuable slaves to Texas in 1861 but had come back for others left behind. Among them were his blacksmith's wife, twin daughters, and younger son, Jim, then about five. Jim remembered hiding in the cellar under a cabin all night and next day while the battle took place at Honey Springs, close enough that the slaves "could not tell the thunder from the cannon firing." At the time, they did not know that Jim's teen-aged brother, a runaway, was over there fighting as a soldier with the Indian Home Guard. When Union soldiers came to burn the Stidham place, Jim said, "All of us were scared and someone hollered, 'Is anybody down in the cellar?' I hollered out, 'I'se down heah.'" The soldiers who brought them out of the cellar loaded them into three wagons. Jim said, "We drove along until we came to a tall bridge." It was the bridge over Elk Creek. "We could see dead soldiers all along and they were picking them up and piling them. Both sides had lost lots of their men."[127]

On July 26 General Blunt reported seventeen men dead with sixty wounded, most slightly. Brigadier General Cooper claimed 134 killed, although the number is still not certain.[128] The 20th Texas Cavalry went into the battle with three hundred men and came out with only sixty, General Blunt reported.[129] The Confederate allies left their dead and wounded where they lay as they withdrew from the field, according to W. K. Makemson. He wrote, "The Federals buried our dead in a corn field in the bottom on the north side of Elk Creek." He continued, "Our wounded were picked up by the Federals and carried to the McIntosh house on the road about a mile north of the battle ground, and were there well cared for by their surgeons until they were relieved under a flag of truce five or six days after the battle. The Federal dead were buried in a corner of the garden at the McIntosh place."[130] They were later removed to Fort Gibson, at which a national cemetery was established in 1868.

Almost exactly a month after the fierce battle, Dallas Bowman wrote that he had visited Fort Gibson with ten companions under a flag of truce. "All the big officers," he wrote to his mother, "came to see us and treated us to as much whiskey as we could drink and as many cigars as we could smoke. They [were] kind and sociable, they tried to get me to join them but no."[131]

The Battle of Honey Springs was such a severe blow to the

Confederate allies that it is considered the turning point of the Civil War in the Indian Territory. The Union seemed fairly firmly entrenched at Fort Gibson, and the vicious warfare that had been confined to the Cherokee Nation seemed likely to spread to the other Indian nations. Fort Gibson's hold on the Arkansas River valley would prove to be somewhat tenuous, but for now it was enough to set off what those who lived through it called "the stampede."

Even though the Tuskaya Hiniha farmstead had survived the battle intact, Lucinda Davis said,

> Old Master pack up de wagon wid everything he can carry den, and we strike out down de big road to git out de way of any more war ....
>
> Dat old Texas road just crowded wid wagons! Everybody doing de same thing we is, and de rains done made de road so muddy and de soldiers done tromp up de mud so bad dat de wagons git stuck all de time.
>
> De people all moving along in bunches, and every little while one bunch of wagons come up with another bunch all stuck in de mud, and dey put all de hosses and mules on together and pull 'em out, and den dey go on together awhile.[132]

Everyone was exhausted by the time the refugees camped that night near the Canadian River. They found no place to stay because the little settlement there was already full of Confederate soldiers. Some were singing around their campfire, and Lucinda, who spoke only Muskogee, asked what the song was. A Creek man translated: "I wish I was in Dixie, look away, look away." Lucinda said, "I asked him whar dat is, and he laugh and talk to de soldiers and dey all laugh, and make me mad!"[133]

Along with seemingly every other stream in the area, the Canadian River was in flood. Yet it did not halt the flight of frightened people. Lucinda remembered, "Dey got some boats and we put stuff on, and float de wagons and swim de mules and finally git across, but it look lak we gwine all drown."[134]

Cherokee minister and national treasurer Stephen Foreman, who had been staying at North Fork Town about ten miles from Honey Springs, heard talk about what civilians with Southern sympathies might expect from the Union troops. He discounted most of it. No one knew just what to do; however, after visits with neighbors he wrote in his diary the night of the battle, "All things considered, I think we had better go to Texas as soon as we can."[135]

He could move his belongings or his children but not both. "After loading up one small wagon with our most valuable things, I started for . . . some other place of safety," he wrote the next night. "I was sorry to leave the children but under the circumstances I thought it was best, and Susie was willing to run the risque [*sic*], believing there was no danger if the Feds and Indians did come provided there were white officers along." He had not gone far on the Texas Road toward the Canadian River before he overtook the family of Isaac Bertholf, a white fellow minister. He wrote later,

> never having been broke up as I have been, they seemed to have no lack of anything. They had two wagons and teams of their own, heavily loaded with their goods of every description, and yet Mrs. Bertholf was mourning over what they had left behind, saying they had not brought over half their things. Yet besides their loaded wagons they had several loose horses, they had their sheep and even their dogs. On the contrary I had lost almost everything and was now moving away a little stuff in a borrowed wagon and was compelled to leave my children exposed to the enemy for lack of ways to bring [them].[136]

The Bertholfs went on, but Foreman did not go far. He left his belongings with a friend and returned home. Even though Blunt had won the Battle of Honey Springs, his men and horses were exhausted, and he was running short of ammunition. Foreman heard talk that Cooper, finally reinforced by General Cabell, would run the federals out of Fort Gibson in less than a week. "I replied," Foreman wrote, "if our men will stand and fight, it will be done, but that is the question, will they do it."[137] By July 29, the situation seemed much better. Foreman wrote, "As we could not get along without the articles I had left at Mr. Scales' in our late stampede, I brought them back, yet not without some doubts . . . . I have concluded to wait awhile before we make a final move."[138]

On the afternoon of August 7, Foreman, who in his role of Cherokee national treasurer had business with Colonel Watie, went to see him at his camp at Soda Spring about twelve miles from North Fork Town. Foreman wrote in his diary later, "My object was to learn if I could, what was doing . . . . I asked the Col. also his opinion with regard to the removal of all the Cherokee families to Boggy Depot [Choctaw Nation]. His reply was that . . . it was his opinion still that they might [need] to go and prepare for the winter, for there was no certainty of safety here, and as to the promises made for help here he put no confidence in them. The Col. had little to say, yet I thought he spoke more discouragingly than I ever heard him."[139]

While Foreman was at the Cherokee camp, the pickets stationed at Chimney Mountain near the Texas Road sent word the enemy was coming. That news set the troops in camp scrambling for their horses, saddling up, and checking their firearms. Watie rode to Chimney Mountain to see what was happening. Nothing that Foreman could see warranted such alarm. "Yet," he wrote, "all the trains, the infantry, and families in camp, had crossed the creek and were going full tilt towards B[riartown?] . . . . No one with whom I conversed thought there was any danger or that the danger, if any, was sufficient to warrant such a stampede. All however moved off as if the enemy were in gunshot, except the cavalry."[140]

Foreman said later,

> I concluded from the movements today that either our men were great cowards, or this was a maneuver of Genl. Steel's [sic] to justify his and Cabble's [sic] falling back to Fort Smith . . . . His and Genl. Cabble's men have been running away all the time, nearly, since they came up, but not without stealing some of the best horses belonging to the Creek and Cherokee regiments. When Genl. Steel first came up from Fort Smith, it was said he would whip the Feds out of Gibson in two weeks, and this is the way he is doing it, the Feds are coming out of Gibson but they are after Steel. Why he has not even tried no one knows probably but himself. This is the protection promised the Indians! We will get fat on it, sure.[141]

Col. Stand Watie shared Foreman's opinion of the Confederate military. Two days later he wrote a letter to the chief of the Muscogee Nation. It stated that Confederate promises to protect the Indian nations had been "a useless and expensive pageant." The Indian nations would have to rely on themselves now to protect their own country, but he had faith they could do it. He concluded, "if we possess the spirit of our fathers, and are resolved never to be enslaved by an inferior race, and trodden under the feet of an ignorant and insolent foe we, the Creeks, Choctaws, Chickasaws, Seminoles, and Cherokees, never can be conquered by the Kansas jayhawkers, renegade Indians, and runaway negroes."[142]

Watie knew the door for a federal invasion of the territory was now open. The Union factions of the Indian nations had fled to Kansas in 1861 and 1862. Now in 1863 the pro-Confederate factions were looking for safety elsewhere. As he stated in this letter, "scarcely a Southern family is left east and north of the Arkansas River."[143] Most had sought refuge in Arkansas, farther south in the other Indian nations, or Texas. Even those Union sympathizers who had come back a few months earlier dared go no farther than the entrenchments around Fort Gibson. All of the Indian Territory had become, one way or another, "an enemy's country" and thus fair game for pillage and destruction.

Most of the refugees did not know what, if anything, might remain when they returned home. Some, such as the Vann-Coodey family of Webber's Falls, already had their answer: nothing. Many already understood that "home" was now a place in the mind and heart, but probably no longer a reality.

Mrs. William P. Ross, a Union Cherokee refugee in Kansas, wrote to her young son that August, "I still intend to go back to the Nation, but whether there will be peace, safety and pleasure living there for a long time to come is doubtful . . . . things will be changed. Many of our friends have scattered . . . . Others dead, yet others are estranged one from the other."[144]

Expressing much the same longing for home, Col. James M. Bell of Watie's 2nd Cherokee Mounted Rifles wrote to his wife, Caroline, "I would like the best in the world . . . if we had our Country." He wanted the peace and ordinary things of life, to "hear the cows lowing the hogs squealing and see the nice garden and the yard with roses in it the waving wheat and stately corn growing . . . no one in want and [to] be blessed with the society of those I love most on earth you and our children."[145]

The log house belonging to Dr. William Vann, Cherokee, was typical of homes among the eastern Indian Territory nations in the Civil War period. *Photograph courtesy of the Research Division, Oklahoma Historical Society.*

"Hunter's Home" near Park Hill, Oklahoma, was built in the 1840s by George M. and Minerva Ross Murrell, the latter Cherokee. It is maintained by the Oklahoma Historical Society and open to the public. *Photograph by the author.*

This parlor furniture at "Hunter's Home" near Park Hill, Oklahoma, belonged to Cherokee principal chief John Ross. *Photograph by the author.*

Robert M. Jones (1808?–1873), Choctaw, here with his wife, Susan Colbert Jones, was one of the wealthiest men in the West, the largest slave owner in the Indian Territory, and an ardent secessionist. *Photograph courtesy of the Research Division, Oklahoma Historical Society.*

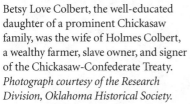

Betsy Love Colbert, the well-educated daughter of a prominent Chickasaw family, was the wife of Holmes Colbert, a wealthy farmer, slave owner, and signer of the Chickasaw-Confederate Treaty. *Photograph courtesy of the Research Division, Oklahoma Historical Society.*

Presbyterian minister Stephen Foreman (1807–1881), Cherokee, also served his nation as its first superintendent of public instruction, clerk of the Cherokee Senate, executive council member, and Supreme Court associate justice. *Photograph courtesy of the Research Division, Oklahoma Historical Society.*

Black Beaver, or Sucktummahkway (1806–1880), Delaware, was a respected trader, guide, and mediator on the frontier. *Photograph courtesy of the Research Division, Oklahoma Historical Society.*

Showetat, or Caddo George Washington (d. 1883), chief of the Caddo Tribe's White Bead Band, refused to leave his Indian Territory homeland when war threatened. He signed a Confederate treaty and led the Frontier Guard. *Photograph courtesy of the Research Division, Oklahoma Historical Society.*

John Chupco (c. 1800–1881) led one of the last Seminole emigrating parties to the Indian Territory. He was chief of the Loyal Seminoles while serving as first sergeant of Company F, 1st Regiment, Union Indian Home Guard. *Photograph courtesy of the Research Division, Oklahoma Historical Society.*

Capt. Peter Maytubby (1837–1907), Chickasaw-Choctaw, commanded a company of the Confederate-allied Choctaw-Chickasaw Mounted Rifles during the Civil War. *Photograph courtesy of the Research Division, Oklahoma Historical Society.*

Elias Cornelius Boudinot (1830–1890) fought with the Confederate-allied Cherokee troops and served as the Cherokee Nation's delegate to the Confederate Congress. *Photograph courtesy of the Research Division, Oklahoma Historical Society.*

During the Civil War, Sarah Caroline Bell Watie (1820–1882), Cherokee, took her family and slaves to Texas, managed a farm, educated her children, and worried about her husband Stand Watie and teen-aged son Saladin, serving in Watie's regiment. *Photograph courtesy of the Research Division, Oklahoma Historical Society.*

Col. Tandy Walker (1814–1877), Choctaw, commanded Choctaw and Chickasaw troops in battle at Honey Springs, Indian Territory; Newtonia, Missouri; and Poison Spring, Arkansas. *Photograph courtesy of the Research Division, Oklahoma Historical Society.*

Satanta, or White Bear (c. 1820–1878), Kiowa, a respected warrior at the 1864 Battle of Adobe Walls, was also a noted orator who represented his nation at the Little Arkansas and Medicine Lodge negotiations. *Photograph courtesy of the Research Division, Oklahoma Historical Society.*

Tosawa (Toshaway), a Penateka Comanche chief, signed Albert Pike's Confederate Treaty, the Little Arkansas Treaty, and the Medicine Lodge Treaty. *Photograph courtesy of the Research Division, Oklahoma Historical Society.*

Joseph M. Perryman (1833–1896), Muscogee, served in Company H of the Confederate-allied 1st Creek Mounted Volunteers. A minister, he was also principal chief of his nation from 1884 to 1887. *Photograph courtesy of the Research Division, Oklahoma Historical Society.*

Pero Bruner (c. 1825–1910) was born a Muscogee slave. As a freedman in the post–Civil War period, he represented Canadian Colored Town in his nation's House of Warriors and was assigned Creek Dawes Roll number 1. *Photograph courtesy of the Research Division, Oklahoma Historical Society.*

Jacob W. Bartles (1842–1908) served in the 6th Kansas Volunteer Cavalry from 1861 to 1865 in the Indian Territory, Arkansas, Kansas, and Missouri. Later, as an intermarried Delaware, he helped found Dewey and Bartlesville, Oklahoma. *Photograph courtesy of the Research Division, Oklahoma Historical Society.*

Hard Rope, or Wehesaki (c. 1822–1883), a loving husband and father as well as a noted Osage warrior, confronted Confederate officers crossing the Osages' Kansas reserve in 1863. In 1868 he led Custer's scouts at the Washita Massacre. *Photograph courtesy of the Research Division, Oklahoma Historical Society.*

In 1884 a delegation of Cheyennes and Arapahos visited the Gettysburg battlefield on their way to Washington, D.C. The visitors included Cheyenne chiefs Black Wolf and Whirlwind and Arapaho chiefs Left Hand and Powder Face, veterans of the recent Plains Wars. *Photograph courtesy of the Research Division, Oklahoma Historical Society.*

Remembering the 1860s Sand Creek and Washita massacres, Cheyenne elders some-times told children such as Minnie Chips of the Red Moon Band, shown here in 1899, that they were safe now, the wars were over, and they could take their moccasins off to sleep. *Photograph courtesy of the Research Division, Oklahoma Historical Society.*

Capt. Charles S. Stewart (1808–1861) commanded Company I, 9th Texas Cavalry, and was killed November 19, 1861, in the first Indian Territory battle with Opothle Yahola's follow-ers. His fellow Texans buried him in an unmarked grave near the junction of the Cimarron and Arkansas Rivers. *Photograph courtesy of the Research Division, Oklahoma Historical Society.*

Cherokee colonel Stand Watie regretted the death of his former friend, "poor Andy Nave," who refused to surrender during Watie's 1863 raid on Tahlequah and Park Hill, Cherokee Nation. He is buried in the Ross Cemetery near Park Hill, Oklahoma. *Photograph by the author.*

Kat-caf-fa-la-sah, a private in Company D, 1st Regiment, Union Indian Home Guard, made up mostly of Muscogees, Seminoles, runaway slaves, and free blacks, died September 5, 1863, at about age thirty-three. He is buried at Fort Gibson National Cemetery, Oklahoma. *Photograph by the author.*

CHAPTER FIVE

Scattered Like Leaves

I n 1878 a writer, reminiscing about the Civil War in the Indian Territory, stated, "The war to preserve the union of States surged over the boundaries of the Indian Territory and swept the Indians from their homes, scattered them like leaves from the forest to the ends of the earth."[1] It was an apt description of what happened from 1861 to 1865 to people of all races and nations who shared the territory. They were at the mercy of events over which they had little or no control.

While their Cherokee neighbors had been in turmoil for at least two years, things were relatively calm in the Muscogee Nation once Opothle Yahola's followers left. A trickle of refugees, though, still made their way toward the Kansas camps or to the Red River valley, depending on their politics and circumstances. With the pro-Confederate faction remaining as the majority in the Muscogee Nation, the national government passed a series of punitive laws aimed at the Union faction. One confiscated the property of "our citizens holding northern proclivities"; another ordered it sold with the proceeds going to the national treasury. Still another law required that free blacks who joined the "northern" faction be sold back into slavery if they were caught. This could compound the danger for black soldiers in the Indian Home Guard or 1st Kansas Colored once they entered the Muscogee Nation.[2]

As dislocation increased, so did disease. In 1862 some Cherokees sent their slaves for safekeeping to the Fort Gibson area. Located close to the backwaters of the Grand, Verdigris, and Arkansas Rivers, the site had long been known as unhealthful, contributing to a high disease and death rate among federal troops stationed there. In 1834 and 1835 alone, 298 soldiers had sickened and died while at that post. The federal military department had abandoned it in 1857 as its frontier role declined. However, in October 1862, Texans in Alexander's and Bass's regiments occupied what was left of the fort and grounds.[3] Rochelle Allred Ward, a slave of the Cherokee Beck family in the Flint District, was about fourteen when her owners loaded their slaves into ox carts and sent them to Fort Gibson for safekeeping. There were few buildings still standing, so soldiers lived in tents that filled the surrounding grounds. There was certainly no place to house the influx of slaves. Rochelle said, "The negroes piled in there from everywhere, and I mean there was lots of them, too. Cooking in the open, sleeping most anywhere, making shelter places out of cloth scraps and brush, digging caves along the river bank to live in. There was no way to keep the place clean for there was too many folks living all in one place, and if you walk around in the night-time most likely you stumble over some negro rolled up in a dirty blanket and sleeping under a bush."[4] In addition to the crowd of soldiers and slaves, Cherokee women and children, seeking protection once most of their men left to fight, also moved near the fort, camping about a mile to the east for some eighteen months.[5]

So many people living in one spot, lacking adequate sanitation, housing, and food, were vulnerable to contagious diseases. For example, smallpox, brought back from Mexico by a Kiowa trading party, spread during the winter of 1861–1862. By February Arapaho chief Little Raven reported that smallpox was in the Comanche and Kiowa camps along the Arkansas River downstream from Fort Wise in southeastern Colorado and that many people were dying.[6] Blackbird Doublehead, a Cherokee teenager then, remembered that a particularly virulent epidemic of "black smallpox" swept through the Cherokee Nation in June, July, and August of 1862. His sister was one of many who died of this deadly hemorrhagic form of the disease which blackened the skin until it looked charred. "This was one of the worst diseases ever to hit the Cherokee Nation," he said. "People died by the hundreds and graves could be found just everywhere in the hills. The Cherokee women would dig shallow graves and bury their dead."[7]

Rochelle Allred Ward recalled another epidemic that occurred sometime after the Union troops occupied Fort Gibson in 1863. "Then come the time of cholera; people die all that season, and the dead—seem like they pass and pass all the time—was carried on little two wheel wagons pulled by a mule to a burying place out near the National Cemetery," she said. Both soldiers and civilians were victims. While the bodies of the soldiers were eventually buried in the National Cemetery, "the slaves," she said, "was buried back in the woods to the north."[8] Throughout the war years, the Indian Territory saw contagious diseases circulate through its population, particularly among those in the military and far-flung refugee camps.

Smallpox apparently struck one family just before they fled in "the stampede" of civilians after the Battle of Honey Springs. Polly Barnett, a Muscogee who was about nine at the time, remembered that her family decided then to go to the Chickasaw Nation. With no men left at home, the women and children began loading the wagons and had not finished when soldiers came. They broke the spokes out of the wagon wheels and then started into the house. The women told the soldiers that one of them had smallpox, which stopped some of the men. Others, though, had already had the disease and went on inside. After they took what they could find, they burned the smokehouse along with the remaining stores of meat and lard. Once the soldiers left, the women repaired the wagons and began their trip south. They had only gone a short distance when someone, hidden by the dense morning fog, shot a young Indian boy driving one of the wagons. They dared not stop and drove on a few miles before pausing long enough to bury his body near the road.[9]

Polly's family was part of the wave of Muscogee refugees that fled toward the Red River valley after the Confederate allies' defeat at the Battle of Honey Springs on July 17. Some stopped in the southern Chickasaw or Choctaw Nations, while others went on across the river into north Texas. Opothle Yahola's followers had begun the exodus from the Muscogee Nation in 1861. These "Southern" Muscogees continued it in 1863, leaving their country virtually deserted.

Many civilians, along with Cherokee Presbyterian minister and national treasurer Stephen Foreman, were not sure whether to flee or stay. After his August 8 visit with Colonel and Principal Chief Stand Watie, Foreman returned to North Fork Town, where he was living temporarily with his children, supervised by his daughter Susie, then twenty-one.[10] In the last year or so they had fled from their own home near Park Hill in the Cherokee Nation to Creek Agency and then on to North Fork Town. In "the stampede" after the Confederate loss at Honey Springs, Foreman had moved his belongings to a safe place farther south and rejoined his children. However, when Maj. Gen. James G. Blunt marched his Union troops back to Fort Gibson and nothing more happened, Foreman had retrieved his possessions, which the family needed for daily use, "yet not without some doubts as to the propriety of the move," according to his diary.[11]

The uneasy peace continued for about a month. Conditions were not good among the Confederate allies. After the Battle of Honey Springs, Brig. Gen. Douglas H. Cooper had dispersed his troops, sending some east and some west to find adequate grazing for their horses, while he pulled back south into the Choctaw country. Morale was low, and Indian civilians complained about the Confederacy's inattention toward the Indian Territory and the failure of the allies to stand and fight.[12] Stand Watie, writing as the principal chief of the Cherokee Nation, reminded the Choctaw and Chickasaw governors that what happened to his nation mattered to them all. All was not yet lost, he said, and concluded, "I believe that, by a united and unyielding opposition of all our Indian forces, we can make the country untenable to our enemies, and hold it against any force they may send against us." Traditional Indian guerrilla warfare had proved its effectiveness long ago. Referring to the 1830s and 1840s conflict in Florida, which had cost the federal government dearly in treasure and soldiers' lives, Watie continued, "The courageous Seminoles have shown what folly it is to try to subjugate or destroy a people determined to defend their rights and their homes."[13]

Eventually, Brig. Gen. William Steele, whose Confederate headquarters was in Fort Smith, Arkansas, decided to take personal command of operations in the Indian Territory. Leaving a few troops behind, he moved west, planning to gather Confederate forces along Elk Creek with the goal of retaking Fort Gibson. Its garrison, he knew, was weakened by sickness. Unfortunately, Steele's own army was shrinking rapidly. His Arkansas troops, officers and enlisted men alike, were deserting, he said, "leaving nightly in tens and fifties."[14] He believed they had little stake in the war or real commitment to the Confederate cause. The Muscogee troops refused to go beyond the Canadian River, which was their southern national border, and some of them and his Cherokee troops were even slipping away to join the enemy. He had started west expecting reinforcements from other Confederate armies in the region, but they were diverted elsewhere. To make matters worse, Steele learned that Fort Gibson had received reinforcements of both troops and artillery. The whole picture became so gloomy by late August Steele could see nothing to do but pull back toward the Red River valley and dig in—even though he lacked engineers, entrenching tools, and labor competent enough to build defensive fortifications.[15]

Meanwhile, at Fort Gibson General Blunt learned of the Confederate build-up some sixty miles south and decided to confront Steele. On the evening of August 22 he crossed the Arkansas River again and headed that way.[16] Stephen Foreman wrote worriedly the next day, a Sunday, "We are still here but how much longer we shall remain unmolested it is difficult to tell, as almost everybody feels unsafe on account of the various rumors afloat that our forces will certainly fall back, if the Feds advance on us. There was much riding about today by the Creek soldiers and others, yet no one could account for it only that something was up more than usual."[17]

As Steele pulled back south along the Texas Road, Blunt came down behind him, expecting the rebels to stop and fight at some point. Instead, Steele sent General William L. Cabell back toward Fort Smith with part of the army and went on south with Brigadier General Cooper's command toward Perryville. At that small community on the Texas Road in the northern Choctaw Nation, he had established a depot.[18]

By then, the alarm had buzzed through the North Fork Town vicinity telling civilians to get out of the way if they could. Stunned, Stephen Foreman wrote later, "For a few moments I was confused not knowing what to do, or where to begin. It was dark and we had but one small two horse wagon in which to put our stuff. We went to work, however, and loaded up, putting in some of our most valuable goods, barely leaving room for the children and myself."[19]

It was nearly midnight by the time they finished, and a very cold north wind was blowing. Since it was really too late to get on the road and there had been so many false alarms lately, Foreman decided to wait for morning. After an early breakfast he and Susie loaded everyone into the overflowing wagon, but they left some things with friends who stoutly refused to leave, "Feds or no Feds," according to Foreman. Having been forced to flee so many times before, the Foreman family grieved for the reminders of home they had to abandon: "some books that had been used in the family, and half-worn garments of those who had died, and other small articles such as augers, gimlet, awls, candel [*sic*] sticks, etc., all were necessary however in a family." They found the road jammed with refugees going both directions. Some had everything they owned in a small wagon or loaded on a pony and were going south. Others had already crossed the Canadian River with some of their belongings and were coming back for more.[20]

The following morning was cool and crisp with the first touch of fall. The family had found shelter with friends, and Foreman, having decided there was no immediate danger, went looking for a yoke of oxen to help move the rest of his belongings over from North Fork Town. As he exchanged rumors with other worried civilians, he learned that the Muscogee troops' supply train had been sent west toward the Little River and that Cooper was being driven back toward Briartown and Perryville. He also heard that the federals had burned North Fork Town about noon, but he discounted that story. By sundown he was back with his children but decided to wait until morning to go on south.[21]

He had waited too long. About an hour after dark, federal troops suddenly surrounded the house in which they were staying. Foreman wrote later, "Pretty soon a number of them rode up . . . and asked several questions. They wanted to know who he was and if he had seen any southern soldiers pass late in the evening. I replied, No. They said it was a lie, they knew better." He retreated into the house, but they dismounted and followed him inside. Foreman said, "about that time Susie and the other children were around me and Susie did the principal talking. This relieved me much for I knew they would not hurt women and children if they were any sort of gentlemen." He hid under a counter in a darkened room, but they came in after him, he wrote,

> with their pistols drawn and cocked, and a few coals of fire on a shovel [for] light . . . I went up to them and told them I surrendered, that I [had] no weapons, that I was not a soldier. They cursed me for an old rascal, and presented their pistols to my breast and ordered me into the room . . . where there was a light . . . . Quite a number of soldiers had by this time collected in the room where the children were . . . . I sat down in a chair in the midst of them not knowing but the next thing would be to shoot me through or cut off my head with a saber. But they offered no further insults as they saw by the fire light that my head was silvered over with age and Susie told them I was her father. The younger children also began to cry aloud and say,

They are going to kill Pa. The scene I thought must have moved them, at least the officer in command for while the children were crying and Susie was standing by me with her hand on my head, saying I was her father, the officer . . . said, No, your father shall not be hurt . . . . I felt a relief I could not describe.[22]

The officer, who clearly did not know that Foreman was a high-ranking member of Stand Watie's Confederate-allied Cherokee government, questioned him, asking why he was running away. Foreman wrote,

I told him I wished to get out of the way of the fighting. You are running the wrong way, he replied . . . . They staied [sic] but a short time, but they kept busy stealing various articles in and about the house. They took two summer coats, two saddles, one bed blanket, one rifle gun, and three horses from the door yard . . . . Susie begged them for her blanket and I begged them for my saddle and gun but to no purpose. When they got all they wanted . . . they left without saying a word to me further.[23]

Foreman, afraid the Union troopers might come back, left the capable Susie in charge of her younger brothers and sister and hid in the brush all night, cold, frightened, and sleepless. Early next morning he heard "the Feds and negroes catching the horses" and went two miles farther away, stopping at an abandoned house. There, Foreman said, "I found an abundance of provisions, some cooked and some not. The family from every appearance had left during the night or very early in the morning before I arrived. Everything was left in confusion, as if the family were frightened, the doors even not locked and there was much valuable stuff left exposed, not only to the Feds, but to Tom, Dick, and Harry." He waited awhile, but when no one came back he helped himself to a breakfast of watermelons, dried beef, and sweet potatoes.[24]

Hoping the enemy soldiers had left the area, he slipped back to see about his children but waited until nearly dark to approach. He found them repacking the wagon and getting ready to leave but not sure where to go. After a joyful reunion, Foreman said,

I helped them to load the wagon and at the same time listened to their different tales of trouble they experienced while I was absent. It seemed the negroes who were going to the Feds had tried to make the children believe that they had to go to

Northfork for protection, if they did not, the Pins and negroes would be back shortly and rob and kill everybody without distinction. Taylor [not quite fifteen] was of the opinion that they ought to go back to Northfork for safety. Susie was opposed to going back and was crying when I came. Mrs. Wade [another refugee] was also opposed to going to Northfork, yet was not decided what it was best to do. She was inclined to linger about the place, hoping Mr. Wade might come in, who had disappeared the evening before like some others. From the account given by Mrs. Wade and the children, of the Pins and negroes, I gave it as my opinion we had better go up the Canadian toward Little river, the way the Creek trains had gone. After seeing that everything was in the wagon, Susie and Taylor thought I had better go on and not travel the road for fear of the Pins and negroes who were expected about that time. They thought they would be able to get along without me. All things considered I thought it was best to go on and take care of myself, as the children said.[25]

It was some time before Foreman was finally reunited with his family. Meanwhile, he traveled and camped alone in unfamiliar country along the Canadian River valley. "It was a wild looking place where owls and wolves dwelt," he wrote, "but after building a fire and hitching my pony to a bush, I laid down and slept as soundly as if I were in a palace." Near the Canadian River crossing on the well-traveled road, he heard roosters crowing and followed the sound half a mile through bushes and briars, hoping to find shelter. As was the case with other homes he had come across, on this farmstead he wrote, "The houses were deserted, the family had evidently left in confusion. No living thing was about but some chickens, hogs, and two or three half starved dogs."[26]

It was about this time that Jennie Grayson's family faced much the same decision as the Foremans. She and her husband, James, mixed-blood Muscogees, had worked a small farm near North Fork Town, reared six children, and given them the best education they could. James died about 1860, leaving Jennie and George Washington, the eldest, to care for the family. When word came that General Blunt was coming down from Fort Gibson and Cooper and Steele were retreating to the Choctaw Nation, Wash, about twenty, was serving in the 2nd Creek Mounted Regiment. In his autobiography he wrote that the retreat left families exposed to an enemy that was destroying everything in its path.

Each family had to decide quickly what to do. They could stay in their homes and trust in the mercy of the federal troops but would likely be forced into the refugee camps around Fort Gibson. The alternative was to load up their belongings and follow the Confederate retreat into the Choctaw Nation. Grayson, like other Muscogee soldiers, made a quick trip home to check on his folks.[27]

He found Jennie and the children debating whether to stay there, join James's parents in the northern Choctaw Nation, or go farther south. Looking back, Grayson wrote, "The idea of loading into one small ox wagon a few supplies and groceries that would last but a very few weeks at most, and starting out with a mother and four helpless children, appeared to be going right into a state of starvation and ruin." Jennie favored staying home with the youngest children but sending Sam and Pilot, the older boys and the ones most likely to be caught up in the war, away with their grandparents. Malone, one of the smaller boys, Grayson remembered, "cried and said when the enemy came and killed him it would hurt, and he was afraid to stay." Sam, though, helped make the decision to go by saying he believed their family could make it if anybody could. At about age fourteen, he was approaching manhood by Muscogee standards and was willing to take responsibility for the family after Wash rejoined his regiment. That being the case, Jennie and Wash agreed with Sam that the family should leave. They quickly loaded their wagon, hitched up their only team, and set off to join their relatives in the Choctaw Nation. Years later Wash gave Sam credit for "holding our family together and preventing the separation . . . which we afterward knew would have been most disastrous."[28]

Grayson then went looking for his regiment but, he wrote, "found the whole command more or less dispersed throughout the country, each man of family being absorbed with considerations for the safety and removal south of his women and children." He could not locate his own family over in the Choctaw country because his grandparents' homeplace was deserted. They had become alarmed and left two days earlier, "going south over some of the rockiest and roughest roads in that entire country."[29] He and a white Confederate soldier he met along the way traveled south together on back trails, dodging Union troops. Consequently, they missed Blunt's attack on Perryville in the Choctaw Nation, although they could hear the artillery fire. They rejoined

Steele's army in August at his headquarters near Boggy Depot, a settlement close to the Clear Boggy Creek crossing on the Texas Road.[30]

Blunt had moved into the Choctaw Nation on August 24 and the next morning skirmished with a Choctaw company left to keep watch for him. Through the day federal troops were close behind Steele's rearguard, and they frequently exchanged fire. The federals reached Perryville about eight o'clock in the evening and found Confederate troops behind barricades with two howitzers blocking the road into the little town. Four companies of the 6th Kansas Cavalry hurried up with their own two howitzers and deployed on foot. During the short moonlit battle, federal fire with Sharps carbines and the howitzers drove the Confederate troops out. As they retreated from the town, the Union soldiers poured in. This was the only Confederate depot between North Fork Town and Boggy Depot, and they found a significant stockpile of supplies. General Blunt had them remove what he could use. Then on the justification that almost every building in the settlement held Confederate property, he had the whole place burned. That done, Blunt turned back north. Steele was out of his reach, and his men were tired from their forty-mile march. Instead, he turned toward Fort Smith, Arkansas, taking it without a shot fired on September 1. That loss severely damaged Confederate hopes for holding the Indian Territory and surrounding region, while it potentially opened the Arkansas River supply route to Fort Gibson.[31]

Even with these events and the resulting "stampede," some people in the Cherokee and Muscogee Nations chose to stay in their homes and take what came. Although Malucy Bear was a small child then, living in the western Muscogee Nation near Okemah, she recalled, "It was a fearful time." After most of the men left for Kansas to avoid serving in the pro-Confederate regiments, Malucy remembered that their women and children were defenseless. Raiders, showing no mercy, came and took whatever they wanted from Indian homes. Their victims dared not protest. Malucy said, "We would often take to the bushes and thickets where we would stay in hiding all during the day and return to what was left of our homes during the night." Although they had wanted no part of the war, eventually, Malucy concluded, "Most of the neighboring country was laid in waste by the raiders and the small skirmishes that took place by the different hostile parties."[32]

SCATTERED LIKE LEAVES

Relatively speaking, the Choctaw Nation avoided the worst upheaval and devastation of the Civil War. However, the Graham family, who were slave owners, looked for shelter after the head of the family left to join the Union army. Thomas Graham, a child then, told his descendants that they camped in caves or under overhanging rocks. However, the best hiding place was in the dense canebrakes in the Kiamichi River valley. Food was scarce, and young Thomas often had only one meal a day—wild potatoes or whatever Choctaw dish his mother could contrive, along with corn bread or a bread made from dried slippery elm bark pounded into flour.[33]

By late 1863 the Choctaw and Chickasaw Nations were being flooded with refugees from other parts of the Indian Territory. Conditions and events caused the Cherokee Vann-Coodey family to move at least three times after their fine home at Webber's Falls was burned. At one place they stayed, Mrs. John Salaule Vann, with her husband and older sons away with the Confederate Cherokee troops, heard that some refugee girls had been molested in the area. That very night she took her sixteen-year-old daughter Ella Coodey and younger children from their latest shelter and set off farther south through the Choctaw Nation. Ella said she learned to sleep rolled up in a quilt under a tree during that trip. With the few household goods they had been able to save, they finally settled in a rented two-room cabin near Bloomfield Academy in the Chickasaw Nation close to today's Achille, Oklahoma. Intermarried Cherokee Israel G. Vore had moved his family and slaves there earlier in the war, and a Cherokee refugee colony collected nearby. A month after moving her family into their latest home, Mrs. Vann gave birth to another son.[34]

Many refugees, though, went on across the Red River into Texas, believing it would be safer than the Indian Territory. Stephen Foreman eventually made his way to the Red River valley during the "stampede" following the Battle of Honey Springs. While staying at Chickasaw governor Winchester Colbert's home in September, he wrote,

> A great many of the Creeks have also passed, on their way to some better camping place where water and grass are more abundant. Many of them are in a very destitute condition. All that they [have] now is a pony, one [or] two pot vessels, and a few old dirty bed clothes and wearing apparel. If they ever had

any more it is left behind at the mercy of their enemies. But many who passed I was acquainted with and knew to be in good circumstances having an abundance of everything, now their all is put into one or two small wagons.[35]

The person who became responsible for these uprooted people was Brig. Gen. Samuel Bell Maxey. A West Point graduate and Mexican War veteran from Paris, Texas, Maxey took charge of the Indian Territory for the Confederacy on December 11, 1863, replacing Brig. Gen. William Steele. Within days he wrote his wife, Matilda, from Doaksville, Choctaw Nation, "there is a great deal to do and the duties not well defined. I not only have control of the Troops, but am ex officio Superintendent of Indian Affairs .... Among other things I have to feed hundreds of indigent Indians." He was expected to settle intertribal conflicts, defend the Indian Territory, recover Union-held ground, and keep north Texas safe from a federal invasion. It would be "a Herculean task. Even the troops I have," he wrote, "are to a large extent Indians, and no Infantry [his emphasis]. It is the first Army I ever heard of without Infantry."[36]

Maxey understood that the Indian Territory was more than a backwater of the Confederacy. He wrote, "If the Indian Territory gives way, the granary of the Trans-Mississippi Department, the breadstuffs, and beef of this and the Arkansas army are gone, the left flank of [department commander] Holmes' army is turned, and with it not only the meat and bread, but the salt and iron of what is left of the Trans-Mississippi Department."[37] While there was no iron being mined in the Indian Territory, it was being produced in neighboring Missouri, which became more vulnerable if the Indian Territory was lost. Maxey also respected the national perspectives and rights of the Indian nations. Unfortunately, like Steele before him, he had an obstacle and rival in Brig. Gen. Douglas H. Cooper, a longtime favorite of the Indians and a man with influential friends.[38] Albert Pike, who had been in the same situation, wrote to Maxey six months after he began his new assignment, "I do not want to see you, also, demolished by being in command of the Indian Territory."[39] Another friend wrote, "I tremble for you." The assignment, he said, could leave Maxey a great success or a great failure.[40]

On taking command in late 1863, Maxey found the Confederate-allied troops in north Texas, western Arkansas, and the Indian Territory "very much demoralized" and the Indian national governments on the verge of making peace overtures to the Union.[41] They were even considering forming their own confederacy and including the Plains tribes, an idea that might have altered the course of American western development. Maxey made the rounds of their troop camps, gave stirring talks, and met with the leaders of the Indian nations to listen to their complaints and reassure them. He supported their objection to a plan of military reorganization combining Indian with white units. Instead, they agreed to the reorganization that produced the Cherokee Brigade made up of Cherokees, Chickasaws, and Osages, commanded by Col. Stand Watie; the Creek Brigade, of Muscogees and Seminoles, commanded by Col. Daniel N. McIntosh; and the Choctaw Brigade, commanded by Col. Tandy Walker. That reorganization spurred Indian enlistment and reenlistment, along with some calls for adult male conscription.[42]

However, with the reorganization and changeover in command, very little military action occurred through the fall and early winter of 1863–1864. The exception was raiding by Watie in the vicinity of Tahlequah and Park Hill. On November 12 he wrote his wife, Sarah Caroline Bell Watie (Sallie), that he had captured some of the Ross family but did not kill them because she had asked that he spare old Mrs. Jack Ross that pain. However, Watie wrote, "Killed a few Pins in Tahlequah. They had been holding council. I had the old council house set on fire and burnt down, also John Ross's house." Andy Nave, a former friend and John Ross's son-in-law, was also dead, he told Sallie, shot because he would not surrender when cornered, "but it could not be helped."[43] Wilfred Knight in his account of Watie's Civil War commented that the colonel's bare-bones account disguised the intense bitterness Watie felt toward Ross and his followers, stoked by the 1839 assassination of Watie's brother Elias Boudinot, his uncle Major Ridge, and cousin John Ridge.[44]

About a month later, Watie returned to the Cherokee Nation, planning to raid the Grand River valley. At the time, troop strength at Fort Gibson was low. The white and black troops had been ordered elsewhere, leaving only the Unionist "Pin" Indians. Capt. Andrew C. Spillman marched them toward Park Hill, the scene of Watie's latest raid, and followed him northeast up the Barren Fork River. Spillman's 290 men and one howitzer were enough to break up an attack by Watie's larger force, ending that incursion.[45]

With the military aspect of his responsibilities more or less dealt with, Brigadier General Maxey turned his attention to the refugee problem, which was daunting. He later wrote Col. S. S. Scott, Confederate commissioner of Indian affairs,

> Thousands of helpless women and children of the Cherokee, Creek, and Seminole Nations had been driven from their Homes by the merciless foe. Their husbands, fathers, sons and brothers were in our army. They were driven out many of them in a state of destitution, others nearly so, whilst a few have the means of subsistence left. They were houseless wanderers. Apart from the sacred obligations of Treaty, it was an act of humanity to provide as best I could for these suffering exiled friends and neighbors.[46]

To make matters worse, the winter of 1863–1864 was the coldest since 1832. A few things worked to the benefit of refugees who arrived in the Red River valley in late 1863. Some, such as the Vann-Coodey family, found fellow Cherokees, friends, and relatives—the Hankses, Gulagers, Carrs, Brewers, and Schrimpschers—already there, some reestablished on farms and plantations.[47] Sallie Watie was one of the later Cherokee refugees. She moved to the vicinity of Rusk, Texas, with her younger children and two or three slaves by late spring 1863. Her sisters were already living in that vicinity. Still, the responsibility for moving and resettling her household fell to her, with her husband, Stand Watie, many miles away, preoccupied with the war and heading the Confederate-allied faction of the Cherokee Nation. She could turn to her relatives or write to him for advice, but ultimately she was the one who purchased farmland, oversaw the slaves who worked it, and got her children enrolled in school before the September session began. Underlying all the challenges of daily living was Sallie's concern for her husband and teenaged son Saladin, a captain in his regiment. She wrote, "I wish I could just see you an hour or two . . . . I cant stay away so long from you. It greaves [sic] me to think that we are so far from each other if any thing should happen we are too far for to help each other."[48]

Many "Southern" Indian refugees stayed on the north side of the Red River in Choctaw and Chickasaw country. Citizens of those nations, with customary Indian hospitality, welcomed them and treated them with generosity. Elizabeth Kemp, daughter of Joel Kemp, the Chickasaw national treasurer, was about thirteen when the Civil War began and lived in far-southern Panola County, Chickasaw Nation. She recalled, "The refugees from the Cherokee Nation came in bunches and settled near us during the war. They were without food, and I have often seen them gathering the tender leaves from mulberry trees and cooking them for greens. Father would kill a beef and hogs and divide out among them; also let them have corn to make bread. They would dig briar root, which was sweet and brittle like potatoes, and mix it with the meal when they didn't have enough for bread."[49]

Martha Gibson, a Muscogee who was also thirteen when the Civil War began, lived in a settlement east of today's Eufaula, Oklahoma, until about 1863. Then Union troops invaded the neighborhood and ordered her father, a white man, to move his family to Fort Gibson. Instead, Martha said, "We hitched our mules to a wagon and loaded what little stuff we could get in right quick and started south." When they arrived at the Red River, her father decided they would stay in the Choctaw country, which seemed relatively quiet. According to Martha, "He went to work and built us a little log house and cleared a little ground and we farmed there until the war was over. We did our cooking on a log fire out in front of our cabin. We had a hard time getting anything to eat part of the time and would have starved if the Choctaws had not divided with us. But they were always willing to give us a part of anything they had that we needed."[50] Meanwhile, that fall an estimated 100,000 bushels of corn lay un-gathered and wasting in fields along the Canadian River valley.[51]

There was already a refugee supply system in place when Brigadier General Maxey assumed command. He reported in August 1864 that at various times rationing officers supplied flour, beef, and soap to 4,823 Muscogees along the Washita River valley, 2,906 Cherokees at Tishomingo, 574 Seminoles at Oil Springs near Fort Washita, 241 Osages near Fort Arbuckle, 4,480 Choctaws, and 785 Chickasaws. To help clothe soldiers and refugees, Choctaw, Chickasaw, and displaced Cherokee farmers in the Red River valley raised 1,500 bales of cotton in 1864. It was shipped through Texas to Mexico and exchanged for textiles from which to make uniforms and clothing, both in short supply.[52]

Some Indian refugees found ways to clothe themselves and their families. The women carded cotton or wool fiber, spun it into thread, and wove cloth on looms they had brought from home or which were supplied by the Confederate agents working with the refugees. Martha Gibson remembered, "We women had to spin and weave our own cloth to make our clothes. We had a spinning wheel but could not bring our loom along. However, there was a white lady named Roswell who lived near us and who had a loom and no spinning wheel, so we would card and spin her thread for her and she would weave our cloth for us."[53]

The type of cooperative effort Martha described was not unusual. Ella Coodey explained, "Those who had saved their household goods by going south at the beginning of the war had their looms and wove cloth for themselves and others. We had indigo and copperas and plenty of alum for setting the colors. We boiled oak bark for different shades of brown and made a pretty purple dye of sumac." Some of the Indian women revived an American frontier custom. Ella said, "The women had gatherings they called 'hankings' where everyone would take some wool and go to the home of a friend who had a loom and spin the wool on the spinning wheel. Then the hostess would weave the goods and the cloth was divided by the guests." This combined a social gathering with work because it included a fine midday dinner and a dance in the evening.[54]

Still, the Indian refugees found basic foods, clothing, and other necessities, not to mention luxuries, were often in short supply. To make up for it, they used their ingenuity. For example, some created their own headgear and footwear. Ella Coodey recalled, "There was plenty of wheat raised in Texas and we soon learned to make hats of wheat straw, and they were both comfortable and pretty." They made shoes by cutting soles out of the uppers of worn-out men's boots and sewing the soles to new canvas uppers. The result was something resembling a sneaker that served for summer wear. Ella said, "Good crops had been raised in that section of the country, and we had plenty to eat in the way of vegetables. We were able to get sugar and flour but no tea or coffee, only a little occasionally from the Army."[55] To fill the latter shortage, people tried substitutes they called "Lincoln coffee," using parched rye, wheat, corn, or dried sweet potato peelings.[56]

Refugee life in the Red River valley had its lighter moments, too.

Young people such as Ella Coodey enjoyed dinners and dances. She said, "I remember riding horseback to go to a dance up to twenty miles distant, fording a river, dancing all night and riding home the next morning. Getting party dresses was a problem. One girl took her mother's lace curtains, dyed them and made a beautiful party dress that was the envy of all of us." To make her own, Ella cut fabric out of a very full-skirted white dress an older friend gave her, made a new bodice, and sewed it all back together as a new dress. Providing music for a dance was not difficult. Ella explained, "There were several good violinists among the Indians and the music was good. We danced the polka, schottische, waltz, and Virginia reel. An old white man of the name McCanaless, who had taught violin at Webber's Falls, went south with the Cherokees and was there at all the parties."[57]

There seemed to be few of these light moments for the Cherokees who in 1863 had returned to their own country from the refugee camps in Kansas and Missouri. With most of the men in the army, it was the women and children who did the plowing, planting, and harvesting—if there were any crops to harvest. In late May 1863 Watie led his raiders through the Cherokee Nation, taking farming implements, wagons, and livestock. Tearing down fences left crops vulnerable to free-ranging cattle, hogs, and wild animals. Watie came through again in July and August. After that, the raiders took less, Union Cherokee agent Justin Harlan wrote with sarcasm, because there was "a less number to rob and less to get by robbing."[58]

By then the elderly Agent Harlan, whose headquarters was in a barn at the fort and who had survived a recent bout of smallpox, was sorry he ever agreed to the Cherokees' return. He was also out of patience with the military's lack of action. Watie, "with 700 ragamuffins," he fumed, "took everything he could ride, or drive, or carry off, and destroyed their crops, and prevented the tending of everything planted. Seeds of all kinds and farming tools were furnished by the government, and all lost, nothing saved. What wheat was sown was not saved; there was nobody to save it but the military, and they were holding Fort Gibson." Sourly he summed up, "3,500 men, a strong fort, and six cannon, were all required to hold Fort Gibson and the territory as far as the cannon would reach."[59]

Special Agent A. G. Proctor echoed Harlan's summary and

sentiments late in November when he reported that Watie and his men had raided the Cherokee Nation three times in the last thirty days without interference from Union troops. On November 2 Watie and more than forty rebels had robbed two homes and, in view of the fort, ridden leisurely away. However, Proctor also reported that the rebel Cherokee families were so desperate for clothing the raiders were stripping it from loyal women and children.[60]

Even with so much hardship and danger, some Indian Territory families refused to leave their homes for a place that might—or might not—be safer. Jennie Lowery, a young Cherokee child living near Gideon northwest of Tahlequah during the war, remembered that soldiers routinely robbed civilians. "One morning we went to the kitchen to get breakfast," she said, "and there was nothing left to cook—they had stolen all our food. They were what was called Pin Indians." Salt was a necessity usually abundant in the Cherokee Nation. However, when it was gone, Jennie said, "We would go to the smokehouse, dig up the dirt and boil it down to get salt to use."[61]

According to family oral history, Rebecca Ketcher Neugin, a Cherokee, and her children stayed on their place near Tahlequah while her husband was a Union Indian officer. She could draw rations from Fort Gibson because of his service, but, according to her daughter Kate, the family often had to "rustle" for themselves. "Sometimes," Kate said, "when they needed fresh meat, the women would run a steer up in the chimney corner and knock him in the head. The women were ready with their butcher knives, and they would soon have the skin off and would begin to cut out the chunks of meat. Hogs were also knocked in the head by the women and the meat shared out among them." Rebecca took apples to Fort Gibson to trade for whatever she could get but left her children at home. Kate explained, "The boys had to be kept out of sight for the Confederates were watching for them. If those boys were large enough to force into the army, they would be taken and perhaps killed and even the smaller boys were sometimes killed and not always by the Confederates but sometimes it was the Pin Indians who killed those boys."[62]

Annie Eliza Hendrix, a Cherokee who was nine when the war began, remembered much the same conditions. Although her father and older brother Daniel Woodall served with the Union troops occupying Fort

Gibson, she, her mother, and younger sister stayed on their farm west of Tahlequah throughout the war. Annie recalled, "The Confederate soldiers never molested us personally, though they robbed our place of all cattle, hogs, chickens and everything we had to eat and everything else of value." To draw rations from Fort Gibson, the family walked the twenty-five-mile round trip weekly leading an old packhorse too crippled for the raiders to steal. However, after Annie's father died of smallpox in 1862, she said, "Daniel took our younger brother, William, who was twelve years of age and kept him at the barracks at Fort Gibson to protect the boy from the Confederate soldiers, as several boys near his age had been killed in homes throughout the Nation."[63]

While Watie's raids hurt loyal civilians, embarrassed the federal military, and infuriated Indian Office personnel, they were part of a tidal wave of lawlessness that afflicted the Indian Territory during the war. It could have some military or political motives, but it soon degenerated into outright looting. The armies of both sides appropriated livestock for food and transportation, sometimes paying the owners but often simply taking what they wanted. In August 1863 Special Agent A. G. Proctor reported, "Cattle are yet abundant in the [Cherokee] nation, although the consumption of the army has been enormous as well as wasteful. I have known a small party of our scouts to shoot down a large fat ox, *for a few slices of steak* [his emphasis], and leave the rest for the wolves. I mention this to illustrate the reckless disregard paid by our troops to Cherokee property."[64]

Jayhawking raids from Kansas by white men, Shawnees, Delawares, and Kickapoos, among others, had the tacit consent of federal authorities as "rebel beef," wearing the brands of Indian owners, was sold to refugee camp contractors for food rations. In the summer of 1864, after Col. William A. Phillips aggressively tracked cattle thieves taking herds from the Indian Territory to the federally controlled Osage Agency in Kansas, he was removed from command of Fort Gibson and reassigned temporarily to an administrative post at Fort Smith. Historian Arrell Morgan Gibson estimated that by the end of the war 300,000 head of cattle worth $5 million had been stolen and driven to Kansas from the Indian nations north of the Canadian River, lands nominally controlled by Union forces from mid-1863 to the end of the war.[65] South of the Canadian River in the Choctaw and Chickasaw country, there was also a high demand for Indian beef to feed the Confederate-allied army and "Southern" Indian refugees. R. P. Vann, a Cherokee in the Chickasaw Nation, said later, "They came and showed their gratitude by killing and eating our cattle and hogs at will, stealing our horses . . . so at the close of the war we were badly used up."[66] There was ample blame for stripping the Indian Territory of its wealth.

Although Stand Watie was the preeminent military raider in the Civil War Indian Territory, the infamous William Clarke Quantrill was also in the area. An 1850s immigrant to the Kansas-Missouri-Indian Territory border region, he had plunged into the sectional violence of the day, using politics to justify plunder and murder. He spent some time in northeastern Indian Territory and became a friend of Joel B. Mayes, a future Cherokee Nation principal chief. Mayes, according to some accounts, introduced him to the type of guerrilla warfare Cherokees used to defend their country against the Plains Indians. Quantrill did not enlist with Mayes in the 1st Cherokee Mounted Regiment but gathered a band of about two hundred irregulars and raided eastern Kansas from Missouri bases. His most infamous attack was on Lawrence, Kansas, on August 21, 1863. He had the town burned and left behind about 150 dead, most of them murdered men and young boys of fighting age. The next month he raided the reservation of the Black Bob Band of Shawnees near Olathe, Kansas. His men stripped the Shawnees of clothing, household goods, provisions, ponies, and equipment. As they fled, Quantrill's guerrillas fired on them and committed atrocities on those who fell behind.[67]

By early October Union troops were scouring the country for Quantrill, and Union posts throughout the region were on alert. Quantrill collected his men and moved toward the Indian Territory, intending to pass through it and winter in Texas. However, on the Texas Road near the border town of Baxter Springs, Kansas, he encountered a party of about eighty Union troops escorting Maj. Gen. James G. Blunt from Fort Scott, Kansas, to Fort Smith, Arkansas. Quantrill's raiders attacked Blunt's outnumbered party, which included his administrative staff and brass band, scattering them and killing even those who surrendered. The running fight reached "Fort Blair," a federal outpost under construction at Baxter Springs. With its cavalry guard absent, Quantrill's men overwhelmed the outnumbered men of the 2nd Kansas Colored

Infantry. After stripping the prisoners and shooting the wounded in the head, Quantrill moved on into the Indian Territory that evening, leaving behind eighty dead, although he boasted of more. It was General Blunt's worst defeat.[68]

After that, Quantrill's trip across the Indian Territory in 1863 was relatively quiet. Neither the new federal post at Cabin Creek nor Fort Gibson had received word he was in the vicinity even though federal scouts quietly trailed him. Beyond Cabin Creek his party swung southwest and crossed the Arkansas River well away from Fort Gibson. On October 10, Quantrill's men captured and killed a twelve-man patrol of Muscogee troops from the 1st Indian Home Guard. Not long afterward they reached Brig. Gen. Douglas H. Cooper's camp near Perryville. From there, they went on to Texas for the winter of 1863–1864 and allied with regional Confederate forces. In December Quantrill even joined Watie for a raid through the eastern Cherokee Nation, harassing Fort Gibson and the civilian population nearby.[69]

Quantrill's arrival in the Indian Territory posed a moral dilemma for the Confederate Trans-Mississippi Department; its commander, Lt. Gen. Edmund Kirby Smith; and his senior officers. There was no question Quantrill brought manpower to a Confederate military stretched thin. When spring came, he could take a western route back north, fatten his horses on the new prairie grass, and strike whatever target he chose in Kansas. Confederate brigadier general Henry E. McCulloch deplored Quantrill's methods, writing that his "mode of warfare is but little, if any, above the uncivilized Indian."[70] He appreciated Quantrill's services but said, "we cannot, as a Christian people, sanction a savage, inhuman warfare, in which men are to be shot down like dogs, after throwing down their arms and holding up their hands supplicating for mercy."[71] Both Kirby Smith and Brigadier General Maxey were willing to look the other way and use Quantrill.[72] Although Col. Stand Watie carried out joint missions with him, he had strong reservations about Quantrill. In April 1864, he wrote his wife, Sallie, that Quantrill had crossed the Arkansas River near Creek Agency and killed eight Creek men and shot a little boy. Watie commented, "I have always been opposed to killing women and children although our enemies have done it, yet I shall always protest against any acts of that kind."[73]

Quantrill, however, was a short-lived problem for the Confederate military. He quickly became unwelcome in Texas and the Chickasaw Nation as his men intimidated and robbed civilians there. Quantrill killed a Confederate officer in the Chickasaw Nation and escaped arrest by dodging back across the Red River into Texas. Headed later toward Boggy Depot, he fell in with Brigadier General Cooper on an expedition against Fort Smith. After it fizzled, he brushed past Fort Gibson and went back to southwest Missouri. By the time he returned to Texas, his rivals had taken command of his men. Unable to rally support in Missouri, in late 1864 he went to Kentucky and was killed in June 1865. Remnants of his guerrilla band hung on in the Indian Territory for a while. In August 1864, 300 federal troops and 150 Kansas partisans surprised and routed 65 of them at Flat Rock Ford near today's Wagoner, Oklahoma. Jesse James, who had been with Quantrill on the Lawrence raid, faked death, escaped, and continued his outlaw ways. Other former Quantrill followers dispersed. Cole Younger even claimed to have joined the regular Confederate army.[74]

Meanwhile, the Confederate allies in far-southern Indian Territory kept up their pressure on Union-occupied Fort Gibson and a cautious eye on Fort Smith. It fell easily to the Union in September 1863, but even then Gen. William L. Cabell's brigade and partisans successfully held up Union forces at Devil's Backbone Mountain long enough for the Confederate supply train to escape.[75] Some in the Indian nations were questioning the wisdom of their Confederate alliances, when in February 1864 Col. William A. Phillips launched another invasion from Fort Gibson aimed at reclaiming them for the Union. Going almost as far south as Fort Washita, his troops burned whatever might be of use to the Confederate allies. At Middle Boggy on February 9, 350 Union cavalrymen commanded by Maj. Charles Willets, along with a section of artillery, found about ninety men of the 1st Choctaw and Chickasaw Mounted Rifles and a detachment from the 20th Texas Cavalry. Captain Adam Nail, a Choctaw officer, quickly went for help from Col. John Jumper's Seminoles, camped nearby. Although the fight was soon over, its bitter outcome fueled the Confederate-allied Indians' ire. Before the Union expedition had set out, Colonel Phillips had issued a circular telling his men to take no prisoners but "to make your footsteps severe and terrible."[76] After the brief fight at Middle Boggy, they left the Confederate wounded on the ground with their throats slashed.[77]

Sgt. Jacob Perryman, once a Muscogee slave, now a soldier in the 1st Indian Home Guard, reported, "On route we killed 110 Rebels mostly Indians. Most of them were killed at their homes because Col. Phillips instructed his men not to take any prisoners for they have had all the chances to come in if they wanted to do so."[78] Daniel N. McIntosh, a Muscogee colonel, was on his way to a meeting of the General Council of the Indian Nations at Armstrong Academy in the Choctaw Nation when he had to dodge the federal troops. He, too, reported, "They took no prisoners but killed all without mercy, what number I am unable to learn . . . . How brutal the actions of the enemy! The much savage tribe of Indian who never heard of Civilization would shudder at such barbarity."[79] The Choctaws would not soon forget what had happened to their people, nor that some of these enemy troops were former slaves now wearing the blue uniform of the United States Army.

In his swath through the Choctaw Nation, Colonel Phillips distributed copies of President Lincoln's Amnesty Proclamation and sent letters to Chickasaw governor Winchester Colbert, Col. John Jumper, and Col. Daniel N. McIntosh. The General Council of the Indian Nations was meeting at Armstrong Academy just then to discuss the growing menace of Plains Indian raids on the western frontier, but the news set off a vigorous debate over what to do about the proffered Union amnesty. In the end, though, the Indian nations kept faith with their Confederate treaties.[80]

In April Col. Tandy Walker led the Choctaw Brigade into southwestern Arkansas to help repel a Union advance from the Arkansas River valley toward northwest Louisiana and east Texas. One prong, which included the 1st Kansas Colored Volunteer Infantry, reached Camden in southwest Arkansas in mid-April. Having learned that about five thousand bushels of corn were stored west of Camden, some six hundred men, including the 1st Kansas Colored, four cannon, and nearly two hundred wagons set off toward White Oak to collect it.[81] They started back on April 18 with what they could find or forage from farms and plantations along the way—"corn, bacon, stole bed-quilts, women's and children's clothing, hogs, geese, and . . . unscrupulous plunder," according to Texas colonel Charles DeMorse.[82]

Although reinforced by more troops and cannon, the Union column found its way blocked near Poison Spring by Brig. Gen. John

Sappington Marmaduke with 3,600 Confederate cavalry from Texas, Arkansas, and Missouri. Included were Col. Charles DeMorse's 29th Texas Cavalry, whom the 1st Kansas Colored had driven from the field at Honey Springs, and Col. Tandy Walker's Choctaw Brigade. In the latter were Choctaws whose country the 1st Kansas had invaded just two months earlier.[83] The Union troops quickly formed a defensive line, and within it the 1st Kansas Colored fought off two attacks on a battleground so rough and brush covered it was hard to shift cannon, ride horses, or maneuver men. A third charge broke the 1st Kansas line, setting off a federal retreat for more than two miles. Col. Tandy Walker reported that when the abandoned wagon train and artillery pieces fell to his men, "I feared . . . that the train and its contents would prove a temptation too strong for these hungry, half-clothed Choctaws, but had no trouble in pressing them forward, for there was that in front and to the left more inviting to them than food or clothing—the blood of their despised enemy." He noted "Private Dickson Wallace, Captain Folsom's company, First Regiment, who in the pursuit was the first man to the artillery, and mounting astride one of the guns gave a whoop, which was followed by such a succession of whoops from his comrades as made the woods reverberate for miles around."[84]

However, the Battle of Poison Spring ended on a particularly chilling note. Col. James M. Williams, who commanded the Union column that day, reported that when it became clear the four-hour battle was lost, he used part of his cavalry as a rearguard while his infantry escaped across a swamp. "By this means," he explained, "nearly all, except the badly wounded were enabled to reach camp." Williams had trained the 1st Kansas Colored and led them at the Battle of Honey Springs a year earlier. Now he wrote, "Many wounded men belonging to the 1st Kansas Colored fell into the hands of the enemy, and I have the most positive assurances from eye witnesses that they were murdered on the spot."[85] Both Union and Confederate accounts agreed that the black troops captured or wounded during the battle were killed. The 301 Union dead, wounded, and missing included 117 from the 1st Kansas Colored Volunteer Infantry.[86] Both white and Choctaw Confederates apparently took part in the killing of prisoners, but an artillery officer from Texas noted in his journal that he saw at least forty bodies "in all conceivable attitudes, some scalped & near all stripped by the bloodthirsty Choctaws."[87] Less than two weeks later, the 2nd Kansas Colored Volunteers at Jenkins's Ferry retaliated, killing wounded or surrendering Confederates, while shouting, "Remember Poison Spring!"[88]

The Union occupation of parts of neighboring Arkansas, particularly Fort Smith, reinforced federal links to Fort Gibson and seemed to offer the isolated post an additional supply line by way of the Arkansas River. However, in June Brig. Gen. Stand Watie demonstrated how unreliable it was.

It was no secret that the *J. R. Williams*, a small stern-wheeler steam ferry boat, would use a recent rise in the water level along the Arkansas River to pass over Webber's Falls and deliver supplies to Fort Gibson. On the return trip, federal lieutenant George W. Houston was to pick up barrels of Cherokee Nation lime and salt for the quartermaster at Fort Smith. Because the probability of an attack by Watie was high, a twenty-six-man escort commanded by Lt. Horace A. B. Cook was along to guard the *Williams* and its cargo of flour, bacon, textiles, boots, tin ware, and other goods valued at about $120,000. When Watie heard the news, he immediately set off from his North Fork Town camp with his available troops and three artillery pieces. He chose Pleasant Bluff northeast of today's Tamaha, Oklahoma, for his ambush. Here, about five miles below the mouth of the Canadian River, the Arkansas, in those days about 350 feet wide, curved south, forcing boat traffic into the channel below the south bluff.[89]

According to Wash Grayson, then lieutenant of Company K, 2nd Creek Mounted Regiment, Watie sent him ahead with about three hundred men and three artillery pieces, commanded by Lt. Henry Forrester. The howitzers, spaced about a hundred yards apart, and men, mostly Muscogees and Seminoles, were completely concealed in the brush on the bluff. They had a fine view of the river.[90] As Grayson told the story, this was his first opportunity to command more men than his own company, and he was pleased that Watie approved the disposition of the men and guns when he arrived a little later.[91]

Even though the federal guards were watching for an attack, they were surprised when the three well-hidden howitzers and Indian soldiers opened fire. The artillery quickly damaged the steamer's smoke stack and blew away the pilot house. Another shot hit the boiler system, which released a cloud of steam that escaped with a deafening shriek. The pilot ran the steamer aground on a sandbar on the north side of the river, and the guards jumped off, leaving the captain and Houston on board. These two also abandoned the steamer and surrendered, so Cook collected his men and started the fifty-mile trek back to Fort Smith to report the incident. A few, though, made it to Mackey's Salt Works about ten miles downstream at the mouth of the Illinois River and reported the attack to the 2nd Indian Home Guard unit stationed there. Their commander set off with a relief party the next morning.[92]

Meanwhile, Watie's men towed the steamer to the south side of the river and began unloading its cargo on a sandbar. Watie sent for wagons to haul off the cargo, but the river kept rising. Much of the captured goods floated off downstream, some all the way to Fort Smith. While Watie's men were still unloading their prize, the federal salt works party arrived and opened fire from across the river. The steamer was beyond saving, so Watie had it set afire and adrift.[93] He reported later, "With the boat was captured 150 barrels of flour, 16,000 pounds of bacon, and considerable quantity of store goods, which was very acceptable to the boys, but has turned out to be [a] disadvantage to the command, as greater portions of the Creeks and Seminoles immediately broke off to carry their booty home. I am left here with only a few men."[94] Among other things, the steamer had been carrying tin ware, which by then was in short supply in the Indian Territory. Indian soldiers snatched up kettles, washtubs, coffee pots, plates, cups, and dippers. As they rode away, their ponies were almost invisible under their clanking loads. A few miles away, some of the Cherokees ran into Union cavalry and sprinted away, leaving a trail of tin ware across the prairie.[95]

The men's hurried departure with their plunder was particularly frustrating to Lt. Wash Grayson, always conscious that white officers looked down on Indian troops for their lack of discipline. No matter how hard he tried that day he could not make them stay. To make matters worse, General Watie, returning to camp, had ordered him and Company K to remain behind until sundown and watch for any federal troops from Fort Smith. Grayson could not persuade even one of his men to stay with him and was too embarrassed to tell Watie.

Consequently, he became the sole, nervous rearguard, very grateful when the sun finally slid below the horizon and he could, honor intact, follow Watie's trail back to camp.[96]

Watie's capture of the *J. R. Williams* came at a particularly inopportune time for the Union occupation of Fort Gibson. In spite of the precarious conditions there, federal authorities in Kansas had decided to send the remaining Indian Territory refugees back to their own country. Dwight D. Hitchcock, the Presbyterian missionary doctor serving with the Union army in the region, was dumbfounded. He wrote to his Robertson relatives, also longtime missionaries to the Indians,

> I hear with amasement [*sic*] that the refugee Indians are even now on their way back to this desolate country, to the number of several thousands. I do not know what the Government means. How supplies are to reach them, and a dozen other questions, are beyond my wisdom to answer. I suppose some gigantic speculation is at the bottom of the movement; and though the Government may for the present meet the expenses, in the end the Indians will have to suffer. Perhaps I do not sufficiently understand the programme to express myself so confidently as I have above: but at this juncture I do think the removal unwise and cruel.[97]

Nevertheless, except for about twenty smallpox victims, by early June Central superintendent William G. Coffin had collected at Osage Mission "all the Creeks ... all the Euchees, Chickasaws and Cherokees; [and] the Seminoles at Neosho Falls." The camps at Belmont were shut down because the "wild tribes" had gone to the bison and antelope range upstream along the Arkansas River and "will not ... trouble us any more soon," he hoped. The remaining Indians refused to move without a military escort, but once it arrived they set off in a wagon train six miles long. Thousands of refugees on foot trailed behind it for two or three miles, strayed ahead, or paralleled the train. Coffin judged it "a sight that is worth seeing, and if I had no responsibility or care, I could enjoy it most hugely."[98]

By June 7 they had traveled forty miles from Osage Mission in spite of daily rain. Coffin wrote:

> On the 5th we had a thunder-storm which killed one active, stout colored man ... instantly ... and a horse by his side. The

lightning struck the man on the top of his head and fired every load in his revolver in his belt . . . . We arrived here at 1 o'clock yesterday; the best camping place I ever saw. The Indians killed four fine deer and about forty wild hogs and one fine, large wild steer [and] one fine, large buck; so we are all right as to meat now; but the Osages, or some cattle thieves, stole all our cattle, thirty head, last night, but we have a file of soldiers and a lot of Indians out after them, and hope to get them. [The cattle] have given us a great deal of trouble, as we can get no lots to put them in of nights. We are within about 120 miles of Fort Gibson, and expect to reach there in ten days if not kept back by the military . . . but they are now within six miles of us with the government ox-train, and will I hope, not delay us much more . . . . They have most of the escort and will camp close to us to-night. There are about 300 wagons in our train, sutlers, and all, and about the same in the government train, including 60 loaded with Indian supplies . . . . As we unload our supply [wagons] by issuing [rations], we load with Indians, the old and broken down; over 3,000 travel on foot, and pack every imaginable article of clothing, bedding, cooking utensils, chickens, ducks, and dogs. I think that we had at least 3,000 dogs when we started, but they are rapidly diminishing; but at least 500 of them, young of course, are packed by the Indians.[99]

He estimated five thousand Indians, probably including the Indian troops in the escort, arrived at Fort Gibson on June 15 "in pretty good shape." Coffin summarized, "I think on the whole we may pronounce the moving a success. Unfortunately one young man of our escort was drowned while fording Grand river, at this place, last evening; he got into running water, was thrown from his horse, and the weight of his carbine and revolvers sunk him."[100]

Coffin needed only hours to realize refugee conditions at Fort Gibson were atrocious, and he immediately wrote a report saying so. Cherokee agent Harlan had been trying to feed nine thousand refugees; the newcomers increased that to sixteen thousand. It was already too late in the season to plant additional corn had refugee Indians even been able to go beyond the range of the fort's artillery without guards. The newcomers would need federal subsistence, adding "truly enormous" expenses. All the refugees were desperate for clothing, and rationing would be tight, with no frills such as coffee, sugar, pepper, or vinegar.

Starvation was a real possibility, and the military had already suggested Coffin take some of the Indians back to Kansas.[101]

He was still writing this report when Col. William A. Phillips brought more bad news. A steamboat from Fort Smith—the *J. R. Williams*—loaded with military and Indian supplies had been attacked by rebels, driven ashore, and abandoned by her crew thirty-five miles downstream. Two hundred cavalrymen who had just escorted Coffin's refugees to Fort Gibson were riding fast toward the ambush site with empty wagons, hoping to save what they could of the cargo.[102] Most of it, though, was already burned, packed in Watie's wagons and his men's saddlebags, or lost to the Arkansas River floodwaters.

One month later, five Muscogee chiefs sent a dignified, undemanding letter to the commissioner of Indian affairs in Washington, requesting help for the twenty thousand Indian refugees facing starvation near Fort Gibson. Last winter, they said, the people there had been so desperate "they were glad to hunt out the little corn that *fell from the horses and mules* [their emphasis] of the military." It had been a "terrible mistake" to bring them down here this year too late to plant a crop, but they blamed no one. "We know the provisions are not here; we know that the provisions destined to relieve our present wants were destroyed by the rebels. If there were any provisions that those who have charge of us could get hold of, we should have them. They are like ourselves, helpless."[103]

Watie's capture of the *J. R. Williams* demonstrated the dangers of the Arkansas River supply route and was a heavy blow to the Fort Gibson military and refugees, but it lifted the spirits of Confederate-allied Indians. His next venture, a second attack on the Texas Road crossing at Cabin Creek, lifted them even higher. Earlier in the spring, Watie had proposed driving into southwestern Kansas with one thousand men as a way to draw federal troops away from Forts Gibson and Smith, making them more vulnerable to a Confederate assault. Permission, which came in late August, had conditions: It must be a joint expedition with Brig. Gen. Richard M. Gano of Texas, a veteran of the war in Tennessee and Kentucky. It must also coincide with a thrust by Gen. Sterling Price into Missouri. Two simultaneous threats in the west, it was hoped, might relieve pressure on Gen. Robert E. Lee in the east.[104]

Gano, also hoping for approval of a raid north of the Arkansas

River, had written General Maxey, "It is true many of my men are dismounted, barefooted, & unarmed, but they would be better satisfied actively employed, than idling in camps. And there would be a pretty fair chance to capture arms, horses & clothing." True, he could make a better case for a joint expedition with Stand Watie if his men were better mounted, but he concluded, "we fight better when we cannot run well."[105]

That summer, while waiting for official approval, Watie and Gano led coordinated raids, directed by Brig. Gen. Douglas H. Cooper. Hay was necessary to keep an army's livestock in good condition during the winter, but cutting and drying it for storage usually meant soldiers left the protection of their bases. While Gano, with his Texans and Col. Sampson Folsom's Choctaws, struck Union haying operations at Massard Prairie just across the line in Arkansas, Watie did the same at Blackburn's Prairie in the Cherokee Nation. Watie and Gano then met at Skullyville, Choctaw Nation, and with Maxey planned a joint attack on Fort Smith, which occurred July 31. Through August they kept pressure on the Union occupiers there. When they finally got permission for their raid north, the question of who would command remained. As of May 10, Watie had been promoted to brigadier general, the first American Indian to attain that rank. He and Gano agreed that each would command his own troops, but because Gano's commission slightly predated Watie's, he deferred to Gano.[106]

On September 14 they set out from their camp near today's Whitefield, Oklahoma, with about two thousand men—Watie's eight hundred Cherokee, Muscogee, and Seminole troops of the 1st Indian Brigade; Gano with about twelve hundred from the 5th Texas Cavalry Brigade and Howell's Battery. Crossing the rain-swollen Arkansas River took six hours, and the men ferried the artillery ammunition over on horseback. Lt. Col. Clement Neeley Vann's Cherokee scouts had already come in to report a large supply train was on its way from Fort Scott to Fort Gibson. Likewise, Union scouts and sympathizers knew a large Confederate force had forded the Arkansas near Creek Agency and headed north. There was little time to spare if Gano and Watie were to capture that train.[107]

However, on the afternoon of September 16 the Confederate allies came across a federal haying operation on the prairie just northeast of today's Wagoner, Oklahoma, along Flat Rock Creek, a tributary of the Grand River. Union scouts reported to its commander, Capt. E. A. Barker, 2nd Kansas Cavalry, there were about two hundred Confederates nearby. Barker left the hay makers—about 125 men altogether from the 2nd Kansas and 1st Kansas Colored Infantry—and went to look for himself. He saw about a thousand men and six pieces of artillery coming toward him. Badly outnumbered, Barker ordered the black infantry troops to take cover in a ravine on the prairie, while he tried to hold the Texans and Indians off with his cavalry. He reported later,

> I immediately fell back, skirmishing with their advance which made several unsuccessful attempts to cut me off from my camp; after reaching which I dismounted my men and placed them in the ravine with the others, which was no sooner accomplished than the main body of the enemy appeared and attacked me from five different points, their infantry line moving up to within 200 yards, while their cavalry made three distinct charges, but were each time handsomely repulsed by the colored infantry and dismounted cavalry.[108]

Gano, a future minister, wrote with flair, "The clouds looked somber and the V-shape procession grand as we moved forward in the work of death. Then commenced a running fight with the enemy's cavalry, while with the center I moved down and engaged their infantry. I sent Major Stackpole with a captured Federal lieutenant under flag of truce to demand surrender, but they fired upon my flag and then commenced the work of death in earnest."[109]

It really was a "work of death." After about a half hour and seeing his troops were about to be overrun, Barker ordered the men who had horses to mount up. The rest—mostly the black infantrymen—he told to head for the timber along the Grand River about a mile away. The mounted soldiers charged the Indian portion of the attacking line, thinking it would be the weakest point, but only fifteen of sixty-five riders got through.[110] The black troops had little chance to escape. Barker reported, "The whole force of the enemy then charged into my camp, capturing all of the white soldiers remaining there, and killing all the colored soldiers they could find."[111] Lt. Pleasant Porter of the 2nd Creek Regiment single-handedly captured seven of the eighty-five prisoners taken, along with their valuable six-shooters.[112]

According to Lt. Wash Grayson, also of the 2nd Creek Regiment, "One or two shots of grape from our guns . . . caused a stampede . . . . The defenders disappeared among the thickets and very high weeds." It seemed the fight was over, and the Confederate allies set fire to the camp, wagons, mowing equipment, and three thousand tons of hay piled in huge ricks or drying on the ground. Then they began to find black soldiers hiding in the tall grass along a small, shallow creek. According to Grayson, "the men began to hunt them out much as sportsmen do quails." A few surrendered, and some begged for their lives. However, Grayson said, "our men were in no spirit to spare the wretched unfortunates and shot them down without mercy." Some black soldiers had hidden in the sluggish creek, its surface partially obscured by willows and lily pads. Only their noses were above water. Grayson wrote that they "were shot and dragged and thrown out on the bank. I confess this was sickening to me, but the men were like wild beasts and I was powerless to stop them from this unnecessary butchery." The Indian troops found one young white man and asked Grayson if they should kill him, too. Grayson said no, that "it was negroes that we were killing now and not white men."[113]

Jefferson P. Baze, then just twenty but already a seasoned veteran of the 30th Texas Cavalry, recalled, "The water was red with blood of the dead negroes. The few Indians who were along with the army . . . dragged the dead bodies from the river and took all that was of any value from them."[114] Only four of thirty-seven black soldiers escaped the slaughter. One of them was George W. Duval, who had fired volley after volley with the men of the 1st Kansas Colored until their ammunition gave out and their position was overrun. He hid in a drift of debris in the creek until dark. Then he crawled out between the Confederate pickets and escaped, still carrying his empty rifle.[115]

Their work done on Flat Rock Creek, Gano and Watie resumed their expedition to intercept the federal supply train on the Texas Road. It had left Fort Scott, Kansas, on September 12 with 205 government wagons, four ambulances, and ninety-one sutler wagons loaded with valuable goods and supplies for Fort Gibson. Maj. Henry Hopkins, 2nd Kansas Cavalry, commanded the escort. It included 180 Kansas troops and about 250 armed wagon drivers. There were a hundred Union Cherokees from the 3rd Indian Home Guard, but half stayed behind on the road to guard a Grand River ford. Meanwhile, Cherokee Pins were hurrying to aid Hopkins against Watie, and Col. Stephen H. Wattles, the new commander at Fort Gibson, was supposed to be sending relief, too. Hopkins knew a large Confederate force was in the vicinity, just as Watie and Gano knew the federal train was approaching the Cabin Creek crossing. However, neither the Confederate allies nor Hopkins had accurate, current information on the other.[116]

There were some changes at Cabin Creek since Watie's 1863 attack. A new federal stockade now stood on the timbered bluff overlooking the ford north of today's Pensacola, Oklahoma. Nearby, the home of Joseph L. Martin, a Cherokee officer serving with Watie, and other buildings had been fortified with a stockade of timbers set endwise into the ground. When Hopkins brought the train into Cabin Creek on the afternoon of September 18, he had it parked close to the stockade and behind a barricade of ten-foot-long hay ricks. These and the steep 150-foot bluff above the creek bed might give defenders some protection.[117]

Gano scouted ahead of the main body of the expedition, located the stockade and supply train, and sent for Watie, who reached Cabin Creek with the rest of their combined force about midnight, September 18–19. Gano immediately deployed their men on the small prairie that sloped slightly down toward the bluff. Gano placed the artillery in the center of a long concave line opening toward the federal defenses, with the Texas troops on his right and Watie's Indian regiments on the left. The 2nd Cherokees were closest to the artillery, with the Seminoles next, then the 2nd Creek regiment, with the 1st Creek on the end.[118] Each force was aware of the other. Lt. Wash Grayson with Col. Samuel Checote's 2nd Creeks wrote that they could see the wagons, mules, and teams by the light of the rising moon and hear "boisterous and careless talk" from the Union lines, inside which some men had clearly been drinking. There were verbal taunts, turkey gobble challenges, and insults, even some shots fired, and he had a hard time restraining his men until the order finally came to open the battle.[119]

By about three o'clock in the morning, the moon, just past full, lit the battlefield. Gano ordered his whole line forward, horsemen in front, dismounted men behind them. When they were about three hundred yards away, federal picket fire began to reach them. According to Grayson, "things certainly began now to appear decidedly warlike."

When the line halted he stood in front of his men in Company K shouting encouragement, sometimes lit by the flashes of their weapons or hidden by powder smoke. His cousin and best friend Valentine McAnally privately advised him to get behind the line because the men were so excited they might shoot him by mistake. But Grayson was eager to put the old suspicions of his courage to rest. "Here was some real fighting where I might exhibit my true self . . . and where there was real danger," he wrote, "and I was determined to improve the opportunity come what may."[120]

The opportunity was there as Gano continued the assault. Major Hopkins discovered that he had underestimated the size of the Confederate-allied force by two-thirds, and he had not known it included artillery. Shells began to fall inside the federal defenses, creating confusion. Some of the teamsters cut single mules loose from their four- or six-mule teams, mounted, and galloped back toward Fort Scott. Panic also spread among the mules left harnessed to the wagons. Some were killed by the shelling, but others kicked and bucked, breaking the wagon tongues, snarling their harness, and stampeding with the loaded wagons. Some mules were killed or injured as they fell, dragging the wagons with them, over the bluff into the creek bed below.[121]

As daylight came the battle continued. Company K, 2nd Creek Regiment, had advanced on foot and fallen back several times, so Lieutenant Grayson had passed the night "pumping bullets at the enemy" and, "always in Indian," shouting encouragement to his men until his voice was nearly gone. Before their ammunition was exhausted, he got his only wound of the war when one of his men excitedly fired his flint lock squirrel rifle too close to Grayson's face. Bits of flint and primer hit his left cheek, creating a permanent tattoo near his eye.[122]

At the center of the line, 1st Lt. Charles H. Stith of Texas commanded a section of Howell's Battery. "[A]s soon as the gray dawn allowed me to see the stockade of the enemy," Stith remembered, "my two guns opened on their left. Gen. Gano was in command, and was by my side."[123] The general ordered Stith, supported by the 1st and 2nd Creek Regiments, to move farther left in order to send a crossfire into the Union defenses. The Seminoles and 29th Texas moved to the left with Stith's guns. In the multiple assaults that followed, the Texan, Seminole, and Muscogee units mixed together, but individuals continued to fight in whatever group they found themselves.[124] Gano, in his flamboyant style reported, "Crash after crash of shell swept Yankees, negroes, Pins, and mules away from the land of the living, while every regiment and company poured in volley after volley, and the brave Indians, having replenished with ammunition, came again to the work, and all with a loud shout rushed on to victory, driving the enemy beyond their fortifications, from where they fled in wild confusion to the densely timbered bottoms."[125]

When the Union line finally crumbled at that end of the defenses about nine o'clock in the morning, the Texans were the first to clamber over the barricades and into the stockade. Muscogee lieutenants Pleasant Porter and Wash Grayson went over with them. That, Porter told Wash years later, vindicated the honor of all the Muscogee warriors who fought at Cabin Creek.[126]

The primary goal of the Confederate allies' attack had been to capture the supply train. Major Hopkins tried several times to get at least part of it away, but Watie and Gano foiled each attempt. The federal troops finally abandoned the train and pulled back north along the Texas Road. Local tradition, supported by the many trees left bullet riddled, was that the Confederate allies dogged them for about a mile. Their real interest, though, was the wagons, teams, and contents of the train.[127]

As the fight subsided, the victorious Texans and Indians flooded the federal enclosure. They helped themselves, according to Grayson, to "portable articles of value, horses, mules, guns, and trunks of goods and whatever else came handy." He was disappointed that he found little worth keeping.[128] Pvt. Jefferson P. Baze of the 30th Texas Cavalry was more fortunate. He explained that at Cabin Creek the captured wagons were "loaded with provisions and clothing .... This was a God-send to us, for we were almost destitute of clothing and provisions. I had gone for three days on only a piece of fat bacon and one of my comrades had only an ear of corn. There was not enough clothing to go round, so we drew for it. An overcoat fell to me"—a welcome item with winter coming soon.[129] W. T. Sheppard, another Texan, drew a pair of boots that were even his size. He had been barefoot before the fight but had continued to wear his homemade spurs. At Flat Rock Creek, another soldier had stepped on one of his spurs and badly sliced his heel. He could not wear his new boots until the cut healed.[130]

Unfortunately, Gano and Watie could not take the whole train and its contents. Some of the wagons and their loads had been destroyed in the fighting or when the stampeding mules dragged them over the bluff. Usable harness was also in short supply, due to damage by the shelling, runaway teamsters, and kicking mules. Watie reported that they burned what they could not move, along with mowing machines and ten ricks of hay, each holding about five hundred tons. Knowing federal reinforcements might still arrive, they left Cabin Creek with about 130 loaded wagons by ten o'clock in the morning, roughly an hour after the battle ended.[131] The men especially appreciated the quality and condition of the 750 captured mules. By 1864, after four years of hard use, little care, and poor feed, their own ponies and mules were worn out. Fifty years later Lt. Charles H. Stith still remembered those taken at Cabin Creek as "the finest mules that I have ever seen."[132]

The wagon train started southwest toward the Arkansas River, but near Pryor Creek in late morning, they ran into federal troops—the 1st and 2nd Kansas Colored Volunteer Infantry and the 11th U.S. Colored Infantry, commanded by Col. James M. Williams. Gano's and Watie's men were exhausted, but so were the Union soldiers, having just marched eighty-two miles from Fort Smith in forty-six hours. The two forces engaged in a short, inconclusive battle and artillery duel about three miles southwest of today's Adair, Oklahoma.[133] According to Wash Grayson, "We might have taken this [Union] force in, but had now so much of value to care for, and being so far within the enemy's lines, we deemed the safe plan the better."[134]

Then Gano and Watie hoodwinked Williams. According to Pvt. James Knox Polk Yeary of the 5th Texas Partisan Rangers, "As night came on we built fires and made a big noise with our caissons, pretending to be preparing for a battle in the morning." They rolled the same wagon repeatedly over rocky ground to make it sound as if the whole train were being lined up and parked over night.[135] Ten days later Col. Charles DeMorse of the 29th Texas Cavalry, formerly editor of the *Standard* of Clarksville, Texas, wrote to his old newspaper, "What a ruse we played upon the enemy that night," he said, "to induce them to think that the train was still with us, it might not be politic to state, as we may have use for it again."[136]

That night they slipped the captured wagons northwest and began a roundabout trip back to their base at North Fork Town. They crossed the Verdigris River near Claremore Mound before turning south behind the Dog Creek Hills in today's Rogers County, Oklahoma. They forded the Arkansas River close to Tulsa's Southwest 38th Street at the place known afterward as "Gano's Crossing."[137]

It was a very difficult trip back. Gano explained to Brig. Gen. Douglas H. Cooper,

> We expected to fight at Arkansas River, and [so] hurried forward with all dispatch day and night. For three days and nights our boys were without sleep, except such as they could snatch in the saddle or at watering places. They dug down banks, cut out trees, rolled wagons and artillery up hills and banks by hand, kept cheerful, and never wearied in the good cause, and came into camp rejoicing on the 28th instant.[138]

Wash Grayson agreed about forty-five years later, "we never unsaddled our horses since crossing the Arkansas river in the going until we again crossed it on the return." Over a period of five or six days, he mused, "I sometimes would sleep while in the saddle, riding along for miles, and cannot yet understand how it happened that I did not fall from my horse."[139]

Cooper, in constant touch with Watie and Gano by Indian messengers, dispatched Col. Daniel N. McIntosh with four hundred Muscogee troops to escort the train in to North Fork Town, but there was no pursuit. The federals were too busy salvaging what they could at Cabin Creek, dealing with the dead and wounded, and guarding the next train. In his report Gano commented favorably on the collaboration with Watie and summarized, "We were out fourteen days, marched over 400 miles, killed 97, wounded many, captured 111 prisoners, burned 6,000 tons of hay and all the reapers or mowers—destroyed altogether from the Federals $1,500,000 of property, bringing safely into our lines nearly one-third of this amount." Their losses were six killed and forty-eight wounded, three of those mortally.[140]

Even though Lt. Wash Grayson received nothing much material from the raid, he earned something he valued highly—his men's respect. While his company relaxed back at Camp Canadian and told funny stories about the expedition, Jackson Munahwe quietly remarked that their former captain, an older man, had shown little vigor in leading them in battle. "We charged that he was cowardly," Munahwe said, then added, "I am sure we have nothing to complain of now."[141] Grayson was surprised and gratified by the indirect compliment. For the first two years of the war his family responsibilities had kept him from enlisting, and he had been aware people questioned his courage. Munahwe's comment showed he had put the old doubts to rest. At some later date, he was promoted to captain and the traditional title, *tvstvnvkke*, "warrior," was added to his Muscogee name "Yvhv," meaning "wolf." For the rest of his long public life he was called "Captain Grayson," or "Yaha Tustunuggee (Wolf Warrior)."[142]

The loss of the "million dollar wagon train" was a stunning blow to Union forces in the region, even though it caused little more than a ripple in the war overall. It briefly lifted morale among Confederate-allied soldiers and civilian refugees in the Indian Territory for whom good news had become scarce. Nearly naked soldiers received parts of blue Union uniforms, shoes, and equipment. New blankets were welcome as the nights grew colder. Supplies of rice, flour, sugar, coffee, and tea filled stomachs and lightened spirits. Gano and Watie sent gifts of coffee, calico, candles, and cans of pineapple and oysters to fellow officers and their wives. Cherokee refugee Ella Coodey was happy to receive a new pair of shoes. It did not matter that they were different sizes. Even then, the amount of goods captured fell far short of the need. Those supplies had been intended for Fort Gibson and even more desperate refugees. The Union people trapped there or trying to survive in the Seminole, Muscogee, and Cherokee Nations still faced hunger, deprivation, and fear. There seemed to be no end in sight. The Osages, according to elder Louis F. Burns, called those times a "moon winter," days during which people could only dream about the distant spring.[143]

CHAPTER SIX

The Terrors of War

The euphoria among the Confederate allies due to their victory at Cabin Creek faded quickly. It did not affect the decline of the Confederacy in the east, and there were no more ambitious expeditions affecting the Indian Territory by either side in the fall and winter of 1864–1865. There was only desultory raiding and the merciless destruction or seizure of anything that might be useful to the enemy. Among the victims were Emma Blythe, a Cherokee who was six when the war began, and her widowed mother living near Tahlequah. It is not known if they had any political views. The oral history Emma related probably reflected the common experience. "During the Civil War," she said, " . . . our clothes was very scant as the soldiers kept the people robbed so clean . . . . Our homes was burned. Our cattle was driven way. Our hogs was killed. Our milk cows was shot down. Our children cried for being hungry. Our bed was taken from us. Mothers set up all night to keep fires to keep from freezing. Our horses was taken out of the plow. Our crops growed up in weeds. Such was the terrors of war."[1]

William Potter Ross, another Cherokee, wrote in a similar vein in December 1864 that most homes by then were abandoned or burned, while brush and briars were taking over the fields of "our once prosperous and beautiful country." Sadly he summarized, "Everything has been changed by the destroying hand of War." The abundant livestock had nearly disappeared. Instead, Ross said, "[there is] a great increase in the number of wild animals. The wolves howl dismally over the land and the panther's scream is often heard."[2]

Almost two years after the murder of her Cherokee husband, Abijah Hicks, missionary printer Hannah Worcester Hicks wrote her sister Anne Eliza Robertson how hard it was to decide what was best for her family "in consequence of this 'Cruel War.' It seems now, more impossible than ever to obey the command, 'Take no thought for the morrow' . . . . Our houses are still spared, and it may be that Watie will be prevented from returning to destroy again. Though I can't yet feel at all confident that he will not come back—and if he does, I am sure that we shall suffer far worse than we ever have yet."[3]

Farther south in the Choctaw Nation, even though conditions were somewhat better, concerns about the war were still ever-present, according to Christine Folsom, who was about thirteen when it began. Four of her brothers and her father, Presbyterian minister Israel Folsom, were serving with the Choctaw troops as allies of the Confederacy. According to Christine, her father, who had been influential in Choctaw government since the Removal, met with other Indians to pray and discuss what to do. He drilled his troops and rode out with them, their bows and quivers across their backs and their hatchets strapped around their waists. Christine's mother, Louisa Nail Folsom, spun, wove, and sewed for the "southern boys." When food became scarce on the Folsom farm that had once been worked by fifty slaves, the family ate wheat-based gruel and drank "Lincoln coffee" made from parched okra. Christine's parents, too, stayed up all night, baking potatoes in the ashes while guarding their sleeping children against the runaway slaves they feared.[4]

The goods captured from the *J. R. Williams* and the wagon train at Cabin Creek did not go far when doled out to the Indian and white soldiers who captured it. Too many of the Confederate allied troops were still ragged and hungry. In early October, Brig. Gen. Douglas H. Cooper reported that he had sent the Muscogees and Seminoles who lacked weapons but had horses in good condition to the Deep Fork and Canadian river valleys to round up cattle to be slaughtered for beef. The men of the Choctaw Brigade, who had not shared in Watie and Gano's spoils, were destitute with winter coming. Cooper said, "They are without axes with which to get wood, and unless clothing and axes can be furnished it will be impossible to keep them in the field much longer. We have already had frost in these mountains." He knew some of the worn-out ponies would soon have to be taken to Texas to graze and rest during the winter. Captain Howell, too, Cooper wrote, had worn out the draft horses that pulled his howitzers, which he was hoping to trade for Parrot guns. These new fieldpieces, Cooper noted, "will be hauled by mules, though it is a dangerous experiment in battle. These animals almost invariably stampede and run off during an engagement."[5]

Even though Lt. Wash Grayson had been with Watie and Gano at Cabin Creek, he had only a small Mexican blanket for protection from the wet and cold that winter.[6] Some of the soldiers even froze to death, according to one Choctaw family's oral history, and sick soldiers received little care because the military hospitals were overcrowded. Lewie Felihkatubbee, son of a Choctaw soldier, remembered, "Smallpox got among the soldiers and killed a good many of them; others came home and spread the smallpox among the Choctaws . . . and a good many of them died. They did not know what to do with the disease when it spread among them." Fear in their community caused the stricken family to be left alone to care for their sick and to bury their dead with little ceremony.[7] Wash Grayson returned from his last raid of the war in the early stages of smallpox. There was no room for him in the military hospital at Boggy Depot, so his men took him on to Wapanucka Academy, a Chickasaw Nation school then serving as a military hospital. He was fortunate that his aunt and mother came over from the family's temporary home in Pontotoc County, Chickasaw Nation, to care for him. He barely survived—scarred, emaciated, and lacking most of his long reddish hair for the time being. He was one of the lucky victims.[8]

Some Indian Territory people were concerned about the moral as well as physical effects of the war on their nations, communities, and families. In late March, Presbyterian missionary and physician Dwight D. Hitchcock, then serving in a Union army hospital, wrote to friends, "I don't believe you have any conception of the wide-spread and terrible depravation of morals that exists in this Army; and I presume we are no worse than other armies. Young men of religious training, and even of religious profession, give themselves up to work all manner of uncleanness with greediness. Licentiousness is the rule, and men are open & unblushing in avowing it." He pointed out, "Gambling is practiced universally. And profanity is as common as speech." Hitchcock, a staunch Unionist and abolitionist, said he supposed the Lord could use even the "vilest instruments" to accomplish His work.[9]

In May, apparently responding to inquiries from his brother-in-law, missionary William Schenk Robertson, about their Indian congregations, Hitchcock wrote, "the picture can hardly be too dark . . . . Morality among our Indians is at a fearfully low ebb: it would seem as though the labor of years had been destroyed by these three years of

War." John Buttrick Jones, the highly influential Northern Baptist missionary to the Cherokees, had recently told him that

> there are but 8 substantial christians in this Regt. In the 3rd, which is considerably larger, the number is greater . . . . You know the Baptists had a very large membership. Probably many women "hold fast their profession," but it is not those who follow the camp. I am not surprized [sic] at the defection of so many members of "our sister churches." I never had confidence in their measures, nor in their church members. There was so much irregularity and vagueness in their instructions and proceedings that one could not look for sound fruit. With all the discipline and care our church tried to exercise, how frequently were we disappointed. I do not know what to suggest for the religious improvement of this people. Their hearts seem to be fully set in them to do evil. Jones tells me that they pay good attention to preaching; but it makes no impression.

Hitchcock suggested one reason for the prevalence of gambling among the troops was boredom from lack of anything better to do. He suggested uplifting reading material might help.[10]

Likewise, his sister-in-law Hannah Worcester Hicks noted that under the stresses of war Christianity seemed to decline in the Cherokee Nation. Church congregations had scattered, and Sunday was just another day, passing without observation of the Sabbath. Hannah, the daughter and widow of Congregationalist-Presbyterian missionaries, feared she was failing as a parent. She wrote to her sister, "you have no idea how weak I am in training my children. Training? My 'training' is just none at all,—and oh how my heart aches as I see them growing up in sin and think that perhaps they are only spared for monuments of judgment against me." Hannah was particularly concerned for her oldest child, Percy, who was about eleven. She wrote, "This time of War and wickedness has been so fearful for Percy—in the lessons of evil he has learnt. Sometimes it does seem as if I should go distracted in my anxiety for him. Oh for wisdom to know what to do with him. He is now staying at the Fort [Gibson], because I dare not keep him at home. Some boys have been killed, and so many threats made that I fear to risk the Rebels coming and finding him here."[11]

In that fear for her son she had much in common with Sallie

Watie, who wrote in considerable distress to her husband, Brig. Gen. Stand Watie, after hearing a rumor that their son Saladin, a teenaged captain in his father's regiment, had killed a prisoner. "[W]rite and tell me who it was and how it was. [T]ell my boys to always show mercy as they expect to find God merciful to them," she begged. "I do hate to hear such things it almost runs me crazy to hear such things. I am afraid that Saladin never will value human life as he ought."[12]

While those who lived in the eastern half of the Indian Territory struggled through the third and fourth years of the Civil War, Indian peoples who inhabited the western half, as well as neighboring states and territories, experienced their own terrors as events unfolded between 1861 and 1865. Within a decade those events propelled them and a dozen other native peoples toward permanent residence in the Indian Territory. They profoundly affected the future State of Oklahoma as well as several other states.

Scholars who have studied the nomadic Plains tribes have concluded that although they participated indirectly in the Civil War, it was important to them. It provided a breathing space from the growing pressures in the 1850s, particularly the incursions of white settlers.[13] Tribes most often found in western Indian Territory and as far east as the Cross Timbers at that time included the Comanches; Kiowas; Cheyennes; Arapahos; and Plains Apaches, who call themselves "Naishadena."[14] Since at least the 1830s they had camped, hunted, traded, visited, and raided one another's horse herds along western Indian Territory's rivers and streams without much regard for boundaries drawn on white men's maps. In 1840 the Kiowas, Comanches, and Plains Apaches on the one hand and the Cheyennes and Arapahos on the other shifted from their earlier rivalry to a loose alliance against common enemies. This sometimes included the recently removed five southeastern nations, to whom the federal government had sold the Plains tribes' range as far west as the Texas Panhandle. Some citizens of those eastern nations occasionally traveled far out to the west to trade for furs, horses, mules, and captives and to hold councils with the Plains Indians, but they had also learned to guard their western frontiers against them.[15]

The Chickasaw Nation's western ranches and settlements had always been particularly vulnerable to Plains Indian raids because that frontier extended the furthest west and was the most exposed.

However, the raiders were after livestock primarily and rarely bothered the ranch families or their homes. Dinah Lewis, a full-blood Chickasaw who was about five when the Civil War began, lived then near today's Sulphur, Oklahoma. She said in 1937,

> The Comanche and Kiowa Indians used to make raids on us. They would steal from us the same as from white people. I remember, when a small child, prowling through the woods and finding ashes of camp fires where they had camped. One day I found an arrow point. It was made of hard steel. We didn't dare leave a cross-cut saw outside. They liked to get hold of them for arrow points. They weren't inclined to fight with us, unless we tried to catch them if they had stolen something. Then they would kill and scalp us.[16]

The tough, self-reliant Chickasaw frontiersmen organized their own defense, but because the Kiowa and Comanche raids, mostly in the summertime, were so infrequent, they were usually taken by surprise.[17]

By the beginning of the Civil War, though, most of the Plains Indians that historically viewed Indian Territory west of the Cross Timbers as part of their range had withdrawn to eastern Colorado and far-western Nebraska, Kansas, and Texas. In the 1850s a growing number of Anglo-Americans were penetrating even the most distant arid plains that once seemed a barrier to white settlement although it provided the Plains Indians resources and protection. Game was growing scarce, and there was increased competition for those resources. Indians also faced a more professional, aggressive U.S. Army in the 1850s than in the past.[18]

They still raided their enemies to supply some of their needs and because raiding was an important part of their culture. The purpose might be to drive intruders out of traditional hunting grounds, soothe hurts, or avenge insults. During raids, a man could demonstrate his abilities as a warrior and potential leader. Recognition and advancement in tribal warrior societies might follow. Livestock and goods captured helped a man provide for his family and show others generosity, a quality much valued by native peoples. Captives, particularly very young ones, could fill family vacancies caused by death. None of those rationales, however, sat well with frontiersmen victimized by Plains Indian raids, particularly those who had seen relatives and neighbors slaughtered without regard for their age or gender. As mentioned earlier, Texans, most often the Plains Indians' victims, retaliated against Indians in their state by forcing nearly all out in 1858–1859. About the same time, Texans and U.S. soldiers twice attacked Comanches in the Indian Territory, killing their people and destroying their camps at the Antelope Hills and the Wichita Village. They, like the other nomadic tribes, were becoming rather desperate.[19]

Some of the pressure on the Plains tribes eased when the federal government pulled troops from the western frontier to help suppress the Southern rebellion. Volunteer units from frontier states and territories filled some of the defensive gaps along the western frontier. For example, the 1st Regiment of Colorado Volunteers, commanded by Col. John M. Chivington, had been created to fight Confederates. After that regiment returned victorious from the Battle of Glorieta Pass in New Mexico Territory, some fought Indians, too, during the administration of Gov. John Evans. He later raised the 3rd Colorado Cavalry specifically to fight Indians. Texas could not ignore the Indian threat, either. That state sent men east to fight for the Confederacy and protected their Gulf Coast against invasion. Meanwhile, on their western frontier, Rangers, Confederate troops, and frontier minutemen manned military or small privately built forts and guarded against Plains Indian raids.[20]

Texans also called on old allies to aid their frontier defense—the Tonkawa Indians. Even when most were forced to leave for the Indian Territory in 1859, a small group headed by Castile had remained in Texas. The survivors of the 1862 massacre at Wichita Agency returned to Texas the next year, and the Tonkawas reunited under Castile's leadership. Longtime enemies of the Comanches, skilled at tracking and fighting, the Tonkawas, now reduced to about 180 people, were willing to defend Texas, their traditional home, against enemies even if they had to do it armed mostly with bows and arrows.[21]

Confederate authorities also relied on the Caddo Indians to help defend the western frontier of the Indian Territory. While some Caddos, Anadarkos, and Hainais went to Kansas or southeastern Colorado to escape the war, the leader of the Whitebead band, Showetat, also called Caddo George Washington, refused to leave the land guaranteed to them after their expulsion from Texas in 1858–1859. At the beginning of the war, his band agreed to serve as scouts to help defend Wichita Agency. Later, the Confederate military created the Caddo Frontier Guard, led by Major Showetat and Anadarko chief Iesh. It was charged with protecting the Indian Territory frontier against Plains raiders, including old enemies such as the Kiowas.[22]

Because Plains Indian raiders typically came through western Indian Territory to cross the Red River, Texans had an additional stake in the decision of the Indian Territory nations to ally with the Confederacy. As soon as federal troops withdrew from the territory in May 1861, Texans preemptively occupied its three federal forts. James Bourland, one of the three Texas commissioners who had lobbied the Indian nations in February, formed Bourland's Border Regiment. It remained at Fort Arbuckle throughout the war. The garrison guarded against hostile Indians as well as potential Union invasion, particularly after the Union victory at the Battle of Honey Springs seemed to open that door. As the war persisted into its third and fourth years, deserters and stragglers flowed across the Indian Territory, adding to the growing security problem. One large gang of these lawless, ruthless "brush men" camped in southwestern Indian Territory between the Wichita Mountains and the Red River. Colonel Bourland recruited some into his regiment and posted them as lookouts in the Indian Territory south of the Wichita Mountains.[23]

Although the Union and the Confederacy recruited men of several tribes in the Indian Territory, Kansas, Texas, and other neighboring territories to fight for them, they did not recruit among the Comanches, Kiowas, Plains Apaches, Cheyennes, and Arapahos. Rather, the warring Anglo-American governments hoped to keep these Plains tribes out of the conflict, particularly as allies of the other side. However, for the last two years of the war the Comanches, Kiowas, and Plains Apaches were suffering from hunger. The federal government did not deliver the annuity goods, merchandise, provisions, and agricultural tools guaranteed to them in the 1853 Fort Atkinson Treaty in exchange for tolerating Anglo-American passage through their lands. Confederate brigadier general Albert Pike, on the other hand, had succeeded in getting a Kiowa representative and all the Comanche bands except the Quahadi to sign his Confederate treaties at Wichita Agency in 1861. He worked hard to supply promised goods that would help keep them content. Even then, the

Plains tribes had their own agendas, and, as noted earlier, the treaties did not stop small parties of Kiowas from revenge raids on the Caddos in 1861 and 1863.[24]

Nor did federal treaties prevent small parties of Plains Indians from attacking scattered ranches and harassing traffic bound for the western gold fields and Union forts in the West. At the time there were three main east-west routes of travel, commerce, and communication across the Central Plains. One paralleled the Platte and South Platte Rivers through Nebraska Territory into northern Colorado Territory. A central route followed the Smoky Hill River through western Kansas toward the Rocky Mountains. Both terminated in Denver. Still farther south lay the Santa Fe Trail, generally along the upper Arkansas River through western Kansas and eastern Colorado Territory. Its Cimarron Cut-off branched through southwestern Kansas and today's Oklahoma Panhandle.

The Treaty of Fort Wise, negotiated in the fall of 1860, was supposed to move the Cheyennes and Arapahos to a reservation in southeastern Colorado Territory farther away from these three routes. While the Arapahos seemed satisfied with it, the Cheyenne people were divided. Peace Chiefs Black Kettle and White Antelope were among those who had already signed it. On becoming a peace chief, each had followed Cheyenne tradition by giving up warfare and working through peaceful means for the welfare of his people. However, other Cheyenne chiefs were absent hunting bison on the plains and unavailable to sign the treaty even if they were willing to do so. Some, particularly the influential Dog Soldier warrior society, were not.[25] Meanwhile, scattered Indian attacks continued, and new federal Indian agent Albert G. Boone, responsible for the Upper Arkansas Agency, wrote in frustration in late April 1861, "Daily and hourly I am receiving complaints of burning ranches, killing stock as well as many cases of outrages of the gravest character perpetrated on white women."[26] With the treaty process incomplete, hostility festered from other Cheyennes toward the treaty signers and among the people of Colorado Territory toward Indians generally.[27]

In the fall of 1862 Anglo-Americans on the western frontier expected a large outbreak of Plains Indian raids, but things remained about as usual. Several representatives of the Plains tribes even went to

Washington, D.C., in March 1863 to visit Pres. Abraham Lincoln. Visits of Indian delegations to eastern cities and the capital were often meant to put Indians in awe of the strength, power, and number of Anglo-Americans. In this delegation were Cheyennes War Bonnet and Standing-in-Water, as well as Peace Chief Lean Bear. Other delegates included Arapahos Spotted Wolf and Neva; Kiowas Lone Wolf, Yellow Wolf, White Bull, Yellow Buffalo, and Little Heart; Comanches Ten Bears and Pricked Forehead; Poor Bear, a Plains Apache; and Caddo Jake. Lean Bear told President Lincoln that he deplored the war between the white men and that he was determined that Indians would not take part in it. He said he wanted white people to be able to travel the Plains in safety. Lean Bear urged the president "to counsel his white children, who were annually encroaching more and more upon [the] tribes, to abstain from acts of violence and wrong toward them."[28] President Lincoln responded that the Plains Indians should become farmers and live like white people. He also commented, "Although we are now engaged in a great war between one another, we are not, as a race, so much disposed to fight and kill one another as our red brethren."[29]

About three months later the problems on the western frontier began to intensify. When in July 1863 Union troops occupied Fort Gibson and defeated the Confederate allies at Honey Springs, Texans became concerned about the escalating threat from the north. Then in August Union general James G. Blunt drove down the Texas Road through Perryville into the Choctaw Nation. Expecting to see north Texas invaded next, Confederate commanders in the state hurried their troops to the Red River crossing at Colbert's Ferry in the Chickasaw Nation. Colonel Bourland, too, moved almost all his frontier regiment east across the Indian Territory toward Boggy Depot. Consequently, when Comanche and Kiowa raiders struck the western Texas and Chickasaw frontiers between August and December, they had little to fear as they destroyed property and made off with captives and herds of cattle. Earlier that March, while their delegates had been in Washington, they had signed a new treaty. Even though it was never ratified by the Senate, for the time being it allowed the Kiowas and Comanches to sell the cattle they captured in Texas, estimated at ten thousand head, to U.S. Army contractors in New Mexico and the Indian Territory. A side benefit of the Indian raids to the Texans in

1863, though, was that the flow of stragglers and deserters coming south across the territory and the Red River temporarily slowed.[30]

The year 1864 was even worse, and the western settlement line in Texas was rolled back toward the east about a hundred miles to the vicinity of Fort Worth. Kiowas and Comanches harassed traffic along the Santa Fe Trail, interfering with commerce, communication, the Union supply line to the Pacific Coast, and the army's Department of New Mexico, commanded by Brig. Gen. James H. Carleton.[31] That summer, while some Kiowas camped near Fort Larned in western Kansas, Setangia, or Sitting Bear, one of the Koeetsenko, or ten bravest Kiowa warriors, was involved in a misunderstanding near the fort, during which he put two arrows through the body of a sentry. In the panic that followed, the Kiowas drove off the fort's horse herd. A few days later Setangia sent a message to the post commander saying he hoped the quality of their horses would be better next time than the latest herd he had taken.[32]

These Indian troubles came as Maj. Gen. Samuel R. Curtis, now commander of the District of Kansas, was trying to shuffle troops east to stop Confederate major general Sterling Price's push out of Arkansas toward Missouri. They also coincided with the Second Battle of Cabin Creek, which saw Brigadier Generals Gano and Watie cut the federal supply line from Fort Scott, Kansas, to Fort Gibson. Curtis with most of the federal military believed force was the answer to Indian problems. He received word about then that Setangia had recently visited Agent Boone of the Upper Arkansas Agency to suggest making peace. Curtis wrote back he wanted no peace without punishment and he wanted indemnity for the property and livestock Kiowas had stolen. He insisted, "Something really damaging to them must be felt by them."[33]

Expecting the U.S. military to retaliate, the Kiowas and Comanches moved south to the Staked Plains in the western Texas Panhandle, camped along the Canadian River, and gathered stores for the coming winter. They may have been hoping to replenish their cattle and horse herds when Comanche chief Little Buffalo recruited the largest war party ever gathered by the two tribes. Some five hundred to seven hundred riders crossed the Red River into Texas under a full moon on October 12. The next day they split up into smaller bands, attacked the Confederate outpost at Fort Murray, and slashed through farms and ranches in Young County, about sixty miles south of today's Wichita Falls, Texas. Among their victims were women and children living on the Fitzpatrick ranch. Seven women, including Elizabeth Fitzpatrick and Mary Johnson, were captured and carried back to the Indian camps. Mrs. Fitzpatrick, who saw her married daughter and young son killed during the raid, was later ransomed and returned home. Britt Johnson, a black orderly at nearby Fort Belknap, found his son dead but went after his missing wife, Mary, and two daughters. With the assistance of Asa-Havey, or Milky Way, a Peneteka Comanche chief, Johnson eventually located his wife and children and ransomed them in May 1865.[34]

John Johnson, interviewed in the 1930s, claimed to be a son, "Cherokee, Comanche, and black," born to Mary Johnson while she was held in captivity. He stated that Britt Johnson learned Mary's location and traded corn, ponies, blankets, and calico cloth for his family. He did not know of baby John's existence and so did not include him in the trade. John said an old Indian woman, his mother's guard, wanted him, but "mother refused to go without me, so I was bought from the Indians for twelve ears of corn." He continued, "The widow took me in charge and kept me until I was eight years old. Then she returned me to my mother."[35] There is a discrepancy in his story, told more than seventy years later, in that he claimed his mother was taken captive in 1863, not 1864, the year of the Elk Creek raid. If he was born during her captivity, his father could have been one of her captors and not Britt Johnson. However, if his basic story is true, Johnson's ransom of the little boy showed his compassion for his wife and the child of her captivity.

Another captive taken in the raid on the Fitzpatrick Ranch was an eighteen-month-old girl, Elizabeth Fitzpatrick's granddaughter Millie Durgan. When the Kiowas who attacked the ranch broke in, killed little Millie's mother, and took Mrs. Fitzpatrick captive, Ausoantsaimah, or Aperian Crow, discovered her hidden under a bed. He pulled her out and took her home to his childless wife, Ahmate. All the captives of the Elm Creek raid were ransomed except Millie, known to the Kiowas as Saintohoodie. They claimed Millie was dead, when actually she was the pampered and much-loved foster child of her Kiowa parents. Ausoantsaimah was also a member of the Koeetsenko, an important man and wealthy by Kiowa standards. He persuaded other members

THE TERRORS OF WAR

of the tribe to keep his daughter's secret. Millie grew up Kiowa and lived from her early teenage years on the Kiowa-Comanche-Apache Reservation in southwestern Indian Territory. There she married Goombi and had her own family. She learned her true origin late in life and reestablished contact with her relatives in Texas. However, by then her identity and family were Kiowa, and her home was the Goombi place near Mountain View, Oklahoma.[36]

The Kiowa and Comanche menace led Brigadier General Carleton in New Mexico Territory to send Col. Kit Carson, the famous mountain man, scout, and Indian fighter, to suppress them. In late November 1864 Carson led about 350 volunteers from the 1st New Mexico Cavalry and 1st California Cavalry, backed by a company of California infantry with two mountain howitzers, east along the Canadian River. They were guided by about seventy-five Ute and Jicarilla scouts. The expedition located the winter camps of the Kiowas, Comanches, and Plains Apaches near the abandoned trading post known as Adobe Walls in today's Hutchinson County, Texas. Early on the morning of November 26, Carson attacked a Kiowa camp of 150 lodges. Dohausan, Stumbling Bear, and White Bear, or Satanta, led determined resistance long enough for the women and children to escape. White Bear added to the confusion by blowing cavalry calls on his bugle. Carson's force then attacked a Comanche camp about three miles away. This time he found himself outnumbered about ten to one. He quickly retreated to Adobe Walls and used the howitzers to hold off Indian attacks the rest of the day. Realizing they were running out of ammunition, Carson declared the fight at Adobe Walls a victory and withdrew but praised his enemies' daring and bravery in repeated charges. Kiowa oral history told how their principal chief Tohausan, by then an elderly man, rode to warn the other camps. As panicked women and children fled the camps, Ahmate, Millie Durgan's Kiowa mother, hid her in the brush until she could come back for her later. It is also said Stumbling Bear charged the white troops so ferociously that his little daughter's shawl, which he wore for good luck, had a dozen bullet holes at the end of the fight.[37]

Meanwhile, the severity of Kiowa and Comanche raids that fall led Texas authorities to plan a sweep into the Indian Territory to search out and destroy Indian raider camps, as they had done in 1858 with the aid of the Tonkawas and other Brazos Reserve Indians. A number of factors prevented that punitive expedition from taking place. What occurred instead was the Battle of Dove Creek.

In late December 1864, only a few weeks after the Elm Creek raid, Capt. N. W. Gillentine and a party of about twenty scouts were patrolling west of the Texas settlement line at that time. They spotted a wide Indian trail crossing the Brazos River and heading southwest. Alarmed, Gillentine immediately sent word to Fort Chadbourne asking for reinforcements. Within a short time, Capt. S. S. Totten was on his way with four Tonkawa scouts and Texas state troops, while Capt. Henry Fosset set off with Confederate troops from the fort. Meanwhile, Gillentine followed the trail toward the headwaters of the Concho River, finding abandoned campsites along the way. They indicated a large group moving deliberately but taking time to dress bison and deer hides. In the camp trash were broken plates, cups, and saucers, as well as some bits of calico. There was also a new spade-dug grave marked with a headboard. Over the protests of some of his men, Gillentine opened it to try to identify the people they were trailing. Inside was the body of a very young Indian girl, neatly dressed in buckskin. Gillentine's men divided up the items buried with the child, although some of the party said that might be "bad medicine."[38]

The trail Gillentine and his scouts picked up had been made by about seven hundred Kickapoos—three bands led by Papequah, Pecan, and Nokowhat. Known as indomitable warriors, the Kickapoos had migrated from the Great Lakes to the Great Plains during the last two centuries. In the early 1800s some went to Texas while it was still a Mexican province. After Texas became independent, hostilities with the Texans caused them to move on to Mexico in 1839 and serve with the Mexican military. By 1860, there was also a northern Kickapoo division with a reservation in Kansas, as well as a band of southern Kickapoos that had settled in the Muscogee Nation in the Indian Territory. The last lived by trading and helping defend its western frontier. When the Civil War began, most of the southern Kickapoo band went to Kansas, and a few had joined the Union Indian Home Guard. Others became jayhawkers, helping strip eastern Indian Territory of livestock and sometimes running afoul of their Osage neighbors. By late 1862 a group led by Machemanet grew so tired of refugee life in Kansas they moved through today's western Oklahoma and Texas to Mexico, fending off a battalion of mounted Texas Confederates on the way. Machemanet urged other Kickapoos to come to Mexico, too. Meanwhile, increasing federal pressure to open the northern Kickapoo reservation to white settlement caused Nokowhat, a northern Kickapoo leader, and his people to join the southern followers of Papequah and Pecan. This combined group then set out for Mexico in the fall of 1864.[39]

With their women, children, and elders along, the chiefs wanted to avoid trouble. Scouts sent by Machemanet guided them due west through Kansas before they turned south to cross today's western Oklahoma and Texas. With each day's travel planned, they took time to hunt game, cure meat, and tan hides against the coming winter. About New Year's Day 1865, near today's Mertzon, Texas, the chiefs decided to stop for a few days to let the ponies rest before the final days' travel to the Rio Grande crossing into Coahuila, Mexico. With a winter storm coming, they gathered wood and put up their lodges in the lee of a bluff edging a flat divided by Dove Creek. Three young men herded the horses into a nearby draw, but the chiefs saw no reason to post guards.[40] Brig. Gen. J. D. McAdoo, who investigated the incident at Dove Creek, reported, "The evidences seemed abundant . . . that they were civilized Indians, and there was nothing discovered that led to the belief that they were unfriendly, further than the simple fact that they were Indians traveling upon the soil of Texas without any notice being given to the civil or military authorities . . . of their presence or . . . of their intentions."[41]

On the morning of January 8, almost four hundred Confederate army, Texas state, and frontier militia troops gathered about three miles east of the Kickapoo camp. Gillentine described for Captains Fossett and Totten how the Indian camp was strung out along Dove Creek for about a quarter mile, while the horse herd was sheltered in the nearby draw. With minimal planning—Totten would take the north end of the camp while Fossett would take the south end and the horse herd—they prepared to attack. According to McAdoo, this was "without any formation of a line of battle, without any preparation, without any inspection of the camp, without any communication with the Indians or inquiry as to what tribe or party they belonged to, without any knowledge of their strength or position." Lieutenant Mulkey, "an old Indian guide, of Indian descent, born and raised in the Cherokee Nation [and] well-acquainted with Indian character and habits," was with Fosset's command. He advised against an attack, stating he saw no reason to believe these Indians were hostile. Fossett refused to communicate with them, though, "saying that he recognized no friendly Indians on the Texas frontier."[42]

McAdoo reported that Totten and Fossett drew their troops into a thin, mile-long line facing the camp and "a pell-mell charge was made for three miles." Rough ground and the sheer distance to the camp broke the force of the charge, as the better horses outpaced the slower. Many men had to dismount and wade the hip-deep creek to reach the camp. Accounts differ as to whether the Kickapoos knew they were coming. McAdoo's information said they did not and at first showed no inclination to fight. He reported, "The women were screaming about the camp, some of them in plain English declaring they were friendly." One man, believed to be a Pottawatomie, came out with two children and tried to surrender. Fossett, however, reportedly said, "We take no prisoners here," and ordered him shot down even after he handed the captain a hunting pass signed by the federal Indian agent for the Pottawatomies in Kansas. Fossett's men refused to shoot the children, who escaped later.[43]

Other accounts said the Kickapoos were waiting for the Texans and took firing positions in the ravines behind the camp with modern Enfield rifles as well as bows and arrows. They used both to cut down thirty of Totten's state troops. The initial Texan attack collapsed in less than an hour.[44] One report said the Texas state troops ran for their horses but even after they mounted, the Kickapoos came after them on foot, pulled some out of their saddles, and "slew them with demoniac fury."[45] At the other end of the camp, Fossett's Confederates captured the horse herd and got into the fight about the time Totten's state troops were pulling back. Polk Cox, a twenty-year-old in Speight's regiment, wrote in 1912, "We charged them about 9 o'clock in the morning and fought them till about 4 in the afternoon." Polk was wounded in the face but still mobile. He said, "There were several killed and wounded, amongst them my brother McDonald Cox. We had to retreat and leave the dead on the ground."[46] Unable to take the camp after about six hours of "scattering fire," the Texans began to disengage from the battle.[47] The Kickapoos surprised some of them, though, as they were re-crossing the creek. Panicked, the Texas Confederates fled, ignoring their officers' commands. Wounded and demoralized troops had already pulled back about three miles from the battleground. On the ridges east of the camp, the dispirited army waited for morning and then began a slow return trip to the settlements through fourteen inches of new snow. Their losses were twenty-six Texans dead and sixty wounded, along with more than sixty injured horses. The Battle of Dove Creek was the worst defeat Texans suffered in all their Indian wars.[48]

Captain Totten went back to Dove Creek a few days later and found the dead of both sides lying where they fell. He reported the Indian camp was abandoned along with "immense quantities of their baggage and property, including several hundred axes, spades, and other implements of husbandry, and immense numbers of buffalo and deer skins." The trail led west, but still no one then knew what Indian people had defeated the Texans. A rumor had been circulating that Kansas jayhawkers and Indians would sweep down on Texas that spring. Some suggested this was a preliminary spying expedition. However, McAdoo concluded these were simply people moving their families and all their possessions "to Mexico to escape the turmoil of the present war."[49] Unlike the Plains Indians who usually slipped away from a fight that became too costly, these Kickapoos, who went on to join their people in Mexico, had made a stand and then counterattacked, something the Texans did not expect. One trooper who was there wrote laconically in his diary entry for January 8, 1865, "made the attack. Got whipped."[50]

The Battle of Dove Creek was disastrous for Texans, and it particularly embarrassed the state troops. Desertions increased, making the situation worse along the Indian Territory-Texas border, already experiencing a surge in Plains Indian raids and plagued by lawless gangs of deserters and stragglers. However, it occurred in a fairly remote location and received much less attention than a similar, nationally publicized incident in Colorado Territory about six weeks earlier.[51]

Trouble had continued along the Kansas-Colorado Territory frontier through 1864. Some Cheyennes, particularly the militant Dog Soldiers, did not want to give up the game-rich Smoky Hill River country in western Kansas. Nor were they willing to accept confinement to the new southeastern Colorado reservation set aside in the Treaty of Fort Wise. However, Gov. John Evans was determined to clear them, the Arapaho, and other Indians from the path of development in Colorado

Territory. Panic threatened in June at rumors of an imminent Indian attack on Denver. Although it did not materialize, there were attacks on trails and outlying ranches. With Colorado's troops posted in Kansas and New Mexico, Governor Evans got permission to raise a new three-month volunteer regiment, the 3rd Colorado Cavalry.[52]

Evans suspected there was something else underlying the "formidable array of savage hostility" facing the federal government. On September 28, 1864, acting as ex-officio superintendent of Indian affairs for the region, he called a number of chiefs, including Cheyenne chief War Bonnet and Arapaho chief Neva, who had met with President Lincoln the previous year, to a conference at Camp Weld near Denver. Cheyenne peace chiefs White Antelope and Black Kettle were there, too. They offered to return white captives taken in raids, a concession which angered the Dog Soldiers.[53] Afterward Evans reported,

> I have taken great pains, in my intercourse with the Indians, and those connected with them who understand their plans, to ascertain whether there were any parties connected with the great rebellion acting in concert with them, or urging them on; but, so far, no positive evidence has been elicited from them. And yet it is a remarkable fact, that an emigrant of strong sympathy with the rebellion, who left southern Missouri last spring, should have stated that it was the plan of the rebels, under [Confederate major general Sterling] Price, to invade Missouri this autumn, at the time when our forces should be drawn away to fight the Indians on the plains; a statement which the subsequent facts would seem to indicate has been based upon information of an alliance between the Indians and the rebel army ... strengthened by professions, on the part of the Indians, that they have been offered the assistance and friendship of the south, if they would continue their war.

Evans concluded his report by stating the Indians were telling one another, "while the whites were fighting among themselves the Indians could easily drive them from their country," a belief "prompted by those who desired to aid the rebellion."[54]

However far-fetched some might consider a Plains Indian-Confederate military plot, Evans laid it on the table, and similar fears reverberated through the Office of Indian Affairs staff all the way across Kansas. Indian agents eyed their assigned tribes for any connection with the rebels but reported none. However, as the military ordered, they told the refugee and prairie reservation Indians to forgo their annual fall bison hunts on the plains for fear they might be mistaken for hostiles. Meanwhile, Evans argued pursuing the Indians into their hiding places was the only way to stop their attacks, intimidate them into peace, and secure their lasting friendship. Col. John M. Chivington of the new 3rd Colorado Cavalry had his own political ambitions and supported Evans's stance. Maj. Gen. Samuel R. Curtis, commander of the Department of Kansas, did not see cause for immediate alarm with the Cheyenne bands scattered over hundreds of square miles of the Plains. However, he telegraphed Chivington on September 28, "I want no peace till the Indians suffer more . . . . It is better to chastise before giving [them] anything but a little tobacco to talk over. No peace must be made without my directions."[55]

Feelings continued to run high that fall against the Cheyennes and Arapahos. Trying to avoid trouble, Peace Chiefs Black Kettle and White Antelope cooperated with Evans and the U.S. military at Fort Lyon by having their followers, about six hundred people, set up their winter camps along Sand Creek southeast of Denver. Among them were some of trader William Bent's half-Cheyenne children, including twenty-one-year-old George. Through 1861 and most of 1862 George had fought for the Confederacy, serving at the Battle of Pea Ridge in the 1st Missouri Cavalry before being transferred east of the Mississippi River. While fighting with a horse artillery unit protecting Confederate general P. G. T. Beauregard's retreat from Corinth, Mississippi, he was taken prisoner and delivered in September 1862 to the Gratiot Street Military Prison in St. Louis. Relatives and friends won his release, and he gratefully returned to his Cheyenne life. Familiar now with both Cheyenne and Anglo-American warfare, by winter 1864 the former Confederate soldier had established his reputation as a Cheyenne warrior and joined the Crooked Lance Society.[56]

By then Governor Evans's patience was thinning as he waited for the rest of the Cheyennes and Arapahos to come in and commit to the treaty and reservation life. Besides, the enlistment period of the 3rd Colorado Cavalry, the new unit raised specifically to fight Indians, was about to expire. On November 29, Colonel Chivington led them on a devastating dawn raid through the camp at Sand Creek, undeterred by the American flag and white flag waving from a lodge pole. Chief Black Kettle and George Bent, both wounded, were able to escape up the bluffs edging the creek. Many from the camp were less fortunate. Following their orders to take no prisoners, at the end of the day the soldiers left more than 150 Cheyennes and Arapahos lying dead and mutilated in the snow. Two-thirds of them were women and children.[57] Arapaho chief Left Hand; Cheyennes War Bonnet and Standing-in-Water, who had visited President Lincoln the previous year; and Cheyenne peace chief White Antelope were among the dead. The last, when he saw he could not stop the charging soldiers, had folded his arms and died singing, "Nothing lives long except the earth and the mountains."[58]

The Sand Creek Massacre was a watershed event in Cheyenne relations with Anglo-Americans. It contributed to a decade of warfare with the United States that expanded to include, among others, the Arapahos, Kiowas, Comanches, and Plains Apaches. When it was over in 1875, those nations were confined permanently to western Indian Territory reservations away from the current Anglo-American frontier. Sand Creek was also the beginning of the time, according to Kathryn Nibbs Bull Coming, born in 1913 in western Oklahoma, when Cheyenne children slept with their shoes on, ready to run. Her grandfather told her at bedtime, "'You're all right tonight. You take your shoes off . . . . In our days over here,' he said, 'white people was fighting us.'" Kathryn's grandmother also reassured her grandchildren as she tucked them in, "'You're all right, you sleep good at night. In our days we don't sleep good.'"[59]

Although Denver celebrated the attack at Sand Creek, word of the atrocities committed by the Colorado volunteers shocked many Anglo-Americans and infuriated native peoples along the frontier from the Northern Plains to Texas. Survivors of the massacre—destitute, wounded, hungry, and cold—struggled toward Cheyenne camps in the Smoky Hill region of western Kansas. According to Eugene Blackbear Sr., of today's Cheyenne and Arapaho Tribes, his great-grandfather Strong Bow's family snatched up a few supplies and fled from the extreme end of the Sand Creek encampment at the first sight of the soldiers. Later they stopped long enough to scratch out a grave for their little son Black Bear, apparently frozen to death while being carried on his mother's back. However, to their joy the rising sun warmed him, and he woke up hungry.[60]

Many Sand Creek survivors found shelter in other Indian camps. Runners carried news of the massacre and war pipes to the far-flung Cheyenne bands as well as the Arapaho and Lakota peoples. Through January and February 1865 Cheyennes, Arapahos, and Lakotas shared the common cause—striking back by burning all the ranches and stage stations along the Platte River route through Nebraska Territory, attacking wagon trains, driving away stock, ripping down the telegraph lines, burning the town of Julesburg twice, and cutting Denver off from the east. George Bent joined the raids, wearing a looted Union officer's uniform coat while retaliating for the massacre at Sand Creek.[61]

Farther south in January the Kiowas and Comanches, also angered by the massacre that came so soon after Carson's attack, camped near the Antelope Hills in western Indian Territory. Their recent raids into Texas and return to the Chickasaw Nation had alarmed not only the Confederate-allied Texans and Chickasaws, but also federal officials and Unionist Indians. Jesse Chisholm, a Unionist Cherokee trader, sug-gested settling them at a safe distance west on a Kiowa-Comanche-Plains Apache reservation along the Arkansas River near the Kansas border. Lewis Downing, also a Unionist and future Cherokee principal chief, proposed a grand council of all the tribes near Claremore Mound to help them reestablish old intertribal relations and friend-ships. This, he hoped, might keep the Plains tribes from turning on Loyal Indians and whites alike when their guard was down after the expected Union victory.[62] Perhaps these Union Indian concerns were warranted. In spite of some earlier wavering on their Confederate treaties, the western tribes, according to a message they sent to L. P. Chouteau, adjutant of the Confederate-allied Osage Battalion, were irate and ready to fight for the Confederacy. He in turn wrote to Col. James M. Bell of the Confederate-allied 1st Cherokee Regiment that the Kiowas would arrive for a council on January 25. Chouteau con-cluded, "I hope next Summer We will give Kansas hell."[63]

About three weeks later, Ohopeyane, second chief of the Comanches, sent a message to Tuckabatche Micco, then chief of the Confederate-allied Muscogees, which he relayed to Stand Watie. Ohopeyane reported that "Northern Officers" had twice approached the Kiowas, Comanches, and Arapahos, the first time the preceding year. They asked these tribes through interpreter Jesse Chisholm to go to war against the South. However, Chisholm apparently advised them against it and the tribes declined the proposal. On a more recent visit to the Indian camps near the Antelope Hills, the federal representatives offered goods, guns, and ammunition if they would attack Confederates and promised to buy captured livestock. They told the Indians to kill all the men and boys and to take the women and children prisoners. They were to give up any white women they captured, but they could keep Indian women. Through Chisholm the spokesman for the Comanches declined, saying he had friends among the southerners and would not attack them. Angry at being refused, the visitors took back their offer of weapons and goods. The chief responded he did not need them while he had his bow and arrows to hunt the buffalo and live on the prairie. This second visit broke up with hard feelings, and Tuckabatche Micco told Watie the Comanches were now hostile to the North and friendly toward the South. Still, even though the Plains tribes twice asked for a council with Confederate-allied representatives, there was no response, and they returned to their own country.[64]

In the meantime, several new factors began to affect the peacemaking process between the United States and these Plains tribes. With the Civil War now in its fourth year, the public in the Union states was eager for peace. They found the Sand Creek Massacre appalling and wanted to see the end of Indian-white warfare. So did many members of Congress, and three different investigations of federal Indian affairs occurred following the massacre. The early 1860s also saw a boom in railroad building. The Union Pacific Railroad, for example, had new federal charters to build a line across the Central Plains, and they wanted to do it without fear of Indian attacks. Ending the Indian menace would benefit them and their stockholders, which included some congressmen. These developments added to the old rivalry between the federal military and the Office of Indian Affairs for control of Indians and Indian policy. They made the road to peace with the Plains tribes even more difficult. Maj. Gen. John Pope and Maj. Gen. Grenville M. Dodge, recently assigned to protect travel and commerce along the Arkansas and Platte river routes, believed the Indian raiders plaguing them must be punished, although not with another Chivington-type massacre. However, Jesse Leavenworth, the new head of the Indian Office's Central Superintendency, and Senator James Doolittle recruited assistance from frontiersmen Jesse Chisholm, William Bent, and Kit Carson, who shared their belief that they could negotiate a peace settlement with the tribes.[65]

Later that spring the federal military launched a major offensive to the north that was designed to suppress the Plains tribes. It floundered as the U.S. Army discovered that large bodies of troops, many of them volunteers who just wanted to go home now that the war was winding down, and large, cumbersome supply trains were at a disadvantage in Plains warfare. This was especially true against fast-moving native people who knew the land and how to survive on it.[66]

In May 1865 new president Andrew Johnson stepped in and authorized Leavenworth and Doolittle to negotiate a treaty with the Cheyennes, Arapahos, Kiowas, Comanches, and Plains Apaches that would curtail the bloodshed. Leavenworth sent George Ransom, his black servant, scouting south from Council Grove, Kansas, to the North Canadian River. He found a large gathering of Kiowas, Comanches, Plains Apaches, Cheyennes, and Arapahos near Fort Cobb on the Washita River. Ransom talked to Tohausan, the Kiowa principal chief, who told him the Kiowas were watching the federal posts along the Santa Fe Trail. They feared "as soon as the grass started [to grow] the troops would be after them." Leavenworth reported,

> From all he (George Ransom) could learn he was satisfied that all the tribes were near Fort Cobb holding a grand medicine lodge. They would hold it for about thirty days, twenty of which are passed. When he arrived at the mouth of the Little Arkansas (the 28th) the friendly Indians reported a command of soldiers south of the Chikaskia [River], about sixty or seventy miles southwest of the mouth of the Little Arkansas. A Caddo chief sent word to [Jesse] Chisholm that all the Indians wished for peace except the Cheyennes, who came amongst them this spring from the north.

Leavenworth wrote that he believed this very large gathering of Indians would fight together against any small troop force advancing toward them from the north, but a large force would show them their own weakness, which in his opinion was not a bad thing.[67]

While the Kiowas and the tribes associated with them were holding that Sundance on the Washita River near Fort Cobb and waiting to see what would happen in the late spring of 1865, an even larger intertribal gathering instigated by the eastern Confederate allies was also taking place. The purpose had been to decide their best course now that rumors of Gen. Robert E. Lee's surrender in Virginia had filtered west. It was a question that people on both sides of the rebellion shared, along with general war weariness.

In February 1865 Joseph Perryman, a Muscogee rancher from the Tulsey Town area and member of the 1st Creek Mounted regiment, wrote to his former teacher at Tullahassee Mission:

> . . . a soldier's life is a troublesome life . . . . I would rather atend [sic] to stock raising than to be under arms . . . . I wish this rebelion [sic] could be put down and peace restored again. I would feel very glad for we could have a chance of going to our homes. [B]ut if we do return to our homes we cannot enjoy ourselves as before the war because there are a great many things that will be amiss to us there[,] for our property what few we did have is destroyed. There will also be family vacancies, [and] departed friends that we shall see no more on earth. But I still cherish the hope of beholding our people again prosperous and happy for I know from experience that a person feels a great deal better satisfied at home than away from it.[68]

Like many Indian Territory people, Perryman knew how badly the war was going for the Confederacy and that it could not last much longer. Still, the Confederate-allied Indian leaders were not willing to concede a Union victory. Some of their troops had been furloughed for the winter months or simply went to stay with their families in refugee camps. In early March, though, Muscogee colonel Timothy Barnett wrote to Brig. Gen. Stand Watie, "The men are all busily engaged in making little patches to plant something in, but are ready to go into camp when called upon—although there is great suffering among their families for something to eat."[69]

Union Indians also knew that spring was planting time, war or no war, and hoped this year their crops might fare better. That same week, Thompson Perryman wrote from Fort Gibson to missionary William Schenk Robertson, "our Creek people are now making preperations [sic] to farm this year . . . . Some are going on the western side of the Verdigris near the mouth, and others on the other side of the Arkansas river about as far as the old Creek Agency, while some are remaining on this side of the Verdigris. They are going to locate as far as Tullahassee Mission . . . . You may know from this that the Rebells [sic] are getting scarce. We hope to raise a crop of corn if no interruption takes place." Perryman was even thinking ahead to the future education of his four young daughters at Tullahassee, empty and damaged but still standing.[70]

In spite of some hopeful signs, serious questions faced the people of the Indian Territory. Could the Indian nations divided into hostile factions during the war reunite, given its particularly vicious and vindictive nature? How would the federal government treat the Confederate-allied nations and factions if, as now seemed likely, it emerged as the victor?

As early as 1863 some observers had doubted reunification would ever be possible for the Muscogee and Cherokee peoples. Noting Opothle Yahola's intransigent attitude toward the pro-Confederate Muscogees, federal officials working with the refugees in Kansas were convinced the "unrelenting and deadly" hostility between his and the McIntosh faction would never die.[71] Dr. Dwight D. Hitchcock, writing two years later in November 1865, shared that opinion. He told friends, "I cannot believe that the two factions will continue to live amicably together. Too much blood has been spilled."[72] There was even, Thompson Perryman said in March 1865, a division between Unionist Muscogees such as himself, "who did not share the unfortunate road to Kansas [his emphasis]" and those who joined Opothle Yahola there later.[73] Federal Indian officials believed the rift between the Cherokee factions was even deeper. Central superintendent William G. Coffin insisted in 1863 that in the postwar period the only answer was placing them in separate homelands. He believed the two divisions should be settled as far apart as possible to prevent a "war of extermination amongst themselves—slow, perhaps, but deadly and sure."[74] While that could be interpreted as a "divide and conquer" strategy, Blackbird Doublehead, a Cherokee teenager during the war, shared that outlook. In 1937 he remembered the war-rekindled feud between the Ross and Watie factions and predicted, "as long as there are three Cherokees alive in the United States, they will never forget this hatred."[75]

Still, internal Indian politics might count for less than the plans of a victorious United States Government. With the new Republican

Party in control of Congress during the war years, the Homestead Act and the Railway Act, geared toward national development and westward expansion, were passed. Both could benefit the new tumultuous, ambitious state of Kansas, but a line of Indian reservations already established along its eastern border was a roadblock to white settlement there. Potential homesteaders wanted access to those Indian lands as did railroad companies, which had more clout. Just before the war, railroad companies negotiated with Kansas tribes and bands such as the Delawares, Shawnees, and Wyandots, who at first saw potential benefits. They could sell part of their reserves and use the money to benefit their people while railroad development nearby increased the value of their remaining land. A few tribes did this with varying success, although it was sometimes over the objections of a conservative minority of their people. There were also experiments in allotting reservation lands to individual Indians. This was an idea foreign to most Indians, who viewed land as something that could not be owned in the way Euro-Americans understood it. They held land and its resources in common as a tribe. Promoters particularly targeted the Kaw (Kansa) and Ottawa tribes, whose reserves were near Topeka, the new state capital. The Kaws tried allotment in severalty by taking individual landholdings, but the experiment ended badly. Some had their land seized for nonpayment of taxes on it. Taxation was yet another practice foreign to most Indians.[76]

Meanwhile, pressure grew to move the tribes out of Kansas and Nebraska Territory and so free up still more land for development. Prime targets were the Osage reservation, a thirty-by-fifty-mile rectangle in southern Kansas, and the eight hundred thousand acres of the Cherokee Neutral Lands in southeastern Kansas.[77] But where would Kansas and Nebraska Territory Indians go if they were uprooted from their reservations?

In 1862 Kansas senators James H. Lane and Samuel Pomeroy produced a plan that would allow President Lincoln to suspend the treaties between the United States and the Five Civilized Tribes, appropriate some of their lands, and move the Indians in Kansas to new reservations in the Indian Territory.[78] By mid-1863, federal Indian department officials were working toward that goal. Just before Opothle

Yahola's death that spring, Central superintendent Coffin recommended that the treaty under negotiation recognizing the Loyal Creeks as the legitimate Muscogee Nation should be the model for future treaties with other fragmented and population-reduced Indian Territory tribes. These new treaties should promote the interests of the Indians and the federal government, he said, "especially in view of the removal of the Indians from Kansas and Nebraska Territory, as contemplated by a recent act of Congress."[79]

In his annual report written the next year commissioner of Indian affairs William P. Dole continued that theme. He stated that the Indian Territory embraced seventy-five thousand square miles but was inhabited by only about seventy thousand Indians even before the rebellion. That was less than one person per square mile on land he judged capable of supporting a dense population. Moreover, many of the prewar inhabitants had joined the rebellion, so relations with the federal government must be "readjusted" at the close of the war. He reasoned, "it can be no wrong to either class that they should be required to receive within the limits of the country other tribes with whom they are on friendly terms." In time, he concluded, the Indian Territory nations and the Kansas and Nebraska Territory tribes would "become one people."[80] Dole apparently believed the Indian nations' opinions, sovereignty, and identity to be as disposable as their land titles.

With the federal government targeting the Indian Territory as the destination for a new round of removals, the Confederate-allied Indian governments understood the need to stand together. Through most of the war their representatives had met periodically in a "Grand Council" at different locations in the Choctaw and Chickasaw Nations. It was, in fact, in session in February 1864, when Col. William A. Phillips marched toward the Red River distributing President Lincoln's Amnesty Proclamation. The delegates from the Choctaw and Chickasaw Nations had been able to hold the wavering Cherokee, Seminole, Muscogee, Caddo, and Osage representatives together that time. By spring 1865, though, the Confederacy was on the verge of collapse. The United States military had already begun mustering out the Indian Home Guard even though the Plains tribes remained actively hostile and the Indian Territory was still infested with rebels, rustlers, and renegades of all kinds. Some observers wondered if disbanding and disarming loyal Indian soldiers could be a precaution as the federal government assumed a more aggressive stance toward the Indian nations.[81]

In early April 1865 Gen. Robert E. Lee surrendered his Confederate army to Gen. Ulysses S. Grant at Appomattox Courthouse, Virginia. About the same time Maj. Israel G. Vore, a Confederate Indian agent, quartermaster, and intermarried Cherokee, received instructions from Gen. E. Kirby Smith, commander of the Confederate Trans-Mississippi Department. Vore was to call representatives of the Indian Territory nations to Council Grove on the North Canadian River just west of today's Bethany, Oklahoma. Meanwhile, the governors of Texas, Arkansas, Louisiana, and Missouri were to meet at Marshall, Texas, to discuss their options. Even though the Confederacy seemed near its demise, it was not dead yet. Its allies in the Trans-Mississippi region needed to plan accordingly. Aid might still come from Europe or Emperor Maximilian of Mexico—an agent was already on his way there—and Texas could be the nucleus of a new Southern republic. This initiative even had the backing of Confederate president Jefferson Davis.[82] At the time, William P. Bumpass was a second lieutenant in the 5th Texas Partisan Rangers. He remembered, "The Confederate troops had high hopes of maintaining the independence of the South at that time and expected to hold all the territory which we might occupy at the close of the war, and we particularly wished to hold all of what is now Oklahoma, for we knew, even then, that it was as valuable a piece of territory as was to be found west of the Mississippi River and, along with Texas, was large enough for an empire."[83]

Holding all the Indian nations—woodland, prairie, and Plains tribes—loyal to the Confederacy or its successor in the West was vital. Their old friend Albert Pike was unavailable to serve in this endeavor, but Brig. Gen. Douglas H. Cooper worked from his headquarters at Fort Washita to keep their allegiance. Texas would be a vital part of the effort, but antipathy between the Plains tribes and Texans could be a stumbling block. Brig. Gen. James W. Throckmorton, a future Texas governor, and Col. W. D. Reagan prepared to take backseats even while serving as commissioners in the preliminary meeting. It was set for May 15 at Council Grove near Jesse Chisholm's ranch and trading post. Cooper, reporting on the planned procedure for the conference, wrote that the delegates would observe Indian diplomatic traditions. First there would be a meeting "between the representatives of the allied nations and the delegates from the Indians of the plains, to whom the tobacco and wampum had been sent inviting them to council." This, Cooper explained to the Confederate staff, was the preliminary to "a general peace and treaty of friendship among all the Indians." It would be a two-stage process. The first was creating a peace among the Indians in which, Cooper wrote, they "washed out all the 'red spots' and made the 'paths' between them 'white.'" Then the representatives of the Confederate states would be introduced. A three-party treaty would be made in writing as well as symbolically "according to their custom . . . with the tobacco, the pipe, and the wampum."[84]

Before the meeting got underway, however, news came that federal troops might be coming south to break it up. That information turned out to be false, but it caused the delegates to scatter immediately after resetting the date of the main meeting for May 26 and changing the location to Cotton Wood Grove farther west on the Washita River. The new location, the site of today's Verden, Oklahoma, was widely known among the territory's Indian peoples because of its abundant water and grass. Some two or three hundred giant cottonwood trees provided good shelter near the red sandstone bluffs edging the Washita River valley. The meeting at this place in late May 1865 would be called "Camp Napoleon," but the rationale for the name has never been established.[85]

During that short delay there was significant news that caused reconsideration of the road ahead and changes in the goals of the Camp Napoleon meeting. Cooper received official notice of Lee's surrender in Virginia, and, while the four state governors debated capitulation in their meeting, federal officials arrived in Texas to take the formal surrender of Gen. E. Kirby Smith and the Confederate Trans-Mississippi Department. That affected an idea Cooper had suggested about the time of the preliminary meeting, when he wrote,

> I am informed the Indians who will attend the council are thirsting for revenge on the frontier of Kansas, and if assisted will at once attack the frontier of Kansas, and even operate farther north simultaneously. Now I desire instructions whether under existing circumstances it would be proper or politic to turn loose these savages upon the Federal settlements on their frontier; and if so,

request to be informed as to the time when the attack should be made. If there is any [Confederate] movement against Missouri in contemplation, the expedition against Kansas and the frontier generally, by the Indians and troops of this district, should of course be so timed that the two columns would support each other and create a diversion mutually advantageous.[86]

When word came, though, of the probable surrender of the governors and the Trans-Mississippi Department, Cooper immediately sent word to Throckmorton to suppress the proposed Indian assault. He suggested the focus of the treaty be changed from Confederate-Indian to intertribal.[87]

The resulting Camp Napoleon meeting combined diplomacy, pageantry, and trade. For the first time in about two decades, delegates from the high plains, prairies, and wooded hills and valleys of eastern Indian Territory mingled in significant numbers. Six thousand people, perhaps more, camped under the cottonwoods along the Washita River. Some say Texans, even representatives from Mexico, were there. If so, there is no record of them other than commissioners Throckmorton and Reagan. Several current or future heads of the Indian nations attended, as well as Indian leaders experienced in diplomacy with the United States and other native peoples. This was the place Texan Britt Johnson came looking for his wife and children, captured in the Elm Creek raid, and with the mediation of Comanche chief Asa-Havey traded for their freedom.[88]

The Camp Napoleon Compact drafted and signed there noted some key issues all the Indian delegates recognized from their past dealings with the United States government, particularly their shrinking independence, land bases, and resources. They agreed that they were "hemmed in to a small and precarious country that we can scarcely call our own." They understood that their best hope of keeping what remained was unity. After declaring eternal peace and friendship among the signers, they declared themselves an Indian confederacy which would settle internal disputes by diplomacy rather than warfare and took as their motto, "An Indian shall not spill an Indian's blood." Representatives of the Confederate-allied Cherokee, Muscogee, and Seminole factions signed the compact, along with delegates from the Chickasaw and Choctaw Nations and the Reserve Caddos, Comanches, and Osages, plus the Kiowas, Arapahos, Cheyennes, and Plains Apaches who were present, and Jim Pockmark's band of Caddos and Anadarkos.[89] While most of the promises in the compact to settle differences between tribes peacefully were soon disregarded, the meeting did reinforce the tradition of intertribal meetings, which strengthened communication and consultation. Along with maintaining a unified Indian front, these would become even more important in the post–Civil War period.

The leaders of the Confederate-allied factions of the Cherokees, Seminoles, and Muscogees, as well as the Choctaw and Chickasaw Nations, had enough experience dealing with the United States Government to understand their best course, when the time came to surrender, was as independent nations separate from the Confederacy. Because there was some confusion among the Union authorities as to whether the U.S. Army or the Department of the Interior would be responsible for accepting their surrender, the Indian nations, under the guidance of Brig. Gen. Douglas H. Cooper, were able initially to act with more strength and independence than might have been expected.[90]

Those were anxious days as people waited in late May to see what would happen. Sallie Watie was particularly worried, given her family's bitter history with the Union Cherokees. She wrote her husband, Stand Watie, "we hear all kinds of rumers [sic] . . . . We don't know what to believe." She begged to be told the worst so she could prepare herself for it, saying, "if I fall among the feds I do not want to be amonge [sic] old Blunts set for the pins will be mean enoug[h]." She had also heard there was a price on her husband's head and complaints he was profiteering at the expense of his own people. She refused to believe the latter, saying she doubted it was so because that was not his character. Besides, if he was filling his pocket "it would have been filled before this time."[91]

Meanwhile, some of Watie's Cherokee and Muscogee troops were still in the field. Scouting along the Canadian River and its tributaries in the Muscogee Nation toward North Fork Town, they had seen no sign of federal troops.[92] As the Confederate military structure crumbled, Stand Watie wrote to Sallie from Boggy Depot on May 27 that there was "great confusion amongst the troops more particularly the white portion." Because he was hearing rumors that they might soon start looting public property, he said he had sent enough of them home on furlough that he believed he could keep the rest under control. He concluded, "I only write to let you know that I am still in the land of the living."[93]

On May 26 when Gen. E. Kirby Smith surrendered the Trans-Mississippi Department, Confederate hopes of hanging on in the West ended. When the Grand Council of the Indian nations met at Armstrong Academy on June 10, the delegates remained unified. They agreed that each nation's full legislature must ratify a peace treaty to make it binding. However, a week later Gov. Peter Pitchlynn of the Choctaw Nation met with Col. A. C. Matthews, representing the federal command in Louisiana, and on June 18 he surrendered to prevent a planned federal incursion across the Red River. Matthews simply ordered the Choctaw troops to go home, not as paroled Confederate soldiers, but under the protection of the United States. Encouraged, Gov. Winchester Colbert of the Chickasaw Nation also contacted federal officials to end hostilities. On June 26, Stand Watie arrived at Doaksville in the Choctaw Nation and, as principal chief of the Cherokee Nation and commander of the Indian Brigade, signed articles that made him the last Confederate general officer to surrender. These articles for a truce included the Muscogees, Seminoles, and Osages involved in hostilities with the United States. They, too, were simply told to go home under federal protection. However, white troops in the Indian Territory were ordered to report to federal paroling officers. The leaders of the Indian nations expected the moderate-approach agreements to serve until September 1 when the Grand Council would meet again. In the meantime they appointed delegates who left for Fort Smith, their first stop on the road to Washington. There they intended to conclude hostilities formally. At Fort Smith, though, the Indian delegates learned that they would no longer be dealing with the military, nor would they have much control over the fate of the Indian Territory.[94]

Meanwhile, the accord established between the Plains tribes and the eastern Indians at Camp Napoleon lasted less than a month. The Chickasaw Nation, stung by comparatively small raids in 1863 and 1864, was the victim. By June 1865 the Caddo Frontier Guard had been disbanded, and the Confederate-allied Chickasaw soldiers were back home under the terms of the truce between Gov. Winchester Colbert and the Union officers. Federal troops had reoccupied Fort Washita, and there was a federal force, too, at Fort Arbuckle farther northwest. While military and refugee demands had left eastern Chickasaw Nation farms and ranches nearly stripped of crops and livestock, those on the western side were still well stocked. They had no real market for their corn or herds in the summer of 1865. Plains raiders could expect to find the pickings good there.[95]

In mid-June a party of about 350 Comanches rode into the Chickasaw Nation from the northwest following the divide between the Canadian and Washita Rivers. They crossed today's McClain County and northeastern Garvin County before reaching the Sealy settlement south of the present towns of Stonewall and Jesse in Pontotoc County. While the Chickasaw residents ran for the nearby hills, the Comanches drove off horses, mules, and cattle but left their houses untouched. From there they moved on southeast to the James settlement and Wapanucka Academy near the eastern border, then to the Mosely settlement only about fifteen miles from Boggy Depot in the Choctaw Nation. Turning southwest, they struck the Keel settlement on Pennington Creek near Tishomingo. By then the raid was four days old, and the Comanches had cut a long swath as much as fifteen miles wide in places. They circled south of the Arbuckle Mountains, crossing today's Interstate 35 about ten miles north of Ardmore, and headed back west toward today's Duncan, Oklahoma. They were driving the Chickasaw livestock they had stolen toward the Wichita Mountains. After crossing Cache Creek east of the mountains, they split up, sending herders north up the west side of the creek with most of the livestock.[96]

Behind them three hundred angry Chickasaws gathered at Wells Spring, about two miles west of Wapanucka. Intent on recovering their livestock, they quickly organized for the job, electing as their captain Milton Brown, a lieutenant in Col. Sampson Folsom's regiment during the war. A cattleman with a ranch near Wapunucka, he could also have been one of the Comanches' victims. He chose Tommy Joseph as his lieutenant, with Wash Colbert, Puckinachubbe, Patterson, and Harris Greenwood as his staff. Each settlement and neighborhood represented at the meeting formed a company of thirty-five to fifty men and chose their own lieutenant. Although the Comanches were several days ahead, but the Chickasaws sent trailers after them, while they organized at the Mosely settlement and then moved out. Riding hard, they followed the Comanche trail westward toward today's Duncan, Oklahoma, across Cache Creek, and on to Elm Spring near the future site of Lawton, Oklahoma. By then they were so close on the heels of the Comanches they pulled back a few miles to keep from being discovered. That could cause the raiders to scatter their stock before the Chickasaws were ready to attack.[97]

With a fight likely to occur soon, Brown and his staff faced a dilemma. They wanted their property back, but the Chickasaw Nation had just reached a truce with representatives of the U.S. Army. They did not want trouble with federal troops if word of their large, well-armed posse reached Fort Arbuckle or Fort Washita. As a precaution, they sent five men back to find out what the Fort Arbuckle garrison knew and if any alarm had been raised. These scouts learned that some Comanches had recently appeared near Fort Arbuckle, causing just enough excitement to keep the small garrison there pinned up and skittish. However, no one at Fort Arbuckle knew anything about the main Comanche raiding party that had twice crossed the Chickasaw Nation rustling livestock as they went. Nor did they know that three hundred armed Chickasaws were hard on their trail.[98]

It was early July before the main Chickasaw column left Elm Spring on the south side of the Wichita Mountains and followed the trail of their stolen livestock north along Cache Creek to its source. There the posse crossed over into the Washita River valley, went west around the north end of the Wichita Mountains, and circled back south along the west side, nearly completing a loop. Occasionally tracks showed small numbers of stock being driven away from the herd, but the Chickasaw leaders refused to be diverted from the main trail. About a month passed while they followed it cautiously, lived off the abundant game, and concealed their camps to keep the Comanche herders unaware of their presence until they could retake the whole herd.[99]

A distant flash of sunlight off metal finally led them to the Comanche camp that was the destination for their stolen stock. It lay south of the mountains between today's Cache and Indiahoma, Oklahoma, about fifteen miles southwest of the future Fort Sill. That night the Chickasaws stealthily surrounded the camp, working in between the Comanche horse herd and their livestock. After posting

THE TERRORS OF WAR

pickets, they settled down for the night in near silence. Dawn was just breaking when a Chickasaw bugler signaled their attack and wakened the Comanche camp. Warriors poured out of the lodges along with panicked women and children. Unable to reach their horses, the Comanches were forced to fight on foot, putting them at a disadvantage. Although they repeatedly threw themselves at the Chickasaw line, the Comanches, outnumbered and poorly armed against the Chickasaw rifles, were unable to break up their attack. By midmorning Comanche losses were so great they sent an English-speaking messenger out under a white flag to parlay. The Comanches agreed to let the Chickasaws take back their livestock, while they collected their own dead and wounded.[100]

It took two days for the Chickasaws to identify their animals by their brands and cut them out from the Comanche stock while they kept close watch on the hostile camp. Their trip back was slow because some of the recaptured livestock was by now in poor condition. A few had been lost, but they arrived home with enough recovered for a feeling of triumph to sweep their settlements. Even then, the Chickasaws, still wary of repercussions from the federal government, kept very quiet about the expedition for years, until most of the participants were dead. There were other Plains Indian raids on Chickasaw ranches and settlements in the following decade, but none was ever so large or penetrated so deep into their country. Nor did any other raid occur at such a critical time.[101]

The story of the Chickasaws' tenacious pursuit of the Comanche raiders and recovery of their livestock was lost amid larger problems and changes affecting the Indian peoples of the West in the backwash of the Civil War. Outbreaks of violence between white Americans and the Eastern Sioux, Navajos, and Mescalero Apaches during the war and the defection of many of the Indian Territory nations to the Confederacy disturbed some United States Office of Indian Affairs personnel assigned to Kansas and Nebraska Territory reservations. F. W. Farnsworth, agent to the Kaws (Kansa) at the Kansas Agency at Council Grove, wrote in August 1864, "All Indians are now looked upon with more suspicion than common, and some bad men do all they can to create ill will towards them."[102]

Although Farnsworth insisted no tribe was more loyal than the Kaws, some suspected them of association with the Kiowas, who were just then threatening the Santa Fe Trail. On a recent visit to Fort Riley he had witnessed military officers giving the Indians gifts in an attempt to win their good will. Farnsworth was outraged and insisted, "I believe that lead, and plenty of it, is what the Kiowas want, and must have, before they will behave." To make matters worse, seven hundred Kaws faced hunger that winter because the military ordered them not to go on their annual fall bison hunt for fear of attacking them by mistake. Farnsworth concluded, "Loyal Indians complain that the government feeds and clothes these murderous [Kiowa] thieves, and they are left to starve."[103]

This occurred while many of the Indian men living on reservations in Kansas and Nebraska Territory were serving in army units to demonstrate their loyalty or defend the United States. Thus, according to commissioner of Indian affairs D. N. Cooley, they "sealed the devotion with their blood."[104] The "friendly and loyal" Kaws, he said, sent eighty-four soldiers to the army, "of whom 24 have died."[105] The Pottawatomis, likewise, sent seventy-one soldiers into the Union army, and their agent reported, "a large percentage of them have died in the service."[106] The Delawares had been an ally of the United States since the American Revolution and continued to defend it during the Civil War. Their agent wrote, "they maintain fully their reputation for devoted loyalty, having furnished many good soldiers to the army."[107] In late 1864 he noted, "The male portion of the tribe are either in the army or are employed in its connexion [sic], and it is a matter of some satisfaction to be able to say they have distinguished themselves in the army of the frontier as most excellent troops. A party of twenty left here latterly under Captain Fall Leaf to assist in the expedition now being engaged against the Sioux."[108] Another tribe that went to war then as allies of the United States against the Sioux were the Pawnees. Eighty-seven mustered in as scouts in the winter of 1864–1865, beginning a proud tradition of service in eight American wars that is still commemorated by the Pawnee Nation.[109]

The Kansas tribe that had the most men enlisted in the Union ranks was the Osage tribe, with about 240.[110] However, the Iowas probably sent the most men into federal military service in proportion to their whole population, assigned to the Great Nemaha Agency in Nebraska Territory. There were only 298 Iowas, with 78 men, 105 women, 51 boys, and 59 girls. "Of the 78 men," their agent reported in late 1864, "14 are soldiers in the 13th Kansas regiment, 23 in the 14th Kansas cavalry regiment, 1 in the 1st Nebraska regiment, and 3 in a Missouri regiment, making a total of 41 Iowa Indians who are soldiers, leaving only 21 men on the reserve who are between the ages of 20 and 45 years." They were not only good soldiers, they also learned to speak English while they were away. Those who remained on their reservation served, too, on the home front. Their agent reported, "The Iowas have thirty-four farms or patches, containing 289 acres, and notwithstanding the small number of men, have produced, without any assistance except the [agency] farmer breaking the ground, laying it out, &c., for the families of soldiers, about 6,500 bushels of corn, 65 bushels of wheat, 40 bushels of oats, 550 bushels of potatoes, and 150 tons of hay."[111]

Both the war in the east and the surge of hostilities on the Plains in 1864 and 1865 involving the Cheyennes, Arapahos, Kiowas, Plains Apaches, and Comanches concerned the tribes in Kansas and Nebraska Territory. Word spread in late summer 1864 that emissaries had invited them to a council with the Confederate-allied tribes that fall in the Muscogee country in the Indian Territory. To rebut any charges of disloyalty to the United States, they held their own meeting in October 1864 on the council ground of the Sac and Fox Agency in Kansas. Delegates from the Loyal Muscogees, Loyal Seminoles, Loyal Chickasaws, Sacs and Foxes of the Mississippi, Osages, Pottawatomies, Senecas, Shawnees, Quapaws, Kaskaskias, Peorias, Weas, Piankashaws, and Miamis signed a proclamation (probably at least partially worded by Office of Indian Affairs staff), which declared,

> we have been faithful to all our treaty stipulations, and truly loyal to the government of the United States; and we solemnly pledge ourselves, our tribes and nations, to our Great Father the President, that we will remain true to him as good, obedient, and loyal children; we consider his enemies our enemies, and his friends our friends; and, although weak and feeble within ourselves, we pledge him our aid and assistance in putting down and crushing out all his enemies, until every rebel in the land shall acknowledge the power of our Great Father.[112]

These delegates, all of them representing native peoples that had been or would be removed to the Indian Territory within a decade, concluded,

"And we would respectfully ask of our Great Father a faithful fulfillment of all our treaty stipulations, and that protection for ourselves, families, and homes due to your loyal and confiding children."[113]

Tremors from the Civil War disturbed even the Otoe and Missouria peoples on their reservation along the Kansas-Nebraska Territory border. According to William Daily, their agent in late August 1864, they were dissatisfied because their annuities were being paid in the paper "greenbacks" issued by the federal government during the war rather than in coin as guaranteed in their latest treaty. The greenbacks, which were not backed by gold, fluctuated in value and contributed to inflation, something the Otoes and Missourias discovered when they made purchases. They had been able to buy what they needed with coin, but, Daily reported, "they say, with much truth, that since they are paid in paper currency, that they cannot buy a sufficient amount with it to do them any good—that they are getting poorer every year." Daily recommended, "It would, in my judgment be advisable to pay them at least one-half of their annuity in coin, as that would insure their loyalty to the government, and their services in this war as scouts, &c."[114]

John A. Burbank, agent for the Iowa and the Sacs and Foxes of Missouri, also noticed a disturbance creeping through many of the neighboring reservations even though he did not see it on his. He reported that fall, "While the recent Indian outbreaks have affected almost every tribe on the frontier, the two little bands comprising this agency have remained insensible alike to the whispers of the disaffected of their own race and the seduction of disloyal whites."[115]

Unfortunately, a problem did arise among Indian Civil War veterans in the fall of 1865. Agency personnel in the Central Superintendency noticed "the habit of Indians, lately returned from service in the army, [of] carrying arms, which they drew and used upon the slightest provocation or excitement. An order was at first issued to disarm the Indians generally, but this was modified so as to require them, when in public assemblies, at payments, or on the occasion of their visiting the towns, to deposit their arms with their agent, receiving receipts [for them]." With relief, Agency staff reported, "The order, it is believed, has had an excellent effect."[116]

Things were definitely changing on the Plains in 1865, and the federal government had to deal with the Indian peoples on Kansas and

Nebraska Territory reservations as well as the hostile Cheyennes and their allies. White settlers were moving west in ever-greater numbers and flowing around—and sometimes over—Indian boundaries. At the federal government's urging some Indians in the southeastern United States had taken individual land allotments in the 1830s, but the experiment had generally been a failure. It had been tried again on Great Plains reservations and remained an option as the Civil War drew to a close. The commissioner of Indian affairs explained, "The advance of the white population, and the gradually increasing attention of the Indians to farming, and their abandonment of the chase, resulted in new treaties, by which the Indians consented to take allotments of specified quantities of land for each person, old and young, and that the surplus land should be sold for their benefit."[117]

Unfortunately, the experiment with allotment in severalty worked little better the second time. For example, debts the Indians had incurred often consumed the income from the surplus land sales, leaving no funds for new expenses. Then there were problems of allotment ownership, such as questions regarding land sales, inheritance of land, and the rights of children orphaned after their parent received a single allotment for the family—the last a problem plaguing the Miamis, Peorias, Kaskaskias, Weas, and Piankashaws of the Osage River Agency. Sometimes Indians became naturalized American citizens in federal courts and were considered legally able to handle their affairs. However, the commissioner admitted, "Experience has shown that in too many cases this process of naturalization has been attempted upon Indians who are notoriously unfit for citizenship." They might lose their allotted land and, along with it, the ability to support their families, which meant returning to their old reservation and an agency no longer responsible for them.[118] What happened to the Sacs and Foxes of the Mississippi was an example of the perils of breaking up a reservation. The commissioner reported, "The largest portion of the extensive reservation of the Sacs and Foxes has been sold at public sale, the funds realized being, however, swallowed up in the payment of certificates of indebtedness of the Indians." The tribes were left with a "diminished reservation," which would support them only if they could be persuaded to give up their traditional hunting way of life and take up farming, which required less land.[119]

These difficulties and hard realities could be solved or improved, federal officials apparently believed, if they wiped the slate clean and removed these tribes to the Indian Territory. They could be resettled on new reservations on the extensive lands held by the five southeastern tribes since their 1830s removals. That was a key issue in late summer 1865 as representatives of the Indian Territory and some Kansas nations were called to Fort Smith, Arkansas, to reestablish relations with the United States. There they found that whatever control they had believed they had over the process now lay in the hands of federally appointed commissioners: D. N. Cooley, the new commissioner of Indian affairs; Elijah Sells, superintendent of the Southern Superintendency, which included the Indian Territory; Thomas Wistar, a prominent member of the Society of Friends; Brig. Gen. W. S. Harney of the U.S. Army; and Col. Ely S. Parker, a Seneca Indian and member of Gen. U. S. Grant's staff. On September 8 the Fort Smith Council opened a series of meetings between these commissioners and representatives from the Muscogees (including three former slaves), Choctaws, Chickasaws, Cherokees, Seminoles, Osages, Senecas, Shawnees, Quapaws, Wyandots, Wichitas, and Comanches. The commissioners immediately laid out the federal perspective: "that they for the most part, as tribes, had, by violating their treaties, by making treaties with the so-called Confederate States, forfeited all *rights* [their italics] under them, and must be considered as at the mercy of the government." However, the commissioners continued, the federal government intended to be lenient and "to recognize in a signal manner the loyalty of those who had fought upon the side of the government, and endured great sufferings on its behalf."[120]

On the second day the commissioners presented the points they expected in the new treaties:

1. Each tribe must agree to a permanent peace among their tribal members, other tribes, and the United States.

2. The tribes living in the "Indian country" would, if called on, aid federal authorities in forcing the "wild tribes" to keep the peace.

3. Slavery must be abolished and former slaves incorporated into the Indian nations and their rights guaranteed. (This was before passage of the 13th, 14th, and 15th Amendments to the Constitution.)

4. A section of the Indian Territory would be purchased and set aside for Indians from Kansas or anywhere else the federal government might choose to colonize there.

5. All the tribes of this region would be consolidated under a single Indian government.

6. No white persons except federal employees, government-authorized officers, or employees of "internal improvement companies authorized by the government" (that could be interpreted as railroad companies) would be allowed to live in the Indian Territory unless they had connections to the Indian nations.[121]

These demands and commissioners' expectations took many of the representatives by surprise to say the least. Even though some members of the "loyal" factions of Indian nations were already aware of federal intentions from wartime treaty negotiations during their Kansas exile, others were not. Several representatives believed they had simply come to Fort Smith to make peace with members of their own tribes who had "gone south" and to reestablish relations with the United States. Instead, the commissioners presented them with demands that would reduce their land bases, affect their relations with other Indian peoples, and undermine their sovereignty without regard for their loyalty to the United States or lack of it during the Civil War.

The delegates received printed copies of the demands to study that night—some with the help of literate interpreters—and on the third day tried to defend themselves. The Loyal Creek representative insisted the Muscogee principal chief in 1861 had acted without authorization and asked "to be considered not guilty" because of that official's actions.[122] The Union Cherokees argued, as many pro-Confederate Indian Territory leaders had since 1861, that the federal government abandoned the Indian nations, leaving them no choice except to ally themselves with the Confederacy. The commissioners rebutted this by stating that under Principal Chief John Ross the Cherokee Nation allied itself with the Confederacy, raised troops, and encouraged other Indians to do the same, thus making the whole nation guilty. Ross, by then nearly seventy-five, had recently returned from the East in poor health and was staying in Fort Smith. Even though he was not at the council, Commissioner

Cooley believed Ross tried to influence the proceedings by keeping his nation divided.[123]

Although the federal commissioners did not credit the Indians' arguments, they realized that as long as the internal divisions existed in some nations, final treaties on which to make the land transfers the federal government wanted must wait. Some delegates also stated they were not empowered to act on these important issues before consulting with their governments. The commission succeeded in getting treaties signed to establish peace among factions of the Senecas, Shawnees, Quapaws, Seminoles, Chickasaws, Muscogees, and Osages, as well as intertribal peace agreements among those tribes and the Kaws (Kansas), Wichita Agency tribes, and Comanches. The major problem remaining was achieving an accord between the Cherokee factions, still bitterly divided. The reunified Muscogee Nation agreed to cede all its land north of the Arkansas River and half of its land south of that river for the future settlement of friendly tribes from Kansas or other places. The Choctaw and Chickasaw Nations, likewise, agreed to cede the Leased District for federal resettlement of other Indian peoples. Generally satisfied by the results of the Fort Smith Council, the federal commissioners started back east. The Indian delegates went home restored to the good graces of the United States and mostly at peace with other Indians but knowing there were still bitter pills to swallow.[124]

The federal government lost no time in pushing its plans to resettle Indians on new Indian Territory reservations, even though the final negotiations on the land transfers had not even started. There was still trouble on the Plains with the Comanches, Kiowas, Plains Apaches, Arapahos, and Cheyennes, and it needed resolution as soon as possible so as not to hinder the advancing Anglo-American frontier, accelerating now that the Civil War was over. Even though the U.S. Army believed force was necessary to subdue the Plains tribes, Agent Jesse Leavenworth continued his attempts to negotiate a peace. In the spring of 1865, new president Andrew Johnson opted for Leavenworth's approach and appointed Senator James R. Doolittle to head a congressional committee charged with making peace. During the summer Doolittle conferred with William Bent, Kit Carson, and other knowledgeable frontiersmen while Jesse Chisholm visited Indian camps south of the Arkansas River. Word came back that only the Cheyennes and Arapahos wanted to continue the hostilities inflamed by the Sand Creek Massacre. Kiowas, Wichitas, and Caddos, serving as intermediaries, took word to the tribes to come to a council at the mouth of the Little Arkansas River, the site of today's Wichita, Kansas.[125]

Indians began gathering in early August. Kiowa chief Tohausan came as did Plains Apache chief Poor Bear, and Jesse Chisholm arrived with some of the Comanches. Although Big Mouth of the Arapahos came, there were still no Cheyennes there. The chiefs who did come signed a truce, which reduced attacks on the Santa Fe Trail. Finally on August 18, Chiefs Black Kettle and Little Robe arrived with some of the Arapahos. They, too, agreed to a truce, which recognized that the Sand Creek Massacre was the cause of recent Cheyenne and Arapaho hostilities. They also agreed to a second meeting, this time with Doolittle's peace commission.[126]

The second meeting at the mouth of the Little Arkansas took place in mid-October 1865. Samuel A. Kingman, hired to help deliver supplies, described the setting, events, and participants in his diary with a mixture of disdain and admiration for the Indians:

> Oct. 11. We have been here one week . . . . Below us a few miles are the villages of several bands of refugee Indians. They have raised small crops of corn, pumpkins, beans & watermelons. They are destitute, dirty, half-clad beggars [of] fine physique. The men [are] all lazy, the women all lewd. They visit camp in great numbers daily. The Osages also visit us. They are like the others save that they do not beg, are better clad & the men shave the head all but the scalp lock. They are a stalwart brawny set of men . . . .
>
> Evening. The prairie is covered with Indians. Arapahoes & Cheyennes in addition to those previously gathered here. They have come to treat and are considered the best Indians of the plains. Tomorrow the council will begin.
>
> Oct. 12. The council met this morning & lasted 4 hours. Only the Arapahoes & Cheyennes were represented & these tribes only partially. The commission propose to treat with them first. It is apparent that these tribes have always been our friends until driven by the Sand creek massacre into hostilities, and the com[missione]rs will treat them gently & use them liberally . . . . The consultations were harmonious & friendly, the commissioners being conciliatory and the Indians apparently frank and

friendly. They will probably keep the terms if we do. Some of their speeches were eloquent, especially in reference to the massacre of Sand creek. Black Kettle, when he spoke of the desolated wigwams, murdered braves, squaws & children on that occasion, sent a thrill throughout the whole of the Indians present & even in translations touched every heart there. . . . While everything is sober and orderly, the bare legs and bodies of the chiefs & braves destroy all idea of dignity & tend to destroy the romance of the affair.[127]

Told by the commissioners that the Cheyennes and Arapahos must move to reservations away from the main transportation routes across the Plains, Arapaho chief Big Mouth said that as for sitting down upon any one piece of ground, he could not understand how that would be. Commissioner and major general John B. Sanborn replied, "We desire to have your reservations so large that you can subsist by hunting for many years." Little Raven, an Arapaho chief, said, "it will be a very hard thing to leave the country that God gave [us] on the [Upper] Arkansas; our friends are buried there, and we hate to leave these grounds." Black Kettle reminded the commissioners that he represented only a fraction of the whole Cheyenne people and could not speak for the rest. He also asked that the move south of the Arkansas River be postponed until spring so that all their people, including the ones north of the Platte River, could receive the news and prepare for the move. Then the commissioners and the Cheyennes, Arapahos, and Plains Apaches signed the treaty by which they would share a new reservation.[128]

That reservation was a large thumbprint-shaped area, tilted a little left, with a boundary that began at the mouth of the Cimarron River and followed the Arkansas River upstream into Kansas to a point north of the junction of Buffalo Creek and the Cimarron River, just west of today's Freedom, Oklahoma. It then followed the course of the Cimarron east back to its junction with the Arkansas. The lands included lay partly in south-central Kansas but also occupied part of the Cherokee Outlet and the Muscogee Nation lands recently ceded to the federal government in treaties drawn up at Fort Smith. On today's maps the boundary would begin west of Tulsa and include the locations of the larger Oklahoma towns of Sand Springs, Stillwater, Ponca City, Enid, and Alva.[129]

With that treaty concluded, those tribes left the council ground, and the Comanche and Kiowa representatives sat down for their turn with the commissioners on October 16, with Jesse Chisholm interpreting. A recorder paraphrased the speech of Kiowa chief Tohausan, who said, "The Kiowas own from Fort Laramie and the north fork of the Platte to Texas, and always have owned it . . . all the branches, creeks, rivers and ponds that you see; all the deer and buffalo, wolves and turtles, all belong to [them]—were given to [them] by the Great Spirit. White men did not give it to [them.]" Tohausan did not "want his country cut up and divided with other tribes or given to the white man." He said he wanted peace with the whites and never did anything to them first, nor did he want soldiers in his lands. He wanted "a big land for my people to roam over; [they] don't want to stay long in one place, but want to move about from place to place." He concluded by saying the Kiowa, his children, "think as I think, and will do as I say. They want peace; their hearts are good."[130]

At the Little Arkansas Council, the Kiowas and Comanches reluctantly agreed to give up claims to Colorado Territory, Kansas, and New Mexico Territory, but they accepted a reservation between the Red River and the Arkansas River. It lay east of New Mexico and partly in today's Oklahoma, Kansas, and Texas and west of the lands just assigned to the Cheyennes, Arapahos, and Plains Apaches. Among the Kiowas involved in the treaty negotiations were some of their most respected leaders: Tohausan; Kicking Bird; Lone Wolf; and Satanta, or White Bear. However, the treaty had signatures of only some of the Comanche bands' representatives, which made it fatally flawed, according to one scholar.[131]

A part of the negotiations for a peace with the Plains tribes had been the surrender of captives held either by Indians or white men. Kingman noted in his diary for October 15,

> A black man from Texas comes in today & reports that he has redeemed his wife & two children from the Comanches, giving therefor[e] 7 ponies. That in the trade a Mrs. Fitzpatrick, about 40 yrs. old, and her granddaughter, were to have also been delivered up, but on getting the ponies the Indians refused to give up the others. Mrs. F. he represented as the widow of a Union man who was hung because he would not join the rebels. The child is

about 4 years old. I hope no treaty will be made till all prisoners are delivered up.[132]

The black man was, of course, Britt Johnson, who had redeemed his family back in May. He was still searching for Elizabeth Fitzpatrick and her granddaughter Millie Durgan, taken in the Elm Creek raid in Texas a year earlier.

For the time being, the treaties with the Plains tribes concluded at the Little Arkansas Council seemed to offer at least a chance of peace. They recognized the Sand Creek Massacre as the justification for Cheyenne and Arapaho outrage and offered some redress for that wrong in much-needed annuities and goods. At the same time, they were meant to draw these tribes away from the main transportation routes across the Plains as military and civilian traffic increased with the end of the Civil War. These reservations were the first to be created in a new round of Indian removals. They were carved largely out of lands held by former Confederate allies using the leverage gained from a Union victory, and they were expected to benefit the national development of the United States. It would not matter that in the next decade, as the wave of removals continued, they would include many Indian veterans from Kansas and Nebraska Territory who had contributed to a Union victory.

In the Indian Territory in late 1865, the terrors of war were finally ending. It was time to start rebuilding homes, farms, institutions, and relationships, although some could never be completely restored. Meanwhile, uneasiness lurked beneath the Indian nations' association with the federal government. In spite of their independence, they knew they had some things in common, and it was better to stand together than to try to stand alone.

CHAPTER SEVEN

Only the Land

L
ooking back in 1878, an anonymous writer for the *Indian Journal*, published in the Muscogee Nation, wrote, "At the close of the war [Muscogee] families were again gathered together only to find their farms desolate, their homes burned, their fences destroyed, their fields overrun with weeds, their church and school buildings even burned." Their country had been stripped of everything of value. There was "nothing left but a trackless waste." He concluded, they "found the land here but only because it was immovable."[1]

William McIntosh, formerly a slave of the wealthy Muscogee McIntosh family, agreed. He had gone north with Opothle Yahola and spent most of the war in the Union Indian Home Guard. As a soldier stationed at Fort Gibson in the last half of the war, he distributed supplies of food and clothing from the commissary to destitute Muscogees and Osages. He told his son,

> The Creek Nation was in a pitiable condition. Many of the Creeks had been killed or died of hunger and exposure. Their homes and barns were burned to ashes by opposing armies. Their horses had been stolen and their cattle killed and eaten or left to go wild in the cane brakes and their farms were grown up with weeds and underbrush. Surely the poor Creeks had suffered for no good cause on the part of any of them. They were aware of this, although an enmity still existed between them. All they really had left was their land, and [in 1865] they were being told they would have to share a part of it with their wild neighbors back in the states.[2]

It was hard to say whether the Muscogee Nation was hit harder by the Civil War than the Cherokee Nation, but they both had much to lose and lost more than most other Indian nations. On October 1, 1865, Agent Justin Harlan, who had shared the wartime troubles of the Union Cherokees, wrote:

No one can fully appreciate the wealth, content and comparative happiness the Cherokees enjoyed before the late rebellion . . . unless he had been here and seen it, which was my case, and no man can believe more than half of the want, misery and destitution of the Cherokee people now. Blackened chimneys of fine houses are now all that is left, fences burned, and farms laid waste. The air of ruin and desolation envelops the whole country. None have wholly escaped.[3]

Many Indian Territory people had also died or gone missing due to violence, disease, and other causes. Indian governments, with the exception of the Choctaws, rarely had a reason or any desire to take a census. Indians did not pay taxes and were excluded from the federal census, so an accurate count is hard to find. Still, the best estimate of the population loss is staggering. In 1860 there were about 4,500 Chickasaws; 500 were still unaccounted for in 1866, or one in nine. There may have been as many as 15,000 Choctaws before the war, but an estimated 12,500 when it was over. There were probably 2,500 Seminoles at the beginning of the war but only about 2,000 when peace came, a loss of about one in five. Including their slaves and legally resident white people, the Cherokee population stood at about 22,000 before the war. The number lost is estimated at about 4,000. An 1863 census of Cherokees at Fort Gibson revealed that one-fourth of the children there were orphans, and one-third of the women were widows. There were about 13,500 Muscogees at the beginning of the war. The difference between a Muscogee census taken in 1859 and one from 1867 showed a decline of 24 percent, or about one person in four lost. Even this percentage does not compare with the Tonkawa losses suffered in the 1862 massacre at Wichita Agency.[4]

Some Indian Territory people never knew exactly what happened to their loved ones. Slaves ran away, noncombatants scattered, and some men left to fight and simply never came back. Some were known to be dead, but no one knew where or if they were buried. The George McPherson family, mixed-blood Cherokees, farmed near today's Claremore, Oklahoma. Mrs. Tom Rattling Gourd, a daughter, said, "My father was killed in the Civil War and was never buried. Mother looked for his bones for a long time after the war but never could find them."[5] Missionary William Schenk Robertson brought his family home to the Indian Territory about eighteen months after the war ended. His daughter Alice, then about twelve, remembered,

> as we neared our destination, in the prairie between the Grand and the Verdigris Rivers, it was our habit to get out and walk to stretch ourselves from the cramped position in the wagon— while thus walking little sister came running with something round and white, saying "what is it, what is it, there is some more of them." It was a battle-punctured skull of one of the men from Fort Gibson killed by Waitie's [*sic*] men who had fled so hastily as to not bury the dead.[6]

Because there had been so much factional enmity and bloodshed, people who had gone elsewhere returned cautiously. Willie Larney, a Seminole whose parents and grandfather had followed Opothle Yahola, said from their accounts, "Jimmie Chupco was in command of the group of men who went to the Seminole . . . lands to make certain that no enemies were near so that a safe return could be made." Only after they determined "the coast was clear" did the Loyal Seminoles start home.[7] Muscogee and Cherokee people were also anxious about what they would find. "After the war was over," according to Joseph Bruner, son of a Union Muscogee refugee, "the Locha-pa-go people returned to their 'Tulsey-town' near today's Tulsa to find everything in ruins."[8]

Mary E. Hudson James, who was seven when the war began, had lived with her family in a large double log house on their prosperous farm in the northeastern corner of the Cherokee Nation, near today's Fairland, Oklahoma. This area close to the Texas Road had been ravaged repeatedly by regular troops, guerrillas, and renegades. The family had lost three of their eight children and now found everything— house, slaves, barns, and livestock—gone or destroyed. "My parents had to begin over," Mary said, with a family to care for and without the slaves that had provided so much labor. After the war, she recalled, "Our first home was a makeshift, everything to be done and nothing to do with, no money, no stock, and no tools to farm with."[9]

Their neighbors, the Audrain family, too, had owned a good farm worked by slaves near today's Wyandotte, Oklahoma. They were forced to leave, taking with them an Osage employee, a blind man who shared their home, and an uncle's family. After wandering over the Choctaw

Nation through the war years, the group returned in the fall of 1866 with only a small miscellaneous collection of livestock. "I still treasure a framed looking glass that my mother took with her to the Red River in Texas and back," Frank Audrain said. "Each time that [we] were compelled to move on she would wrap it up in a feather bed." They, too, found little remaining at their old home place. "Before leaving we had nice valley fields," Frank said, but "... on our return Father found his fields a mass of young trees, sprouts, and brush and not a rail left of the fences."[10]

The Audrains, like the Hudsons and other people throughout the Indian Territory, were tough, resilient, and determined. They had been through hard times before and knew they must rely on themselves to rebuild. The Hudsons camped at their old place while they built another house, and the senior Audrain went to Missouri to buy seed he shared with them. The Hudsons planted small garden patches, and Mary said, "This is all we had that year and these had to be tended with the hoe, as we had neither horse nor cow [to pull a plow]." She summarized, "Life was harder than when my parents were married about 1850." However, both families were fortunate that their orchards had survived and produced plenty of fruit that year.[11]

Meanwhile, the Audrains moved into two slave cabins that were still standing. They made a cornfield, Frank said,

> but we had nothing to work with. We hoed corn and had corn-bread and onions for lunch. We made our hay with a homemade wooden pitch-fork and rake. The first year we raised only corn and pumpkins. Next year we had squash and a cotton patch. During the winter evenings we sat round the fireplace with the cotton piled in front of the fire to warm it and picked the cotton seeds out by hand . . . for mother and my sisters to make into thread and cloth for our clothes.
>
> A black wolf killed, in the daytime, one of our sheep and one of the goats. Mother . . . took one of the ox teams and drove to Joplin, Missouri, and when she returned she brought with her two hog jowls. We thought we had the finest meal ever. The trip took four days.[12]

Farther north in the Cherokee Neutral Lands in southeastern Kansas, George Walker returned to the ruins of his farm near Chetopa in search of his wife, Rachel, and their five children. He learned that they were all at Fort Scott, interned there with other pro-Confederate Cherokees after the Union troops destroyed Chetopa. George, still wearing the Confederate uniform that was his entire wardrobe, went immediately to Fort Scott. There he and Rachel were happily reunited, but his children ran away from him. They had been taught to fear men in Confederate uniforms and were too young the last time they saw him to remember him.[13]

The George W. Stidham family had spent the war in the Red River valley and returned to the Muscogee Nation when peace finally came. Stidham, a wealthy, self-made merchant who before the war had several farms and owned about forty slaves, now "went to work to try to make us some corn," according to his daughter Georgeanna, called "Annie." In a memoir for her grandchildren, she wrote, "My sister and I did all the cooking . . . . The bread stuff had to be prepared by pounding corn in a mortar." A neighbor had an old hand mill, and they used it to grind their corn. "My hands were always blistered," she wrote, "and still bear the marks of hard usage." The first year after the war ended, Annie explained, there were no mills within fifty miles, no stores, and "nothing in the country at all to be bought for love or money." However, Stidham had returned to the territory with bags of twenty-dollar gold pieces, so he went back to Texas, bought merchandise, and opened a store in North Fork Town. Annie said, "Then began life in a little better shape."[14]

Her future husband, George Washington Grayson, rode back to the North Fork Town settlement with his teenaged brothers Sam and Pilot soon after the war ended and his Muscogee regiment disbanded. They were among the lucky few who found their old house still standing and got to work repairing it so they could bring their mother, younger brother, and sister home from the Chickasaw Nation. That summer there were long hard days while they cleared their overgrown fields of brush and weeds, split rails for new fences, and put in a corn crop. There was little to eat and, with no blacksmiths, no one to sharpen or repair broken tools. At night they dared not sleep too soundly. With the country deserted, wolves, panthers, and wild dogs—abandoned pets and their offspring—flourished. One night Grayson found a wolf prowling their porch. Worse, with its government and lighthorse police force shut down or absent during the Civil War, the usually law-abiding Muscogee Nation was overrun with human predators, too. An unsavory family of Union Indians had squatted not far away and would, Grayson suspected, "not scruple to strangle their grandmothers for $5.00." They were so close the Grayson brothers, who lived "in constant dread" of being killed for their skimpy provisions, could hear their drunken carousing. Then one night, after the ringleader leveled a "gross insult" at a former Confederate Indian soldier, the young man shot him dead with the "trusty musket that had been his close companion" during the war. The troublemakers moved on, and no one, Grayson said, was ever prosecuted for the shooting.[15]

Along with Indian Territory homes and businesses, the Indian nations' public institutions had suffered damage or destruction. In late summer 1865 Agent J. W. Dunn, assigned to the Muscogee Nation, reported he had visited Creek Agency and its surrounding settlement and found all in ruins. He wrote, "nothing is left now to mark the place where it stood, except lonely, dilapidated chimneys, and here and there solitary pairs of gate-posts." He had also visited the Tullahassee Mission neighborhood across the Arkansas River and found the once-impressive three-story building in sad condition. He reported, "The buildings are all still standing, but badly abused; the window-sash all gone, as well as most of the doors, and many of the floors of the rooms torn up and carried off; the bell still swings in its accustomed place."[16]

Likewise, Muscogee soldier Joseph K. Perryman, a former student, wrote to his former teacher, "The old Tallahassee building is still standing but it has lost its former grandeur. The house is vacant . . . . The bedsteads stoves and house furniture were all sold at highest bidder." He was pained to find a library abandoned in a yard, saying, "I have some books that I picked up at Mr. Vandiver's place. There was a whole library destroyed there. It was a dreadful sight to look at, to see books trampled upon with muddy feet."[17] Some of the former teachers also reported, "We stopped . . . at Tallahassee & almost wept at beholding its ruins."[18]

Alice Robertson vividly remembered coming home to Tullahassee:

> How different the home coming from the leaving in that July
> afternoon in '61, when flowers were blooming, fruit and grain

ripening, the cow pen full of young calves, the hog pasture full of growing swine, getting ready for winter meat, everywhere there were signs of prosperity and plenty. In the five years the formerly well-kept hedge surrounding the front yard had grown into a mass of tall trees, in field, in yard, and everywhere weeds had grown so rank and large that the tall stalks had to be broken and chopped down to make a road for the wagons to enter, and to make room to pitch our tents and make our campfires. A row of graves nearby added to the gloom. The building was windowless and doorless, the large dining room had been used as a stable, and was deep with stable refuse; the kitchen wing in the rear had much of the wall torn down, its brick had been hauled over to Fort Gibson during the Federal occupation to make bake ovens for the troops. The wells were choked with rubbish.[19]

Fortunately, that was not the end of Tullahassee or education in the Muscogee Nation. According to Muscogee educator Myra Starr, "if assailing a culture's educational system inflicts lethal damage, re-building is surely the way back. The *Mvskoke* saw Anglo schooling so important that at the end of the Civil War, they re-opened their schools as a bi-partisan act. Teachers took their positions without pay even while buildings were still going up." Former soldier Pleasant Porter, once a Tullahassee student, was named the first superintendent of schools, when the new 1867 constitution codified their schooling processes.[20]

People such as the Hudsons, Audrains, Stidhams, and Robertsons came back when the Civil War ended because the Indian Territory was home. So did Indian free blacks and former slaves of the Indians, who were now "freedmen."[21] Federal troops had liberated some, and others had liberated themselves by running away, even before the postwar treaties ended slavery among the Cherokees, Chickasaws, Choctaws, Muscogees, and Seminoles. According to their oral histories, most new freedmen understood the great change that had taken place, but some did not. Polly Colbert, who was only about seven when the war began, regarded her owners Holmes and Betsy Colbert as surrogate parents in the only home she knew. She was afraid of the federal soldiers she saw stealing their cattle and corn and pillaging their smokehouse. At the age of eighty-three, she said, "We didn't know anything 'bout dem fighting to free us. We didn't specially want to be free dat I knows of."

After the war she worked at Bloomfield Academy for a while but returned to work for Betsy Colbert for several years.[22]

Lucinda Davis, about seventeen when the Civil War ended, had lived with the Muscogee family of her master "old man Tuskaya-hiniha" since she was too small to remember anything else. He took her with his family to the Red River valley in the civilian stampede after the Battle of Honey Springs, and they stayed there "until the War quit off." Even though she was free now, Lucinda did not know who her parents were, and Tuskaya-hiniha "didn't know whar to send me to, anyways." One day some men came and talked to him "in English talk," which Lucinda, who spoke only Muskogee, did not understand. "Den he called me and tell me to go wid dem to find my own family," she said. "He just laugh and slap my behind and set me up on the hoss in front of one of de men and dey take me off and leave my good checkedy dress at de house!" They delivered her to Creek Agency, where her parents, who had apparently been looking for her, came to claim her. Lucinda said, "I know den whose child I is."[23]

Patsy Perryman, a slave of the Taylor family in the Cherokee Flint District, had also been taken to Texas along with her mother. Mistress Judy Taylor, Patsy said, was "the only mother my mama ever had" after her own died just after her birth. At the end of the war, Mrs. Taylor "started back to the old home place, but wasn't going to take us with her until Mammy cried so hard she couldn't stand it and told us to get ready. We drove through in an ox wagon." They found their old home-place in ruins, with the house burned to the ground. Patsy explained, "There was no stock and no way for any of us to live. The mistress told us that we were free anyway and to go wherever we wanted to."[24]

For the first time, some freedmen had to fend for themselves. Patsy's mother supported her family as a cook in Fort Gibson and Tahlequah, but Morris Sheppard, the slave of Joe Sheppard, a Cherokee, was not yet thirteen when the war ended. He recalled, "After the War was over, old Master tell me I am free but he will look out after me 'cause I am just a little negro and I ain't got no sense. I know he is right, too. Well, I go ahead and make me a crop of corn all by myself and then I don't know what to do wid it. I was afraid I would get cheated out of it 'cause I can't figure and read, so I tell old Master about it and he bought it off'n me." Sheppard later got work through the Freedmen's Bureau or hired out to various employers until he finally settled on a freedman's allotment in the northeastern Cherokee Nation. There he was able to farm and support a wife and eleven children. Looking back at the age of eighty-five, he said he knew about Abraham Lincoln from his children and considered him a great man. However, he said, "I always think of my old Master as de one dat freed me, and anyways Abraham Lincoln and none of his North people didn't look after me and buy my crop right after I was free like old Master did. Dat was de time dat was de hardest and everything was dark and confusion."[25]

Once their slaves were free, some Indian slave owners had no money to pay them for their labor or tried to avoid paying them at all. Betty Robertson, a Cherokee slave about twenty-one in 1865, recalled, "One day young Master come to the cabins and say we all free and can't stay there less'n we want to go on working for him just like we been, for our feed and clothes. Mammy got a wagon and traveled around a few days and go to Fort Gibson .... We settled down a little ways above Fort Gibson ... and we worked a good size patch there until she died."[26]

Some owners who had taken their slaves to the Red River valley brought them back after the war ended. Others simply abandoned them once they were freed, and they had to make their own way home. Mary Grayson belonged to Mose Perryman, a Muscogee, who took Mary, her mother, and Mary's younger siblings when he refugeed in the Fort Washita area. She was about eleven, she remembered, when, "one day Mr. Mose came and told us that the War was over and that we would have to root for ourselves after that. Then he just rode away and I never saw him after that until after we had got back up into the Choska country. Mammy heard that the Negroes were going to get equal rights with the Creeks, and that she should go to the Creek Agency to draw [allotments] for us, so we set out to try to get back."[27] With no money or transportation, Mary's mother got odd jobs along the way to buy food as they began walking home, about 150 miles away. Another group of freedmen had a horse, so Mammy paid them to let her children "ride and tie." That meant some of the children rode the horse a distance, tied it up, and walked on. When the second group reached the tied horse, they got to ride on past the first group until it was their turn to tie the horse and walk on. Fast-flowing water frightened that horse, so when they came to a river they had to wait, sometimes a whole day, until someone with a wagon came along and accepted money or some of their belongings for a ride to the other side. Their journey to the Creek Agency ended happily, though, because they were reunited with Mary's father, a runaway who had spent the war as a soldier in the Union Indian Brigade and fought at Honey Springs near their old home.[28]

There was also a happy homecoming for the family of Tom and Flora, formerly slaves of George W. Stidham. Separated at the beginning of the war, blacksmith Tom had been taken to Texas, and their teen-aged son had runaway to Kansas. Flora, her twin daughters, and little son Jim were left at the farm near Honey Springs. Federal troops had taken Flora and the younger children to Fort Gibson after the battle there. At the fort they found Flora's older son, now a soldier. He saw to it his family had enough to eat and survive life in the refugee camps. Tom's return at the end of the war completed their family circle. Years later Jim concluded, "We sure were lucky."[29]

Many of the Muscogee freedmen who came back settled in the Arkansas-Verdigris river valleys near Fort Gibson on lands that they had once farmed for Indian planters. They were the nucleus of the new town of Muskogee. When the planters came back, only the Perryman family was willing to live near the freedmen and ranched in the Arkansas River valley near today's Tulsa, Oklahoma. Most Lower Creek planters settled farther west, causing a ripple effect as some traditional people who had lived there moved on west into the blackjack-timbered hills.[30]

These personal stories illustrate some of the changes in the Indian Territory as a result of the Civil War. Knitting the Seminoles, Muscogees, and Cherokees back together as nations after so much hostility, bloodshed, and loss would be difficult. Some Indians, as well as federal officials and other observers, doubted the factions could ever reconcile. The new agent for the Muscogee Nation faced a critical situation when he arrived at his post in late July and reported a month later after the Fort Smith Council,

> On my arrival here I found the loyal Creeks divided into parties, on the point of breaking into open war with each other—in such a condition that it was with great difficulty I could transact the business of the agency with them. I at once set about to heal the dissensions, if possible, and am gratified, after much talking and exertion on my part and the influence of others, to inform you

that I have succeeded, and that we are now at peace with ourselves; and, moreover, concluded lately, at the grand council at
Fort Smith, friendship and good neighborhood with the disloyal
Creeks, and have invited them back to their former homes and
rights, under treaties heretofore made with the government.[31]

Relations were still unsettled in November 1865 when Dr.
Dwight D. Hitchcock wrote to friends, "there has been a general
returning to the Creek country; and I believe the rebels are coming
back, too. There has been no act of violence that I can learn of ... but
I cannot believe that the two factions will continue to live amicably
together."[32] However, while they rebuilt their property, they overcame
the factionalism enough to reconstruct their nation, too, even though
some friction remained. Moreover, in spite of the sacrifice and loyalty
of so many of them, they did it without much help from the federal
government, which punished all of them for "disloyalty" because that
suited its own ends.

In reviewing the conditions in the Indian Territory in his annual
report for 1865, commissioner of Indian affairs James W. Harlan
admitted, "The change is pitiful."[33] However, he, along with many in
Washington, had a vision that gave American national development
priority over the Indian nations' goals and sovereignty:

> Whenever, in the progress towards a final settlement ... in regard
> to the reorganization of the Indian country, the proper time shall
> come, it will be advisable to provide for the construction of inter-
> nal improvements in that region calculated to develop its mag-
> nificent resources. With a territorial government organized and
> in operation, its feuds healed, the scars of war gone from view, a
> judicious educational system in operation, the missionary estab-
> lishments which have done so much for the people in the past
> reopened, and the industry of the country in full process of devel-
> opment, will have come a time when railroads must traverse the
> country, binding its several parts together, and all to one common
> Union, and giving a choice of markets and depots for exchange
> and shipment of produce, either on the Gulf of Mexico, say at
> Galveston, or northward, to connect with the great central con-
> verging points of railroads in Kansas. Whatever can properly be
> done by the government of the United States in paving the way

for these improvements should, in my judgment, be done now, and thus avoid difficulties which may arise in the future.[34]

This vision of constructing rail lines across the Indian Territory, exploiting its natural resources, and eventually integrating it into the rest of the United States affected the Reconstruction Treaties concluded with the five largest Indian nations in 1866. The Choctaws and Chickasaws signed a joint treaty, because the Chickasaws retained an interest in Choctaw lands and resources from their prewar sharing of the Choctaw domain. Except for small pro-Union factions, these nations had supported the Confederacy. However, the Seminoles, Muscogees, and Cherokees had to overcome deep internal divisions to deal with one another and the United States. Each Reconstruction treaty contained a provision establishing peace with the United States and other Indian nations. Likewise, the abolition of slavery was already a fact, and each nation acknowledged it. From that point, however, some issues were sticky.[35]

While the Choctaws and Chickasaws agreed to the sale of the Leased District for $300,000 and to the freedom of their former slaves, they objected to adopting them as citizens. Among other things, freedmen in their country outnumbered the Chickasaws; and the number continued to grow over the next decade with an influx of noncitizens. They could conceivably form a voting majority. Meanwhile, getting both nations to act together on their common treaty proved a "legislative impossibility," according to historian Daniel F. Littlefield. Nor did the federal government follow through on its obligations.[36]

Both nations supported having the freedmen removed from their lands, an idea some members of the other Indian nations and even their federal agents shared. The idea was to give the freedmen allotments in what would later be called the "Unassigned Lands" in today's central Oklahoma, and many freedmen were willing to move there. When that did not happen, the Chickasaw freedmen settled down where they were, established farms, and supported themselves and their families however they could. The Choctaws enacted laws requiring former owners to care for their ex-slaves who were too old or infirm to work. Their freedmen could contract to work for them or others, and some lived near freedmen schools supported by federal funds through missionary organizations. At first as noncitizens living in the Choctaw Nation they lacked certain rights, but they eventually received Choctaw citizenship in 1883. The Chickasaws, however, never adopted their freedmen, leaving them people without a country.[37]

The Seminoles, although divided during the Civil War, mended their relationship with the least trouble. Both the Union faction led by John Chupco and the "southern" faction led by John Jumper attended the Fort Smith Council. In the treaty negotiated there, the United States extended amnesty to all Seminoles, and the loyal Seminoles extended amnesty to the pro-Confederate faction. In their Reconstruction treaty, signed March 31, 1866, they abolished slavery and granted full citizenship rights to their freedmen. Then the federal government, making the whole Seminole Nation responsible for the actions of the pro-Confederates, demanded and received its entire domain: all the lands between the Canadian River and the North Canadian River, from the Muscogee Nation west to the Texas Panhandle. For the option on these 2,170,000 acres, the federal government paid the Seminoles fifteen cents an acre.[38]

The Muscogees had more difficulty making peace. The Loyal Creeks and the southern faction had been in communication but had not yet met formally, although there had been informal reunions of family and friends divided by the war. A joint meeting at the old Uekihulwe (High Spring) council ground was scheduled, but only members of the southern faction went. When the Union people failed to appear, Wash Grayson and two others crossed the Arkansas River to the Loyal Creek camp below the mouth of the Verdigris River and found relatives, he said, among "those who so lately had been our deadly enemy."[39] Representatives of the two factions met formally at Fort Smith in September. At first they asked to be allowed to form separate nations, but during the Sunday recess they reconciled their differences and signed a preliminary treaty. Once they returned home, they met again. Samuel Checote, formerly a Confederate colonel, recognized Sands, who had worked closely with Opothle Yahola, as principal chief. Sands told the southern Muscogees to go back to the Red River valley and bring their people home, which they did over the next few months.[40]

Two delegations of Muscogees went to Washington in early 1866, with the Loyal Creeks arriving first. By the time representatives of the southern faction arrived, the Loyal Creeks had trustingly agreed to a "Treaty of cession and indemnity." It charged the Muscogee Nation had ignored its allegiance to the United States, damaging that relationship, and thereby forfeited all federal benefits, annuities, and protection. The Loyal Creeks, who had promised freedom to the slaves who accompanied them to Kansas, agreed to adopt them and free blacks living in the nation up to one year from the date of the treaty ratification. They accepted the idea of a unified territorial government and made land grants to one east-west and one north-south rail line. The treaty also stated the Muscogee Nation must cede "a portion of their land" to the federal government. That actually amounted to the western half of their domain. Over the protests of the southern Muscogee delegates, the federal government effectively took an option on 3,250,560 acres for thirty cents per acre, or about $975,000. Of this, $100,000 was allocated to compensate the Loyal Creeks and freedmen who had lost property during the war.[41]

The Muscogee Nation was actually fortunate to receive thirty cents an acre for their land. Secretary of the Interior William Harlow, according to the attorneys who handled the transaction, believed no Indian land was worth more than fifteen cents an acre. However, because the Seminoles were now landless, the federal government then sold them 200,000 acres of the lands it had just acquired from the Muscogee Nation, charging them fifty cents an acre.[42]

The Cherokee Nation had the most difficult time getting past the wartime divisions. Even though Acting Principal Chief Lewis Downing, a Ross adherent, won a declaration of amnesty for the Watie faction, the council refused to rescind an earlier act confiscating their homes and other property. Thinking themselves landless and homeless, they were reluctant to go back. Both factions sent delegates to Fort Smith in September 1865. Commissioner of Indian affairs Dennis Cooley had become convinced that John Ross had been an ardent supporter of the Confederacy before his capture and refused to recognize him as chief when he finally appeared at the council. Downing and the other Union Cherokee delegates protested that the commissioners were overlooking their service to the Union and treating them as if they had always been Confederate allies. Unable to conclude a treaty, they simply signed a peace agreement covering most of the points the commissioners wanted. The southern Cherokees also met with the commissioners and agreed to everything except two points: they did not want the freedmen to become Cherokee citizens, nor did they agree to a territorial government.[43]

Clement Neeley Vann, who had enlisted as a private in 1861 and ended the war as a lieutenant colonel of the 1st Regiment of Cherokee Mounted Volunteers in Stand Watie's brigade, wrote to John Ross in early October about the "reckless spirits" who, ever since the Treaty of New Echota, had seen the nation's politics as a game to be won. Had the council not passed such punitive legislation, he believed, they would have far fewer followers now. Vann said he could see no benefit in fault-finding and accusations. Admitting that both sides had erred, he appealed to Ross to mediate for the good of the Cherokee Nation. He concluded, "There are many Cherokees South who are and have always been true men and attached to their country. They feel conscious of having committed crime and are slow to submit to humiliation or any kind of oppressive legislation."[44]

Two Cherokee delegations went to Washington in the summer of 1866 to continue the process of making peace with the United States if not with each other. The federal representatives finally negotiated separate treaties with the two factions, and Commissioner Cooley played one off against the other to gain the points laid out at the Fort Smith Council. Hoping to establish a separate nation, the Watie faction agreed to a treaty that included generous railroad rights-of-way; sale of the Cherokee Neutral Lands, Cherokee Strip, and Cherokee Outlet; civil and political rights for their freedmen; and a territorial government. Cooley then used this treaty, never forwarded to the Senate for ratification, to pressure John Ross and the Union Cherokees into signing a second treaty on July 19, which was ratified. Ross was able to moderate some points, including retaining the Cherokee Outlet and trimming grants for railroad rights-of-way down to one hundred feet on either side of the track. This saved millions of acres that could have been sold to non-Cherokees, allowing them to flood his nation. Reluctantly, Ross agreed to adopt the freedmen who returned within one year of ratification, the sale of the Cherokee Strip, and the future settlement of other tribes on Cherokee lands. This treaty meant the Watie faction lost any hope of a separate nation. However, the Cherokee council repealed the law confiscating their property, and they were allowed to return to whatever was left.[45]

In 1866, though, the Cherokee Nation ceded the Neutral Lands and the Cherokee Strip, that narrow band of land just north of the Cherokee Outlet, to the federal government. The purchase price when the land was sold to white settlers helped rebuild and fund the national school system. Unfortunately, the sale of that land meant Cherokees who called the Neutral Lands home were forced out. Some families from the Chetopa area—the Hursts, Rogerses, McGhees, and Walkers—moved south into the Cooweescoowee District of the Cherokee Nation. Along the headwaters of Big Cabin Creek, George Walker built a log house for his growing family, founded a horse farm, and with his neighbors in 1869 established a school for their children. He prospered while he built a better future for his sons and daughters.[46]

So peace finally settled over the eastern half of the Indian Territory after five years of turmoil and terror. While their people went home and tried to rebuild their lives in 1866 and 1867, their Indian neighbors to the north and west were already feeling the impact of the signatures on those treaties written in Fort Smith and Washington. A new round of removals to the Indian Territory was beginning, eventually affecting states from the Great Plains to the Pacific Coast.

While Indian peoples lived in a number of western American states and territories, several tribes still lived on Kansas reservations that comprised almost four million acres. The railroad companies, including the ones hoping to build across the Indian Territory, lobbied for federal grants of lands in Kansas and other western areas to finance new lines connecting the developing West with the booming East. Once these were built, the railroad companies expected new towns and farms to support rail operations through fares and shipping charges for crops and goods. Kansas settlers agreed Indian lands would be better used for tracks, farms, and towns, but they did not want to pay the high price per acre the railroads would charge them for lands near the rail lines. By the 1850s there was already competition between the railroad companies and settlers for Indian lands. The Homestead Act passed during the Civil War set a low price per acre for settlers claiming federally controlled lands. The problem for them was that through the Civil War years the railroad promoters got the first chance at newly opened Indian reservations because they had congressmen, federal officials, including Office of Indian Affairs staff, military men, and local and state politicians in their pockets. Even some Indian leaders became tools of the railroad companies. The railroad-settler struggle for land was still going on when the Fort Smith and Washington, D.C., treaties acquired access to millions of acres of Indian Territory lands for the future settlement of tribes from other states and territories. This, of course, included the Indians in Kansas, who could not be shoved out of the way fast enough for the settlers or railroads.[47]

As federal representatives opened removal negotiations with the Kansas tribes in the 1850s and 1860s, one of the main areas of the Indian Territory involved was the Neosho Agency in today's Ottawa and Delaware counties of Oklahoma. The Quapaw, Seneca, and Seneca-Shawnee peoples had shared reservations there since the 1830s. They often allowed individuals from other eastern tribes to live among them.[48] These three resident tribes signed Confederate treaties in 1861. However, almost all of them soon fled to Kansas because raiders from the adjacent states of Kansas, Missouri, and Arkansas repeatedly attacked their homes and farms. They were also vulnerable because of their location near the Texas Road. Federal troops burned and destroyed what was left on their reservations while returning to Kansas from Fort Gibson in 1862. Nevertheless, almost every able-bodied man of these tribes joined in the Union army while living as refugees in Kansas. In 1867 the Quapaws signed a treaty for a new reservation in the extreme northeastern corner of today's Oklahoma. During the next decade, other bands or tribes received small reservations nearby but east of the Grand (Neosho) River. The Shawnees and Senecas, who had shared a reservation, divided into the Eastern Shawnees and the Seneca-Cayuga tribe after the war. They received new reservations supervised by the Neosho Agency. Renamed Quapaw Agency in 1871, it became the home, or at least the gateway, for several Indian peoples arriving in the Indian Territory through the 1870s.[49]

Among them were the Ottawas, who lived along the Canadian shore of Lake Huron in the early 1600s. Farmers, hunters, and traders, they were middlemen between the French and Great Lakes tribes and sometimes allies of the Potawatomis and Wyandots. In the 1700s and 1800s, although some stayed near the Great Lakes, others trekked to

Michigan, Ohio, Illinois, Wisconsin, and Iowa before settling on a Kansas reservation. In 1862 they agreed to sell it and move to the Indian Territory. However, speculators got control of twenty thousand acres of their Kansas land and founded Ottawa University, a swindle for which they were never reimbursed. Among the Ottawas removed in the early 1860s was Jane Phelps (King), who was born near the Great Lakes and came to the Indian Territory by way of Ohio and Kansas. Although crippled by a fall in infancy, she lived a full life in her 122 years, many during tribal migrations. A midwife and healer, she was always ready to help anyone who asked and was "the merriest, liveliest person that you ever met," according to a neighbor.[50] Her tribe settled finally in Ottawa County near today's Miami, Oklahoma.[51]

Their neighbors in Kansas and then in the Indian Territory included the Peorias, Miamis, and Wyandots. Under pressure, the Peorias, after their formerly large population was severely reduced, ceded more than 6.8 million acres in Illinois in 1818 in exchange for one square mile in Missouri. Almost at once settler pressure forced the Peorias still farther west. They joined bands of Kaskaskias, Michigameas, Cahokias, and Tamaroas—all once part of the Illinois Confederacy. Calling themselves the Confederated Peorias, they moved to a new 365,000-acre reservation along the Kansas River. Later the Weas and Piankashaws joined their confederation. Unfortunately, the federal government had invested the Peorias' money from earlier land cessions in Southern state bonds. By the end of the Civil War these were worthless, and the Peorias were impoverished. Meanwhile, Union veterans were pressuring the federal government for lands to homestead, which brought demands that the Confederated Peorias give up their Kansas reservation. In the Omnibus Treaty of 1867 the Confederated Peorias and Miamis agreed to buy 72,000 acres of the Quapaw Reservation and remove to the Indian Territory. The Miamis had much in common with the Confederated Peorias, including control of major trade routes earlier in the Old Northwest. Removals to Kansas and then the Indian Territory led to tribal divisions and eventual landlessness. Once settled in the northeastern corner of today's Oklahoma, though, the Peorias took advantage of the good water and grasslands on their new reserve by renting pastures to Texas cattlemen eager to fatten their herds for the northern markets.[52]

The Wyandots, composed of Huron, Neutral, and Petun peoples, had similar experiences to the Ottawas during the seventeenth and eighteenth centuries. Involved in the traditional Huron-Iroquois conflict and then the French-British rivalry, they were forced from the eastern end of the Great Lakes to the western side. They tried to remain neutral in the British-American struggle but supported Tecumseh's Indian resistance movement in the early 1800s. When that was shattered, they were forced farther west. They bought land from the Delawares in Kansas, but proslavery and antislavery violence ravaged their new Kansas homes in the 1850s. Chief Matthew Mudeater led about two hundred Wyandots to the Seneca lands in the Indian Territory in 1857 to escape the violence, while others went back to Ohio or even Canada. The Civil War washed over the Wyandots of the Indian Territory before they could conclude a purchase of Seneca lands. They went back to Kansas, where some served in the Union army. In 1867, however, the Wyandots bought twenty thousand acres from the Senecas and settled finally in the northeastern Indian Territory.[53]

While these Indian peoples reestablished themselves in the northeastern corner of the Indian Territory, two tribes removed from Kansas settled farther west on lands ceded by the Muscogee and Seminole Nations at the end of the Civil War. The Potawatomis, who often intermarried with the French, had been entrepreneurs in the Great Lakes fur trade in the 1600s. The American Revolution and Tecumseh's movement caused divisions among them, but all were forced to leave their lands in Indiana, Illinois, Michigan, and Wisconsin and move on to a large reservation just west of Topeka, Kansas. Situated along the emigrant trails between Missouri and Colorado Territory, Potawatomi businessmen prospered until the outbreak of the Civil War. In 1861 many, called the "Citizen Band," took allotments, but the "Prairie Band" refused and moved to another reservation. The experiment left the Citizen Band landless by the end of the war, so in 1867 they accepted a new reservation in central Indian Territory near today's Shawnee, Oklahoma.[54]

The Sacs and Foxes also reluctantly agreed to a new reservation just northeast of the Citizen Potawatomis in the former Muscogee country. In the general shuffle resulting from Indian competition for the European fur trade, these tribes from the Upper Peninsula of Michigan had resettled in Wisconsin near the headwaters of the Mississippi River in the late 1600s. By the early 1700s the Foxes, or Mesquakie people, dominated the upper end of the trade route connecting Canada and Louisiana. The French and their Indian allies tried to exterminate them and nearly succeeded. The Sac, or Sauk, people offered the survivors refuge farther south, but eventually both tribes moved westward into Iowa. Unable to escape white pressure even there, in 1832 Sac chief Black Hawk tried and failed during the Black Hawk War to return with his followers to their former Illinois lands. Ten years later a majority of the Sacs and Foxes accepted a 435,000-acre reservation in Kansas. By 1867 pressure from white settlers for this land was so strong most of the Sacs and Foxes agreed to move to a somewhat larger reservation in central Indian Territory. Unfortunately, while they waited for the federal government to provide funds for their removal, squatters pushed in and tore their homes down around them. Even after most relocated to the Indian Territory in 1869, a faction led by Mokohoko refused to leave. This "Prairie band" finally moved south in 1886 and settled near today's Cushing, Oklahoma.[55]

Apparently the 480,000 acres of the new reservation in the Indian Territory were more than adequate for the Sacs and Foxes. William Foster, or Hapetuke, was the son of band chief Grey Eyes. He remembered, "When we first came to Oklahoma there were several hundred in our band, or clan . . . . Our homes were scattered over a wide range of territory in the new country. For many it was fifteen to twenty miles to their nearest neighbor, and the only store was the trading post near the Sac and Fox agency."[56] There was space to accommodate some of the Iowas, too, who gave up much of their land in Nebraska Territory and Kansas in 1861. In the late 1870s some of the more traditional Iowas moved voluntarily to the Indian Territory, settling west of the Sacs and Foxes, who were old friends. In 1883 an executive order established an Iowa reservation that lay in today's central Oklahoma between the Cimarron and Deep Fork Rivers and west of the Sac and Fox reserve. The same year, the Kickapoos, scattered by the end of the Civil War from Mexico to Texas and Kansas, received a 100,000-acre reservation immediately south of the Iowas. Some moved there, but others chose to live instead along the Texas-Mexican border or in Kansas.[57]

Many of the Kansas and Nebraska tribes involved in the post–Civil War round of removals ceded their lands and went to the Indian

Territory peacefully. Still, there was a wrenching sense of loss as they left people, places, and associations dear to them. Individual Indians who had taken allotments and become United States citizens did not have to remove and were left behind to succeed or fail on their own. A few factions and individuals flatly refused to go to the Indian Territory or returned to their former reservation areas. If they were fortunate, these people eventually received another smaller acreage in Kansas or Nebraska, but some became homeless wanderers. Indian people forced to repeat the removal pattern went south with understandable misgivings. Ottawa chief John Wilson, while walking south to the new reservation, repeatedly said he did not want to go. He died of a chill along the way. A Kickapoo, called to Washington with a delegation, told officials his people would accept a different way of life on their new reservation but worried about their children's future. "I could not sleep last night," he said, "all of these Indians here cried."[58] As a general rule, though, violence associated with this round of removals from eastern Kansas and Nebraska was directed *at* the Indians rather than *by* them against those who forced them out.

The response of the Plains tribes living farther west was very different. As some of the chiefs of the Cheyennes, Kiowas, and Comanches explained as they signed the Treaty of the Little Arkansas in October 1865, they did not represent all their people. Some chiefs or bands were still angry because of the Sand Creek Massacre or for other reasons. They refused to give up their freedom or lands they considered theirs.

The "peace" supposedly established by the Treaty of the Little Arkansas was ephemeral. Comanches and Kiowas were soon raiding the Chickasaw and Texas frontiers again or making forays into southwestern Kansas. In western Indian Territory, only Fort Arbuckle was garrisoned. It had just two hundred cavalrymen, including two companies of black soldiers in the new 10th Cavalry, and twenty Caddo scouts. The commander sent the Caddos out to watch for Plains raiders but paid more attention to the internal operations of the fort. Things were much worse on the Kansas frontier. There angry Cheyennes and Kiowas watched homesteaders and bison hunters intrude on lands and resources they regarded as theirs, while construction of the transcontinental railroad pushed westward, dividing their lands and bringing still more white people. Infuriated, they struck back at frontier farms, military posts, and wagon and rail transportation along the Smoky Hill River route, violating the previous year's Little Arkansas Treaty.[59]

According to Cheyenne peace chief Gordon Yellowman, *Hó'nehe, tsex ho'ëhne,* or the time "when the wolf came," had been very difficult. By 1865 the Cheyenne warrior societies were in a state of confusion as they saw their independence ending and white encroachment into their territory. The warrior societies—the Bowstrings, Elk Soldiers, Dog Men, Kit Fox Men, Red Shields, and Crooked Lance Men—were at odds with the Chiefs Council of Forty-four over the right thing to do. The eager young men and some of the chiefs wanted to continue fighting, but other chiefs wanted peace. They hoped the treaties offered to them would secure peace, protect the people, and preserve their Cheyenne culture, traditions, and way of life. In 1865 the split between the northern and southern Cheyennes widened with two different reactions to the massacre at Sand Creek. Southern Cheyennes who followed Black Kettle looked for peace by remaining along the Arkansas River. The northern group led by Dull Knife vowed never to accept peace and went farther north to join Red Cloud's Oglala Sioux and continue war with the United States.[60]

Early in 1867 Gen. Winfield Scott Hancock, a Civil War hero, led a large force of cavalry, infantry, and artillery through western Kansas to awe or force the Plains tribes into submission. The Cheyenne Dog Soldiers and Oglala Lakotas encamped at Pawnee Fork feared they were about to experience another Sand Creek Massacre and fled as the column approached. In his ignorance of Indians Hancock mistook their flight for guilt and had the camp and all their belongings burned, further stoking Plains Indian anger.[61]

Complaints from the Indians that the federal government was not keeping its Little Arkansas commitments and their own depredations in Kansas and other areas resulted in calls for a new treaty moving Plains Indians farther from the frontier. Exactly two years after the meeting at the Little Arkansas, federal commissioners called representatives of the Comanches, Kiowas, Plains Apaches, Arapahos, and Cheyennes to Medicine Lodge in southwestern Kansas to make peace and redraw reservation boundaries. It was an impressive spectacle attended by an estimated five thousand Indians of several tribes and many prominent chiefs, including all four Arapaho head chiefs and the Wichita head chief.

The federal commissioners' military escort consisted of two companies of the 7th Cavalry backed up by Gatling guns from the 4th Artillery. Among the Indian spectators were some Osages, who had long considered the Central Plains their territory. Twenty rode into camp one night, ate the food they demanded, and left just as abruptly as they had arrived. The federal party was impressed but mystified. The Plains people, however, understood the Osages had just insulted the white men who had excluded them from the proceedings.[62]

While journalists from eastern newspapers recorded the meeting, the federal commissioners laid out their case for moving the tribes onto new reservations. The government's plan was to turn nomadic hunters into farmers, with the assistance of agents, teachers, and Christian missionaries. Senator John B. Henderson warned the Plains chiefs, "the buffalo will not last forever . . . . Before all the good lands are taken by the whites we wish to set aside a part of them for your exclusive use." Henderson told them the government would build them schools and houses to store the supplies and food it would send them.[63]

The Indian spokesmen explained that they preferred their own ways, which did not include living in government houses. Satanta, or White Bear, who had become Kiowa head chief after the death of Tohausan, told the commissioners, "I love the land and the buffalo and will not part with any . . . . I love to roam over the wide prairie . . . but when we settle down we grow pale and die." Comanche chief Ten Bears said the commissioners' words about putting them on reservations and building them houses were bitter as gourds. He explained, "I was born upon the prairies, where the wind blew free, and there was nothing to break the light of the sun. I was born where there were no enclosures, and where everything drew a free breath. I want to die there, and not within walls."[64]

Nevertheless, the treaty drawn up at Medicine Lodge called for smaller reservations located entirely in the Indian Territory and aimed to put an end to Indian raiding, particularly attacks on railroad construction and military posts. The Plains Apaches, assigned earlier to the Cheyenne-Arapaho reservation, were reassigned to the Kiowa and Comanche reservation. Set aside for twelve hundred Kiowas, seventeen hundred Comanches, and three hundred Plains Apaches, it consisted of about three million acres in the Leased District, lands recently ceded by the Chickasaw and Choctaw Nations in today's southwest Oklahoma. The two thousand Cheyennes and twelve hundred Arapahos received about five million acres in the Cherokee Outlet between the Cimarron and Arkansas Rivers in today's northern Oklahoma. The lands in southern Kansas assigned to them in 1865 were thus made available for non-Indian settlement.[65]

Getting all members of these five Plains tribes to move onto their latest reservations was challenging for the federal government. Some bands or factions were willing to make the move to this familiar territory they knew had abundant game, good grazing, water, timber, and resources their people had used at least since the early nineteenth century. However, some resisted limitations on the hunting, trading, visiting, and warfare so vital to their cultures. They were also unwilling to stop their raids into Texas and Kansas. Lt. Gen. William T. Sherman commanded the U.S. Army in frontier Kansas, and one of his senior officers was Maj. Gen. Philip Sheridan. During the Civil War they had not spared civilians or their property when they believed the situation called for harsh measures. In August 1868, Sheridan ordered Brig. Gen. Alfred Sully to go into the Indian Territory and punish the hostile Cheyenne Dog Soldiers in their own camps. Sully's expedition, however, bogged down in the sand hills near today's Woodward, Oklahoma, with its wagons buried up to the axles. The elusive Cheyenne warriors mooned the struggling column from the surrounding ridges and hills.[66]

This embarrassment, combined with the near disaster at Beecher's Island, Colorado Territory, a month earlier, convinced Sheridan to change tactics in order to stop Indian raids and force the Plains tribes onto the Indian Territory reservations. Nomadic Indian peoples typically settled for the winter into sheltered campsites close to good grazing and timber and lived mostly off stored foods, confident they were safe from enemies until late spring. Sheridan planned a winter campaign deep into the Indian Territory with fast moving columns to be supplied from a new base closer to the Indian winter camps than Fort Dodge, Kansas. His soldiers had orders to destroy lodges, supplies, and horse herds so that the Indians lost mobility and had to fight at a disadvantage. They were to kill the men and capture the women and children, while making no distinction between innocent or guilty, hostile or neutral.[67]

In November 1868 the three-pronged offensive began. One column headed east from Fort Lyon, Colorado Territory. A second rode east from Fort Bascom, New Mexico Territory. The third set off south from Fort Dodge, Kansas. Brigadier General Sully commanded the Kansas column, composed of the 7th Cavalry and the 19th Kansas Volunteer Cavalry. Their guides were civilian scouts and Osage trailers led by Hard Rope, unmatched among the Osages in tracking skills and battle strategy, and Little Beaver. The Osages had their own agenda, retaliation for the recent killing of an Osage by a Cheyenne. In mid-November the expedition established Camp (later Fort) Supply near the junction of Wolf and Beaver Creeks in today's Woodward County, Oklahoma, as its forward base. By the time General Sheridan and Lt. Col. George A. Custer arrived with the rest of the 7th Cavalry, a winter storm was blowing across the plains. Ben Clark and the other scouts insisted they knew where the Cheyennes, who had recently been raiding near Fort Dodge, would be camped and feeling secure in the deep snow. Sheridan ordered Custer to take the scouts and eight companies of the 7th Cavalry out to find them, and the column set off on November 23.[68]

As they expected, a series of Cheyenne, Arapaho, Comanche, Kiowa, and Plains Apache camps lay along a ten-mile stretch of the Washita River, called the "Lodge Pole River" by the Cheyennes, generally between today's Strong City and Cheyenne, Oklahoma. About seventy-five lodges associated with Cheyenne peace chief Black Kettle lay at the extreme western end. The shadow of the Sand Creek Massacre still hung over him, and some Cheyennes resented his cooperation with the white men. A Kiowa war party, just back from raiding the Utes, was visiting his camp, and they reported a soldier trail near the Antelope Hills. That frightened people, including Black Kettle's wife, who had been shot at Sand Creek. Moving Behind, a Cheyenne girl about fourteen then, was also alarmed. An orphan, she lived with her aunt Corn Stalk and uncle, who usually camped near Black Kettle. The peace chief had just returned from Fort Cobb, recently reopened as an Indian Department annuity distribution station for the western tribes.[69] Black Kettle had told rationing officer Col. William B. Hazen he wanted peace, but Hazen replied the chief needed to discuss that not with him but with General Sheridan.[70]

Even as an elderly woman, Moving Behind remembered the

tension in the camp on the night of November 26. Eonahpah, or Trailing the Enemy, a young Kiowa visitor, refused invitations to stay in the camp and went back to his little shelter out on the hillside. He took off his moccasins and went to sleep.[71] Some Cheyennes in the camp were afraid the soldiers would find them and wanted to leave immediately. "Black Kettle's wife became very angry," Moving Behind recalled, "and stood outside for a long time . . . . She talked excitedly, and said, 'I don't like this delay, we could have moved long ago . . . . It seems we are crazy and deaf, and cannot hear.'"[72]

Meanwhile, the 7th Cavalry column rode as silently as possible through the frigid, crystal-clear night a little distance behind Hard Rope and Little Beaver, scouting on foot through the deep snow. About midnight they paused on a ridge north of the Washita River. Hard Rope caught the scent of smoke with his keen sense of smell. A barking dog, tinkling pony bell, and baby's cry told them they had found a camp. Satisfied it sheltered Indian raiders, Custer divided his troops into four columns with orders to converge at his signal on the lodges, set in a loop of the river, from four directions. At dawn on November 27 he led the charge down off the ridge and across the river as the band played the first notes of "Garry Owen." It was so cold most of the bandsmen only got a few notes out before their instruments froze up. Scout Ben Clark recalled "the rush and rumble of the charge" as "the horses sprang forward on a run, the troopers shouting in anticipation of battle."[73] Custer declared later, "There never was a more complete surprise. My men charged the village and reached the lodges before the Indians were aware of our presence." It reminded him, he said, "of scenes during the [Civil] war."[74]

Moving Behind remembered,

> [J]ust before daylight . . . . We heard a woman saying in a low voice, 'Wake up! Wake up! White men! White men are here! The soldiers are approaching our camp.' . . . At that instant, the soldiers let out terrible yells, and there was a burst of gunfire from them . . . . I could see the dark figures of persons running here and there in a mad rush. When a burst of gunfire was heard, my aunt would catch my hand, and say, 'Hold my hand tightly, don't turn it loose whatever may happen. We will go somewhere and hide.'"[75]

As people spilled out of their lodges, Amithneh, then a little girl about eight or nine, grabbed her backpack and scrambled after her younger sister and mother Mosaio, who carried her little son on her back. Amithneh told her great-granddaughter as they ran with the other women, it was impossible to hear because of the screaming, crying, shouting, and shooting.[76]

Moving Behind agreed, "The young men had guns, and they uttered the most terrifying war whoops when the fight began. Black Kettle and his wife ... rode off on a horse .... Many Indians were killed during the fight. The air was full of smoke from guns, and it was almost impossible to flee, because bullets were flying everywhere .... As we ran, we could see the red fire of the shots."[77]

Amithneh ran with her sister and mother for the river, but before they could get there, she heard her mother call her name. Looking back, she saw her little brother go tumbling and Mosaio on the ground. While her sister picked their little brother up, Amithneh ran to her mother and tried to lift her. It was already too late. Her mother, shot in the back, was dying. She told Amithneh to go with the rest of the women and not to look back. Amithneh and her sister took their little brother by his hands and ran with him dangling between them. Before they reached the river and jumped in, they saw two soldiers on horseback shoot down a pregnant woman, slice her abdomen open, and, laughing, lift up her unborn baby on the point of a saber.[78]

By then the noise had wakened Eonahpah. The Kiowa grabbed his bow and quiver and ran through the snow toward the camp. As screaming women and children fled along the riverbank, he, a man named Little Rock, and a young boy called Packer ran behind them and tried to hold off the pursuing soldiers. Little Rock was killed, and Eonahpah used up all his arrows. Packer handed him more. He kept shooting until they, too, were gone and he was knocked down. Somehow as he fell his hand closed on a revolver in the snow, and he used it to shoot a mounted soldier and escape. Only when it was all over did Eonahpah realize he was still barefoot.[79] Amithneh saw that fight on the riverbank above her and marveled to her great-granddaughter, "They were fighting—those two men were fighting soldiers as best they could."[80] According to Cheyenne elder Alfrich Heap of Birds, his grandmother also witnessed their attempt to hold off the soldiers. Remembering her account, he added, "They always said this was the bravest Kiowa they had ever seen."[81]

Once the charging cavalrymen cut through Chief Black Kettle's camp, Lieutenant Colonel Custer, accompanied by Ben Clark, rode to the top of a knoll from which he could observe the action. Many women and children ran down the river toward the other Indian camps, and some jumped into the shallow river, breaking through a thin sheet of ice that gashed their legs. Scout Ben Clark watched as other fleeing Cheyennes came under fire while they climbed the steep bank south of the camp. "It was here the greatest slaughter took place," he said. Those who made it up onto the prairie ran into one of the cavalry columns as well as the Osage scouts, who, according to Clark, shot them down and mutilated their bodies. Seeing what was happening, Clark asked Custer "if it was his wish that they should be killed, and he ordered me to stop the slaughter." Clark did and had the survivors taken back to the camp and placed in a large tepee under guard. The captives included one elderly woman, who, the scout said, "stood at bay like an enraged tigress. She had an old cavalry saber raised defiantly for battle." With difficulty he persuaded her to put it down and sent her with the other prisoners. Rounding them up continued all morning, Clark said, along with "the hunting and slaughter of fugitives."[82]

Moving Behind and Corn Stalk tried to escape by running up a steep path over a bank. Moving Behind remembered,

> There was red grass along the path, and . . . it was still high enough for us to hide. In this grass we lay flat, our hearts beating fast; and we were afraid to move. It was now bright daylight. It frightened us to listen to the noise and the cries of the wounded. When the noise seemed to quiet down, and we believed the battle was about to end, we raised our heads high enough to see what was going on . . . .
>
> The wounded ponies passed near our hiding place, and would moan loudly, just like human beings. We looked again, and could see the soldiers forcing a group of Indian women to accompany them, making some of the women get into wagons, and others on horses.
>
> . . . The soldiers would pass back and forth near the spot where I lay. As I turned sideways and looked, one soldier saw us,

and rode toward where we lay. He stopped his horse, and stared at us. He did not say a word, and we wondered what would happen. But he left, and no one showed up after that. I suppose he pitied us, and left us alone.[83]

The noise of the attack alerted the Indian camps downstream. Cheyenne men there hurried their women and children onto horses and sent them toward safety. Then they grabbed weapons and rode fast toward Chief Black Kettle's camp, along with Kiowas led by Satanta, Arapahos led by Little Raven, and some Comanches.[84] Meanwhile, Maj. Joel Elliott, separated from his command, spotted fugitives running down river and set off after them with nineteen volunteers. Out of sight and sound of Black Kettle's camp behind some small buttes, Elliott and his followers rode into a low spot along a little stream (today called Sergeant Major Creek) east of the camp. They got caught there between Cheyennes running downstream and the Indian reinforcements coming upstream. Elliott made a critical mistake then by having his men dismount and lie prone in a circle, facing out. That cost them their good line of fire.[85] An account passed down by Kaywichamy, a Comanche eyewitness, said Putuaputiquay, or One Who Looks after His Son, and Napiwatah, or No Foot, rode circles around the troopers to pin them down until more Indians could arrive. Outnumbered and exposed, the soldiers were all dead within an hour. Kaywichamy said, "I looked there … and looked like they were on fire … but it was steam." Moisture rose straight up from the warm bodies in the windless cold. The Cheyenne women came then and stripped and mutilated the dead soldiers to make their spirits harmless in the next world.[86]

Unaware of what was happening to Elliott, Custer ordered the lodges—mostly Cheyenne but with two Arapaho and two Lakota—along with their furnishings, clothing, blankets, bison robes, weapons, and winter provisions—destroyed. Among them the soldiers found some letters and items evidently taken during raids in Kansas. They captured more than eight hundred horses and mules, too. After choosing some to transport the prisoners, selecting the best for himself, and allowing his officers and the Osage trailers to select some, Custer ordered all the rest of the unmanageable herd shot, a job that took two platoons of troopers almost two hours.[87]

By then one of his officers had reported the Indian reinforcements coming up river. However, the enraged Indians could only watch the destruction of the camp and valuable horse herd while the soldiers held more than fifty women and children captive. Aware by now that he was seriously outnumbered, Custer pretended to lead his force downriver toward the other camps and then turned quickly back toward Camp Supply as dusk approached, leaving Major Elliott and the missing men unaccounted for.[88]

Moving Behind and Corn Stalk dared to come out of hiding late in the afternoon and joined other stunned and grieving survivors, including her sweetheart Crane. On seeing her, he asked, "'Is this you, Moving Behind?' I said, 'Yes,'" Moving Behind remembered. "We both cried, and hugged and kissed each other,'" she said, and then they went to help retrieve the bodies of Chief Black Kettle and his wife from the river and bury them.[89]

News of Custer's victory at the Battle of the Washita, or the Washita Massacre, depending on one's point of view, spread quickly by telegraph and newsprint. It also sent native peoples in western Indian Territory running for safety. Some Kiowas moved to the west side of the Wichita Mountains, and soon the Cheyenne and Arapaho survivors from the Washita camps joined them. Near the North Fork of the Red River, they held an intertribal council and considered but rejected the idea of an all-out war against white people.[90] According to Plains Apache oral history, Custer's attack on Black Kettle's camp shook their tribe's confidence in a future likely to be dominated by numberless white people. They knew from the other tribes that Custer's attack had left elders and children dead. According to tribal elder Alonzo Chalepah of today's Apache Tribe of Oklahoma, they realized that kind of attack could happen to them and questioned how such an aggressive U.S. Army would even know "who was Cheyenne and who was a Kiowa and who was an Apache?"[91] Many of the Indian Territory Plains peoples had moved near Fort Cobb by mid-December, trying to demonstrate they were peaceable. There Col. William M. Hazen, hoping to prevent another Sand Creek Massacre, sent that message to the U.S. troops still in the field.[92]

However, some Kiowas and the Nokoni Comanches stayed away and camped near Devil's Canyon northwest of today's Warren,

Oklahoma. By then, Maj. A. W. Evans, commanding the Fort Bascom, New Mexico Territory, column of two hundred men from the 3rd Cavalry and 37th Infantry, had arrived in the Indian Territory. Near the Canadian River they picked up the trail left by Indians fleeing from Black Kettle's camp on the Washita River and followed it toward today's Quartz Mountain State Park. On Christmas Day 1868, the troops attacked and overran a Comanche camp near Soldier Spring at the base of Soldier Peak. Its chief was Horseback, known to be friendly to white people but currently away at Fort Cobb. While the noncombatants fled, the Comanche men fought back, reinforced by Kiowas led by Woman's Heart. By sundown, though, the troopers controlled the Comanche camp. Following Sheridan's plan for subduing the Plains tribes, they burned the captured lodges, furnishings, and provisions and threw ten tons of dried bison meat into the spring-fed pond that supplied drinking water to the camp. From that time on, the Comanches called it "Dried Beef Pond." The loss of life at the Battle of Soldier Spring was minimal, perhaps one dead on each side. However, dead cavalry horses killed by the bitter winter weather marked Evans's trail there and back to New Mexico. Custer's victory much overshadowed his, but this fight also helped force the Plains Indians onto the new Indian Territory reservations. With their winter food supplies gone, some of these Comanches went to Fort Cobb for help, but others joined the unyielding Quahadi Comanches on the Staked Plains.[93]

The army's winter campaign was somewhat successful because most Kiowas settled on their new reservation, along with the Peneteka, Nokoni, and some Yamparika Comanches. The Cheyennes and Arapahos were reluctant to live on the Cherokee Outlet lands set aside by the Medicine Lodge Treaty, partly because it placed them too close to their traditional Osage and Pawnee enemies. In 1869 Pres. U. S. Grant by executive order assigned them lands in today's west-central Oklahoma between the 98th and 100th meridians and generally from the Cherokee Outlet's south boundary to the Kiowa-Comanche-Apache Reservation and Old Greer County. The Caddos, Wichitas, and small tribes historically associated with them were assigned a wedge in the southeast corner of this rough rectangle. Agents, teachers, and missionaries began trying to replace their traditional ways with those of Christian, Anglo-American farmers. Meanwhile, federal control in western Indian Territory strengthened when Fort Sill was established near the Wichita Mountains in 1869.[94]

Still, while bison and other game remained plentiful, small parties frequently left the reservations to hunt or raid in Texas and Kansas. They also attacked Fort Sill, Fort Supply, travelers, cattle herders, and surveyors marking off tribal lands. The federal government used military force to suppress these hostilities; however, public concern, roused initially by the Sand Creek massacre, led to an experimental federal "peace policy." Agents, missionaries, and teachers were recruited from the Society of Friends and other religious denominations, while the new Board of Indian Commissioners made recommendations on federal policies and actions.[95]

Even then, periodic warfare with the western Indian Territory tribes continued until the mid-1870s. Even though their reservation lands were supposedly set aside for their exclusive use, non-Indian cattle herders, travelers, and freighters used the Chisholm Trail (roughly today's U.S. Highway 81) and the Great Western Trail paralleling the 100th meridian. Horse thieves and woodcutters slipped in to steal their stock and timber, while commercial hunters nearly eradicated the bison herds that were so much a part of their culture and livelihood. The "Outbreak of 1874," or Red River War, arising from Indian frustration with reservation life and these conditions, was their last violent revolt. After the frontier United States Army suppressed it, seventy-one chiefs and warriors and one woman selected as the worst offenders were imprisoned at Fort Marion, St. Augustine, Florida. When the survivors returned home from about three years' imprisonment, they understood the futility of fighting and the necessity of adopting some white ways, particularly literacy.[96]

The series of removals to Indian Territory to lands ceded in the wake of the Civil War continued through the 1870s and 1880s. In 1871, the Osages sold their 8-million-acre Kansas reservation and bought 1.5 million acres—today's Osage County, Oklahoma—in the Cherokee Outlet. The target of homesteaders in Kansas for years, they preferred the tall grass prairie that was fine for grazing their livestock but would not tempt farmers. The last tribe left in Kansas was the one it was named for, the Kansas (Konzas or Kaws), the "wind people." Their 250,000-acre reserve

lay near Council Grove at the Santa Fe Trail head. Settlers, land speculators, and railroad builders all coveted it. The intense outside pressure
fractured the tribe politically by 1873 when they finally removed to
today's Kay County, Oklahoma. At the beginning of the Civil War, there
had been ten thousand Indians living in Kansas. Less than fifteen years
later, there were fewer than one thousand, trying to live as individuals
apart from their tribal communities.[97]

During the next few years, tribes from Nebraska also left their
homelands for the Indian Territory. The Pawnee, a once-powerful
Caddoan Plains tribe, were proud they had never made war against
the United States. Rather, they had served honorably as scouts for the
U.S. Army and protected the crews building the new transcontinental
railroad. However, by the mid-1800s many had died in epidemics or
conflict with old enemies such as the Cheyennes and Lakotas. In late
summer 1873, while they were on a bison hunt along the Republican
River, a large war party of Brule and Oglala Lakotas killed more than
seventy Pawnees at Massacre Canyon. This loss, combined with the
shrinking bison herds, increasing hunger, and other problems, made
a move to the Indian Territory appealing. Small groups went south to
join their Wichita relations near Anadarko, and several Pawnees
scouted for the army during the Red River War. Eventually, the
Pawnees gave up their Nebraska lands for 280,000 acres along Black
Bear Creek between the lands of the Osages and the Sac and Fox reservation in today's northern Oklahoma.[98]

The seven clans of the Otoes and Missourias, the first Indian
people to host Lewis and Clark on their 1803 journey up the Missouri
River, held almost 163,000 acres in southeastern Nebraska. Some of
the more traditional of these seminomadic hunters and farmers had
already left for the Indian Territory. In 1881 the rest moved south to
a new 130,000-acre reserve along Red Rock Creek in the Cherokee
Outlet.[99] Rosa La Due Daily was about eight when they made that trip
by wagon train and riding horseback. Her family settled near Black
Bear Creek in an abandoned one-room log cabin with a good spring
nearby. Rosa said they built a rock fireplace for cooking, "as we did not
have any stove. The team my father had was a small pony team, but he
had a plow, and we broke some sod and made a garden, also planted
some corn. We had a hard time to get food at first until we could raise

some. Mother often parched corn and made coffee of it. We did a great deal of hunting and fishing and secured most of our living this way."[100] John Hudson, about twenty then, described his people before removal as "a sturdy and healthy tribe." That changed once they were on the new reservation and lost their independence. "We had to stop our roaming and settle in one place," he explained. "Our food was rationed to us, and we learned to eat many things we had never heard of before—canned goods, flour, sugar, coffee, beans [and] meat.... The government gave us money, too, with which to buy clothing and other necessities. Too often, however, it went for whiskey," he said.[101]

The federal government removed some tribes to the Indian Territory by force or as a type of imprisonment. The first were the Modocs, a tribe from the California-Oregon border region, through whose homeland the Oregon Trail ran. Federal attempts to make way for non-Indian farms and ranches there included placing them on a reservation with their old enemies, the Klamaths. As the Civil War ended, Modoc chief Kintpuash, or Captain Jack, and his followers left that reservation for their old country and refused to return to the reservation. When federal troops came for them in 1872, they retreated to the Lava Beds near today's Tulelake, California. For five months one thousand troops failed to drive out the fifty-seven Modoc warriors. When that very costly war ended in 1873, most of the Modoc leaders were hanged. The surviving 155 Modocs were shipped that fall in heavily guarded railroad boxcars to Baxter Springs, Kansas. From there they went by wagon to Quapaw Agency. In spite of being repeatedly victimized by Quapaw agent Hiram Jones and his corrupt employees, the surviving Modocs settled in, worked hard, and prospered on their four-thousand-acre reservation carved from the Eastern Shawnee lands.[102]

Emily Ensworth, a Miami adopted by the Peoria, remembered the Modocs and other Indian prisoners who came through Quapaw Agency. Being an Indian herself, she said, "did not keep me from being afraid of the other wild Indians who were brought here. I was always afraid of the Nez Perces and the Poncas. When they were brought here they wore blankets and were watched by the soldiers .... The Modocs were soon taken to the Modoc Reserve and were quiet and friendly and anxious to learn after they were brought here in 1873."[103]

ONLY THE LAND

The Ponca Indians that young Emily feared had lived along the South Dakota-Nebraska border near the big bend of the Missouri River. Peaceful farmers and hunters closely related to the Omahas, they had an ancient warrior tradition. They fought back fiercely when attacked by the better armed Pawnees or Lakotas. An 1865 treaty guaranteed them a 96,000-acre reservation, but they were stunned to learn three years later that the federal government had given their land to the Lakotas. Nor did the government honor its guarantee to protect them when their enemies tried to drive them out. Rather, it made plans to remove them by force. Over their protests and under guard, they were sent to Quapaw Agency with instructions to choose new lands in the Cherokee Outlet. After spending a miserable year camped along Spring River, hereditary chief White Eagle and a delegation surveyed lands west of the Osage country. They agreed to take almost 102,000 acres along the Arkansas River and its Salt Fork south of today's Ponca City, Oklahoma. In the fall of 1878, just after their arrival, they held their annual Hethushka, or War Dance, at their campground on the Salt Fork, a tradition unbroken to this day.[104] Harry Buffalo Head, a Ponca elder, said in 1958, "The white people has different stories of how we got here, but what my grandpa told me is a lot different. And he told me, he says Jesus Christ brought us here . . . . Them people . . . wanted to do away with us . . . the Lord took mercy on us and brought us to this good country, lots of good water, wild game, anything we wanted was here."[105]

However, some Poncas remained discontented. The attempt of Standing Bear to take his son's body back to Nebraska for burial caused a panic and then a sensation as the public learned the circumstances. Imprisoned in Omaha for leaving the reservation without permission, he received help from sympathetic lawyers who asked for a writ of *habeas corpus* for his release. It was denied at first because he was an Indian. However, in Standing Bear's trial the judge ruled that an Indian is a person under the Constitution and entitled to the same protection as any person. This well-publicized case arising from the post–Civil War removals to the Indian Territory was a landmark for Indian civil rights.[106]

About the same time as the Poncas, the Nimi'puu, or "Nez Perce," were exiled from their homeland in Idaho and parts of Washington, Oregon, Montana, and Wyoming. Friendly to white people, they had fed and sheltered Lewis and Clark's exhausted and starving exploring party in 1805. By 1863, though, gold had been discovered on their 7.5 million acres, and the United States wanted it reduced by 90 percent. Chief Joseph led opponents of the smaller reservation when the tribe divided over what to do. After some young Nez Perce men attacked settlers, panic on both sides escalated into the Nez Perce War of 1877. Chief Joseph led his adherents east across the Rocky Mountains and then north toward Canada, while fighting off the U.S. Army. Just short of the Canadian border, soldiers surrounded them and forced them to surrender. Joseph and his closest followers were shipped to Quapaw Agency. In 1878 they were sent on to Oakland Reserve adjacent to the new Ponca Reservation in today's Kay County, Oklahoma. Decimated by sickness and never content in the "hot country," they were finally allowed to go to reservations in the Pacific Northwest in 1884. The Tonkawas, long homeless, soon accepted their abandoned 91,000-acre Indian Territory reserve.[107] To this day, they maintain ties with the Nez Perce and care for the graves of their dead buried in Oklahoma.

Not all Indian peoples that moved to the Indian Territory following the Civil War received their own reservation. Instead, they shared the lands of another tribe. That was a situation many feared would blur or even erase their culture. Fall Leaf, who had fought beside Union soldiers and guided army columns in the war with the Plains tribes, wrote federal officials in 1867, "We call ourselves Delaware Indians. Before the government of the United States was formed, we were a nation, and for time to come, as far as human mind can conceive, we wish to be a nation."[108] However, the Delaware were already divided. One part—today's Western Delawares—had migrated earlier through Texas and settled with the Wichitas and Caddos on their reservation near Anadarko, while the Eastern Delawares, including Fall Leaf, remained in the Cherokee Nation. Likewise, through an administrative error Absentee Shawnees, who before the Civil War lived in the western Muscogee Nation, resettled on former Seminole lands already designated for the Citizen Potawatomis. Both peoples were assigned to Shawnee Agency near today's Shawnee, Oklahoma. The Black Bob Band of Shawnees in Kansas saw their 1.6-million-acre reservation shrink to 200,000 acres by 1854 and took allotments in 1858. Quantrill's raiders ravaged their homes near Olathe, Kansas, but they remained steadfastly loyal to the Union, earning them the name "Loyal Shawnees." They moved to the Cherokee Nation in 1869 but retained their own identity.[109]

In the wake of the Civil War, then, and in some cases as a direct result, Indian nations that were removed to the Indian Territory lost or gave up claim to millions upon millions of acres of land in today's Oklahoma, Kansas, Nebraska, Colorado, Texas, New Mexico, Arizona, California, Oregon, Idaho, and Washington. Gone with them were the sacred places and resources of those lands—game, fish, birds, furs, hides, feathers, bones, sinew, quills, plants, timber, water, soils, and minerals— that Indian people had used and incorporated into their cultures over many generations. These things had spiritual as well as material meaning for them. Lost, too, was their identity with a place, their homeland perhaps for centuries. Comanche chief Ten Bears recalled that association when he said at Medicine Lodge, "I know every stream and every wood between the Rio Grande and the Arkansas."[110]

Ownership of these lands and resources passed within a generation to other Americans who would develop their own association with them. Part of this appropriated land expanded the grain production of the United States, while other areas furnished grazing, once the bison were gone, for the beef cattle industry just starting a boom period. These products helped feed and clothe Americans gravitating to towns and cities flourishing with post–Civil War industrialization and immigration. Moreover, with some of the most troublesome native peoples confined to the Indian Territory, a major hindrance to the construction and operation of the new transportation and communication lines tying together the East and West was removed. That these inconvenient or troublesome native peoples could be concentrated in the Indian Territory was the direct result of the Civil War because it engulfed the Indian nations and at its end left them nearly helpless before the power of the federal government.

The ink was still fresh on the Reconstruction treaties when the pressure to impose a new order began. About five years after the Civil War ended, Washington called the Indian nations to a constitutional convention to create the territorial government they had agreed to in theory in the Reconstruction treaties. The Five Civilized Tribes staunchly opposed giving up their national identity and sovereignty within their remaining lands. However, in September 1870 Cherokee, Chickasaw, Muscogee, and Seminole delegates arrived in Okmulgee, the new Muscogee capital, to meet with federal officers and representatives of other Indian nations. In some ways this meeting continued the Grand Council of the Indian Territory last convened at Camp Napoleon in 1865. The Plains tribes at war with the United States stayed away, as did the cautious Choctaws. However, Ottawa, Eastern Shawnee, Quapaw, Seneca, Wyandot, Confederated Peoria, Wea, Sac, and Fox delegations attended. Traditionally the southeastern Indian peoples chose delegates representing different viewpoints as a way of building consensus, so Civil War veterans from both sides were delegates. For example, the Cherokee delegation included wartime enemies William Potter Ross and Stand Watie. The latter had warned the Indian nations in 1863 their best hope was to stand together, and he held to that tactic still.[111]

Central superintendent Enoch Hoag presided over this constitutional convention intended to end the Five Civilized Tribes governments, which still controlled large amounts of land, opposed non-Indian settlement on them, and resisted the "railroad lobby" clamoring in Congress for access to the Indian Territory. The Indian delegates prepared a lengthy report demonstrating their progress in education and agriculture, two federal goals for "civilizing" Indians. In December they produced the Okmulgee Constitution establishing a federal union on the United States model. Even though ratification by Indian citizens failed, the delegates learned from the experience. When they reconvened in 1871, the Cheyennes, Arapahos, Kiowas, and Comanches—also under federal pressure—attended, too. By 1875 federal officials realized the more sophisticated nations were using the annual conventions to tutor the other Indians in resistance to territorialization, so the federal government cut off funding for them and tried other methods to reach its goals.[112]

By then the leaders of the Indian nations understood the nature of the increasing outside pressures. Cherokee, Chickasaw, Choctaw, Muscogee, and Seminole "delegates" traveled to Washington every year to meet with congressmen, federal officials, and sympathetic U.S. citizens. They knew major rail corridors to connect the Mississippi River with California and the Missouri Valley with the Gulf Coast must cross

ONLY THE LAND

their lands. They realized the railroad corporations would never be satisfied until Indian land became public land. The tracks entered the Indian Territory in the early 1870s, and new white-style towns such as Vinita, Wagoner, Muskogee, and McAlester sprang up next to them. Railroad construction brought hordes of non-Indians into the territory, as did cattle ranching and the new coal mining and timber industries. Some "foreign"—non-Indian—workers and hangers-on stayed on under the Indian governments' permit systems, but large numbers of "intruders" came in illegally. Either way, the foreign population mushroomed. Meanwhile, the Civil War–era lawlessness hung on in the Indian nations. The lighthorsemen and justice systems of the Indian nations were never able to restore the relatively low prewar crime rate. The federal government's response to Indian and non-Indian complaints about intruders and criminals was to extend its judicial authority from Fort Smith, seat of the federal district court, and send its U.S. deputy marshals into the Indian nations. Jurisdictional conflicts arose, while the Indian Territory gained a reputation as a "robbers' roost." At the same time, remnants of Civil War hostilities surfaced periodically in Indian national politics. The worst case was the Green Peach War in the Muscogee Nation in 1882–1883. Reviving Civil War memories, it sent Indian families scrambling for safety. After a fight between the constitutional and insurgent factions along Battle Creek near today's Okemah, Oklahoma, it ended with federal intervention. Unfortunately, that reinforced complaints that the Indian nations could not adequately govern themselves.[113]

The 1870s also brought major change in the relationship between the federal government and Indian nations. The Cherokee Reconstruction Treaty had allowed Cherokees to produce and sell goods in the states without paying federal excise taxes. In 1870, though, the U.S. Supreme Court in the "Cherokee Tobacco Case" ruled that Stand Watie and his nephew Elias C. Boudinot could not sell tobacco products from their factory tax free in the states. The court reasoned Indian treaties did not have the same legal status as those with foreign nations and that federal laws were superior to them. Congress quickly passed an act ending federal treaty making with Indian tribes and made them subject to acts of Congress and presidential executive orders.[114] Boudinot's brother William, editor of the *Cherokee Advocate*, wrote that the Supreme Court decision meant "Congress can take away our lands, while we hold them in common, and give them to others." Their only recourse, he reasoned, would be to become individual landowners, which would also mean giving up Cherokee citizenship for U.S. citizenship.[115]

While the Indian nations were absorbing this blow, the clamor increased to allot their lands in severalty and open surplus lands to homesteaders. Most Indian citizens believed their landholding system was better than the Euro-Americans' individual landownership system because any Indian could use as much land as he or she chose without infringing on a neighbor. Choctaw governor Isaac L. Garvin pointed out in his 1878 inaugural address, "Under the traditional system of land held in common we have neither paupers nor tramps."[116] Because everyone had free access to his nation's land, Muscogee George W. Stidham wrote, "We . . . have our own farms, no taxes to pay; our papers are not filled with advertisements of lands for sale on account of delinquencies."[117] In 1878 the Senate Committee on Territories visited the Muscogee Nation to hold hearings on issues such as allotting land. Back in Washington, they reported favorably on allotment even though they had received a petition signed by 705 Muscogee citizens asking that no alien political or social system be imposed on them.[118] Then in October 1879 Secretary of the Interior Carl Schurz visited the new town of Muskogee. He told an audience of Tawaconis, Kickapoos, Ottawas, Quapaws, Caddos, Plains Apaches, Wacos, Keechis, Osages, and Comanches as well as citizens of the Five Civilized Tribes they must soon allot their lands and admit non-Indian homesteaders. This was not news to the Five Civilized Tribes, but the other Indians privately expressed dismay, wondering if the federal government would fail to keep faith with their treaties.[119]

This visit occurred about the same time as the eruption of the "boomer" movement. It included would-be homesteaders backed by railroad corporations and other interests expecting to benefit if the Indian Territory was opened for settlement. One spokesman insisted this "grand fenced zoological garden" set aside for savages too lazy to work was impeding the progress of the whole region. As for the Indians, they could be removed again, he said, perhaps to Alaska.[120] Elias C. Boudinot, disheartened by the Cherokee Tobacco Case ruling, had come to support allotment and opening the Indian Territory. An article he published in the *Chicago Times* in February 1879 noted that 12 million acres of former Seminole land set aside for settlement by Indians or their freedmen still lay vacant. He reasoned these "Unassigned Lands" some called "Oklahoma" were public domain and so eligible for homesteading."[121]

The most famous of the boomers was Boudinot's associate, David L. Payne, who founded the "Oklahoma Colony." Based on the southern Kansas border, he tried to force an opening by leading or instigating several settler invasions of the Unassigned Lands or Cherokee Outlet from 1880 to 1884.[122] The Indian nations closed ranks to counter this threat, and Muscogee principal chief Samuel Checote told the international council in March 1880, "The land which we now possess is all that is left for our children."[123] They reminded federal officials of their obligation to protect the territory's borders and sent word to the western tribes to watch out for intruders. Sac and Fox chief Wequahoka replied, "We always depend on you. Anything you will do we will agree with you. P.S. We are brothers we must be one mind."[124]

Even though regional newspapers warned their readers the Indian Territory was home to eighteen thousand Civil War veterans—experienced guerrilla fighters who could probably cut a path all the way to Topeka!—the Indian nations used the federal court system against Payne. He knew the penalty for the first offense of intrusion was expulsion, but the second brought a thousand-dollar fine. Hoping to make his case in court for opening the Unassigned Lands, he intruded twice, was arrested the second time, and was taken to face the federal court at Fort Smith. Indian representatives assisted the prosecution in his trial before federal judge Isaac C. Parker in March 1881, with the president of the St. Louis and San Francisco Railroad assisting the defense. Judge Parker ruled that the Unassigned Lands, occupied or not, were still Indian land and so not available for homesteading. Therefore, Parker found Payne guilty of intrusion, levied the fine—which he could not pay—and released him. While he planned his next move on the Indian Territory, the Indian nations celebrated their victory in federal court.[125]

Payne died suddenly in 1884, but the boomer movement grew along with Anglo-American public support for opening the Indian

Territory to non-Indian settlement. Indian leaders still argued that their traditional system of holding land in common allowed any Indian the opportunity to support his family on as much land as he wanted to work. Critics charged, however, that a few well-educated, ambitious Indians were growing rich exploiting the common resources at the expense of the ignorant or less ambitious. The territory's abundant grazing land was a prime example. With the post–Civil War boom in the beef cattle business, Indian ranchers prospered. Some formed partnerships, often with non-Indians. Even after their governments passed pasture laws, they fenced large portions of the common land for a few cents per head per year. By 1890 the standard size of a fenced pasture in the Muscogee Nation was 32,000 acres, but two companies fenced more than 50,000 acres each. On central and western Indian Territory reservations, lands not being used by Indians were routinely leased to white cattlemen for grazing. To protect their interests, the cattlemen formed associations such as the Cheyenne and Arapaho Live Stock Association, which even had its own newspaper. Among the best known was the Cherokee Strip Live Stock Association, which leased all six million unoccupied acres in the Outlet from the Cherokee Nation for five years at less than two cents per acre. Opponents charged these enterprises were monopolies, a potent accusation in that populist era. Eventually the federal government ended grazing leases on reservation lands and paid the Cherokee Nation $1.25 per acre for its remaining interest in the Cherokee Outlet. The cattle business suffered major setbacks in the late 1880s, but the large-scale Indian ranches continued, reinforcing public opinion that the Indian Territory should be opened for homesteading.[126]

The first step was passage in February 1887 of the Dawes (General Allotment) Act, which required that Indian reservations be allotted in severalty. It applied to all the Indian Territory nations except the Five Civilized Tribes and the Osage. The former were politically experienced and still strong enough to maintain their independence, while the latter were exempt because their removal treaty stated they would hold their land in common until they requested allotment.[127] The preceding winter the commissioner of Indian affairs had visited the tribes to persuade them to accept allotment and open their lands to outsiders. Osage principal chief Nekakepahah replied that with white people living among them, the Indians would soon be disenfranchised. As for the argument they would prosper by taking allotments, the chief said sarcastically they had only to look at Kansas homesteaders to see "the whites who live on alotments [sic] they have two ropes one to lead there [sic] cow and one to stake out the calve [sic]."[128] Unconvinced by the commissioner's arguments, the western tribes sent representatives to the international council in June 1887. Tawakoni Jim of the Wichita tribes declared, "We have always thought our lands would remain ours, and never be divided in severalty, and *it can never be done with our consent* [his emphasis]. The government treats us as if we had no rights, but we have always lived at our present place, and that is our home."[129]

In spite of Indian objections, the Dawes Act made allotment a hard reality. Over the next few years the Jerome Commission oversaw the process, which required compiling census lists for each tribe and assigning an allotment to every individual. Even when each Indian received 160 acres, the standard allotment size, most reservations were large enough to have surplus land, which could then be opened to non-Indians. The Kickapoos, however, had a very small reservation east of today's Oklahoma City. Assigning each of them 160 acres would not have left much surplus, so each Kickapoo received only 80 acres. Long before the process ended, the Indian Territory's barrier to non-Indian settlement crumbled. After paying the Seminole and Muscogee Nations for their residual interests in the Unassigned Lands, the federal government threw them open to homesteaders on April 22, 1889, in the first land run. Openings of reservation surplus lands by land runs or other methods followed through 1906. Each newly settled area was added to "Oklahoma Territory" as stipulated in the 1890 Organic Act. Non-Indians soon greatly outnumbered the Indian population.[130]

Midway through the process, in 1894, the Chiricahua Apaches arrived in the Indian Territory. Chiricahua Apache-white hostilities predating the Civil War had worsened during the war, and Goyathlay, also known as Geronimo, emerged as a militant leader. By the 1870s they were forced onto the Chiricahua Reservation but remained dissatisfied with the changes forced on them. Things grew worse when they were told to move again to the San Carlos Reservation. As Sam Hazous, a young teenager then, told it, "They surround us with their . . . cavalry horses. Chief Bigdoya . . . he don't want to leave this reservation. He said,

'You white man never give me this land. When you was out on the sea somewhere, I got this land already to stay on it . . . . Why they trying to take us away from here?'[131] Geronimo led the faction against removal, fighting in Arizona and Mexico until forced to surrender in 1886. Those who had survived the warfare and then were imprisoned at Fort Marion, Florida, and Mount Vernon Barracks, Alabama, arrived at Fort Sill in 1894. They remained prisoners of war there until 1913. The dissolution of the reservations was already underway when they received allotments on the Kiowa-Comanche-Apache Reservation. Otherwise, they would have been left landless.[132]

For the time being, the lands of the Cherokees, Chickasaws, Choctaws, Muscogees, and Seminoles were safe from the flood of non-Indian settlement even though it lapped at their borders. While that consumed most of their attention, a major issue from the Civil War remained unresolved in the Muscogee Nation: the Loyal Creek claim against the federal government for their property losses, initially estimated at five million dollars. In their Reconstruction Treaty the United States had agreed to reimburse these steadfast people and promised an initial payment of $100,000. (Federal representatives failed to mention it would come out of the $975,000 placed in the U.S. Treasury from the appropriation of their nation's western lands.) In 1870 the Loyal Creeks submitted a careful inventory of lost property totaling $1,836,830.41 and received that initial $100,000. Getting the rest was more difficult. Although the Loyal Creeks, usually represented by David M. Hodge, became a political faction, the nation's delegates to Washington, whatever their own views, faithfully pressed the claim. In the late 1880s it was finally referred to the U.S. Senate, which pared it to $1,200,000. However, the House of Representatives halved that amount to $600,000. When 15 percent was taken out for attorneys' fees, the Loyal Creeks received only $510,000, less than ten cents on the dollar for their losses a generation earlier.[133]

That final settlement came at the end of the nineteenth century as part of the Muscogee Nation's negotiations with the Dawes Commission, set up to oversee the dissolution of the Five Civilized Tribes. Although they fought long and hard against allotting their land and ending their national governments, they were swimming against too strong a tide. In 1892 there was already a statehood bill for the "Twin

Territories," and their delegates reminded a congressional committee of the Choctaw removal treaty guarantee, "at no time shall the Indian Territory be included within the bounds of a state."[134] Still, in 1894 the Dawes Commission told representatives of the Five Civilized Tribes, Osages, and Pawnees they had better negotiate because Congress could do whatever it chose. The next year the U.S. Geological Survey began surveying their lands. When they still delayed, passage in 1898 of the Curtis Act, authored by Congressman Charles Curtis, a mixed-blood Kaw Indian from Kansas, forced the issue, taking control of their national governments' operations and setting March 4, 1906, as their dissolution date. Although the Indian nations held a constitutional convention in 1905 to create a separate "State of Sequoyah," the federal government rejected the ratified document and instead created the State of Oklahoma in 1907.[135]

About 1912 George Washington Grayson, deeply involved in Muscogee and Indian Territory affairs since the Civil War, viewed those developments as catastrophic for Indian people. The changes had been forced on them, he believed, not because the Indians could not govern themselves adequately, had an inferior landholding system, or had violated treaties. It was because, he wrote, "the ruthless restless white man demanded it. Demanded it because in the general upheaval that would follow the change he, the white man, hoped and expected to obtain for a song, lands for ignorant Indians."[136]

Mary Cobb Agnew, a Cherokee housewife born in 1840, bitterly agreed, "the Government took another shot at us and set up the Dawes Commission in 1894. We owned all the land as a whole and could farm all we wanted to as long as we didn't infringe on our friends' land. We had a good government of our own just like we had back in Georgia, but the white man wanted our land just as they had wanted it back in Georgia."[137] The Curtis Act required the Five Civilized Tribes to enroll and choose allotments, but those nations avoided non-Indian settlement of their lands because they allotted it all to their own citizens. Indian businessmen, ranchers, and farmers who had sometimes controlled thousands of acres took small allotments along with the rest. Some adamantly refused to cooperate. The most notable instances of resistance were the Keetoowah Nighthawks in the Cherokee Nation and the Crazy Snake Rebellion in the Muscogee Nation. In the end, though, most dissidents were forced to take allotments or had them arbitrarily assigned. Mary Cobb Agnew said, "I and all my kin enrolled without any trouble, for I saw . . . that if we were to get anything, it would be necessary to enroll."[138] Oil production on their lands had already begun when the Osages accepted allotment. They retained their mineral rights in common, and their original allottees received headrights representing individual shares of the total royalties.[139]

Indian leaders repeatedly warned federal officials that, while some would adapt to the new order, too many Indians were ignorant of Anglo-American landholding practices involving sales, leases, and taxes. Restrictions placed on the sale of Indian lands for the first five years were revised later and based on the individual's degree of Indian blood. Unfortunately, this "crime of 1908," as some called it, left many of the uneducated, whatever their blood quantum, vulnerable to "grafters." These rapacious business and professional men got control of Indian lands and resources or fleeced the owners out of fair prices, rents, lease money, or royalties, particularly after the early 1900s oil boom began. The worst cases were probably the county probate judge-appointed guardians who controlled the lands and income of Indian minors and "incompetent" adults while taking outrageous fees for their services. Some Osages, called the "world's richest Indians," were even murdered in attempts to acquire their headrights.[140]

Among the western tribes, reservation agents supervised leases of Indian lands to white farmers and ranchers. Few western Indians at first had the farming skills, equipment, or interest needed to put their allotted land into production. Indians and homesteaders alike discovered the standard 160 acre-homestead was not enough to succeed raising stock or grain on the Southern Plains. Nor did some Cheyennes feel safe living on scattered allotments. Some bands and extended families camped together along the Washita River or White Shield Creek for decades, while "lease men" controlled their lands. In the Cherokee Outlet the Miller brothers leased nearly 110,000 acres, mostly Ponca land, for the spectacular 101 Ranch near today's Ponca City, Oklahoma. The Poncas received minimal income from the leases, even after much of their land proved in the early 1900s to overlie rich petroleum reserves, little of which ever benefited them. Meanwhile, grafters along with hard-working non-Indian farmers, ranchers, oil men, timber men, and miners saw themselves as developing the new state of Oklahoma.[141]

Although Indians became United States citizens in 1924, federal control over their land did not end, particularly among those with time restrictions on land sales. The result was that some allotments were leased year after year, decade after decade. Original owners died, while the number of their heirs often multiplied. Eventually one parcel might have multiple owners. That meant it became—and remains—almost impossible to sell it or do anything productive with it. During the New Deal in the 1930s the federal government reversed its Indian policy. It encouraged tribes to reorganize their governments and ended allotment. Although Oklahoma Indians by then refused to give up individual land-holding, they returned to self-government. Some Oklahoma Indian nations have since prospered through hard work, good leadership, and the advantages of their sovereign status within the United States, although that road has taken many twists and turns.[142]

As it turned out, though, land was not all Indian people had left. In spite of attempts to destroy and replace their cultures, some traditional cultural elements remained very important. According to historian Clyde Ellis, even in the reservation period warrior societies continued their traditional dances while they incorporated innovations.[143] For example, when the Poncas were forced to move to the Indian Territory, they brought with them and continued their war dance tradition. Recruited by the Miller brothers to perform in the 101 Ranch Wild West Show, they developed a public version that kept the structure, organization, and regalia of the war dance but was primarily for entertainment.[144] Meanwhile, they shared their traditional version with their new Otoe-Missouria, Kaw, Pawnee, and Osage neighbors for whom it also became an important tradition, particularly in welcoming home veterans of World War I and World War II.[145]

At the same time, the public entertainment version known generically as a "powwow" acquired songs and traditions from the Kiowas, Cheyennes, and other tribes. It spread across Oklahoma and on to other Indian peoples. Today the Quapaw Tribe and the Sac and Fox Nation are among many Oklahoma tribes and Indian organizations that have annual powwows dating back to the 1940s or earlier. During the mid-twentieth century, when Oklahoma Indian people moved to cities or were dispersed across the nation, the powwow helped maintain traditional ways while knitting together the new urban intertribal communities. Today Indians and non-Indians alike enjoy powwows, a staple event that has spread across North America and overseas.[146] Would that have happened without the post–Civil War concentration of so many Indian peoples in the Indian Territory?

Like the war dance and powwow, the peyote religion, too, spread from tribe to tribe on post–Civil War Indian Territory reservations. The Tonkawas, native to southwest Texas where the peyote cactus grows, believe they introduced its spiritual use to Indian peoples struggling to adjust to post–Civil War reservation life. About 1900, John Wilson, a Caddo-Delaware, and Comanche chief Quanah Parker "spread the fireplace" through the Twin Territories, teaching this mixture of traditional and Christian ways. Concern over peyote's mild hallucinogenic nature caused the Oklahoma Territorial Legislature to prohibit its use in 1898, but in 1908 Quanah Parker led a successful fight for repeal. After a court hearing in 1918, the Native American Church received a charter from the State of Oklahoma. Cheyenne elder Grover Turtle said in 1999, "They use that peyote sacrament just like white people they use wine." He explained, "They went to court and got the best doctors they could get to analyze that peyote. They could not find no dope in there . . . the judge said . . . . 'Only Indians know how to use it. They got different way of thinking with God.'"[147] The Native American Church became a vital force spreading to hundreds of thousands of Indian people, who like Quanah Parker and John Wilson, looked for a way to adapt to the new circumstances accelerated and ushered in by the Civil War.[148]

While these new paths opened for Indian people, non-Indians— black and white from many backgrounds—filled in the space around and among them. The 1870s, 1880s, and 1890s were hard economic times, and the Indian Territory land openings offered a chance for a fresh start. According to one scholar, three groups emerged in the Cherokee Nation after the Civil War with in-migration: Cherokees, Cherokee freedmen, and "states blacks." Cherokee freedmen worried that the last group threatened the progress they had made. The situation was somewhat similar in the Muscogee Nation. Muscogees not only adopted their freedmen, they assigned them to three political "towns," or districts, and allowed them to participate in the national government. In addition, the freedmen founded several physical all-black towns: Tullahassee, Gibson Station, Wybark, Clarksville, Summit, Grayson, Red Bird, Clearview, Rentiesville, Taft, and Boley.[149]

In the 1890s black promoter Edwin P. McCabe worked to create an all-black state in Oklahoma Territory. He founded Langston, an all-black town and university just east of Guthrie, the territorial capital. McCabe recruited "states blacks," which did not sit well with the freedmen from the Indian nations. Oklahoma statehood brought the imposition of Jim Crow laws, which reduced the rights and status of Indian freedmen, too. McCabe gave up "persuading freedmen throughout the South that dignity and fortune waited in the territories . . . . His motto became 'Come prepared or not at all.'" McCabe ended his efforts in Oklahoma. However, within three years, according to editor Roberta Clardy, "O. W. Gurley and John and Loula Williams transformed a Creek freedman cow pasture near Tulsa" into what visitors such as Booker T. Washington and Madam C. J. Walker knew as "the Black Wall Street." The residents of this "Greenwood" district were the third and fourth generations of the Indian freedmen's all-black towns.[150]

In addition to home-seekers from other American states, Italians and Slavs moved into the Choctaw Nation to mine coal, while Czechs settled in what had been Seminole and Muscogee lands until the Civil War. Germans from Russia brought their fine farming skills halfway around the world to the Cherokee Outlet and the Cheyenne and Arapaho Reservation. Today some Comanches still sing German hymns their ancestors learned from German-Russian missionaries. How the emigration of all these different peoples related to their old homes is another story, but their immigration into the Indian Territory and their continuing impact on Oklahoma was possible because of the Civil War.

Opothle Yahola characterized the Civil War as a wolf, a creature his people feared and respected, sometimes too much even to call it by name.[151] Others compared the war to a tremendous storm that tore their lives up by the roots. Ella Coodey, Stephen Foreman, Hannah Hicks, Wash and Annie Grayson, Blackbird Doublehead, Lucinda Davis, and George Bent were among the lucky ones who lived to tell their stories of survival. It is important to remember that this fragment of history that began in the 1800s and continued through the 1900s did not happen in isolation. It had two parts: what happened in the Indian Territory during the Civil War and the ramifications afterward—for its own peoples and those who would choose or be forced to come from other places, leaving vacancies and opportunities behind for still others.

So perhaps the Civil War in the Indian Territory was rather like a rock tossed into a calm pond, causing waves to spread in all directions, strike the far banks, and wash back, stirring and rearranging what they passed over. The Civil War in the Indian Territory was a very big rock.

BIBLIOGRAPHIC ESSAY

The Civil War is a topic that never seems to fall out of favor for research. The 150th anniversary can only heighten interest among professional historians as well as those who simply want to know more about it. The nature of the war in the Indian Territory, touching as it did so many different peoples, should generate even more research and publication.

Research materials are more accessible than ever before partly because of the Internet and digital libraries. *The War of the Rebellion: A Compilation of the Official Records of the Union and Confederate Armies*, published between 1880 and 1901, is now available online. Included are original reports on conditions, incidents, battles, and campaigns, including those in or affecting the Indian Territory. Likewise, pertinent *Annual Reports of the Commissioners of Indian Affairs* are available online. While reflecting the Union perspective, the yearly volumes provide summaries of conditions and events as well as reports from agents, agency staff, and others working with specific Indian tribes. Locating these materials today is as simple as typing the title into a search box.

Reliable Web sites also provide valuable information. Several online encyclopedias sponsored by state agencies and museums provided basic information for this book or aided fact checking. They include *The Encyclopedia of Oklahoma History and Culture, The Encyclopedia of Arkansas History and Culture, Texas Beyond History, The Handbook of Texas Online, Territorial Kansas Online,* and *The Colorado State Archives* sites. *The State Historical Society of Missouri* site provides access to period newspapers, manuscripts, and regimental histories among other things. The *Oklahoma Civil War Sesquicentennial 2011–2015* provides scanned documents and historic maps. The *Missouri Civil War Sesquicentennial, Museum of the Kansas National Guard,* and various National Park

Service and state historical site Web pages provided information about specific events or places. The texts on these sites are the work of history professionals or others with a background of research into their topic. Sources or suggested reading citations then direct the reader to yet more information.

Researchers today also have Web access to publications and materials once available only in libraries and archives. Full texts of volumes 1–40 (1923–1962) of *The Chronicles of Oklahoma*, published by the Oklahoma Historical Society, are now available online. Tables of contents of later volumes are available but require a hard copy of the original issue. Included in the *Chronicles* are articles written during the centennial of the Civil War by historians such as LeRoy H. Fischer, Muriel H. Wright, Angie Debo, and Edward Everett Dale. Likewise, the *Kansas Historical Quarterly*, volumes 1 (1931–1932) through 43 (1977), are online.

First-person material is more available now that repositories have posted Civil War correspondence and diaries. McFarlin Library at the University of Tulsa posted the valuable Civil War correspondence and diaries of the Worcester-Robertson family who lived in the Muscogee and Cherokee Nations. Particularly useful are the diaries of Hannah Worcester Hicks and her second husband, Dr. Dwight D. Hitchcock, a missionary doctor who worked in Union hospitals in the region.

The Western History Collections at the University of Oklahoma put its set of the Indian-Pioneer History online in a searchable database. This Federal Writers Project oral history collection includes some twenty-five thousand interviews of black, white, and Indian people. Many interviewees had lived through the Civil War era in the Indian Territory. Although some were children at the time, others, such as Mary Cobb Agnew, a Cherokee housewife, were adults with an adult perspective on events and conditions. The Western History Collections and the Oklahoma Historical Society each hold a set of the 1937–1938 transcripts of the interviews. However, the two sets were bound differently, so volume and page numbers do not match. The Oklahoma Historical Society has a comprehensive card file index to its set. Both sets have been available on microfiche and microfilm, respectively, for years.

Included with the Indian-Pioneer History are interviews of former slaves. At the Oklahoma Historical Society the interviews are in the Ex-slave Narrative Collection. Researchers will also find them published in T. Lindsay Baker and Julie P. Baker, *The WPA Oklahoma Slave Narratives*. Another publication based on this source is *Slave Narratives from the Federal Writers Project, 1936–1938, Oklahoma*. It includes people with surnames beginning with A through J.[1]

Some historians are skeptical of oral history, such as the Indian-Pioneer History, with good reason. Interviewees may have a faulty memory, or they may exaggerate conditions or their roles in events. However, oral history properly evaluated and used judiciously can provide information available nowhere else. The Oklahoma Historical Society has a large Oral History Collection covering many topics. A recent addition was the National Park Service–sponsored Cheyenne/Washita Oral History Project for Washita Battlefield National Historic Site. It was completed in four phases from 1998 to 2003. Historians, an anthropologist, and Indian fieldworkers collected information from Indian and non-Indian people about the 1868 Washita Massacre discussed in chapter 7. Later phases of the project collected information about western Oklahoma, the Washita River valley, and its resources. Indian interviews from the Washita project or other oral history projects at the Oklahoma Historical Society provided material for this book.

Source material also came from document collections at Oklahoma repositories. The Grant Foreman Collection is divided between the Gilcrease Museum of American History and Art in Tulsa, Oklahoma, and the Oklahoma Historical Society in Oklahoma City. The Foreman Collection at the Gilcrease yielded, among other things, an 1861 letter from Muscogee colonel Daniel N. McIntosh to Cherokee colonel John Drew about Opothle Yahola, which stated, "it is now certain that he has combined with his party all the surrounding wild tribes and has openly declared himself the enemy of all the South."[2] The Samuel Bell Maxey Collection is also at the Gilcrease. In it is Maxey's correspondence with his Civil War associates and his wife, Matilda. An example is his letter dated February 25, 1864: "Oh for 5000 good guns, and I would place Northern Texas in safety. I have the promise, but when will it be fulfilled?"[3]

The Western History Collections at the University of Oklahoma is also rich in Civil War material. Those used in this book are the

Grayson Family Collection, Peter P. Pitchlynn Collection, and Stephen Foreman's diary. The transcript of the last details his daily life and difficulties as a widowed father, minister, Cherokee official, Stand Watie supporter, and refugee. The Cherokee Nation Papers include correspondence of the Ridge-Watie-Boudinot family published as *Cherokee Cavaliers: Forty Years of Cherokee History as Told in the Correspondence of the Ridge-Watie-Boudinot Family*, edited by Edward Everett Dale and Gaston Litton.

Collections at the Oklahoma Historical Society that contributed to this book were from its portion of the Grant Foreman Collection; the Alice Robertson Collection; and the national records of the Cherokee, Chickasaw, Choctaw, Muscogee, and Seminole Nations. The Indian national governments generated these important Indian records from about 1850 to the early 1900s, although some are earlier. The society has held them and the Indian agency records, predominantly postwar, for the National Archives since 1934.[4] Unfortunately the Civil War devastation in the Indian Territory resulted in the loss of most Indian prewar and wartime documents. Still, there are some surviving pertinent original materials, such as "The Record Book of Chief Sam Checote in the Early Sixties" in the Indian Archives. It includes harsher slave laws imposed at the beginning of the war to cope with the problem of runaways. Civil War–related documents in the Indian national records include the Choctaw Nation's declaration of independence from the United States; lists of supplies issued to Col. Chilly McIntosh and his officers on July 13, 1862; and lists of supplies distributed to heads of Muscogee families in refugee camps on Caney Creek, Chickasaw Nation, as of March 31, 1865.[5] In the Cherokee Nation Records are claims written in English and Cherokee for property lost during the war. Included is Dr. W. L. G. Miller's claim for surgical instruments and "teeth extracting instruments." He listed livestock, too, appropriated by the federal Indian Expedition in 1862, and gold spectacles later "taken by rebels."[6]

Other Civil War materials at the Oklahoma Historical Society include photostatic copies of the muster rolls from the 1st, 2nd, and 3rd Indian Home Guard held by the National Archives in Washington, D.C. There is also Grant Foreman's 1928 two-volume work, *A History of the Confederate Army in the Indian Territory*, which covers 1861 to

1863. It is available on microfilm. Lastly, there are wartime letters written by individuals. These include Dallas Bowman, a Texan in the Choctaw-Chickasaw regiment, and R. J. Ross, a Muscogee living among the Cherokees. Lastly, a surprising number of Civil War–era photographs of people and places are found in the Oklahoma Historical Society Photographic Archives, even though visits by photographers to the Indian Territory were rare before the Civil War.

These Indian Territory materials and national records were not available to Civil War veteran Wiley Britton, who drew on personal experience as well as documents for *The Union Indian Brigade in the Civil War*. They were deteriorating in storage in federal facilities in Muskogee, Oklahoma, when Annie Heloise Abel wrote her three-volume, early-twentieth-century work on the Civil War in the Indian Territory. She based it on federal records, memoirs of Civil War veterans, and late-nineteenth-century histories. Her work fell out of favor by the late 1900s, when Theda Perdue and Michael D. Green edited it for a Bison Book edition through the University of Nebraska Press. Abel's *The American Indian as Slaveholder and Secessionist: An Omitted Chapter in the Diplomatic History of the Southern Confederacy* (1992) and *The American Indian and the End of the Confederacy, 1863–1866* (1993) are still useful to researchers for their full-text footnotes if for no other reason.[7]

In the decade before 2000 researchers of Indian Territory history were able to build on the works of mid-twentieth-century predecessors such as Angie Debo, Grant Foreman, Morris L. Wardell, Edwin C. McReynolds, Arrell M. Gibson, and Donald J. Berthrong. The flourishing of ethnic studies, including Indian history, in the second half of the twentieth century encouraged specialization. The new generation of historians focused on ethnicity and interactions between Indian peoples and non-Indians in books such as Colin G. Calloway's *New Worlds For All: Indians, Europeans, and the Remaking of Early America* and Richard White's *The Middle Ground: Indians, Empires, and the Republics in the Great Lakes Regions, 1650–1815*.[8]

More specific to the Indian Territory was Elizabeth A. H. Johns's *Storms Brewed in Other Men's Worlds: The Confrontation of Indians, Spanish and French in the Southwest, 1540s–1795*. It described the "Wichita exchange," the system by which Wichita middle men along the Indian Territory's rivers linked the Comanches on the Great Plains with French traders from Louisiana. Thomas W. Kavanagh's *The Comanches: A History, 1706–1875* and David La Vere's *Contrary Neighbors: Southern Plains and Removed Indians in Indian Territory* described the complexities and frictions of Indian-white and inter-tribal relations west of the Cross Timbers.[9] Duane Champagne compared southeastern Indian political systems in *Social Order and Political Change: Constitutional Governments among the Cherokee, the Choctaw, the Chickasaw, and the Creek*. In *After the Trail of Tears: The Cherokees' Struggle for Sovereignty, 1839–1880*, William G. McLoughlin reexamined events in the Cherokee Nation between removal and 1880, the point at which it became clear federal plans for the Indian nations and their lands superseded guarantees of Indian sovereignty.[10] Cecile Elkins Carter, a Caddo, used oral history as well as documentary research for her award-winning *Caddo Indians: Where We Come From*. Stan Hoig, a journalist and prolific writer on Oklahoma's Indian history, produced *Tribal Warfare on the Southern Plains* as well as *The Peace Chiefs of the Cheyennes*. Osage geographer Louis F. Burns, who had herded cattle and traced the old Indian trails with his Osage grandfathers in the 1930s, incorporated Osage culture and sense of place in *A History of the Osage People*. First published by the author in 1989, it was reissued by the University of Alabama Press in 2004.[11]

Looking at Indian experiences in the post–Civil War period, David Wallace Adams described the impact of boarding schools on Indian young people in *Education for Extinction: American Indians and the Boarding School Experience, 1875–1928*. Daniel F. Littlefield Jr. and James W. Parins, specialists in the study of Indian writers and their literature, produced *Native American Writing in the Southeast: An Anthology, 1865–1935*. *The Encyclopedia of North American Indians: Native American History, Culture, and Life from Paleo-Indians to the Present*, edited by Frederick E. Hoxie and published in 1996, included entries reflecting the new research and perspectives by this generation of historians. An even more recent encyclopedia is Blue Clark's *Indian Tribes of Oklahoma: A Guide*, replacing the venerable work by Muriel H. Wright.[12]

In the late 1900s the topic of the Civil War in the West, including the Indian Territory, retained its appeal. Phillip W. Steele and Steve

Cottrell's *Civil War in the Ozarks* included the eastern Indian Territory lying on the western margin of the Ozarks, but their focus was tighter on Arkansas and Missouri. Soon afterward, though, Cottrell's *Civil War in the Indian Territory* outlined the military aspects of the war in the Indian Territory. David Paul Smith's fine *Frontier Defense in the Civil War: Texas' Rangers and Rebels* described why and how Texans tried to secure control of the Indian Territory for their own purposes as much as for the Confederacy.[13]

Three books published between 2000 and 2002 focused on specific battles or campaigns related to the Indian Territory. Lela J. McBride's *Opothleyaholo and the Loyal Muskogee: Their Flight to Kansas in the Civil War* was clearly a labor of love and the result of decades of research. It was based almost entirely on government documents, a few nineteenth-century publications, newspaper articles, and an interview with a descendant of Opothle Yahola. However, it contained details that brought the Loyal Indians and their exile in Kansas into sharp focus. Another privately published work was Steven L. Warren's *Brilliant Victory: The Second Civil War Battle of Cabin Creek, Indian Territory, September 19, 1864. The Prairie Was on Fire: Eye Witness Accounts of the Civil War in the Indian Territory* was an unusual book compiled by living history specialist Whit Edwards. It was composed of excerpts from records and reports as well as first-person accounts of events. The impact of the Civil War on the Cherokee residents of the Neutral Lands in Kansas is usually overlooked. Gary L. Cheatham addressed this topic in a fine article published in *Kansas History* in 2007, "'If the Union Wins We Won't Have Anything Left': The Rise and Fall of the Southern Cherokees in Kansas."[14]

In the last decade a new generation of historians has reexamined the Indian removals that contributed to Civil War divisions. New books include an intellectual history by Amy H. Sturgis, *The Trail of Tears and Indian Removal;* a biography by John L. Elder, *Everlasting Fire: Cawokoci's Legacy in the Seminole Struggle Against Western Expansion;* and Clarissa W. Confer's well-written but tightly focused *The Cherokee Nation in the Civil War.*[15]

The Civil War in the Indian Territory cannot easily be isolated from conditions and events beyond its borders. The Battle of Wilson's Creek, Missouri, in 1861 is often mentioned as the Confederate victory that caused the Cherokee Nation to become a Confederate ally. In 2000 William Garrett Piston and Richard W. Hatcher III described it in *Wilson's Creek: The Second Battle of the Civil War and the Men Who Fought It*. William L. Shea wrote several books about Civil War battles in Arkansas, including in 1992 *Fields of Blood: The Prairie Grove Campaign*. Shea and Earl J. Hess also published *Pea Ridge: Civil War Campaign in the West* the same year. They detailed the battle in northwest Arkansas in which Indian Territory troops played a relatively minor role. Nevertheless, the scalping incident attributed to the Confederate-allied Cherokees caused acrimonious discussion about whether Indians should even be allowed to fight in a civilized army. Anne J. Bailey, citing Shea and Hess in *Invisible Southerners: Ethnicity in the Civil War*, noted that bigotry then was not aimed simply at Indians. It was also directed at the "Dutch," or Germans in the Union army.[16]

Black soldiers faced more than criticism during the Civil War in the Indian Territory and surrounding states. By the 1970s scholars were studying African slavery in the Indian nations. In 1979 Theda Perdue authored *Slavery and the Evolution of Cherokee Society, 1540–1866*, while Daniel F. Littlefield Jr. wrote *Africans and Seminoles: From Removal to Emancipation* in 1977 and *Africans and Creeks: From the Colonial Period to the Civil War* in 1979. During the same period Dudley Taylor Cornish broke new ground with two books about black soldiers in the Civil War military: *Kansas Negro Regiments in the Civil War* published for that state's Civil Rights Commission and *The Sable Arm: Black Troops in the Union Army, 1861–1865*.[17]

New books about African slavery in the Indian nations in the first decade of the twenty-first century included Gary Zellar's *African Creeks: Estelvste and the Creek Nation*, Kevin Mulroy's *The Seminole Freedmen: A History*, and Celia E. Naylor's *African Cherokees in the Indian Territory: From Chattel to Citizens*.[18] Related topics included the enlistment of Indian freedmen and former slaves in the Union Indian Home Guard and the 1st Kansas Colored Volunteer Infantry. Mark A. Lause described the role of abolitionists in creating, training, and commanding the new black troops in *Race and Radicalism in the Union Army*. Noah Andre Trudeau's *Like Men of War: Black Troops in the Civil War, 1862–1865* described campaigns and battles, including those in the Indian Territory, in which black troops fought in Union uniforms. They did so knowing they could expect no quarter from white troops. Notorious incidents of atrocities against them in the west in 1864 included the Hayfield Fight at Flat Rock Creek just before the 2nd Battle of Cabin Creek and the Battle of Poison Spring, Arkansas. Gregory J. W. Urwin described the latter in "We Cannot Treat Negroes . . . as Prisoners of War," a chapter in *Civil War Arkansas: Beyond Battles and Leaders*, edited by Anne J. Bailey and Daniel E. Sutherland.[19]

Books about the Civil War in the Indian Territory frequently give little attention to events or peoples who lived west of the Cross Timbers. Yet the tribes clustered around Wichita Agency and the Plains tribes that considered the Indian Territory part of their range also had a stake in the war. Biographies about the two men who negotiated with the western Indians for the Confederacy were Walter Lee Brown's *A Life of Albert Pike* and Thomas W. Cutrer's *Ben McCulloch and the Frontier Military Tradition*. Two new biographies discuss a major player in the federal attempt to suppress raiding along the vital transportation routes across the Great Plains. They are David Remley's *Kit Carson: The Life of an American Border Man* from 2011 and Tom Dunlay's *Kit Carson and the Indians* from 2000. Both describe Carson's attack on the Comanche, Kiowa, and Plains Apache winter camps at the 1864 battle at Adobe Walls.[20]

The Cheyennes were at the center of conflict on the High Plains in the 1860s. Three new books that address this period in their history are Jerome A. Greene, *Washita: The U.S. Army and the Southern Cheyennes, 1867–1869* published in 2004; William Y. Chalfant, *Hancock's War: Conflict on the Southern Plains* published in 2010; and Brad D. Lookingbill, *War Dance at Fort Marion: Plains Indian War Prisoners* published in 2006.[21] These tribes, of course, were all eventually confined to Indian Territory reservations. Two new biographies also discuss this period in Cheyenne history. Thom Hatch's *Black Kettle: The Cheyenne Chief Who Sought Peace But Found War* recreates a central figure from the 1860s. David Fridtjof Halaas and Andrew E. Masich demonstrate how a Confederate soldier who fought at Wilson's Creek became a Cheyenne warrior in *Halfbreed: The Remarkable True Story of George Bent—Caught Between the Worlds of the Indian and the White Man*, published in 2004. A new book on one of the Cheyennes' perennial enemies that served as an Anglo-American ally on the Plains is Mark Van de

Logt's *War Party in Blue: Pawnee Scouts in the U.S. Army,* published in 2010.[22]

Three recent works address developments in the Indian Territory that stem from the Civil War. James W. Parins in 2006 described the ideological drift of Elias C. Boudinot away from the Cherokee Nation in part because of postwar changes in federal Indian policy in *Elias Cornelius Boudinot: A Life on the Cherokee Border.* In *The Real Wild West: The 101 Ranch and the Creation of the American West,* Michael Wallis discussed in 1999, among other things, how the Ponca Indians, removed to a postwar Indian Territory reservation, contributed to our image of the West through Wild West Show entertainment. Native songs, dances, and clothing the Miller Brothers used to entertain the non-Indian public actually had deep meaning for the Poncas. They passed the styles on to other Indian peoples along with their war dance tradition. Likewise, *A Dancing People: Powwow Culture on the Southern Plains,* published by Clyde Ellis in 2003, describes how Indian peoples used the powwow to resist federal attempts to erase their cultures in the Indian Territory. Instead, they maintained, recreated, and enhanced traditional ways to save what they could while producing today's powwow culture.[23] With the sesquicentennial of the Civil War in the Indian Territory underway, new research and publications from increasingly accessible resources should soon appear to add to our knowledge and understanding of this critical event.

NOTES

CHAPTER ONE

1. Israel Folsom to Peter P. Pitchlynn, March 19, 1860, Folder 64, Box 3, Peter P. Pitchlynn Collection, Western History Collections, University of Oklahoma, Norman, Oklahoma (hereafter cited as WHC).

2. Israel Folsom (1802–1870), minister, writer, and politician, was the son of a white father and a Choctaw mother. Daniel F. Littlefield and James W. Parins, *Native American Writing in the Southeast: An Anthology, 1875–1935* (Jackson: University Press of Mississippi, 1995), 3. The new Constitution of 1860 would replace the Skullyville Constitution of 1857, but there was strong opposition to it from Doaksville and Blue County. Paul Bonnifield, "The Choctaw Nation on the Eve of the Civil War," in *The Civil War Era in Indian Territory*, ed. LeRoy H. Fischer (Los Angeles: Lorrin L. Morrison, Publisher, 1974).

3. Interview of Alonzo Chalepah, by Loretta Fowler, Apache, Oklahoma, March 31, 2003, quoted in Mary Jane Warde, *Washita* (Oklahoma City: Oklahoma Historical Society and Washita Battlefield National Historic Site, National Park Service, 2003, 2005 edition), 39–40.

4. Interview of Charles Whitehorn, by B. D. Timmons, January 25, 1969, volume 48, T-463–1, Doris Duke Oral History Collection, University of Oklahoma, Norman, Oklahoma.

5. The Wichitas living in the Twin Villages on the Red River in today's Jefferson County, Oklahoma successfully fended off a very large Spanish-Indian punitive expedition armed with cannon in 1759. Elizabeth A. H. Johns, "Portrait of a Wichita Village, 1808," *Chronicles of Oklahoma* 60 (Winter 1982–83): 412–414.

6. Actually, Long was referring to the sparse population rather than the land type when he called it a "desert." He and the expedition botanist described western Oklahoma as rich in game, wild grapes, and native grasses with potential for grazing farm animals. James Smallwood, "Major Stephen Harriman Long, 1820," in *Frontier Adventurers: American Exploration in Oklahoma*, ed. Joseph A. Stout Jr. (Oklahoma City: Oklahoma Historical Society, 1976), 55–60.

7. Arrell Morgan Gibson, *The American Indian: Prehistory to the Present* (Norman: University of Oklahoma Press, 1980), 366; David La Vere, *Life Among the Texas Indians: The WPA Narratives* (College Station: Texas A & M University Press, 1998), 39–40.

8. A Creek "town" (*tvlwv*) in this sense was a group of people tied together by

descent, ceremonies, government, and history rather than the location where they actually lived.

9. Blue Clark, *Indian Tribes of Oklahoma: A Guide* (Norman: University of Oklahoma Press, 2009), 65, 95, 111, 212–213, 326; Arrell M. Gibson, *The Chickasaws* (Norman: University of Oklahoma Press, 1971), 4–5; Ronald N. Satz, *Tennessee's Indian Peoples: From White Contact to Removal, 1540–1840* (Knoxville: University of Tennessee Press and the Tennessee Historical Commission, 1979, paperback edition), 11, 34.

10. Charles Hudson, *The Southeastern Indians* (Knoxville: University of Tennessee Press, 1976), 434–441.

11. Andrew K. Frank, *Creeks & Southerners: Biculturalism on the Early American Frontier* (Lincoln: University of Nebraska Press, 2005), 5; Mary Jane Warde, *George Washington Grayson and the Creek Nation, 1843–1920* (Norman: University of Oklahoma Press, 1999), 9–10.

12. Warde, *George Washington Grayson*, 10–11; Grace Steele Woodward, *The Cherokees* (Norman: University of Oklahoma Press, 1963; Satz, *Tennessee's Indian Peoples*, 17; Robert J. Conley, *The Cherokee Nation: A History* (Albuquerque: University of New Mexico Press, 2005), 40–42, 54–55, 81–82.

13. Jane F. Lancaster, *Removal Aftershock: The Seminoles' Struggles to Survive in the West, 1836–1866* (Knoxville: University of Tennessee Press, 1994), 3–4.

14. David Wallace Adams, *Education for Extinction: American Indians and the Boarding School Experience, 1875–1928* (Lawrence: University Press of Kansas, 1995), 5–9; Margaret Connell Szasz, "Education," *Encyclopedia of North American Indians*, ed. Frederick E. Hoxie (Boston: Houghton Mifflin Company, 1996), 177–179.

15. Spanish Jesuits founded Catholic missions in coastal Florida, Georgia, South Carolina, and Virginia in 1566, but these early efforts failed. Franciscan missions in Florida and Georgia in the 1580s were more successful but did not last. Hudson, *The Southeastern Indians*, 433–434. Joseph Bullen, a Presbyterian, worked among the Chickasaws from 1799 to 1803 but never established a church or school or made converts. Gibson, *The Chickasaws*, 107–108.

16. Hudson, *The Southeastern Indians*, 448–449; Woodward, *The Cherokees*, 140; Satz, *Tennessee's Indian Peoples*, 73; Grant Foreman, *The Five Civilized Tribes: Cherokee, Chickasaw, Choctaw, Creek, Seminole* (Norman: University of Oklahoma Press, 1934), 35; Angie Debo, *The Road to Disappearance: A History of the Creek Indians* (Norman: University of Oklahoma Press, 1941), 84–85.

17. R. David Edmunds, *The Shawnee Prophet* (Lincoln: University of Nebraska Press, 1983), 118–119.

18. The attack on Fort Mims was the Red Sticks' response to a white militia attack on their supply train at Burnt Corn Creek, Alabama. "Fort Mims State Historic Site, Tensaw, Alabama," http://www.exploresouthernhistory.com/fortmimsl.html (accessed July 7, 2010); Satz, *Tennessee's Indian Peoples*, 53, 72–73; Angie Debo, *The Rise and Fall of the Choctaw Republic* (Norman: University of Oklahoma Press, 1934, second edition, 1961), 40–41; Gibson, *The Chickasaws*, 96–99.

19. Quoted in Gibson, *The Chickasaws*, 98–99.

20. Woodward, *The Cherokees*, 140; Satz, *Tennessee's Indian Peoples*, 76–78.

21. Satz, *Tennessee's Indian Peoples*, 21, 28–30.

22. Quoted in ibid., 30.

23. Arrell Morgan Gibson, *Oklahoma: A History of Five Centuries* (1965; rpt. Norman: University of Oklahoma Press, 1981), 71–72, 77; Woodward, *The Cherokees*, 145–146; Gibson, *The Chickasaws*, 206–207.

24. Satz, *Tennessee's Indian Peoples*, 80–81.

25. Louis W. Ballard, "Cultural Differences: A Major Theme in Cultural Enrichment," *Indian Historian* 2 (Spring 1969): 4–7.

26. *To Keep the Drum; To Tend the Fire* (1978; rpt. Oklahoma City: Mvskoke Publishing Company, 1996), 1–2, 15; Colin G. Calloway, *New Worlds for All: Indians, Europeans, and the Remaking of Early America* (Baltimore: Johns Hopkins University Press, 1997), 81.

27. Amy H. Sturgis, *The Trail of Tears and Indian Removal* (Westport, Conn.: Greenwood Press, 2007), xiv.

28. Gibson, *Oklahoma*, 43–51.

29. Ibid., 50; Debo, *The Road to Disappearance*, 87–89.

30. Quoted in Gibson, *Oklahoma*, 50.

31. Debo, *The Road to Disappearance*, 89–90.

32. Ibid., 91–99.

33. Interview of Mary Hill, 42:390, Indian-Pioneer History, Western History Collections, University of Oklahoma, Norman, Oklahoma (hereafter cited as IPH WHC).

34. Debo, *The Road to Disappearance*, 100–102.

35. Interview of Mary Hill, 42:390–391, IPH WHC.

36. Interview of Elsie Edwards, 27:189, IPH WHC. The vessel may have been the *Monmouth*, a steamboat which sank in the Mississippi River, drowning some three hundred Muscogees. Debo, *The Road to Disappearance*, 102.

37. Interview of Mary Hill, 42:391–393, IPH WHC.

38. Debo, *The Road to Disappearance*, 108–109.

39. Elias Boudinot to Stand Watie, March 7, 1832, quoted in *Cherokee Cavaliers*, ed. Edward Everett Dale and Gaston Litton (1939; rpt. Norman: University of Oklahoma Press, 1995), 4–5.

40. Mary Hershberger, "Mobilizing Women, Anticipating Abolition: The Struggle Against Indian Removal in the 1830s," *Journal of American History* 86 (June 1999): 15–40; Gibson, *The Chickasaws*, 153.

41. Gibson, *Oklahoma*, 65–67.

42. John Ridge to Stand Watie, April 6, 1832, quoted in Dale and Litton, *Cherokee Cavaliers*, 9.

43. Ibid., xvi–xvii; Gibson, *Oklahoma*, 66–68. The Cherokees also received the Neutral Lands in southeastern Kansas and the Cherokee Outlet, which stretched across today's northern Oklahoma to the Panhandle. The former was a buffer against incursions from enemies to the north, and the latter was a clear path to prime grazing lands for bison and other prairie animals.

44. Quoted in Woodward, *The Cherokees*, 215.

45. Ibid., 218; Hudson, *The Southeastern Indians*, 464.

46. Gibson, *Oklahoma*, 80–83; Woodward, *The Cherokees*, 223–231, 236–237; Dale and Litton, *Cherokee Cavaliers*, xiii; Sturgis, *The Trail of Tears*, 49–51; interview of Blackbird Doublehead, 22:368–369, Indian-Pioneer History, Oklahoma Historical Society (hereafter cited as IPH and OHS).

47. Debo, *The Choctaw Republic*, 50–53; Gibson, *The Chickasaws*, 154–155.

48. Debo, *The Choctaw Republic*, 52.

49. Quoted in ibid., 55.

50. James Culberson, "Two Thousand Choctaws Died During Their Removal," *American Indian* 3, no. 3 (December 1928): 11.

51. Interview of Josephine Usray Lattimer, 52:373–374 IPH WHC.

52. Culberson, "Two Thousand Choctaws Died During Their Removal," 10.

53. Quoted in Debo, *The Choctaw Republic*, 56.

54. Gibson, *The Chickasaws*, 154–155.

55. Gibson, *Oklahoma*, 62.

56. Gibson, *The Chickasaws*, 171.

57. Ibid., 168–183.

58. John L. Elder, *Everlasting Fire: Cowakoci's Legacy in the Seminole Struggle Against Western Expansion* (Edmond, Okla.: Medicine Wheel Press, 2004), 71–72, 85–88, 91, 95; Edwin C. McReynolds, *The Seminoles* (Norman: University of Oklahoma Press, 1957), 286–288; Lancaster, *Removal Aftershock*, 15–124.

59. Mary F. McCormick, "John Chupco: A Family Story," unpublished manuscript, Friends of the Oklahoma Historical Society Archives Civil War Collection (hereafter cited as 2012.138 FOHSA CWC), OHS.

60. Lancaster, *Removal Aftershock*, 124.

61. Gibson, *The Chickasaws*, 218–222; Gibson, *Oklahoma*, 79–80; Lancaster, *Removal Aftershock*, 52, 124–127.

62. A. P. Chouteau to Commissioner of Indian Affairs C. A. Harris, June 28, 1838, M234, Letters Received, Office of Indian Affairs, microfilm, OHS; Gibson, *Oklahoma*, 55–57.

63. [1] Odie B. Faulk, Kenny A. Franks, and Paul F. Lambert, eds., *Early Military Forts and Posts in Oklahoma* (Oklahoma City: Oklahoma Historical Society, 1978), 3–4; David La Vere, *Contrary Neighbors: Southern Plains and Removed Indians in Indian Territory* (Norman: University of Oklahoma Press, 2000), 70–71, 95, 140, 165. Gibson, *Oklahoma*, 114.

64. Lancaster, *Removal Aftershock*, 103.

65. Interview of Siah Hicks, 42: 183–184, IPH WHC.

66. Interview of Josephine Usray Lattimer, 52: 374- 380, ibid.

67. Among the Indian traders were Jesse Chisholm, a Cherokee, and Charles McIntosh, a Muscogee. Gibson, *Oklahoma*, 113–114; Agent Philip H. Raiford to Superintendent John Drennen, September 15, 1851, *Annual Report of the Commissioner of Indian Affairs for the Year 1851* (Washington, D.C.: Government Printing Office, 1851), 122–125 (hereafter cited as *AR CIA* and year); Warde, *George Washington Grayson*, 28–29; Lancaster, *Removal Aftershock*, 124–127.

68. Bill Corbett, "The Texas Road and the Civil War," unpublished manuscript, 2012.138 FOHSA CWC OHS; Louis F. Burns, *A History of the Osage People* (Tuscaloosa: The University of Alabama Press, 2004), 55–56, originally published by the author in 1989.

69. Steven L. Warren, *Brilliant Victory: The Second Civil War Battle of Cabin Creek, Indian Territory, September 19, 1864* (Wyandotte, Okla.: Gregath Publishing Company, 2002), 8–9; Blue Clark, "North Fork Town," unpublished manuscript, 2012.138 FOHSA CWC OHS.

70. Blue Clark, "Edwards Trading Post," unpublished manuscript, 2012.138 FOHSA CWC OHS; Jon May, "Edwards's Post," *Encyclopedia of Oklahoma History and Culture*, http://digital.library.okstate.edu/encyclopedia/entries/E/ED008.html (accessed September 5, 2012).

71. Woodward, *The Cherokees*, 245–246.

72. Gibson, *Oklahoma*, 90–96; Warde, *George Washington Grayson*, 37–43.

73. Gibson, *Oklahoma*, 90–97; Woodward, *The Cherokees*, 242–243.

74. Duane Champagne, *Social Order and Political Change: Constitutional Governments among the Cherokee, the Choctaw, the Chickasaw, and the Creek* (Stanford, Calif.: Stanford University Press, 1992), 228–237.

75. Gibson, *Oklahoma*, 71–83; Warde, *George Washington Grayson*, 50; Foreman, *The Five Civilized Tribes*, 276–278; Lancaster, *Removal Aftershock*, 118–119, 125–127.

76. Gibson, *Oklahoma*, 100–101. Individual entries in Carolyn Thomas Foreman, *Oklahoma Imprints, 1835–1907: A History of Printing in Oklahoma Before Statehood* (Norman: University of Oklahoma, 1936).

77. Gary Zellar, *African Creeks: Estelvste and the Creek Nation* (Norman: University of Oklahoma Press, 2007), 24.

78. Interview of Mary Grayson, *Slave Narratives from the Federal Writers Project, 1936–1938, Oklahoma* (Bedford, Mass.: Applewood Books and the Library of Congress, n.d.), 115, 117. Transcriptions sometimes paraphrased the interviews; others approximate the dialect the interviewer heard during the interview.

79. T. Lindsay Baker and Julie P. Baker, *The WPA Oklahoma Slave Narratives* (Norman: University of Oklahoma Press, 1996), 79–80, 83.

80. *Slave Narratives from Oklahoma*, 34.

81. Baker and Baker, *The WPA Oklahoma Slave Narratives*, 257–260.

82. *Slave Narratives from Oklahoma*, 155–157.

83. Baker and Baker, *The WPA Oklahoma Slave Narratives*, 436–437.

84. Ibid., 437–438.

85. Ibid., 464–465.

86. Zellar, *African Creeks*, 26–31.

87. Judith L. Michener, "Uncle Wallace and Aunt Minerva Willis," unpublished manuscript, 2012.138 FOHSA CWC OHS. It is not known if the pair were husband and wife or brother and sister.

88. Baker and Baker, *The WPA Oklahoma Slave Narratives*, 325.

89. Ibid., 356.

90. Ibid., 83.

91. Ibid.

92. *Slave Narratives from Oklahoma*, 9.

93. Zellar, *African Creeks*, 32–40.

94. William C. McLoughlin, *After the Trail of Tears: The Cherokee's Struggle for Sovereignty, 1839–1880* (Chapel Hill: University of North Carolina Press, 1993), 125–136.

95. Ibid., 125–136, 136–137, 147–148.

96. James Anderson Slover, *Minister to the Cherokees: A Civil War Autobiography*, ed. Barbara Cloud (Lincoln: University of Nebraska Press, 2001), 50.

97. Theda Perdue, *Slavery and the Evolution of Cherokee Society, 1540–1866* (Knoxville: University of Tennessee Press, 1972), 123–124.

98. McLoughlin, *After the Trail of Tears*, 156.

99. James A. Parins, *Elias Cornelius Boudinot: A Life on the Cherokee Border* (Lincoln: University of Nebraska Press, 2006), 43.

100. McLoughlin, *After the Trail of Tears*, 154–155, 158.

101. Ibid., 158; Conley, *The Cherokee Nation: A History*, 174.

102. Velma Nieberding, "Indian Home, 90, Still Stands in Craig Co.," *Tulsa (Oklahoma) World*, Sunday supplement, July 8, 1956, p. 36; Woodward, *The Cherokees*, 260; George Lisle to Hon. Nelson Case, August 1, 1892, in Nelson Case, ed., *History of Labette County, Kansas and Its Representative Citizens* (Chicago: Biographical Publishing Co., 1901), http://skyways.lib.ks.us/genweb/archives/labette/1901/20–26.shtml (accessed January 16, 2013); McLoughlin, *After the Trail of Tears*, 163–164; Morris L. Wardell, *A Political History of the Cherokee Nation* (Norman: University of Oklahoma Press, 1938), 91.

103. McLoughlin, *After the Trail of Tears*, 147–148.

104. Southern Superintendent of Indian Affairs Elias Rector to Commissioner of Indian Affairs Charles E. Mix, October 26, 1858, *AR CIA 1858* (Washington, D.C.: Government Printing Office, 1858), 127.

105. A. B. Greenwood to Elias Rector, November 17, 1859, Samuel Checote's Book of Records, Creek Nation Records (hereafter cited as CNR and reel number), microfilm, OHS, 9.

106. Motey Carnard (Kennard) and Echo Harjo to Creek Agent William H. Garrett, January 19, 1860, CNR 9.

107. McLoughlin, *After the Trail of Tears*, 164–165.

108. William Seward, quoted in Annie Heloise Abel, *The American Indian as Slaveholder and Secessionist: An Omitted Chapter in the Diplomatic History of the Southern Confederacy* (Cleveland, Ohio: Arthur H. Clark Company, 1915; rpt., Lincoln: University of Nebraska Press, 1992), 58–59.

109. Lawrence M. Hauptman, *Between Two Fires: American Indians in the Civil War* (New York: Free Press, 1995), 11.

110. The Choctaw Treaty of Dancing Rabbit Creek, 1830, *Indian Affairs: Laws and Treaties,* Sept. 27, 1830, 7 Stat., 333, comp. Charles J. Kappler (Washington, D.C.: Government Printing Office, 1904).

111. Israel Folsom to Peter P. Pitchlynn, March 19, 1860, Folder 64, Box 3, Peter P. Pitchlynn Collection, WHC.

CHAPTER TWO

1. Trevor M. Jones, "Thomas Pegg," *Encyclopedia of Oklahoma History and Culture*, http://digital.library.okstate.edu/encyclopedia/entries/P/PE008.html (accessed November 16, 2010).

2. Thomas Pegg, "Laws Passed by the National Council at Various Periods Commencing at the Council Held in Cowskin Prairie in February 1863," p. 1, frame 101, roll 8, Cherokee National Records, Oklahoma Historical Society, Oklahoma City, Oklahoma (hereafter cited as OHS).

3. Arrell Morgan Gibson, *Oklahoma: A History of Five Centuries* (1961; rpt., Norman: University of Oklahoma Press, 1981), 117–118; Arrell M. Gibson, *The Chickasaws* (Norman: University of Oklahoma Press, 1971), 228–229.

4. James Roane Gregory, "Some Early History of the Creek Nation," *Wagoner (Creek Nation) Record*, January 24, 1901.

5. Ibid.; Gibson, *Oklahoma*, 143; William G. McLoughlin, *After the Trail of Tears: The Cherokees' Struggle for Sovereignty, 1839–1880* (Chapel Hill: University of North Carolina Press, 1993), 167. Even though the Euchees (Yuchis) were not a Muskogean people, they were members the confederacy of tribal towns.

6. Angie Debo, *The Road to Disappearance: A History of the Creek Indians* (Norman: University of Oklahoma Press, 1941), 142; Daniel F. Littlefield Jr., *Africans and Seminoles: From Removal to Emancipation* (Jackson: University Press of Mississippi, 2001), 180–182; Jane F. Lancaster, *Removal Aftershock: The Seminoles Struggles to Survive in the West, 1836–1866* (Knoxville: University of Tennessee Press, 1994), 122; William D. Welge, "Douglas H. Cooper," unpublished manuscript, 2012.136, Friends of the Oklahoma Historical Society Archives, Civil War Collection (hereafter cited as FOHSA CWC), OHS.

7. Gibson, *Oklahoma*, 92, 119; Alice Hurley Mackey, "Father Murrow: Civil War Period," *Chronicles of Oklahoma* 12, no. 1 (March 1934): 58 (55–65); Kevin Mulroy, *The Seminole Freedmen: A History* (Norman: University of Oklahoma Press, 2007), 159–160.

8. Gibson, *Oklahoma*, 109, 117.

9. Gibson, *The Chickasaws*, 229.

10. Ibid.

11. Debo, *The Road to Disappearance*, 142–143; "The Record Book of Chief Samuel Checote in the Early Sixties," 32467.a, Indian Archives, OHS; Paul Bonnifield, "The Choctaw Nation on the Eve of the Civil War" in *The Civil War Era in the Indian Territory*, ed. LeRoy H. Fischer (Los Angeles: Lorrin L. Morrison, Publisher, 1974), 63.

12. Al Turner, "Texas and the Civil War," unpublished manuscript, 2012.138 FOHSA CWC OHS.

13. W. David Baird, *Peter Pitchlynn: Chief of the Choctaws* (Norman: University of Oklahoma Press, 1972), 126–127; Angie Debo, *The Rise and Fall of the Choctaw Republic* (1931; rpt., Norman: University of Oklahoma Press, 1961), 60.

14. "Proclamation by the Principal Chief of the Choctaw Nation," June 14, 1861, *The War of the Rebellion: A Compilation of the Official Records of the Union and Confederate Armies. Published under the Direction of the Secretary of War* (hereafter cited as *OR*), series 1, volume 3, part 1, 593.

15. Helen Hornbeck Tanner, "Caddo," *Encyclopedia of North American Indians: Native American History, Culture, and Life from Paleo-Indians to the Present*, ed. Frederick E. Hoxie (Boston: Houghton Mifflin Company, 1996), 91–92; Blue Clark, "Wichita," in *Indian Tribes of Oklahoma: A Guide* (Norman: University of Oklahoma Press, 2009), 377–378; Thomas F. Schilz, "Placido," *Handbook of Texas Online*, http://www.tshaonline.org/handbook/online/articles/fpl01 (accessed November 19, 2010); Cecile Elkins Carter, *Caddo Indians: Where We Come From* (Norman: University of Oklahoma Press, 1995), 345–349.

16. J. Patrick Hughes, "Forts and Camps in Oklahoma before the Civil War,"

Early Military Forts and Posts in Oklahoma, ed. Odie B. Faulk, Kenny A. Franks, and Paul F. Lambert (Oklahoma City: Oklahoma Historical Society, 1978), 51–53.

17. The identity of "Rover" has never been determined. Louise Barry, ed., "With the First U.S. Cavalry in Indian Country, 1859–1861—Concluded, Letters to the Daily Times, Leavenworth, III, The Letters, May 3, 1860–April 28, 1861," *Kansas Historical Quarterly* 24, no. 3 (Autumn 1958): 417.

18. Ibid., 419.

19. Ibid., 420.

20. Ibid., 421.

21. *OR*, series 1, volume 1, part 1, 659–660.

22. Ibid.

23. "With the First Cavalry," 421.

24. Ibid., 422.

25. *OR*, series 1, volume 1, part 1, 665–666; "With the First Cavalry," 422; Muriel H. Wright, "Lieutenant Averell's Ride at the Outbreak of the Civil War," *Chronicles of Oklahoma* 39 (Spring 1961): 3–4.

26. "With the First Cavalry," 423.

27. Ibid., 423–424.

28. Wright, "Lieutenant Averell's Ride," 2, 4, 6–11. Muriel Wright placed their meeting near today's Minco, Oklahoma. Muriel Wright, "A History of Fort Cobb," *Chronicles of Oklahoma* 34, no. 1 (1956): 58, 59; Gibson, *The Chickasaws*, 230; Stephen B. Oates, *Confederate Cavalry West of the River* (Austin: University of Texas Press, 1961), 11; Lary C. Rampp and Donald L. Rampp, *The Civil War in the Indian Territory* (Austin, Tex.: Presidial Press, 1975), 4.

29. Quoted in "With the First Cavalry," 423–424.

30. Gibson, *Oklahoma*, 118.

31. Wright, "Fort Cobb," 59; H. S. Tennant, "Two Cattle Trails," *Chronicles of Oklahoma* 14, no. 1 (March 1936): 84–121.

32. Quoted in "With the First Cavalry, "424.

33. Ibid.

34. Ibid.

35. Ibid.

36. Quoted in Gibson, *The Chickasaws*, 231.

37. George Hudson, "Proclamation by the Principal Chief of the Choctaw Nation," June 14, 1861, *OR*, series 1, volume 3, part 1, 593–594.

38. Pitchlynn to the Commissioner of Indian Affairs, June 20, 1865, folder 26, box 4, Peter P. Ptichlynn Collection, Western History Collections, University of Oklahoma, Norman, Oklahoma (hereafter cited as WHC).

39. Georgianna Stidham Grayson, "Why the Five Civilized Tribes Joined the Confederacy," *Indian Journal* (Eufaula, Oklahoma), June 6, 1913. Mrs. Grayson presented this paper to the United Daughters of the Confederacy. Her husband, George Washington Grayson, was a former officer in the Confederate-allied 2nd Creek Mounted Volunteers and long active in his nation's government.

40. Edwin C. McReynolds, *The Seminoles* (Norman: University of Oklahoma Press, 1957), 291.

41. Grayson, "Why the Five Civilized Tribes Joined the Confederacy."

42. Ingrid P. Westmoreland, "Albert Pike," *Encyclopedia of Oklahoma History*

and Culture," http://digital.library.okstate.edu/encyclopedia/entries/P/PI006.html (accessed November 24, 2010).

43. Grayson, "Why the Five Civilized Tribes Joined the Confederacy."

44. Ibid.; McLoughlin, *After the Trail of Tears*, 172–173; Mary Jane Warde, *George Washington Grayson and the Creek Nation, 1843–1920* (Norman: University of Oklahoma Press, 1999), 56–57.

45. Quoted in Walter Lee Brown, *A Life of Albert Pike* (Fayetteville: University of Arkansas Press, 1997), 309–310. By 1857, Pike was well acquainted with the Stidham family from extended visits to the Muscogee Nation. George W. Stidham was also a brother Mason.

46. Thomas W. Cutrer, *Ben McCulloch and the Frontier Military Tradition* (Chapel Hill: University of North Carolina Press, 1993), 39–44.

47. Quoted in ibid., 203.

48. Gibson, *Oklahoma*, 120.

49. Grayson, "Why the Five Civilized Tribes Joined the Confederacy"; Warde, *George Washington Grayson*, 56–58; Gibson, *The Chickasaws*, 232; Brown, *Albert Pike*, 358.

50. Mulroy, *Seminole Freedmen*, 162.

51. Commissioner of Indian Affairs William P. Dole to Secretary of the Interior Caleb B. Smith, November 27, 1861, *Annual Reports of the Commissioner of Indian Affairs* (Washington, D.C.: Government Printing Office, 1864), 10 (hereafter cited as *AR CIA* and year).

52. McReynolds, *The Seminoles*, 292; Lancaster, *Removal Aftershock*, 130–137.

53. Mulroy, *Seminole Freedmen*, 165.

54. Quoted in McLoughlin, *After the Trail of Tears*, 171.

55. Ibid., 172–175.

56. Velma Nieberding, "Indian Home, 90, Still Stands in Craig Co.," *Tulsa (Oklahoma) World*, Sunday supplement, July 8, 1956, p. 36; Gary L. Cheatham, "'If the Union Wins, We Won't Have Anything Left': The Rise and Fall of the Southern Cherokees in Kansas," *Kansas History* 30 (Autumn 2007): 162, 168–170.

57. Interview of Blackbird Doublehead, 22:374–375, Indian Pioneer History (hereafter cited as IPH) WHC.

58. Quoted in McLoughlin, *After the Trail of Tears*, 173.

59. McReynolds, *The Seminoles*, 291.

60. Gibson, *Oklahoma*, 120; Edward Everett Dale and Gaston Litton, *Cherokee Cavaliers: Forty Years of Cherokee History as Told in the Correspondence of the Ridge-Watie-Boudinot Family* (1939; rpt., Norman: University of Oklahoma Press, 1995), 98–99.

61. Wilson's Creek National Battlefield, "A Brief Account of the Battle of Wilson's Creek," http://www.nps.gov/wicr/historyculture/collections.htm (accessed December 7, 2010); William Garrett Piston and Richard W. Hatcher III, *Wilson's Creek: The Second Battle of the Civil War and the Men Who Fought It* (Chapel Hill: University of North Carolina Press, 2000), 160.

62. Bob Rea, "George Bent in the Civil War: Cheyenne Confederate Warrior," unpublished manuscript, 2012.136 FOHSA CWC OHS; David Fridtjof Halaas and Andrew E. Masich, *Halfbreed: The Remarkable True Story of George Bent—Caught Between the Worlds of the Indian and the White Man* (Cambridge, Mass.: DeCapo

Press, 2004), 83–84; James A. Parins, *Elias Cornelius Boudinot: A Life on the Cherokee Border* (Lincoln: University of Nebraska Press, 2006), 45.

63. McLoughlin, *After the Trail of Tears*, 179–182.

64. Robert J. Conley, *The Cherokee Nation: A History* (Albuquerque: University of New Mexico Press, 2005), 174.

65. McLoughlin, *After the Trail of Tears*, 182–185.

66. Dale and Litton, *Cherokee Cavaliers*, 108.

67. Jon D. May, "Tandy Walker," *Encyclopedia of Oklahoma History and Culture* http://digital.library.okstate.edu/encyclopedia/entries/W/WA009.html (accessed December 8, 2010); Jon D. May, "Daniel Newman McIntosh," ibid., http://digital.library.okstate.edu/encyclopedia/entries/m/mc030.html (accessed December 8, 2010); Lancaster, *Removal Aftershock*, 108.

68. McLoughlin, *After the Trail of Tears*, 175, 186; Gibson, *Oklahoma*, 120.

69. Welge, "Douglas H. Cooper"; Ingrid P. Westmoreland, "Albert Pike," *Encyclopedia of Oklahoma History and Culture* http://digital.library.okstate.edu/encyclopedia/entries/P/PI006.html (accessed December 9, 2010).

70. Oates, *Confederate Cavalry*, 86–87; John C. Waugh, *Sam Bell Maxey and the Confederate Indians* (Fort Worth: Ryan Place Publishers, 1995), 37; Holmes Willis Lemon, "Chickasaw Horse," *Official Site of the Chickasaw Nation*, http://www/chickasaw.net/history_culture/inter_681.htm (accessed October 2, 2012).

71. John Joseph Mathews, *The Osages: Children of the Middle Waters* (Norman: University of Oklahoma Press, 1961), 632.

72. H. F. Buckner to "Brother Robert," January 4, 1861, 96.47.03, H. F. Buckner Collection, OHS.

73. Mary Jane Warde, "'Now the Wolf Has Come': The Civilian Civil War in the Indian Territory," *Chronicles of Oklahoma* 71, no. 1 (Spring 1993): 68.

74. Interview of Morris Sheppard, 1–5, folder 8, box 27, 81.105, Federal Writers Project Ex-Slave Narratives (hereafter cited as FWP EN), OHS.

75. Interview of Richard Adkins, 1:280–281, IPH OHS.

76. Interview of Rowland S. Bailey, 4:86–87, IPH WHC.

77. Alice Robertson, "Incidents of the Civil War," Box 1, 82.86, Alice Robertson Papers, OHS. Tullahassee Mission was just northwest of today's Muskogee, Oklahoma. Robertson (1854–1931) represented Oklahoma in the U.S. House of Representatives, the second woman to serve in Congress.

78. Ibid.

79. Interview of Joe M. Grayson, 35:414, IPH WHC; Mary Jane Warde, *George Washington and the Creek Nation, 1843–1920* (Norman: University of Oklahoma Press, 1999), 58–59.

80. Quoted in Angie Debo, *The Road to Disappearance: A History of the Creek Indians* (Norman: University of Oklahoma Press, 1941), 146.

81. McReynolds, *The Seminoles*, 292–293; Debo, *The Road to Disappearance*, 14.

82. Annie Heloise Abel, *The American Indian as Slaveholder and Secessionist: An Omitted Chapter in the Diplomatic History of the Southern Confederacy* (Cleveland: Arthur H. Clark Company, 1915), 245–246.

83. Ibid.

84. Ibid., 244–245; Angie Debo, *The Road to Disappearance*, 146–148; Abel, *The American Indian as Slaveholder and Secessionist*, 244–245; Lela J. McBride,

Opothleyaholo and the Loyal Muskogee: Their Flight to Kansas in the Civil War (Jefferson, N.C.: McFarland and Company, 2000), 150.

85. McReynolds, *The Seminoles*, 292–293; Orpha Russell, "Ekvn-hv'lwuce: Site of Oklahoma's First Civil War Battle," *Chronicles of Oklahoma* 29, no. 4 (1951): 404–405; Debo, *The Road to Disappearance*, 149.

86. Debo, *The Road to Disappearance*, 149; McReynolds, *The Seminoles*, 293; Gary Zellar, *African Creeks: Estelvste and the Creek Nation* (Norman: University of Oklahoma Press, 2007), 45.

87. W. David Baird, *The Quapaws* (New York: Chelsea House Publishers, 1989), 60–65.

88. Louis F. Burns, *A History of the Osage People* (Tuscaloosa: The University of Alabama Press, 2004), 234–235, 243, 260–261.

89. Ibid., 261–263; interview of Louis F. Burns, by Sammie Dennison Harmon and Mary Jane Warde, Pawhuska, Oklahoma, March 1, 2011.

90. McLoughlin, *After the Trail of Tears*, 187–193.

91. Interview of Jim Tomm, 91:323–324, 327, IPH WHC.

92. Interview of Phoebe Banks, 1–3, folder 2, box 25, 81.105, FWP EN OHS.

93. D. N. McIntosh to Col. John Drew, September 11, 1861, volume 97, box 43, Grant Foreman Collection, Gilcrease Institute of American History and Art, Tulsa, Oklahoma (hereafter cited as GFC GI).

94. Various letters, "Creek Civil War," box 6, 83.229, Grant Foreman Collection (hereafter cited as GFC), OHS.

95. John Ross to John Drew, October 20, 1861, ibid.

96. D. H. Cooper to Lt. Col. W. P. Ross, November 10, 1861, ibid.

97. Warde, *George Washington Grayson*, 60.

98. They may have been aiming toward the ruins of old Fort Arbuckle. Zellar, *African Creeks*, 50–51.

99. Interview of Malucy Bear, 14: 82–85, IPH OHS.

100. Interview of James Scott, 81:78–79, IPH WHC.

101. T. Lindsay Baker and Julie D. Baker, *The WPA Oklahoma Slave Narratives* (Norman: University of Oklahoma Press, 1996), 31.

102. D. H. Cooper to J. P. Benjamin, Secretary of War, Confederate States of America, January 20, 1862, Section X, 84.19, OHS.

103. Quoted in McLoughlin, *After the Trail of Tears*, 193.

104. *Fighting With Ross' Texas Cavalry Brigade, C.S.A.: The Diary of George L. Griscom, Adjutant, 9th Texas Cavalry Regiment*, ed. Homer L. Kerr (Hillsboro, Tex.: Hill Jr. College Press, 1976), 3–4.

105. Ibid., 4–5.

106. McReynolds, *The Seminoles*, 293; Abel, *The American Indian as Slaveholder and Secessionist*, 254.

107. Abel, *The American Indian as Slaveholder and Secessionist*, 25–41; D. H. Cooper to J. P. Benjamin, January 20, 1862, Section X, 84.19, OHS; *Diary of George L. Griscom*, 5.

108. A thorough impartial study of the route of the refugee Indians is given in Mary Elizabeth Good, *Historical Review: Bird Creek Basin from 1800* (n.p.: Corps of Engineers, Tulsa District, 1979).

109. Patricia Loughlin, "The Battle of Historians of Round Mountain,"

unpublished manuscript, 2012.138 FOHSA CWC OHS; Patricia Loughlin, *Hidden Treasures of the American West: Muriel H. Wright, Angie Debo, and Alice Marriott* (Albuquerque: University of New Mexico Press, 2005), 52–54.

110. John Bartlett Meserve, "Chief Opothleyahola," *Chronicles of Oklahoma* 9, no. 4 (December 1931): 445–446.

111. Interview of James Scott, 81: 79–80, IPH WHC.

112. "Creeks in the Civil War," *Galveston (Texas) News*, November 27, 1901, "Creek Civil War" file, box 6, GFC OHS.

113. McBride, *Opothleyaholo and the Loyal Muskogee*, 165.

114. Statement of William P. Adair, Richard Fields, J. A. Scales, Daniel N. McIntosh, James M. C. Smith, and Tim Barnett, notarized March 19, 1868, Section X, 84.19, OHS. Signs of a refugee camp were found near Appalachia close to the mouth of the Cimarron River. The settlement is recalled today in the name of Appalachia Bay Recreation Area on Keystone Lake. Good, *Bird Creek*, 15.

115. D. H. Cooper to J. P. Benjamin, January 20, 1862, Section X, 84.19, OHS.

116. McBride, *Opothleyaholo*, 165; Abel, *The American Indian as Slaveholder and Secessionist*, 256. A small group of Chickasaws had chosen to follow Opothle Yahola in spite of their nation's new treaty with the Confederacy.

117. *Diary of George L. Griscom*, 5.

118. Ibid.

119. Ibid.

120. Statement of William P. Adair et al., March 19, 1868; *Diary of George L. Griscom*, 6.

121. *Diary of George L. Griscom*, 6.

122. "Creeks in the Civil War," *Galveston (Texas) News*, November 27, 1901, "Creek Civil War" file, box 6, GFC OHS.

123. D. H. Cooper to J. P. Benjamin, January 20, 1862, Section X, 84.19, OHS.

124. Good, *Bird Creek*, 15; Leroy H. Fischer and Kenny A. Franks, "Confederate Victory at Chusto-Talasah," *Chronicles of Oklahoma* 49 (Winter 1971–1972): 460.

125. Fischer and Franks, "Confederate Victory at Chusto-Talasah," 464–465. Usually spelled "Chustenalah," an account written in 1868 by Indian veterans of the fight spelled it with an initial letter A.

126. Interview of Joseph Bruner, 89: 265–267, IPH OHS.

127. Fischer and Franks, "Victory at Chusto-Talasah," 460–462; Statement of William P. Adair et al., March 19, 1868.

128. Statement of William P. Adair et al., March 19, 1868.

129. McReynolds, *The Seminoles*, 299.

130. Statement of William P. Adair et al., March 19, 1868.

131. Fischer and Franks, "Victory at Chusto-Talasah," 462–463.

132. Report of Col. D. N. McIntosh, December 16, 1861, *OR*, series 1, volume 8, part 1, 16.

133. Ibid.

134. Report of Capt. William B. Pitchlynn, January 18, 1862, ibid., 21.

135. Report of Col. William B. Sims, December 15, 1861, ibid., 18.

136. *Diary of George L. Griscom*, 8.

137. McReynolds, *The Seminoles*, 299.

138. Report of Col. D. N. McIntosh, December 16, 1861, *OR*, series 1, volume 8, part 1, 16.

139. Third interview of Joseph Bruner, 89: 265–267, IPH OHS.

140. Good, *Bird Creek*, 19.

141. Cooper to Confederate Secretary of War Judah P. Benjamin, January 20, 1862, January 20, 1862, Section X, 84.19, OHS.

142. "Creeks in the Civil War," *Galveston (Texas) News*, November 27, 1901, "Creek Civil War," box 6, GFC OHS; Fischer and Franks, "Victory at Chusto-Talasah," 471–472.

143. McLoughlin, *After the Trail of Tears*, 194.

144. *Diary of George L. Griscom*, 9.

145. Ibid.

146. Abel, *The American Indian as Slaveholder and Secessionist*, 256; McLoughlin, *After the Trail of Tears*, 194–195; Statement of William P. Adair et al., March 19, 1868.

147. Report of Col. James McIntosh, January 1, 1862, *OR*, series 1, volume 8, part 1, 22.

148. Ibid.

149. Douglas Hale, *The Third Texas Cavalry in the Civil War* (Norman: University of Oklahoma Press, 1993), 80.

150. Victor M. Rose, *Ross' Texas Brigade, Being a Narrative of Events Connected with Its Service in the Late War Between the States* (Louisville, Ky: Courier Journal Company, 1881), 43.

151. Report of Maj. Elias C. Boudinot, December 28, 1861, *OR*, series 1, volume 8, part 1, 22.

152. Hale, *The Third Texas Cavalry*, 80–81; Rose, *Ross' Texas Brigade*, 43; Report of Col. James McIntosh, January 1, 1862, *OR*, series 1, volume 8, part 1, 22.

153. Quoted in McBride, *Opothleyaholo*, 169, from the *Leavenworth (Kansas) Daily Conservative*, January 28, 1862.

154. William L. Shea and Earl J. Hess, *Pea Ridge: Civil War Campaign in the West* (Chapel Hill: University of North Carolina Press, 1992), 70.

155. Report of Col. James McIntosh, January 1, 1862, *OR* series 1, volume 8, part 1, 22.

156. Hale, *The Third Texas Cavalry*, 81.

157. James H. Kearly, *Reminiscences of the Boys in Gray, 1861–1865*, comp. Mamie Yeary (Dallas: Smith & Lamar, 1912), 395–396.

158. Report of Col. James McIntosh, January 1, 1862, *OR*, series 1, volume 8, part 1, 22.

159. Quoted in Hale, *The Third Texas Cavalry*, 82.

160. Report of Col. James McIntosh, January 1, 1862, *OR*, series 1, volume 8, part 1, 22.

161. "Creeks in the Civil War," *Galveston (Texas) News*, November 27, 1901, "Creek Civil War" file, box 6, GFC OHS.

162. Report of Lt. Col. Walter P. Lane, Third Texas (South Kansas-Texas) Cavalry, December 26, 1861, *OR*, series 1, volume 8, part 1, 29.

163. Quoted in Hale, *The Third Texas Cavalry*, 82.

164. Report of Col. James McIntosh, January 4, 1862, *OR*, series 1, volume 8, part 1, 28–29.

165. Third interview of Joseph Bruner, 89:265–267, IPH OHS.

166. Ibid.

167. Quoted in Mulroy, *The Seminole Freedmen*, 169.

168. Interview of Phoebe Banks, 3, folder 2, box 25, FWP EN.

169. Report of Col. James McIntosh, January 4, 1862, *OR*, series 1, volume 8, part 1, 32; report of Col. Stand Watie, December 28, 1861, ibid.

170. Interview of Phoebe Banks, 4, folder 2, box 25, FWP EN 4.

171. Interview of James Scott, 81:81 IPH WHC.

172. James H. Kearly, *Reminiscences of the Boys in Gray*, 396.

173. Burns, *A History of the Osage People*, 78; McBride, *Opothleyaholo and the Loyal Muskogee*, 172–173.

174. Interview of James Scott, 81:81 IPH WHC.

175. Fischer and Franks, "Victory at Chusto-Talasah," 474.

176. P. G. Beauchamp, *Reminiscences of the Boys in Gray*, 47–48.

177. Statement of William P. Adair et al., March 19, 1868.

178. E. H. Carruth to Tasaquach, September 11, 1861, *OR*, series 1, volume 8, part 1, 26.

179. Cooper to Benjamin, January 20, 1862, Section X, 84.19, OHS.

180. Central Superintendent W. G. Coffin to Commissioner of Indian Affairs William P. Dole, September 24, 1863, Report Number 81½, *AR CIA 1863*, 176.

CHAPTER THREE

1. "Murrow, Joseph Samuel (1835–1929)," *Encyclopedia of Oklahoma History and Culture*, http://digital.library.okstate.edu/encylcopedia/entries/M/MU016.html (accessed January 5, 2011).

2. Joseph S. Murrow to "Bro Jones," January 14, 1862, volume 97, box 34, Grant Foreman Collection, Gilcrease Institute of American History and Art, Tulsa, Oklahoma (hereafter cited as GFC GI).

3. Joseph S. Murrow to Brother Hornady, January 11, 1862, ibid.

4. Ibid.

5. "Foreman, Stephen (1807–1881)," *Encyclopedia of Oklahoma History and Culture*, http://digital.library.okstate.edu/encylcopedia/entries/f/fo021.html (accessed January 7, 2011).

6. Entry of January 3, 1862, F-21, Stephen Foreman Diary, Western History Collections, University of Oklahoma, Norman, Oklahoma (hereafter cited as SFD WHC).

7. William G. McLoughlin, *After the Trail of Tears: The Cherokees' Struggle for Sovereignty, 1839–1880* (Chapel Hill: University of North Carolina Press, 1993), 195–196.

8. Quoted in ibid., 196.

9. *Annual Report of the Commissioner of Indian Affairs for the Year 1862* (Washington, D.C.: Government Printing Office, 1862, hereafter cited as *AR CIA* and year), 139.

10. Annie Heloise Abel, *The American Indian in the Civil War, 1862–1865* (Lincoln: University of Nebraska Press, 1992, Bison Book Edition), 80–81, 84–85.

11. Surgeon A. B. Campbell to Maj. Charles G. Halpine, Fort Leavenworth, Kansas, February 5, 1862, *AR CIA 1862*, 151–152.

12. Ibid.

13. Ibid., 151.

14. Ibid., 151–152.

15. Ibid., 139, 152; Indian Affairs Commissioner William P. Dole, ibid., 25–29.

16. Surgeon A. B. Campbell, ibid., 152.

17. *AR CIA 1861*, 10.

18. *AR CIA 1862*, 139.

19. Ibid.

20. Abel, *The Indian in the Civil War*, 19–21; Grant Foreman, "Fort Davis," *Chronicles of Oklahoma* 17, no. 2 (June 1939): 147–148; Walter Lee Brown, *A Life of Albert Pike* (Fayetteville: University of Arkansas Press, 1997), 384.

21. Abel, *The Indian in the Civil War*, 25–27, 29–30; William L. Shea and Earl J. Hess, *Pea Ridge: Civil War Campaign in the West* (Chapel Hill: University of North Carolina Press, 1992), 25–27.

22. Joseph S. Murrow to the *Banner*, March 22, 1862, box 34, volume 97, GFC GI.

23. Abel, *The Indian in the Civil War*, 27–29; Shea and Hess, *Pea Ridge*, 68–78.

24. Shea and Hess, *Pea Ridge*, 60–63, 79.

25. Ibid., 85–86.

26. Ibid., *Pea Ridge*, 82.

27. Thomas W. Cutrer, *Ben McCulloch and the Frontier Military Tradition* (Chapel Hill: University of North Carolina Press, 1993), 286.

28. Shea and Hess, *Pea Ridge*, 97–101.

29. Report of Albert Pike, March 14, 1862, *The War of the Rebellion: A Compilation of the Official Records of the Union and Confederate Armies. Published under the Direction of the Secretary of War* (Washington, D.C.: Government Printing Office, 1880–1901 (hereafter cited as *OR*), series 1, volume 8, part 1, 288.

30. Ibid., 288–289.

31. Joseph S. Murrow to the "Indian Column," *Baptist Banner*, March 22, 1862, box 34, volume 7, GFC GI. It should be noted Murrow was off on his dates of the battle by a week.

32. Shea and Hess, *Pea Ridge*, 107.

33. Ibid., 143.

34. Ibid.; Roy A. Clifford, "The Indian Regiments in the Battle of Pea Ridge," *Chronicles of Oklahoma* 25 (Winter 1947–1948): 317; Abel, *The Indian in the Civil War*, 31.

35. Shea and Hess, *Pea Ridge*, 224.

36. Clifford, "The Indian Regiments in the Battle of Pea Ridge," 318–320; McLoughlin, *After the Trail of Tears*, 197.

37. Murrow to the *Banner*, March 22, 1862, box 34, volume 7, GFC GI. Fort Donelson, Tennessee; Bowling Green, Kentucky; Columbus, Kentucky; and Nashville, Tennessee, were all important points for Confederate control of the vital Mississippi-Ohio-Tennessee river system. They all fell to Union control in February 1862, shortly before the Battle of Pea Ridge.

38. Ibid.

39. Quoted in McLoughlin, *After the Trail of Tears*, 197.

40. Wiley Britton, *The Union Indian Brigade in the Civil War* (Kansas City, Mo.: Frank Hudson Publishing Company, 1922), 58–59.

41. Daniel E. Sutherland, "Guerrillas: The Real War in Arkansas," in *Civil War Arkansas: Beyond Battles and Leaders*, ed. Anne J. Bailey and Daniel E. Sutherland (Fayetteville: University of Arkansas Press, 2000), 136–139.

42. *OR*, series 1, volume 8, part 1, 194.

43. Ibid., 195.

44. Ibid., 206; Shea and Hess, *Pea Ridge*, 102.

45. Robert J. Conley, *The Cherokee Nation: A History* (Albuquerque: University of New Mexico Press, 2005), 175.

46. McLoughlin, *After the Trail of Tears*, 201–203; Walter Lee Brown, *A Life of Albert Pike* (Fayetteville: University of Arkansas Press, 1997), 395–399.

47. Quoted in Shea and Hess, *Pea Ridge*, 320.

48. Quoted in Anne J. Bailey, *Invisible Southerners: Ethnicity in the Civil War* (Athens: University of Georgia Press, 2006), 38.

49. Abel, *The Indian in the Civil War*, 99–118; Britton, *The Union Indian Brigade*, 61; Kevin Mulroy, *The Seminole Freedmen: A History* (Norman: University of Oklahoma Press, 2007), 172–173; Gary Zellar, *African Creeks: Estelvste and the Creek Nation* (Norman: University of Oklahoma Press, 2007), 40.

50. Britton, *The Union Indian Brigade*, 60–61.

51. Quoted in Abel, *The Indian in the Civil War*, 36.

52. Britton, *The Union Indian Brigade*, 60.

53. Report of Lt. James K. Mills, June 14, 1862, *OR*, series 1, volume 13, part 1, 92–94.

54. Report of Col. Stand Watie, June 1, ibid., 94–95. The Elk flows into the Grand (Neosho) River from the east near today's Grove, Oklahoma.

55. Britton, *The Indian Brigade*, 62–64.

56. Ibid., 64–65; Abel, *The Indian in the Civil War*, 119–120; Muriel H. Wright and LeRoy H. Fischer, "Civil War Sites in Oklahoma," *Chronicles of Oklahoma* 44 (Summer 1966): 175.

57. Abel, *The Indian in the Civil War*, 120.

58. Weer to Capt. Thomas Moonlight, June 13, 1862, *OR*, series 1, volume 13, part 1, 430.

59. Ibid., 431.

60. Quoted in Abel, *The Indian in the Civil War*, 123.

61. Ibid., 126–127.

62. Ibid., 130–132; Wright and Fischer, "Civil War Sites," 187, 189.

63. Col. William Weer to Capt. Thomas Moonlight, July 4, 1864, *OR*, series 1, volume 13, part 1, 137; Weer to Moonlight, July 6, 1864, ibid., 138; McLoughlin. *After the Trail of Tears*, 204; Britton, *The Union Indian Brigade*, 66.

64. *AR CIA 1862*, 162, quoted in Abel, *The Indian in the Civil War*, 133n.

65. Zellar, *African Creeks*, 56–57.

66. Entry of June 27, 1862, SFD WHC; McLoughlin, *After the Trail of Tears*, 204–205; Gary E. Moulton, *John Ross, Cherokee Chief* (Athens: University of Georgia Press, 1978), 177.

67. Report of Maj. William T. Campbell, July 14, 1862, *OR*, series 1, volume 13, part 1, 161.

68. Britton, *The Union Indian Brigade*, 67–74; McLoughlin, *After the Trail of Tears*, 206.

69. Interview of Mary E. Hudson James, 31:41–46, Indian Pioneer History, Oklahoma Historical Society (hereafter cited as IPH OHS).

70. Ibid.

71. Interview of Moses Lonian, 61: 386, IPH OHS. The Texas Road was also called the Military Road or Trail.

72. Ibid.

73. Britton, *The Union Indian Brigade*, 66, 75, 83; Abel, *The Indian in the Civil War*, 138–140.

74. Britton, *The Union Indian Brigade*, 82–83.

75. Muriel H. Wright, "Notes on the Life of Mrs. Hannah Worcester Hicks Hitchcock and the Park Hill Press," *Chronicles of Oklahoma* 19, no. 4 (December 1941): 349–350.

76. Ibid.

77. Ibid., 351.

78. Entry of July 6, 1862, SFD WHC.

79. Ibid., July 16, 17, 18, 29, 1862.

80. Ibid., July 29, 1862.

81. Wright, "Notes on Mrs. Hannah Worcester Hicks Hitchcock," 351.

82. Ibid.

83. Samuel Austin Worcester had died in 1859, and the press had continued to operate for a short time before ceasing operation. Carolyn Thomas Foreman, *Oklahoma Imprints, 1835–1907: A History of Printing in Oklahoma Before Statehood* (Norman: University of Oklahoma Press, 1936), 1–26.

84. Wright, "Notes on Mrs. Hannah Worcester Hicks Hitchcock," 351. Hungry Mountain is west-southwest of Stillwell, Oklahoma.

85. Ibid., 351–352.

86. Ibid., 352.

87. "Creeks in the Civil War," *Galveston (Texas) News*, November 27, 1901, box 6, Grant Foreman Collection, OHS (hereafter cited as GFC OHS). Gregory later served as a respected Muscogee Nation judge.

88. J. Leitch Wright Jr., *Creeks and Seminoles: The Destruction and Regeneration of the Muscogulge People* (Lincoln: University of Nebraska Press, 1986), 33; Mary Jane Warde, *George Washington Grayson and the Creek Nation, 1843–1920* (Norman: University of Oklahoma Press, 1999), 62–63.

89. Grayson described his life in W. David Baird, ed., *A Creek Warrior for the Confederacy: The Autobiography of Chief G. W. Grayson* (Norman: University of Oklahoma Press, 1988); Warde, *George Washington Grayson*, 62–65.

90. Robert L. Kerby, *Kirby Smith's Confederacy: The Trans-Mississippi South, 1863–1865* (New York: Columbia University Press, 1972), 57.

91. Pike, unaddressed correspondence, May 4, 1862, *OR*, series 1, volume 13, part 1, 821, 823.

92. Ibid., 819.

93. Baird, *A Creek Warrior*, 97.

94. Ibid.; Warde, *George Washington Grayson*, 66.

95. Warde, *George Washington Grayson*, 66–67.

96. Britton, *The Union Indian Brigade*, 226.

97. Ibid.

98. Pike, unaddressed correspondence, May 4, 1862, *OR*, series 1, volume 13, part 1, 819.

99. William P. Bumpass, *Reminiscences of the Boys in Gray*, comp. Mamie Yeary (Dallas: Smith & Lamar, 1912), 100–101.

100. Warde, *George Washington Grayson*, 66–68.

101. William D. Welge, "Dallas W. Bowman Lied about His Age," unpublished manuscript, 2012.138 FOHSA OHS.

102. Allan C. Ashcraft, "Confederate Troop Conditions in 1864," *Chronicles of Oklahoma* 41, no. 4 (1963): 442, 445.

103. Jerlena King, "Jackson Lewis of the Confederate Creek Regiment," *Chronicles of Oklahoma* 41, no. 1 (1963): 66–69.

104. Thomas Wildcat Alford, *Civilization and the Story of the Absentee Shawnees*, As Told to Florence Drake by Thomas Wildcat Alford (Norman: University of Oklahoma Press, 1936), 6–8.

105. Ibid., 7–8.

106. Ibid., 9–10.

107. Ibid., 12.

108. Ibid., 12–13.

109. Mildred P. Mayhall, *The Kiowas* (Norman: University of Oklahoma Press, 1962), 160–162; W. S. Nye, *Carbine and Lance: The Story of Old Fort Sill* (Norman: University of Oklahoma Press, 1937), 28–29.

110. Mayhall, *The Kiowas*, 161–162.

111. Nye, *Carbine and Lance*, 29.

112. Muriel H. Wright, "A History of Fort Cobb," *Chronicles of Oklahoma* 34 (Spring 1956): 59–60; Thomas Frank Schilz, "People of the Cross Timbers: A History of the Tonkawa Indians," unpublished dissertation, Texas Christian University, Fort Worth, Texas, 1983, 162–163; S. S. Scott to James A. Seddon, January 12, 1863, *OR*, series 4, volume 1, part 2, 352.

113. Nye, *Carbine and Lance*, 30–31; *OR*, series IV, volume 1, part 2, 354–355. Laurence M. Hauptman, *Between Two Fires: American Indians in the Civil War* (New York: Free Press, 1995), repeated the common error that Agent Leeper was killed in the attack (29).

114. *OR*, series 4, volume 1, part 2, 355.

115. Ibid.; C. Ross Hume, "Historic Sites around Anadarko," *Chronicles of Oklahoma* 16 (December 1938): 410–424.

116. Abel, *The Indian in the Civil War*, 143–146.

117. Ibid., 147–152; Jon D. May, "Fort McCulloch," *Encyclopedia of Oklahoma History and Culture*, http://digital.library.okstate.edu/encyclopedia/entried/F/FO036.html (accessed February 2, 2011).

118. Abel, *The Indian in the Civil War*, 152–153.

119. Ibid., 156–169.

120. Ibid.; Brown, *Albert Pike*, 401–416.

121. Abel, *The Indian in the Civil Wa*r, 179–180, 193–194.

122. "First Battle of Newtonia," Missouri Civil War Sesquicentennial, http://mocivilwar150.com/history/battle/174 (accessed July 12, 2012); Col. J. G. Stevens, Report No. 12, *OR*, series 1, volume 13, part 1, 304.

123. Col. Douglas H. Cooper to Brig. Gen. James S. Rains, October 2, 1862, Report No. 8, ibid., 297–298.

124. Ibid., 299.

125. "First Battle of Newtonia," Missouri Civil War Sesquicentennial, http://mocivilwar150.com/history/battle/174 (accessed July 12, 2012); Brig. Gen. Albert Pike to Adjutant Inspector General S. Cooper, October 24, 1862, *OR*, series 1, volume 13, part 1, 893.

126. Quoted in Abel, *The Indian in the Civil War*, n. 527, 195.

127. Britton, *The Union Indian Brigade*, 99.

128. Ibid., 102–104; Wright and Fischer, "Civil War Sites," 174–175; Able, *The Indian in the Civil War*, 218–219; Steve Cottrell, *The Civil War in the Indian Territory* (Gretna, La.: Pelican Publishing Company, 1995), 56–60.

129. Report 8, Col. Stephen Wattles to Col. William F. Cloud, December 12, 1862, *OR* series 1, volume 22, part 1, 93–94.

130. Velma Nieberding, "Indian Home, 90, Still Stands in Craig Co.," *Tulsa (Oklahoma) World*, Sunday supplement, July 8, 1956, p. 36; George Lisle to Hon. Nelson Case, August 1, 1892, in Nelson Case, ed., *History of Labette County, Kansas*, 5, http://skyways.lib.ks.us/genweb/archives/labette/1901/20–26.shtml (accessed January 16, 2013); Gary L. Cheatham, "'If the Union Wins, We Won't Have Anything Left': The Rise and Fall of the Southern Cherokees in Kansas," *Kansas History* 30 (Autumn 2007): 171–173. In his fine article, Cheatham places the raid that drove the Walkers out of Chetopa in late 1861. However, George Lisle, another civilian refugee with whom Rachel Walker and her children left Chetopa, places their expulsion in the Willetts raid on November 19, 1863.

131. James M. McPherson, *Battle Cry of Freedom: The Civil War Era* (New York: Oxford University Press, 1988), 500, 563–564; Keith P. Wilson, *Campfires of Freedom: The Camp Life of Black Soldiers during the Civil War* (Kent, Ohio: Kent State University Press, 2002), xii, xv.

132. "James Henry Lane," *Territorial Kansas Online*, http://www.territorial kansasonline.org/~imlskto/cgi-bin/index.php?SCREEN=bio_sketches/lane_james (accessed February 16, 2011); Noah Andre Trudeau, *Like Men of War: Black Troops in the Civil War, 1862–1865* (Boston: Little, Brown and Company, 1998), 13.

133. Dudley Taylor Cornish, *Kansas Negro Regiments in the Civil War* (Topeka: State of Kansas Commission on Civil Rights, 1969), 4.

134. Ibid., 8; Kansas Historical Society, "Cool Things: First Kansas Colored Infantry Flag," http://www.kshs.org/cool2/coolflg1.htm (accessed August 20, 2009); Museum of the Kansas National Guard, "1st Kansas Volunteer Colored Infantry," http://www.kansasguardmuseum.org/1kscvls.html (accessed August 8, 2009); Mulroy, *The Seminole Freedmen*, 177.

135. Dudley Taylor Cornish, *The Sable Arm: Black Troops in the Union Army, 1861–1865*, 2nd ed. (Lawrence: University Press of Kansas, 1987), 145; Trudeau, *Like Men of War*, 4.

136. Interview of Phoebe Banks, 3, folder 2, box 25, Federal Writers Project Ex-Slate Narratives (hereafter cited as FWP EN) OHS; Abel, *Indians in the Civil War*, 107–109; Zellar, *African Creeks*, 59.

137. Cornish, *The Sable Arm*, 145–146; Trudeau, *Like Men of War*, 103, 166–169.

138. Interview of Henry Clay, folder 3, box 25, FWP EN OHS.

139. Interview of William L. Cowart, 21:177–178, IPH OHS.

140. Ibid., 177–178.

CHAPTER FOUR

1. Col. William A. Phillips to Maj. Gen. Samuel R. Curtis, January 19, 1862, *The War of the Rebellion: A Compilation of the Official Records of the Union and Confederate Armies* (hereafter cited as *OR*), series 1, volume 22, part 1, 55.

2. Dr. Daniel Dwight Hitchcock to "My dear friend," February 11, 1863, number 22, Ann Augusta Robertson Moore Papers, "Letters rec'd," 1861–1865 and undated" file, 82.84, Oklahoma Historical Society, Oklahoma City, Oklahoma (hereafter cited as OHS). Dr. Hitchcock was the brother-in-law of Hannah Worcester Hicks, Ann Eliza Worcester Robertson, and Ann Augusta Robertson Moore.

3. Interview of Siegal [Siegel] McIntosh, 35:231–232, Indian-Pioneer History (hereafter cited as IPH), OHS.

4. Entry of December 25, 1862, Stephen Foreman Diary, Western History Collections, University of Oklahoma, Norman, Oklahoma (hereafter cited as SFD and WHC).

5. Ibid.

6. Entry of December 26, 1862, ibid.; Col. William A. Phillips to Gen. James Blunt, December 25, 1862, *OR*, series 1, volume 22, part 1, 873–874.

7. Entry of January 10, 1863, SFD WHC. Foreman's son Evarts had married Judge Stidham's daughter Celestia in 1862.

8. Entries of January 14 and 15, 1863, ibid.

9. Phillips to Maj. Gen. Samuel M. Curtis, January 19, 1862, *OR*, series 1, volume 22, part 1, 55–56.

10. William G. McLoughlin, *After the Trail of Tears: The Cherokees' Struggle for Sovereignty, 1839–1880* (Chapel Hill: University of North Carolina Press, 1993), 208–209.

11. Phillips to Maj. Gen. Samuel M. Curtis, February 6, 1863, *OR*, series 1, volume 22, part 2, 101.

12. S. G. Colley to Commissioner of Indian Affairs William P. Dole, January 25, 1863, Report No. 57, and Dole to Colley, March 30, 1863, Report No. 58, *Annual Report of the Commissioner of Indian Affairs* (Washington, D.C.: Government Printing Office, 1864), 135–136 (hereafter cited as *AR CIA* and year).

13. Agent Isaac Coleman to Superintendent William G. Coffin, September 2, 1863, Report No. 84, ibid., 183–184; Directing Physician A. V. Coffin to W. G. Coffin, September 25, 1863, Report No. 90, ibid., 189; Superintendent Coffin to Commissioner of Indian Affairs Dole, September 24, 1863, Report No. 81 ½, ibid., 173–178.

14. Annie Heloise Abel, *The American Indian in the Civil War, 1862–1865* (Lincoln: University of Nebraska Press, 1992, Bison Book Edition), 215.

15. Superintendent Coffin to Commissioner of Indian Affairs Dole, September 24, 1863, Report No. 81 ½, *AR CIA 1863*, 175; Acting Physician A. V. Coffin to Superintendent Coffin, September 25, 1863, Report No. 90, ibid., 189.

16. Ibid., 177–178.

17. Agent Coleman to Superintendent Coffin, September 2, 1863, Report No. 84, ibid., 183.

18. Dr. A. V. Coffin to W. G. Coffin, September 25, 1863, Report No. 90, ibid., 189–191.

19. Ibid., 191.

20. Ibid.

21. Agent Cutler to Southern Superintendent Coffin, Report No. 83, September 5, 1863, ibid., 182,

22. Coffin to Commissioner Dole, March 22, 1863, Report No. 99, ibid., 198.

23. Ibid., 176.

24. Coffin to Commissioner Dole, February 7, 1863, Report No. 92, ibid., 194.

25. Ibid. Laurence M. Hauptman, *Between Two Fires: American Indians in the Civil War* (New York: Free Press, 1995), 32–33, 38.

26. Coffin to Commissioner Dole, February 12, 1863, Report No. 93, *AR CIA 1863*, 195.

27. Agent P. P. Elder to Superintendent Coffin, September 20, 1863, Report No. 88, ibid., 187; Superintendent Coffin to Commissioner Dole, February 24, 1863, Report No. 96, ibid., 197.

28. Superintendent Coffin to Commissioner Dole, February 24, 1863, Report No. 96, ibid., 197.

29. Superintendent Coffin to Commissioner Dole, March 17, 1863, Report No. 97, ibid., 198.

30. Phillips to Agent A. G. Proctor, included in Superintendent Coffin to Commissioner Dole, February 24, 1863, Report No. 94, ibid., 195–197.

31. Wiley Britton, *The Union Indian Brigade in the Civil War* (Kansas City, Mo.: Franklin Hudson Publishing Co., 1922), 204-208.

32. Report of Brig. Gen. William Steele, February 15, 1864, *OR*, series 1, volume 22, part 1, 28–36; James W. Parins, *Elias Cornelius Boudinot: A Life on the Cherokee Border* (Lincoln: University of Nebraska Press, 2006), 56.

33. Britton, *The Union Indian Brigade*, 207–208.

34. Ibid., 212–213, 217; Alice Robertson, "Incidents of the Civil War," Box 1, Alice Robertson Papers, 82.86, OHS.

35. Britton, *The Union Indian Brigade*, 58–59. Wortleberries are wild blueberries that grew in the area.

36. Ibid., 215–217.

37. Interview of Blackbird Doublehead, 22:375–377, Indian Pioneer History (hereafter cited as IPH) OHS.

38. Ibid., 377.

39. Abel, *The Indian in the Civil War*, 271; Britton, *The Union Indian Brigade*, 222–223.

40. Carolyn T. Foreman, "The Coodey Family of Indian Territory," *Chronicles of Oklahoma* 25 (Winter 1947–1948): 323–341.

41. Interview of Ella Coodey Robinson, 107: 451–463, 465–479, IPH OHS.

42. Ibid., 465–479.

43. Entry of April 22, 1863, SFD WHC; Mary Jane Warde, *George Washington Grayson and the Creek Nation, 1843–1920* (Norman: University of Oklahoma Press, 1999), 70.

44. Mrs. G. W. Grayson, "Prominent Indian Confederates," *Indian Journal* (Eufaula, Oklahoma), May 9, 1914. In this article it is likely Mrs. Grayson combined knowledge from her own experiences with information supplied by her husband, George Washington Grayson, or her father, George W. Stidham.

45. Warde, *George Washington Grayson*, 63–64.

46. Entry of January 26, 1863, SFD WHC.

47. Warde, *George Washington Grayson*, 64–65.

48. Superintendent Coffin to Commissioner Dole, September 24, 1863, Report No. 81 ½, *AR CIA 1863*, 173.

49. Phillip W. Steele and Steve Cottrell, *Civil War in the Ozarks* (Gretna, [La.]: Pelican Publishing Company, 1994), 56; Louis F. Burns, *A History of the Osage People* (Tuscaloosa: The University of Alabama Press, 2004), 264; "The Only Survivor's Story of Tragedy," *Kansas Genealogy*, http://www.kansasgenealogy.com/indians/only_survivor.htm (accessed August 21, 2009). Their number included three colonels, one lieutenant colonel, one major, and four captains, according to recovered documents. However, the total number in the party varies by account. See also Superintendent Coffin to Commissioner Dole, June 10, 1863, Report No. 106, *AR CIA 1863*, 206–207.

50. Burns, *A History of the Osage People*, 263–264, 278–279; John Joseph Mathews, *The Osages: Children of the Middle Waters* (Norman: University of Oklahoma Press, 1961), 638–640; "The Only Survivor's Story of Tragedy," *Kansas Genealogy*, http://www.kansasgenealogy.com/indians/only_survivor.htm (accessed August 21, 2009).

51. "The Only Survivor's Story of Tragedy," *Kansas Genealogy*, http://www.kansasgenealogy.com/indians/only_survivor.htm (accessed August 21, 2009).

52. Ibid.; Burns, *A History of the Osage People*, 264; Superintendent Coffin to Commissioner Dole, June 10, 1863, Report No. 106; *AR CIA 1863*, 206–207 .

53. Superintendent Coffin to Commissioner Dole, September 24, 1863, Report No. 81 ½, ibid., 173.

54. Burns, *A History of the Osage People*, 264.

55. Superintendent Coffin to Commissioner Dole, September 24, 1863, Report No. 81 ½, *AR CIA 1863*, 173.

56. Superintendent Coffin to Commissioner Dole, June 10, 1863, Report No. 106, ibid., 206–207.

57. Ibid., 207.

58. Abel, *The Indian in the Civil War*, 221–223.

59. Superintendent Coffin to Commissioner Dole, March 22, 1863, Report No. 98, *AR CIA 1863*, 198–199.

60. Agent George A. Cutler to Superintendent William G. Cutler, September 5, 1863, Report No. 83, ibid., 183.

61. Quoted in Abel, *The Indian in the Civil War*, 280–281.

62. Agent Harlan to Superintendent Coffin, May 26, 1863, Report No. 103, *AR CIA, 1863*, 203–204; Britton, *The Union Indian Brigade*, 229–234; interview of Rowland S. Bailey, 4:87, IPH OHS.

63. Report of Brig. Gen. William Steele, February 15, 1864, *OR*, series 1, volume 22, part 1, 32.

64. Ibid.

65. Agent Harlan to Superintendent Coffin, May 26, 1863, Report No. 103, *AR CIA 1863*, 203–204.

66. Ibid., 204–205.

67. Britton, *The Union Indian Brigade*, 242; Lary C. Rampp, "Negro Troop Activity in Indian Territory," *Chronicles of Oklahoma* 47, no. 1 (Spring 1969): 536.

68. Britton, *The Union Indian Brigade*, 241–243.

69. Ibid., 234. Cabin Creek, flowing south, joined the Grand River a little south of the ford.

70. Report of Col. James M. Williams, 1863, *OR*, series 1, volume 22, part 1, 378–380.

71. Britton, *The Union Indian Brigade*, 258.

72. Report of Col. William A. Phillips, July 7, 1863; Report of Col. James M. Williams, 1863, *OR*, series 1, volume 22, part 1, 378–380.

73. Britton, *The Union Indian Brigade*, 259–263; Report of Col. James M. Williams, 1863, *OR*, series 1, volume 22, part 1, 379–380.

74. Report of Col. James M. Williams, 1863, *OR*, series 1, volume 22, part 1, 380.

75. Ibid., 380–381; Rampp, "Negro Troop Activity," 538–541; Trudeau, *Like Men of War: Black Troops in the Civil War, 1862–1865* (Boston: Little, Brown and Company, 1988), 104–105.

76. Stand Watie to Sarah C. Watie, Edward Everett Dale and Gaston Litton, *Cherokee Cavaliers: Forty Years of Cherokee History as Told in the Correspondence of the Ridge-Watie-Boudinot Family* (1931; rpt., Norman: University of Oklahoma Press, 1995), 131.

77. Stand Watie to "My dear Sally," July 12, 1863, number 47, box H-57, Jay L. Hargett Collection, WHC.

78. *Reminiscences of the Boys in Gray, 1861–1865*, comp. Mamie Yeary (Dallas, Tex.: Smith & Lamb, 1912), 118. As there were other casualties, Candler was probably the only man killed from the 5th Texas Partisan Rangers.

79. Britton, *The Union Indian Brigade*, 265, 267. Britton reported nine Union dead. Report of Col. James M. Williams, 1863, *OR*, series 1, volume 22, part 1, 380.

80. Interview of Ella Coodey Robinson, 107: 465–479, IPH OHS.

81. Robert Steven Jones, "General James G. Blunt and the Civil War in the Trans-Mississippi West," master's thesis, Oklahoma State University, Stillwater, Oklahoma, 1990; Britton, *The Union Indian Brigade*, 267–268.

82. Britton, *The Union Indian Brigade*, 270–271.

83. Ibid., 271.

84. Ibid., 274; Jones, "General James G. Blunt," 104.

85. Maj. Gen. James G. Blunt, Report Number 1, July 26, 1863, *OR*, series 1, volume 22, part 1, 447.

86. Brig. Gen. Douglas H. Cooper, August 12, 1863, ibid., 457–458; Britton, *The Union Indian Brigade*, 274–275; Rampp, "Negro Troop Activity," 541–542.

87. Trudeau, *Like Men of War*, 106; Lt. Col. Frederick W. Schaurte, Report

Number 3, July 20, 1863, *OR,* series 1, volume 22, part 1, 451; Capt. Edward A. Smith, Report Number 5, July 19, 1863, ibid., 454.

88. Brig. Gen. Douglas H. Cooper, August 12, 1863, ibid., 458; Lt. William T. Campbell, Report Number 4, July 19, 1863, ibid., 452.

89. Brig. Gen. Douglas H. Cooper, August 12, 1863, ibid., 458. It has been suggested that this powder, manufactured for Mexico's dry climate, lacked the humidity-resistant coating of gunpowder manufactured for damper climates elsewhere.

90. Ibid.

91. Maj. Gen. James G. Blunt, Report Number 1, July 26, 1863, *OR,* series 1, volume 22, part 1, 447; Britton, *The Union Indian Brigade,* 275–276.

92. Brig. Gen. Douglas H. Cooper, Report Number 10, August 12, 1863, *OR,* series 1, volume 22, part 1, 457–458; Wilfred Knight, *Red Fox: Stand Watie and the Confederate Indian Nations During the Civil War Years in Indian Territory* (Glendale, Calif.: Arthur H. Clark Company, 1988), 166–167.

93. Interview of Lucinda Davis, 7–8, folder 7, box 25, 81.105, Federal Writers Project Ex-Slave Narratives (hereafter cited as FWP EN), OHS.

94. Lewis E. Daniell, "W. K. Makemson," *Personnel of the Texas State Government, with Sketches of Distinguished Texans, Embracing the Executive and Staff, Heads of the Departments, United States Senators and Representatives, Members of the Twenty-first Legislature* (Austin, Tex.: Smith, Hicks, and Jones, State Printers, 1889), n.p.

95. W. K. Makemson to "My dear friend Thoburn," November 19, 1910, 86.01.1247.D, folder 15, box 19, "Confederate Memorial Association," Joseph B. Thoburn Collection, 86.01, OHS.

96. Maj. Gen. James G. Blunt, Report Number 1, July 26, 1863, *OR,* series 1, volume 22, part 1, 447–448.

97. Quoted in Britton, *The Union Indian Brigade,* 276–277.

98. Quoted in W. David Baird, ed., *A Creek Warrior for the Confederacy: The Autobiography of Chief G. W. Grayson* (Norman: University of Oklahoma Press, 1988), 63. It is likely both Britton and Grayson paraphrased these speeches but remembered well the sentiments and ideas they expressed.

99. Maj. Gen. James G. Blunt, Report Number 1, July 26, 1863, *OR,* series 1, volume 22, part 1, 448.

100. Capt. Henry Hopkins, Report Number 9, July 21, 1863, *OR,* series 1, volume 22, part 1, 456; LeRoy H. Fischer, *The Battle of Honey Springs, 1863–1988.* Oklahoma Historical Society, Official Program, Re-enactment, July 16–17, 1988.

101. Maj. Gen. James G. Blunt, Report Number 1, July 26, 1863, *OR,* series 1, volume 22, part 1, 448.

102. Capt. Edward R. Stevens, Report Number 5, July 19, 1863, ibid., 453.

103. Lt. Col. William T. Campbell, Report Number 4, ibid., 452–453.

104. Lt. Col. John Bowles, Report Number 2, ibid., 449–450.

105. Ibid.

106. Britton, *The Union Indian Brigade,* 279.

107. Lt. Col. John Bowles, Report Number 2, *OR,* series 1, volume 22, part 1, 450.

108. Ibid.; Britton, *The Union Indian Brigade,* 279.

109. Dallas W. Bowman to "Dear Mother," August 18, 1863, 96.72.10.01, Dallas W. Bowman Collection, OHS.

110. Maj. Gen. James G. Blunt, Report Number 1, July 26, 1863, *OR*, series 1, volume 22, part 1, 448.

111. Brig. Gen. Douglas H. Cooper, August 12, 1863, ibid., 460.

112. James Johnson, *Reminiscences of the Boys in Gray*, 383.

113. Col. Stephen H. Wattles, Report Number 8, July 18, 1863, *OR*, series 1, volume 22, part 1, 455.

114. Lt. Col. Frederick W. Schaurte, Report Number 3, July 20, 1863, ibid., 452.

115. Lt. Col. William T. Campbell, Report Number 4, July 19, 1863, ibid., 452.

116. Capt. Henry Hopkins, Report Number 9, July 21, 1863, ibid., 456–457.

117. Brig. Gen. Douglas H. Cooper, Report Number 10, August 12, 1863, ibid., 459–460.

118. Dallas W. Bowman to "Dear Mother," August 18, 1863, 96.72.10.01–97.72.10.02, Dallas W. Bowman Collection, OHS.

119. Brig. Gen. Douglas H. Cooper, Report Number 10, August 12, 1863, *OR*, series 1, volume 22, part 1, 461.

120. Lt. Col. John Bowles, Report Number 2, ibid., 450.

121. Brig. Gen. Douglas H. Cooper, Report Number 10, August 12, 1863, ibid., 460.

122. W. K. Makemson to "My dear friend Thoburn," November 19, 1910, 86.01.1247E-F, Joseph B. Thoburn Collection, OHS.

123. Britton, *The Union Indian Brigade*, 282–283.

124. Interview of Lucinda Davis, 8, folder 7, box 25, FWP EN OHS.

125. W. K. Makemson to "My dear friend Thoburn," November 19, 1910, 86.01.1247E, Joseph B. Thoburn Collection, OHS.

126. Baird, ed., *A Creek Warrio*r, 61–63.

127. Interview of Jim Tomm, 112: 277, OHS IPH.

128. Brig. Gen. Douglas H. Cooper, Report Number 10, August 12, 1863, *OR*, series 1, volume 22, part 1, 460.

129. Maj. Gen. James G. Blunt, Report Number 1, July 26, 1863, ibid., 448.

130. W. K. Makemson to "My dear friend Thoburn," November 19, 1910, 86.01.1247E, Joseph B. Thoburn Collection, OHS.

131. Dallas W. Bowman to "Dear Mother," August 18, 1863, 96.72.10.02, Dallas W. Bowman Collection, OHS.

132. Interview of Lucinda Davis, 9, folder 7, box 25, FWP EN OHS.

133. Ibid.

134. Ibid.

135. Entry of July 18, 1863, SFD WHC.

136. Ibid.

137. Entry of July 19, 1863, ibid.

138. Entry of July 29, 1863, ibid.

139. Entry of August 8, 1863, ibid.

140. Ibid.

141. Ibid.

142. Stand Watie, Principal Chief of the Cherokees, to His Excellency, the Governor of the Creek Nation, August 9, 1863, *OR*, series 1, volume 22, part 2, 1105.

143. Ibid.

144. Quoted in Grace Steele Woodward, *The Cherokees* (Norman: University of Oklahoma Press, 1963), 284.

145. Quoted in Dale and Litton, eds., *Cherokee Cavaliers*, 123.

CHAPTER FIVE

1. *Indian Journal* (Eufaula, Indian Territory), May 1, 1878.

2. "Record Book of Chief Sam Checote in the Early Sixties," typescript, 30–32, Indian Archives, Oklahoma Historical Society, Oklahoma City, Oklahoma (hereafter cited as OHS).

3. Richard C. Rohrs, "Fort Gibson: Forgotten Glory," *Early Military Forts and Posts in Oklahoma*, ed. Odie B. Faulk, Kenny A. Franks, and Paul F. Lambert, volume 9, The Oklahoma Series (Oklahoma City: Oklahoma Historical Society, 1978), 31; T. A. Neace, *Reminiscences of the Boys in Gray, 1861–1865*, comp. Mamie Yeary (Dallas: Smith & Lamar, 1912), 561.

4. Interview of Rochelle (Rachel) Allred Ward, 3–4, folder 4, box 28, 81.105, Federal Writers Project Ex-Slave Narratives (hereafter cited as FWP EN), OHS.

5. Interview of Blackbird Doublehead, 22:378, Indian-Pioneer History (hereafter cited as IPH) OHS.

6. Mildred P. Mayhall, *The Kiowas* (Norman: University of Oklahoma Press, 1962), 194–195; Virginia Cole Trenholm, *The Arapahoes, Our People* (Norman: University of Oklahoma Press, 1970), 166; Thomas W. Kavanagh, *The Comanches: A History, 1706–1875* (Lincoln: University of Nebraska Press, 1999), 394.

7. Interview of Blackbird Doublehead, 22:378, IPH OHS.

8. Interview of Rochelle Allred Ward, 3–4, folder 4, box 28, FWP EN OHS. There was a cholera epidemic at Fort Gibson in 1867.

9. Interview of Polly Barnett, 13:449–450, IPH OHS.

10. The other children were John Anthony, 19; Stephen Taylor, 14, Jennie Lind, 12, Archibald Alexander, 10, and Austin, 8. Minta Ross Foreman, "Reverend Stephen Foreman, Cherokee Missionary," *Chronicles of Oklahoma* 18, no. 3 (September 1940): 237.

11. Entry of July 29, 1863, Stephen Foreman Diary, Western History Collections, University of Oklahoma, Norman, Oklahoma (hereafter cited as SFD and WHC).

12. Wilfred Knight, *Red Fox: Stand Watie and the Confederate Indian Nations during the Civil War Years in Indian Territory* (Glendale, Calif.: Arthur H. Clark Company, 1988), 172–173.

13. Stand Watie to the Governor of the Choctaw and Chickasaw Nations, August 9, 1863, *The War of the Rebellion: A Compilation of the Official Records of the Union and Confederate Armies,* (Washington, D.C.: Government Printing Office, 1880–1901, hereafter cited as OR), series 1, volume 22, part 2, 961–962.

14. Brig. Gen. William Steele to Maj. W. B. Blair, August 7, 1863, ibid., 956.

15. Ibid., 956–957; Brig. Gen. William Steele to S. S. Scott, August 7, 1863, ibid., 957; Brig. Gen. William Steele to Maj. W. B. Blair, August 9, 1863, ibid., 961.

16. Annie Heloise Abel, *The American Indian in the Civil War, 1862–1865* (Lincoln: University of Nebraska Press, 1992, Bison Book edition), 291–292; Knight, *Red Fox*, 173–175.

17. Entry of August 23, 1863, SFD WHC.

18. Wiley Britton, *The Union Indian Brigade in the Civil War* (Kansas City, Mo.: Franklin Hudson Publishing Co., 1922), 288.

19. Entry of August 24, 1863, SFD WHC.

20. Ibid.

21. Ibid., entry of August 25, 1863.

22. Ibid., entry of August 26, 1863. Foreman was about fifty-six at the time.

23. Ibid.

24. Ibid.

25. Ibid.

26. Ibid., entry of August 27, 1863.

27. W. David Baird, ed., *A Creek Warrior for the Confederacy: The Autobiography of Chief George Washington Grayson* (Norman: University of Oklahoma Press, 1988), 63–64.

28. Ibid., 64–65.

29. Ibid., 66.

30. Ibid., 66–71. The settlement was in the vicinity of today's Atoka, Oklahoma.

31. Britton, *The Union Indian Brigade*, 288–291.

32. Interview of Malucy Bear, 14:82–85, IPH OHS.

33. Interview of Bently Beams, 14: 62–63, ibid.

34. Interview of Ella Coodey Robinson, 107:465–479, ibid. Israel G. Vore was the son of Israel Vore, a well-respected trader who had come west with the Cherokees and was murdered during previous political troubles.

35. Entry of September 5, 1863, SFD WHC.

36. Samuel Bell Maxey to Matilda Maxey, December 29, 1863, 3826.958, Samuel Bell Maxey Collection, Gilcrease Institute of American History and Art, Tulsa, Oklahoma (hereafter cited as SBM and GI). For a biography of Maxey, see John C. Waugh, *Sam Bell Maxey and the Confederate Indians* (Fort Worth: Ryan Place Publishers, 1995).

37. Quoted in Abel, *The Indian in the Civil War*, 313.

38. Ibid., 333–334.

39. Albert Pike to Samuel Bell Maxey, June 21, 1864, 3826.986, SBM GI.

40. Quoted in Abel, *The Indian in the Civil War*, 319–320.

41. Report of Samuel Bell Maxey to Col. S. S. Scott, August 23, 1864, SBM GI.

42. Abel, *The Indian in the Civil War*, 319–320, 314–321, 326–327.

43. Stand Watie to Sarah C. Watie, November 12, 1863, Edward Everett Dale and Gaston Litton, eds., *Cherokee Cavaliers: Forty Years of Cherokee History as told in the Correspondence of the Ridge-Watie-Boudinot Family* (1939; rpt., Norman: University of Oklahoma Press, 1995), 144–145. Sarah's nickname was spelled both "Sallie" and "Sally."

44. Knight, *Red Fox*, 186–187.

45. Report of Capt. Andrew C. Spillman, December 23, 1863, *OR*, series 1, volume 22, part 1, 781–783.

46. Samuel Bell Maxey to Col. S. S. Scott, August 23, 1864, ibid.

47. Interview of Ella Coodey Robinson, 107: 465–479, IPH OHS.

48. Sarah C. Watie to Stand Watie, May 20, 1863, Dale and Litton, eds., *Cherokee Cavaliers*, 124–126.

49. Interview of Elizabeth Kemp Mead, 64:420, IPH OHS.

50. Interview of Martha Gibson Matoy Walker, 94:376, ibid.

51. Special Agent A. G. Proctor to Superintendent W. G. Coffin, November 28, 1863, Report Number 117 ¾, Annual Report of the Commissioner of Indian Affairs (Washington, D.C.: Government Printing Office 1864), 223–225 (hereafter cited as AR CIA and year).

52. Report of Samuel Bell Maxey to Col. S. S. Scott, August 23, 1864, SBM GI; Arrell M. Gibson, *The Chickasaws* (Norman: University of Oklahoma Press, 1971), 269–270.

53. Interview of Martha Gibson Matoy Walker, 94:376, IPH OHS.

54. Interview of Ella Coodey Robinson, 107: 465–479, ibid.

55. Ibid.

56. Ibid., 120; interview of Belle Haney Labor Airington, 10:167, ibid.

57. Interview of Ella Coodey Robinson, 107: 465–479, ibid.

58. Agent Justin Harlan to Superintendent of Indian Affairs William G. Coffin, September 8, 1863, *AR CIA 1863*, 179–181.

59. Agent Justin Harlan to Superintendent of Indian Affairs William G. Coffin, August 8, 1863, ibid., 215.

60. Special Agent A. G. Proctor to Superintendent W. G. Coffin, November 28, 1863, Report Number 117 ¾, ibid., 223–225.

61. Interview of Jennie Martin, 6: 407, IPH OHS.

62. Interview of Kate Rackleff, 41: 114–115, ibid.

63. Interview of Annie Eliza Hendrix, 41:160–1164, IPH WHC.

64. Special Agent A. G. Proctor to Superintendent of Indian Affairs William G. Coffin, August 8, Report Number 11, *AR CIA 1863*.

65. Britton, *The Union Indian Brigade*, 430–434; Arrell Morgan Gibson, *Oklahoma: A History of Five Centuries* (1965, rpt., Norman: University of Oklahoma Press, 1981), 131.

66. Quoted in Gibson, *The Chickasaws*, 238–239. Vann was a Cherokee, but Gibson identified him as a Chickasaw, according to Grant Foreman, "Reminiscences of Mr. R. P. Vann," *Chronicles of Oklahoma* 11 (June 1933): 833–844.

67. "Kansas Indians" file, Section X Vertical File, OHS; LeRoy H. Fischer and Lary C. Rampp, "Quantrill's Civil War Operations in Indian Territory," *Chronicles of Oklahoma* 46 (Summer 1968): 157–161; Abel, *The Indian in the Civil War*, 204–205.

68. Britton, *The Union Indian Brigade*, 311–321; Fischer and Rampp, "Quantrill's Civil War Operations," 161–164; Maj. Gen. James G. Blunt, Report 1, October 19, 1863, *OR*, series 1, volume 22, part 1, 689; Robert Steven Jones, "General James G. Blunt and the Civil War in the Trans-Mississippi West" (Master's thesis, Oklahoma State University, Stillwater, Oklahoma, 1990), 120–127. The 2nd Kansas Colored Infantry was newly formed in 1863 by Samuel J. Crawford, a future Kansas governor.

69. Fischer and Rampp, "Quantrill's Civil War Operations," 164–171.

70. Quoted in ibid., 171.

71. Quoted in David Paul Smith, *Frontier Defense in the Civil War: Texas' Rangers and Rebels* (College Station: Texas A & M Press, 1992), 78–79.

72. Abel, *The Indian in the Civil War*, 326.

73. Stand Watie to Sarah C. Watie, April 24, 1864, Dale and Litton, eds., *Cherokee Cavaliers*, 155–156.

74. Fischer and Rampp, *Quantrill's Civil War Operations*, 171–179.

75. Tom Franzman, "The Battle of Devil's Backbone Mountain," *Chronicles of Oklahoma* 62 (Winter 1984–1985): 420–428.

76. Quoted in Whit Edwards, *The Prairie Was on Fire: Eyewitness Accounts of the Civil War in the Indian Territory* (Oklahoma City: Oklahoma Historical Society, 2001), 90.

77. Lary C. Rampp and Donald L. Rampp, *The Civil War in the Indian Territory* (Austin: Presidial Press, 1975), 66; Steven L. Warren, "Battle of Middle Boggy," *The Encyclopedia of Oklahoma History and Culture,* http://digital.library.okstate.edu/encyclopedia/entries/M/MI006.html (accessed May 24, 2012).

78. Quoted in Edwards, *The Prairie Was on Fire*, 91.

79. Ibid.

80. Abel, *The Indian in the Civil War*, 322–323; Fred Hood, "Twilight of the Confederacy in Indian Territory," *Chronicles of Oklahoma* 41, no. 4 (Winter 1963–1964): 432–433; Rampp and Rampp, *The Civil War*, 68.

81. "Poison Spring, Engagement at," *The Encyclopedia of Arkansas History and Culture,* http://www.encyclopediaofarkansas.net/encyclopedia/entry-detail.aspx?entryID=37 (accessed August 8, 2009).

82. Report of Col. Charles DeMorse, April 21, 1864, *OR*, series 1, volume 34, part 1, 847.

83. Dean A. Bohlender, "The Battle of Poison Spring, Arkansas, April 18, 1864," in *Civil War Battles in the West*, ed. LeRoy H. Fischer (Manhattan, Kan.: Sunflower Press, 1981), 87–88; Gregory J. W. Urwin, "'We Cannot Treat Negroes . . . as Prisoners of War': Racial Atrocities and Reprisals in Civil War Arkansas," in *Civil War Arkansas: Beyond Battles and Leaders*, ed. Anne J. Bailey and Daniel E. Sutherland (Fayetteville: University of Arkansas Press, 2000), 223.

84. Report of Col. Tandy Walker, April 19, 1864, *OR*, series 1, volume 34, part 1, 849.

85. Report of Col. J. M. Williams, April 24, 1864, quoted in "1st Kansas Volunteer Colored Infantry," Museum of the Kansas National Guard: Historic Units, http://www.kansasguardmuseum.org/1kscvls.html (accessed August 20, 2009).

86. "Poison Spring, Engagement at," *The Encyclopedia of Arkansas History and Culture,* http://www.encyclopediaofarkansas.net/encyclopedia/entry-detail.aspx?entryID=37 (accessed August 8, 2009); "Online Exhibits: Keep the Flag to the Front," Kansas Historical Society, http://www.kshs.org/exhibits/flags/flags4.htm (accessed August 20, 2009).

87. Quoted in Urwin, "'We Cannot Treat Negroes . . . as Prisoners of War,'" 217.

88. Ibid., 224–227; Dudley Taylor Cornish, *The Sable Arm: Black Troops in the Union Army, 1861–1865*, 2nd ed. (Lawrence: University Press of Kansas, 1987), 177.

89. Capt. Greene Durbin to Lt. George W. Houston, June 14, 1864, Inclosure 1, *OR*, series 1, volume 34, part 4, 687; Britton, *The Union Indian Brigade*, 401–403. Today this area is at the upper end of the Robert S. Kerr Reservoir. Some reports called the spot "Pheasant (or Pleasant) Bluff."

90. Knight, *Red Fox*, 219–220.

91. Baird, ed., *A Creek Warrior*, 81–82.

92. Britton, *The Union Indian Brigade*, 403–406.

93. Ibid., 405–408.

94. Report of Col. Stand Watie, June 17, 1864, *OR*, series 1, volume 34, part 1, 1012.

95. Rampp and Rampp, *The Civil War*, 87.

96. Baird, ed., *A Creek Warrior*, 81–88.

97. Dwight D. Hitchcock to "My dear friends," June 2, 1864, Alice Robertson Collection, Special Collections, McFarlin Library, University of Tulsa, Tulsa, Oklahoma (hereafter citied as ARC and TU).

98. Superintendent W. G. Coffin to Commissioner W. P. Dole, June 3, 1864, Report Number 169, *AR CIA 1864*, 340–341.

99. Report Number 170, ibid., 341–342.

100. Report Number 171, ibid., 342.

101. Ibid., 342–343.

102. Ibid., 343.

103. Oktahasushurgah, Kapitchafireco, Kowetamicco, Miccohutka, Tustenukechuahhikogee, and Tulladegulachapoka to the Commissioner of Indian Affairs, July 16, 1864, Report Number 172, ibid., 344.

104. Lt. Col. W. P. Adair to Maj. Gen. [Samuel Bell] Maxey, February 5, 1864, *OR*, series 1, volume 34, part 2, 945–946; Brig. Gen. W. R. Boggs to Maj. Gen. [Samuel Bell] Maxey, August 25, 1864, ibid., series 1, volume 42, part 2, 1082. Gano, formerly with John Bell Hood and the Texas Brigade, had returned to Texas for health reasons, but was now much improved. Price's expedition concluded with the Battle of Westport on October 23, 1864.

105. Brig. Gen. Richard M. Gano to Brig. Gen. Samuel Bell Maxey, August 29, 1864, 3826.996, SBM GI.

106. Knight, *Red Fox*, 228–235.

107. Marvin J. Hancock, "The Second Battle of Cabin Creek, 1864," *Chronicles of Oklahoma* 39 (Winter 1961–1962): 416–418; Brig. Gen. Richard M. Gano to Brig. Gen. Douglas H. Cooper, September 29, 1864, *OR*, series 1, volume 41, part 1, 788.

108. Capt. Edgar A. Barker, Report Number 7, September 20, 1864, ibid., 771–772.

109. Brig. Gen. Richard M. Gano to Brig. Gen. Douglas H. Cooper, September 29, 1864, ibid., 789.

110. Knight, *Red Fox*, 243.

111. Capt. Edgar A. Barker, Report Number 7, September 20, 1864, *OR*, series 1, volume 41, part 1, 771.

112. Knight, *Red Fox*, 244.

113. Baird, ed., *A Creek Warrior*, 95–96.

114. Jefferson P. Baze, *Reminisces of the Boys in Gray*, 45–46.

115. Capt. Edgar A. Barker, Report Number 7, September 20, 1864, *OR*, series 1, volume 41, part 1, 771; Britton, *The Union Indian Brigade*, 439–440.

116. Britton, *The Union Indian Brigade*, 440–441; Hancock, "The Second Battle of Cabin Creek," 419–420. Watie estimated the federal number at eight hundred to one thousand. Brig. Gen. Stand Watie to Capt. T. B. Heiston, October 3, 1864, *OR*, series 1, volume 41, part 1, 787.

117. Hancock, "The Second Battle of Cabin Creek," 419–420.

118. Britton, *The Union Indian Brigade*, 442; Knight, *Red Fox*, 247–248.

119. Baird, ed., *A Creek Warrior*, 99–101.

120. Ibid., 101.

121. Britton, *The Union Indian Brigade*, 442–443.

122. Baird, ed., *A Creek Warrior*, 102.

123. Charles H. Stith, *Reminisces of the Boys in Gray*, 724.

124. Knight, *Red Fox*, 251; Baird, ed., *A Creek Warrior*, 103.

125. Brig. Gen. Richard M. Gano to Brig. Gen. Douglas H. Cooper, September 29, 1864, *OR*, series 1, volume 41, part 1, 789.

126. Baird, ed., *A Creek Warrior*, 103; Brig. Gen. Stand Watie to Capt. T. B. Heiston, October 3, 1864, *OR*, series 1, volume 41, part 1, 787. Pleasant Porter and Grayson, friends as well as political rivals, both later served in the Muscogee national government. Each in the early 1900s was principal chief of the Muscogee Nation.

127. Brig. Gen. Stand Watie to Capt. T. B. Heiston, October 3, 1864, *OR*, series 1, volume 41, part 1, 786–787; "Old Battle Ground," interview of James R. Carselowey, 19:159–160, IPH OHS.

128. Baird, ed., *A Creek Warrior*, 103–104.

129. Jefferson P. Baze, *Reminiscences of the Boys in Gray*, 45–46.

130. W. T. Sheppard, ibid., 684.

131. Brig. Gen. Stand Watie to Capt. T. B. Heiston, October 3, 1864, *OR*, series 1, volume 41, part 1, 786–787.

132. Charles H. Stith, *Reminiscences of the Boys in Gray*, 724; Jefferson P. Baze, ibid., 46.

133. Hancock, "The Second Battle of Cabin Creek," 422.

134. Baird, ed., *A Creek Warrior*, 104.

135. James Knox Polk Yeary, *Reminiscences of the Boys in Gray*, 832.

136. Bradford K. Felmly and John C. Grady, *Suffering to Silence: 29th Texas Cavalry, C.S.A., Regimental History* (Quanah, Tex.: Nortex Press, 1975), 166.

137. James Knox Polk Yeary, *Reminiscences of the Boys in Gray*, 832; Wright and Fischer, "Civil War Sites in Oklahoma," 210.

138. Brig. Gen. Richard M. Gano to Brig. Gen. Douglas H. Cooper, September 29, 1864, *OR*, series 1, volume 41, part 1, 791.

139. Baird, ed., *A Creek Warrior*, 105.

140. Brig. Gen. Richard M. Gano to Brig. Gen. Douglas H. Cooper, September 29, 1864, *OR*, series 1, volume 41, part 1, 791.

141. Baird, ed., *A Creek Warrior*, 105–106; Mary Jane Warde, *George Washington Grayson and the Creek Nation, 1843–1920* (Norman: University of Oklahoma Press, 1999), 45–46.

142. Warde, *George Washington Grayson*, 69. Muscogee poet and satirist Alexander Posey, who was Grayson's friend about 1900, named one of his characters in his "Hot Gun" political satires "Yaha Tustunuggee."

143. Knight, *Red Fox*, 257; Maj. Gen. [Samuel Bell] Maxey to Matilda Maxey, October 12, 1864, 3826.1010 SBM GI; interview of Ella Coodey Robinson, 107:465–479, IPH OHS.

CHAPTER SIX

1. Interview of Emma Blythe Sixkiller, 100:46–48, Indian-Pioneer History, Oklahoma Historical Society, Oklahoma City, Oklahoma (hereafter cited as IPH and OHS).

2. Quoted in Steven L. Warren, *Brilliant Victory: The Second Civil War Battle of Cabin Creek, Indian Territory, September 19, 1864* (Wyandotte, Okla.: Gregath Publishing Company, 2002), 11.

3. Hannah Worcester Hicks to "My dear sister," March 29, 1864, Alice Robertson Collection, 16.3, Special Collections, McFarlin Library, University of Tulsa, Tulsa, Oklahoma (hereafter cited as ARC TU).

4. Interview of Christine Folsom Bates, 14:12–13, IPH OHS.

5. Brig. Gen. Douglas H. Cooper to Capt. M. L. Bell, October 6, 1864, *The War of the Rebellion: A Compilation of the Official Records of the Union and Confederate Armies* (Washington, D.C.: Government Printing Office, 1880–1901) (hereafter cited as *OR*), series 1, volume 41, part 3, 982–984.

6. W. David Baird, ed., *A Creek Warrior for the Confederacy: The Autobiography of Chief G. W. Grayson* (Norman: University of Oklahoma Press, 1988), 109–111.

7. Interview of Lewis Felihkatubbee, 51:434–435, IPH OHS.

8. Baird, ed., *A Creek Warrior*, 112–114; Mary Jane Warde, *George Washington Grayson and the Creek Nation, 1843–1920* (Norman: University of Oklahoma Press, 1999), 83.

9. Dwight D. Hitchcock to "My dear friends," March 24, 1864, ARC TU.

10. Dwight D. Hitchcock to "My dear Robertson," May 20, 1864, ibid.

11. Hannah Worcester Hicks to "My own dear sister," September 25, 1864, 16.3, ibid.

12. Edward Everett Dale and Gaston Litton, *Cherokee Cavaliers: Forty Years of Cherokee History as Told in the Correspondence of the Ridge-Watie-Boudinot Family* (1939; rpt., Norman: University of Oklahoma Press, 1995), 128.

13. Rupert Norval Richardson, *The Comanche Barrier to South Plains Settlement: A Century and a Half of Savage Resistance to the Advancing Frontier* (Glendale, Calif.: Arthur H. Clark Company, 1933), 290; Ernest Wallace and E. Adamson Hoebel, *The Comanches: Lords of the South Plains* (Norman: University of Oklahoma Press, 1952), 307.

14. Blue Clark, *Indian Tribes of Oklahoma: A Guide* (Norman: University of Oklahoma Press, 2009), 27.

15. Warde, *George Washington Grayson*, 34–35.

16. Interview of Dinah Lewis Frazier, 3:582, IPH OHS.

17. Robert L. Ream, "A Nearly Forgotten Fragment of Local History," *Chronicles of Oklahoma* 4, no. 1 (March 1926): 34.

18. Richardson, *The Comanche Barrier*, 265–266.

19. Ibid.

20. Stan Hoig, *The Peace Chiefs of the Cheyennes* (1980; rpt., Norman: University of Oklahoma Press, 1990), 62–63; David Paul Smith, *Frontier Defense in the Civil War: Texas' Rangers and Rebels* (College Station: Texas A & M University Press, 1992), 61–67, 118, 123–128, 168; M. S. Elswick, Colorado State Archives, "Colorado Volunteers, 1861–1865," http/www.colorado.gov/dpa/doit/archives/civwar/civilwar.html (accessed

June 25, 2011). The Union victory at Glorieta Pass near Santa Fe on March 26–28, 1862, ended Confederate incursions into New Mexico.

21. Smith, *Frontier Defense*, 121–122.

22. "A Place to Call Home," *Texas Beyond History*, http://www.texasbeyond history.net/tehas/voices/place.html (accessed April 25, 2011); David La Vere, *Contrary Neighbors: Southern Plains and Removed Indians in Indian Territory* (Norman: University of Oklahoma Press, 2000), 170.

23. Commissioners James E. Harrison, James Bourland, and Charles A. Hamilton to Texas governor Edward Clark, April 23, 1861, *OR*, series 4, volume 1, 322–325; Smith, *Frontier Defense*, 118, 123–128, 168. Dissenters against the war, draft dodgers, and deserters were a major problem in Texas throughout the war, and many infested areas along the Red River.

24. Charles J. Kappler, comp., *Indian Treaties, 1778–1883* (New York: Interland Publishing, 1972), 600–602; Richardson, *The Comanche Barrier*, 247–275, 289–290; W. S. Nye, *Carbine and Lance: The Story of Old Fort Sill* (1937; rpt., Norman: University of Oklahoma Press, 1969), 34–35.

25. Mildred P. Mayhall, *The Kiowas* (Norman: University of Oklahoma Press, 1962), 194; Donald J. Berthrong, *The Southern Cheyennes* (Norman: University of Oklahoma Press, 1963), 152–153.

26. Quoted in Berthrong, *The Southern Cheyennes*, 152.

27. Ibid., 149–150.

28. Paraphrased in the *Washington Evening Star*, March 27, 1863, quoted in Hoig, *The Peace Chiefs*, 71–72.

29. Ibid., 72.

30. Smith, *Frontier Defense*, 67–70, 128.

31. Robert M. Utley, *The Indian Frontier of the American West 1846–1890* (Albuquerque: University of New Mexico Press, 1984), 93–95.

32. Mayhall, *The Kiowas*, 121, 163; Nye, *Carbine and Lance*, 35.

33. Maj. Gen. S. R. Curtis to Maj. Gen. James G. Blunt, September 22, 1864, *OR*, series 1, volume 41, part 3, 314–315.

34. Smith, *Frontier Defense*, 131; Nye, *Carbine and Lance*, 35; Mayhall, *The Kiowas*, 198–199; George Hunt, "Millie Durgan," *Chronicles of Oklahoma* 15, no. 4 (December 1937): 481; Michael E. McClellan, "Britton Johnson," Texas State Historical Association, *The Handbook of Texas Online*, http://www.tshaonline.org/ handbook/online/articles/fjo07 (accessed April 9, 2011).

35. Quoted in David La Vere, *Life Among the Texas Indians: The WPA Narratives* (College Station: Texas A & M Press, 1998), 68–69. John would have been in his early seventies at the time he told this story, and his memory could have been faulty, as is sometimes the case with oral history.

36. Mayhall, *The Kiowas*, 198–199; George Hunt, "Millie Durgan," *Chronicles of Oklahoma* 15, no. 4 (December 1937): 480–481. Millie's surname is sometimes spelled "Durkin."

37. Clyde Ellis, "The 1864 Battle of Adobe Walls," unpublished manuscript, 2012.136 Friends of the Oklahoma Historical Society Archives Civil War Collection (hereafter cited as FOHSA CWC), OHS; Nye, *Carbine and Lance*, 36–37; Tom Dunlay, *Kit Carson and the Indians* (Lincoln: University of Nebraska Press, 2000), 330–337. There was a second battle of Adobe Walls in 1874 during the Red River War.

38. Smith, *Frontier Defense*, 152; Brig. Gen. J. D. McAdoo to Lt. Col. T. M. Jack, March 4, 1865, *OR*, series 1, volume 48, part 1, 26; A. M. Gibson, *The Kickapoos: Lords of the Middle Border* (Norman: University of Oklahoma Press, 1963), 203–204.

39. Gibson, *The Kickapoos*, 144–158, 200–202.

40. Ibid., 203–203.

41. Brig. Gen. J. D. McAdoo to Lt. Col. T. M. Jack, March 4, 1865, *OR*, series 1, volume 48, part 1, 26.

42. Ibid., 27–28.

43. Ibid.

44. Smith, *Frontier Defense*, 153.

45. Quoted in Gibson, *The Kickapoos*, 205.

46. Polk Cox, *Reminiscences of the Boys in Gray, 1861–1865*, comp. Mamie Yeary (Dallas: Smith & Lamar, 1912), 156–157.

47. Brig. Gen. J. D. McAdoo to Lt. Col. T. M. Jack, March 4, 1865, *OR*, series 1, volume 48, part 1, 27–27.

48. Smith, *Frontier Defense*, 153–154; Gibson, *The Kickapoos*, 206.

49. Brig. Gen. J. D. McAdoo to Lt. Col. T. M. Jack, March 4, 1865, *OR*, series 1, volume 48, part 1, 27–28.

50. Quoted in Gibson, *The Kickapoos*, 207.

51. Smith, *Frontier Defense*, 155.

52. Ray C. Colton, *The Civil War in the Western Territories: Arizona, Colorado, New Mexico, and Utah* (Norman: University of Oklahoma Press, 1959), 151–154.

53. Berthrong, *The Southern Cheyenne*, 210–212.

54. Gov. John Evans, September 29, 1864, Report Number 21, *Annual Report of the Commissioner of Indian Affairs for the Year 1864* (Washington, D.C.: Government Printing Office, 1864), 221 (hereafter cited as *AR CIA* and year).

55. Ibid.

56. Bob Rea, "George Bent in the Civil War: Cheyenne Confederate Warrior," unpublished manuscript, 2012.136 FOHSA CWC OHS; David Fridtjof Halaas and Andrew E. Masich, *Halfbreed: The Remarkable True Story of George Bent—Caught Between the Worlds of the Indian and the White Man* (Cambridge, Mass.: DeCapo Press, 2004), 84–90, 111, 132.

57. Alvin M. Josephy Jr., *The Civil War in the American West* (New York: Alfred A. Knopf, 1991), 310–311; Colton, *The Civil War in the Western Territories*, 157–158; Halaas and Masich, *Halfbreed*, 141–153; Thom Hatch, *Black Kettle: The Cheyenne Chief Who Sought Peace But Found War* (Hoboken, N.J.: John Wiley and Sons, 2004), 154–162.

58. Hoig, *The Peace Chiefs*, 65–66, 106–112; Berthrong, *The Southern Cheyennes*, 213–223; M. S. Elswick, Colorado State Archives, "Colorado Volunteers, 1861–1865," http/www.colorado.gov/dpa/doit/archives/civwar/civilwar.html (accessed June 25, 2011).

59. Interview of Kathryn Bull Coming, by Mary Jane Warde, Seiling, Oklahoma vicinity, March 26, 1999, Cheyenne/Washita Project (hereafter cited as C/WP), OHS.

60. Interview of Eugene Blackbear Sr. by Mary Jane Warde and Larry Roman Nose, Concho, Oklahoma, April 21, 1999, ibid.

61. Utley, *The Indian Frontier*, 93–94; Colton, *The Civil War in the Western Territories*, 159; Josephy, *The Civil War in the American West*, 312–313.

62. La Vere, *Contrary Neighbors*, 174–175.

63. L. P. Chouteau to Col. J. M. Bell, January 21, 1865, quoted Dale and Litton, eds., *Cherokee Cavaliers*, 209–210.

64. Ohopeyane to the Chiefs and Headmen of the Creek Nation, February 21, 1865, ibid., 213–215; La Vere, *Contrary Neighbors*, 174–176.

65. Berthrong, *The Southern Cheyennes*, 231–234.

66. Mayhall, *The Kiowas*, 164–165; Utley, *The Indian Frontier*, 95–98.

67. J. H. Leavenworth to Brig. Gen. Ford, May 30, 1865, *OR*, series 1, volume 48, part 2, 687. These Cheyennes were probably Peace Chief Black Kettle's followers.

68. Joseph Perryman to Ann Eliza Worcester Robertson, February 17, 1865, box 6, 83.229, Grant Foreman Collection (hereafter cited as GFC), OHS. Perryman was a future principal chief of the Muscogee Nation.

69. Timothy Barnett to Stand Watie, March 3, 1863, number 71, M93-2-1-E, Cherokee Nation Papers, Phillips Collection, Western History Collections, University of Oklahoma, Norman, Oklahoma (hereafter cited as WHC).

70. Thompson Perryman to W. S. Robertson, March 8, 1865, "Creek Civil War" file, Box 6, GFC OHS. Missionaries William Schenk Robertson and his wife, Ann Eliza Worcester Robertson, had worked and taught at Tullahassee since its founding in 1850.

71. Superintendent of Indian Affairs W. G. Coffin to Commissioner of Indian Affairs William P. Dole, September 24, 1863, *AR CIA 1863*, 176.

72. Dwight D. Hitchcock to "My dear friends," November 26, 1865, ARC TU.

73. Thompson Perryman to W. S. Robertson, March 8, 1865, "Creek Civil War" file, Box 6, GFC OHS.

74. Superintendent of Indian Affairs W. G. Coffin to Commissioner of Indian Affairs William P. Dole, September 24, 1863, *AR CIA 1863*, 175.

75. Interview of Blackbird Doublehead, 22:380, IPH OHS.

76. Craig Miner, *Kansas: The History of the Sunflower State, 1854–2000* (Lawrence: University Press of Kansas, 2002), 106–112; Superintendent of Indian Affairs W. G. Coffin to Commissioner of Indian Affairs William P. Dole, November 15, 1864, *AR CIA 1864*, 37.

77. Miner, *Kansas*, 106–112.

78. Arrell Morgan Gibson, *Oklahoma: A History of Five Centuries* (1965; rpt., Norman: University of Oklahoma Press, 1981), 127.

79. Superintendent W. G. Coffin to Commissioner William P. Dole, Report 98, *AR CIA 1863*, 198–199.

80. Commissioner of Indian Affairs William P. Dole to Secretary of the Interior J. P. Usher, November 15, 1864, *AR CIA 1864*, 33.

81. Arrell Morgan Gibson, *The Chickasaws* (Norman: University of Oklahoma Press, 1971), 271–272; Annie Heloise Abel, *The American Indian and the End of the Confederacy, 1863–1866* (Lincoln: University of Nebraska Press, 1993, Bison Book edition), 124–130.

82. Abel, *The End of the Confederacy*, 130; Brad R. Clampitt, "'An Indian Shall Not Spill an Indian's Blood': The Confederate-Indian Conference at Camp Napoleon, 1865," *Chronicles of Oklahoma* 83, no. 1 (Spring 2005): 40.

83. William P. Bumpass, *Reminiscences of the Boys in Gray, 1861–1865*, comp. Mamie Yeary (Dallas: Smith & Lamar, 1912), 101.

84. D. H. Cooper to Col. S. S. Anderson, May 15, 1865, *OR*, series 1, volume 48, part 2, 1306.

85. Clampitt, "Camp Napoleon," 41–42; interview of C. Ross Hume, 45:343, IPH.

86. D. H. Cooper to Col. S. S. Anderson, May 15, 1865, *OR*, series 1, volume 48, part 2, 1306.

87. Brig. Gen. Douglas H. Cooper to Brig. Gen. James W. Throckmorton, May 16, 1865, ibid.; Clampitt, "Camp Napoleon," 42.

88. Michael E. McClellan, "Britton Johnson," Texas State Historical Association, *The Handbook of Texas Online*, http://www.tshaonline.org/handbook/online/articles/fjo07 (accessed April 9, 2011).

89. Clampitt, "Camp Napoleon," 49–51.

90. W. David Baird, *Peter Pitchlynn: Chief of the Choctaws* (Norman: University of Oklahoma Press, 1972), 140–141.

91. Sarah C. Watie to Stand Watie, May 21, 1865, quoted in Dale and Litton, eds., *Cherokee Cavaliers*, 225–226.

92. Richard Fields to Thomas F. Anderson, May 22, 1865, ibid., 226–227.

93. Stand Watie to Sarah C. Watie, May 27, 1865, ibid., 227–228.

94. Baird, *Peter Pitchlynn*, 140–141; Wilfred Knight, *Red Fox: Stand Watie and the Confederate Indian Nations during the Civil War Years in Indian Territory* (Glendale, Calif.: Arthur H. Clark Company, 1988), 274–275; Abel, *The End of the Confederacy*, 147–148; Lt. Col. A. C. Matthews and Adjutant W. H. Vance to Brig. Gen. Stand Watie, June 23, 1865, *OR*, series 1, volume 48, part 2, 1101.

95. Ream, "A Nearly Forgotten Fragment, "35.

96. Ibid., 36–37.

97. Ibid., 38–39; H. R. O'Beirne and H. F. O'Beirne, *Leaders and Leading Men of the Indian Territory, with Interesting Biographical Sketches, 1, Choctaws and Chickasaws* (Chicago: American Publishers' Association, 1891), 217–218.

98. Ream, "A Nearly Forgotten Fragment," 39–40.

99. Ibid., 39–40

100. Ibid., 40–42.

101. Ibid., 41–44. The identity of the Comanche raiders has never been discovered.

102. Agent F. W. Farnsworth to Commissioner of Indian Affairs William P. Dole, August 11, 1864, Report Number 195, *AR CIA 1864*, 369.

103. Ibid.

104. Commissioner of Indian Affairs D. N. Cooley, Annual Report, October 31, 1865, *AR CIA 1865*, 41.

105. Ibid., 45–46.

106. Ibid., 44.

107. Ibid., 43.

108. Agent John G. Pratt to Commissioner of Indian Affairs William P. Dole, September 13, 1864, Report Number 184, *AR CIA 1864*, 356–357.

109. *AR CIA 1865*, 50.

110. Ibid., 40.

111. Agent John A. Burbank to the Commissioner, September 30, 1864, Report Number 200, AR CIA 1864, 374; Commissioner D. N. Cooley, *AR CIA 1865*, 49.

112. Report Number 190, ibid., 362–365.

113. Ibid.

114. Agent William Daily, August 29, 1864, Report Number 203, ibid., 308.

115. Agent John A. Burbank to the Commissioner, September 30, 1864, Report Number 200, ibid., 374.

116. Commissioner D. N. Cooley, Report, October 31, 1865, *AR CIA 1865*, 43.

117. Ibid., 43.

118. Ibid.

119. Ibid., 42–43, 45.

120. Ibid., 34.

121. Ibid., 35.

122. Ibid.

123. Ibid.

124. Ibid., 35–36.

125. Berthrong, *The Southern Cheyennes*, 234–239.

126. Ibid., 239–240.

127. "The Diary of Samuel A. Kingman at Indian Treaty in 1865," *Kansas Historical Quarterly* 1, no. 5 (November 1932): 442–446.

128. Treaties Made with the Arapahoes, Cheyennes, etc., Report Number 13, *AR CIA 1865*, 518–519.

129. See Berthrong, *The Southern Cheyennes*, 11.

130. Treaties Made with the Arapahoes, Cheyennes, etc., Report Number 14A, *AR CIA 1865*, 530–531.

131. Ibid., 528; Thomas W. Kavanagh, *The Comanches: A History, 1706–1875* (Lincoln: University of Nebraska Press, 1999), 402–403.

132. "The Diary of Samuel A. Kingman," 447.

CHAPTER SEVEN

1. *Indian Journal* (Muskogee and Eufaula, Indian Territory), May 1, 1878.

2. Interview of Scott Waldo McIntosh, 35:215–224, Indian-Pioneer History, Oklahoma City, Oklahoma (hereafter cited as IPH and OHS).

3. Agent Justin Harlan, Report Number 99, *The Annual Report of the Commissioner of Indian Affairs to the Department of the Interior for the Year 1865* (Washington, D.C.: Government Printing Office, 1865), 292 (hereafter cited as *AR CIA* and year).

4. Mary Jane Warde, "Now the Wolf Has Come: The Civilian Civil War in the Indian Territory," *Chronicles of Oklahoma* 71, no. 1 (Spring 1993): 83; Angie Debo, *The Road to Disappearance: A History of the Creek Indians* (Norman: University of Oklahoma Press, 1941), 71, 221; William G. McLoughlin, *After the Trail of Tears: The Cherokees' Struggle for Sovereignty, 1839–1880* (Chapel Hill: University of North Carolina Press, 1993), 223–224; *AR CIA 1865*, 38–39. This report estimates the total number of Muscogees at the end of the war at more than fourteen thousand, which does not seem accurate given the other census data and severe losses during the war.

5. Interview of Mrs. Tom Rattling Gourd, 52:216, IPH OHS.

6. Alice Robertson, "Incidents of the Civil War," Box 1, Alice Robertson

Papers, 82.86, OHS. Fort Gibson National Cemetery was established in 1868, when civilian and military remains from the military reservation were moved to the present location. Remains were also collected from Fort Arbuckle and known Civil War battlefields in the Indian Territory. Most of the remains were of Union dead. Information supplied by Director Bill Rhoades, Fort Gibson National Cemetery, September 13, 2011.

7. Interview of Willie Larney, 52:331, IPH Western History Collections, University of Oklahoma, Norman, Oklahoma (hereafter cited as WHC).

8. Interview of Joseph Bruner, 89:265–267, IPH OHS.

9. Interview of Mary E. Hudson James, 31:141–146, ibid.

10. Interview of Frank G. Audrain, 12:527–529, ibid.

11. Interview of Mary E. Hudson James, 31:143–144, ibid.

12. Interview of Frank G. Audrain, 12:527–529, ibid.

13. Velma Nieberding, "Indian Home, 90, Still Stands in Craig Co.," *Tulsa (Oklahoma) World*, Sunday supplement, July 8, 1956, p. 36; interview of Henry J. Walker, 94:348, Indian-Pioneer History, University of Oklahoma, Norman, Oklahoma (hereafter cited as WHC).

14. Georgianna Stidham Grayson, untitled manuscript, Mary Hansard Knight, Okmulgee, Oklahoma.

15. W. David Baird, ed., *A Creek Warrior for the Confederacy: The Autobiography of Chief G. W. Grayson* (Norman: University of Oklahoma Press, 1988), 121–122.

16. Agent J. W. Dunn, Report Number 101, September 20, 1865, *AR CIA 1865*.

17. Quoted in Myra Starr, "War and Schooling," unpublished manuscript, 2012.138 Friends of the Oklahoma Historical Society Archives Civil War Collection (hereafter cited as FOHSA CWC), OHS.

18. Ibid.

19. Alice Robertson, "Incidents of the Civil War," Box 1, Alice Robertson Papers, 82.86, OHS.

20. Starr, "War and Schooling."

21. Celia E. Naylor, *African Cherokees in the Indian Territory: From Chattel to Citizens* (Chapel Hill: University of North Carolina Press, 2008), 204.

22. Interview of Polly Colbert, 5, folder 2, box 25, Federal Writers Project Ex-Slave Narratives (hereafter cited as FWP EN), OHS.

23. Interview of Lucinda Davis, ibid.

24. T. Lindsay Baker and Julie P. Baker, *The WPA Oklahoma Slave Narratives* (Norman: University of Oklahoma Press, 1996), 314–316.

25. Interview of Morris Sheppard, 7, 9, folder 8, box 27, FWP EN OHS; Theda Perdue, *Slavery and the Evolution of Cherokee Society, 1540–1866* (Knoxville: University of Tennessee Press, 1979), 143.

26. [2] Baker and Baker, *The WPA Oklahoma Slave Narratives*, 356.

27. This belief was based on the year's grace given to freedmen and free blacks in the nation following ratification of the Muscogee Nation's Reconstruction Treaty.

28. Interview of Mary Grayson, *Slave Narratives from the Federal Writers Project, 1936–1938, Oklahoma* (Bedford, Mass.: Applewood Books and The Library of Congress, n.d.), 121–122.

29. Interview of Jim Tomm, 112: 277, IPH OHS.

30. Debo, *The Road to Disappearance*, 170–171.

31. Agent J. W. Dunn, Report Number 101, September 20, 1865, *AR CIA 1865*.

32. Dwight D. Hitchcock to "My dear friends," Dwight D. Hitchcock to William Schenk Robertson and Ann Eliza Worcester Robertson. 1860–1866, n.d., 18.1, Alice Robertson Collection, Special Collections, McFarlin Library, University of Tulsa, Tulsa, Oklahoma (hereafter citied as ARC TU).

33. *AR CIA* 1865, 37.

34. Ibid., 42.

35. Arrell Morgan Gibson, *Oklahoma: A History of Five Centuries* (1965; rpt., Norman: University of Oklahoma Press, 1981), 128–129.

36. Daniel F. Littlefield Jr., *The Chickasaw Freedmen: A People Without a Country* (Westport, Conn.: Greenwood Press, 1980), 40, 45.

37. Walt Willson, "Freedmen in Indian Territory During Reconstruction," *Chronicles of Oklahoma* 49 (Summer 1971): 240–243.

38. Edwin C. McReynolds, *The Seminoles* (Norman: University of Oklahoma Press, 1957), 275–276, 315–316; Willson, "Freedmen in Indian Territory," 234–235.

39. Baird, ed., *George Washington Grayson*, 120.

40. Debo, *The Road to Disappearance*, 167–170.

41. Ibid., 174; Willson, "Freedmen in Indian Territory," 233.

42. Statement of I. B. Luce, September 6, 1884, Grayson Family Collection, WHC; McReynolds, *The Seminoles*, 316–317.

43. McLoughlin, *After the Trail of Tears*, 219–221.

44. C. N. Vann to Dear Sir [John Ross], October 3, 1865, *The Papers of Chief John Ross*, Gary E. Moulton, ed., vol. 2 (Norman: University of Oklahoma Press, 1985), 650–651.

45. McLoughlin, *After the Trail of Tears*, 222–227. The Cherokee Strip was a section of land about 2.5 miles wide lying inside the southern Kansas border between the Neosho River and the 100th meridian. These 430,000 acres belonged by treaty to the Cherokee Nation and had wrongly been assigned to Kansas. Over time the public confused the Cherokee Strip with the much larger Cherokee Outlet lying immediately south of the Kansas border in today's Oklahoma.

46. Grace Steele Woodward, *The Cherokees* (Norman: University of Oklahoma Press, 1963), 311–312; Grace Nieberding, "Indian Home," *Tulsa (Oklahoma) World*, Sunday supplement, July 8, 1956, p. 36; interview of Henry J. Walker, 94:348, IPH WHC.

47. For a very good account of these times, see H. Craig Miner and William E. Unrau, *The End of Indian Kansas: A Study of Cultural Revolution, 1854–1871* (Lawrence: Regents Press of Kansas, 1978).

48. The Seneca band had emigrated from Sandusky, Ohio, while the Seneca-Shawnees were from Lewiston, Ohio. Frank H. Harris, "Neosho Agency 1838–1871," *Chronicles of Oklahoma* 43, no. 1 (Spring 1965): 35.

49. Miami, Oklahoma, Visitors Center, "Indian Tribes," http: www.visitmiamiok.com/native/ (accessed July 28, 2011); Harris, "Neosho Agency 1838–1871," 54–55.

50. Interview of Sarah Hollingsworth, 32:263–264, IPH OHS.

51. Miner and Unrau, *The End of Indian Kansas*, 67–68; Blue Clark, *Indian Tribes of Oklahoma: A Guide* (Norman: University of Oklahoma Press, 2009), 257–259.

52. Clark, *Indian Tribes of Oklahoma,* 274–275, 196–199; Glen Roberson, "The

Homeless Peorias," in *Oklahoma's Forgotten Indians*, ed. Robert E. Smith (Oklahoma City: Oklahoma Historical Society, 1981), 44–51.

53. Clifford E. Trafzer, "The Wyandots: From Quebec to Indian Territory," ibid., 108–118.

54. R. David Edmunds, "Potawatomi," *Encyclopedia of North American Indians: Native American History, Culture, and Life from Paleo-Indians to the Present*, ed. Frederick E. Hoxie (Boston: Houghton Mifflin Company, 1996), 506–508.

55. Donald J. Berthrong, "Sauk," *Encyclopedia of North American Indians*, 566–568; Clark, *Indian Tribes of Oklahoma*, 314–318.

56. Interview of William Foster, 25:502, IPH OHS.

57. Clark, *Indian Tribes of Oklahoma*, 162–163, 180–181.

58. Quoted in Miner and Unrau, *The End of Indian Kansas*, 133–134.

59. W. S. Nye, *Carbine and Lance: The Story of Old Fort Sill* (1937; rpt., Norman: University of Oklahoma Press, 1969), 40–46.

60. Cheyenne peace chief Gordon Yellowman, "*Hó'nehe, tsex ho'ëhne*, When the Wolf Came: The Cheyenne in the Post–Civil War Era," unpublished manuscript, 2012.138 FOHSA CWC OHS.

61. William Y. Chalfant, *Hancock's War: Conflict on the Southern Plains* (Norman: Arthur H. Clark Company, an imprint of the University of Oklahoma Press, 2010), 161.

62. Douglas C. Jones, *The Treaty of Medicine Lodge: The Story of the Great Treaty Council as Told by Eyewitnesses* (Norman: University of Oklahoma Press, 1966), 38–39; Louis F. Burns, *A History of the Osage People* (1989; rpt., Tuscaloosa: The University of Alabama Press, 2004), 276–277.

63. Jones, *Medicine Lodge*, 127.

64. Quoted in Gibson, *Oklahoma*, 144–145.

65. Ibid., 145–16.

66. Stan Hoig, *Tribal Wars of the Southern Plains* (Norman: University of Oklahoma Press, 1993), 233, 244–248, 252–253; Robert Leckie, *The Military Conquest of the Southern Plains* (Norman: University of Oklahoma Press, 1963), 81–83; Wilbur Sturtevant Nye, *Plains Indian Raiders: The Final Phases of Warfare from the Arkansas to the Red River* (Norman: University of Oklahoma Press, 1968), 123–134. Nye interviewed Indian veterans of the Plains Wars while stationed at Fort Sill, Oklahoma.

67. Hoig, *Tribal Wars*, 252–253.

68. Ibid., 252–257; Sammie Dennison Harmon and Louis F. Burns, "Hard Rope," unpublished manuscript, 2012.138 FOHSA CWC OHS; Nye, *Carbine and Lance*, 59–60; Jerome A. Greene, *Washita: The U.S. Army and the Southern Cheyennes, 1867–1869* (Norman: University of Oklahoma Press, 2004), 88, 95.

69. Theodore A. Ediger and Vinnie Hoffman, "Some Reminiscences of the Battle of the Washita," *Chronicles of Oklahoma* 33, no. 2 (1955): 137–138. Rations were part of the annuity goods promised in the Treaty of Medicine Lodge.

70. Ibid., 57; Nye, *Carbine and Lance*, 57–58.

71. Interview of Martha Koomsa (Perez), by Loretta Fowler and Jim Anquoe, Carnegie, Oklahoma, November 25, 2002, Cheyenne/Washita Project (hereafter cited as C/WP) OHS.

72. Quoted in Ediger and Hoffman, "Reminiscences," 138.

73. Harmon and Burns, "Hard Rope"; "Custer's Oklahoma Fight," unidentified newspaper clipping, 1904, "Battle of the Washita," Section X, OHS.

74. Report of Lt. Col. G. A. Custer to Maj. Gen. P. H. Sheridan, in the field on Washita River, November 28, 1868, *Senate Executive Document Number 18*, 40th Congress, 3rd Session, 27.

75. Ibid., 138–139.

76. Interview of Colleen Cometsevah, by Mary Jane Warde, Clinton, Oklahoma, August 20, 1999, C/WP, OHS.

77. Ediger and Hoffman, "Reminiscences," 139.

78. Interview of Colleen Cometsevah, by Mary Jane Warde, Clinton, Oklahoma, August 20, 1999, C/WP, OHS.

79. Interview of Martha Koomsa (Perez), by Loretta Fowler and Jim Anquoe, Carnegie, Oklahoma, November 25, 2002, C/WP, OHS; Greene, *Washita*, 131–132.

80. Interview of Colleen Cometsevah, by Mary Jane Warde, Clinton, Oklahoma, August 20, 1999, C/WP, OHS. Some accounts give "Little Chief" or "Little Rock" as the Cheyenne man and "Packer" as the boy's name.

81. Interview of Alfrich Heap of Birds, by Mary Jane Warde and Jim Anquoe, Thomas, Oklahoma, vicinity, July 23, 1999, C/WP, OHS.

82. "Custer's Washita Fight."

83. Ediger and Hoffman, "Reminiscences," 139.

84. Interview of Colleen Cometsevah, by Mary Jane Warde, Clinton, Oklahoma, August 20, 1999, C/WP, OHS.

85. Nye, *Carbine and Lance*, 67–68.

86. Interview of Carney Saupitty Sr. by Mary Jane Warde, Lawton, Oklahoma, March 12, 1999, C/WP, OHS.

87. Nye, *Carbine and Lance*, 69; Custer to Sheridan, November 28, 1868, 28; interview of Ben Clarke, Walter Camp Collection, University of Indiana, copy in Section X, OHS, 17.

88. Nye, *Carbine and Lance*, 69; Ediger and Hoffman, "Reminiscences," 139; Custer to Sheridan, November 18, 1868, 28–29. On December 10–11 General Sheridan led an expedition to the Washita River to examine the scene of the fight and retrieve the dead from Custer's command.

89. Ediger and Hoffman, "Reminiscences," 140.

90. Nye, *Carbine and Lance*, 71–72.

91. Interview of Alonzo Chalepah, by Loretta Fowler, Anadarko, Oklahoma, March 31, 2003, C/WP, OHS.

92. Nye, *Carbine and Lance*, 72–73.

93. Ibid., 100–107; Leckie, *The Military Conquest of the Southern Plains*, 114–118; Nye, *Plains Indian Raiders*, 141.

94. Richardson, *The Comanche Barrier*, 329–331, 338; Leckie, *The Military Conquest of the Southern Plains*, 136–137. Because of a survey error, there was confusion as to where the boundary between Texas and the Indian Territory lay in today's southwest Oklahoma. It was finally resolved in *United States v. Texas* in 1896 when Greer County, Texas, was ruled part of Oklahoma Territory.

95. Gibson, *Oklahoma*, 154–155. See Nye, *Carbine and Lance*, for the military perspective on this policy.

96. Leckie, *The Military Conquest of the Southern Plains*, 183. A recent study on

this topic is Brad D. Lookingbill, *War Dance at Fort Marion: Plains Indian War Prisoners* (Norman: University of Oklahoma Press, 2006). "The Red River War of 1874," *Texas Beyond History*, http://www.texasbeyondhistory.net/redriver/ind (accessed August 22, 2011).

97. Burns, *A History of the Osage People*, 321; Miner and Unrau, *The End of Indian Kansas*, 102, 138–139.

98. Mark Van de Logt, *War Party in Blue: Pawnee Scouts in the U.S. Army* (Norman: University of Oklahoma Press, 2010), 173–186.

99. Thomas Richter, "The Otoes' Removal to Indian Territory: Or, A Failure to End the 'Idle Pastimes of Their Indian Customs,'" in *Oklahoma's Forgotten Indians*, 68–85.

100. Interview of Rosa La Due Daily, 105:2–4, IPH OHS.

101. Interview of John Hudson, 85:248–249, ibid.

102. Patricia Scruggs Trolinger, "History of the Modoc Tribe of Oklahoma," unpublished manuscript, 2004, 1–5; National Park Service, "Lava Beds National Monument California," http://www.nps.gov/labe/index.htm (accessed August 24, 2010); Albert L. Hurtado, "The Modocs and the Jones Family Indian Ring: Quaker Administration of the Quapaw Agency, 1873–1879," *Oklahoma's Forgotten Indians*, 86–107.

103. Interview of Emily Ensworth, 23:448–455, IPH OHS.

104. Thomas Brown, "In Pursuit of Justice: The Ponca Indians in Indian Territory, 1877–1905," in *Oklahoma's Forgotten Indians*, 53–67.

105. Interview of Harry Buffalo Head, by Irving Peithman, White Eagle, Oklahoma, August 30, 1958, OHS.

106. Gibson, *Oklahoma*, 147–148.

107. Clark, *Indian Tribes of Oklahoma*, 229–232; Allen Slickpoo, "Nez Perce," *Encyclopedia of North American Indians*, 431–433.

108. Quoted in Miner and Unrau, *The End of Indian Kansas*, 136.

109. Annie Heloise Abel, *The American Indian in the Civil War, 1862–1865* (Lincoln: University of Nebraska Press, 1992, Bison Book edition), 204–205; Timothy James McCollum, "Delaware, Western," *Encyclopedia of Oklahoma History and Culture*, http://www.digital.library/okstate.edu/encyclopedia (accessed August 24, 2011); Clark, *Indian Tribes of Oklahoma*, 350–351.

110. Quoted in Gibson, *Oklahoma*, 145.

111. Mary Jane Warde, *George Washington Grayson and the Creek Nation, 1843–1920* (Norman: University of Oklahoma Press, 1999), 113–115.

112. Ibid., 115–117; "Journal of the General Council of the Indian Territory," *Chronicles of Oklahoma* 3 (April 1925): 32–44. Renamed the "international council," it met periodically through the 1890s in an attempt to maintain Indian independence, sovereignty, and lands.

113. Gibson, *Oklahoma*, 130–141, 157–172; Warde, *George Washington Grayson*, 140–147.

114. James W. Parins, *Elias Cornelius Boudinot: A Life on the Cherokee Border* (Lincoln: University of Nebraska Press, 2006), 85–108.

115. Quoted in McLoughlin, *After the Trail of Tears*, 267.

116. Choctaw governor Isaac L. Garvin, inaugural address, October 8, 1878, Records of the Principal Chiefs, Choctaw Nation Records, OHS, M235, reel 53.

117. G. W. Stidham, "What G. W. Stidham Thinks of Vest's Oklahoma Bill," *Indian Journal* (Eufaula and Muskogee, Creek Nation), January 8, 1880.

118. Testimony before the Senate Investigating Committee, Creek Nation Records, OHS, 35, 18E.

119. *Indian Journal* (Eufaula and Muskogee, Creek Nation), October 9, 1879.

120. *St. Louis Globe-Democrat*, August 8, 1880.

121. Warde, *George Washington Grayson*, 122–123; Parins, *Elias Cornelius Boudinot*, 192–193. Allen Wright suggested the name "Oklahoma" from the Choctaw for "land of the red man." Gibson, *Oklahoma*, 129.

122. Michael W. Lovegrove, "Payne, David Lewis (1836–1884)," *Encyclopedia of Oklahoma History and Culture*, OHS, http://www.digital.library.okstate.edu/encyclopedia/entries/p/pa028.html (accessed August 31, 2011).

123. "To the Delegates of the Several Tribes in Council Assembled," March 18, 1880, Creek Nation Records 37, 30817, OHS.

124. Chief We-qua-ho-ka to the Chief of the Creeks, May 4, 1881, ibid., 30822.

125. Warde, *George Washington Grayson*, 127–129.

126. Ibid., 182–185; John W. Morris, Charles R. Goins, and Edwin C. McReynolds, *Historical Atlas of Oklahoma*, 2nd ed. (Norman: University of Oklahoma Press, 1976), 47.

127. Burns, *A History of the Osage People*, 340–341.

128. Quoted in Debo, *The Road to Disappearance*, 320.

129. Ibid., 321–322.

130. Gibson, *Oklahoma*, 176–182.

131. Interview of Sam Hazous, by the Hazous family, 1956, Doris Duke Oral History Collection, WHC.

132. James Riding In, "Geronimo (Goyathlay)," *Encyclopedia of North American Indians*, 220–223; Gibson, *Oklahoma*, 156. For a biography of Geronimo, see Angie Debo, *Geronimo: The Man, His Time, His Place* (Norman: University of Oklahoma Press, 1976).

133. Debo, *The Road to Disappearance*, 172–175, 188–189, 375–376.

134. Quoted in Bert Hodges, "Notes on the History of the Creek Nation and Some of its Leaders," *Chronicles of Oklahoma* 43, no. 1 (Spring 1965): 15.

135. Gibson, *Oklahoma*, 196–197.

136. Baird, ed., *A Creek Warrior*, 163–164.

137. Interview of Mary Cobb Agnew, 66:16–22, IPH OHS.

138. Ibid.

139. Warde, *George Washington Grayson*, 178–189, 193–196. The classic study of this period and the debacle afterward is Angie Debo, *And Still the Waters Run: The Betrayal of the Five Civilized Tribes* (Princeton, N.J.: Princeton University Press, 1940).

140. Debo, *And Still the Waters Run*; Clark, *Indian Tribes of Oklahoma*, 240. An adult was considered competent if he or she had the education or experience to handle business affairs.

141. Interview of Moses Starr, by Loretta Fowler, Weatherford, Oklahoma, March 26, 2001, C/WP, OHS; Donald Berthrong, *The Cheyenne and Arapaho Ordeal: Reservation and Agency Life in the Indian Territory, 1875–1907* (Norman: University of Oklahoma Press, 1976), 212, 230, 249; Clark, *Indian Tribes of Oklahoma*, 285.

142. Citizens of the Five Civilized Tribes became U.S. citizens when their governments were ended in 1906.

143. Clyde Ellis, *A Dancing People: Powwow Culture on the Southern Plains* (Lawrence: University Press of Kansas, 2003), 18–21.

144. Michael Wallis, *The Real Wild West: The 101 Ranch and the Creation of the American West* (New York: St. Martin's Press, 1999), 140–143, 227–228, 248–250; interview of Chairman Daniel C. Jones, by Mary Jane Warde, White Eagle, Oklahoma, December 13, 2006, OHS; interview of Douglas G. Eagle, by Mary Jane Warde, White Eagle, Oklahoma, December 13, 2006, OHS.

145. Ellis, *A Dancing People*, 19, 26.

146. Ibid., 25, 156–157.

147. Interview of Grover Turtle, by Mary Jane Warde and Larry Roman Nose, Watonga, Oklahoma, August 24, 1999, C/WP, OHS.

148. Daniel C. Swan, "Native American Church," *The Encyclopedia of Oklahoma History and Culture,* OHS, http://www.digital.library/okstate.edu/encyclopedia (accessed September 9, 2011).

149. Naylor, *African Cherokees*, 192–199; Roberta Clardy, "Come Prepared or Not at All," unpublished manuscript, 2012.138 FOHSA CWC, OHS .

150. Clardy, "Come Prepared or Not at All."

151. Interview of Austin Harry, 28:178–184, IPH OHS.

BIBLIOGRAPHIC ESSAY

1. T. Lindsay Baker and Julie P. Baker, *The WPA Oklahoma Slave Narratives* (Norman: University of Oklahoma Press, 1996); *Slave Narratives from the Federal Writers Project, 1936–1938, Oklahoma* (Bedford, Mass.: Applewood Books and The Library of Congress, n.d.).

2. Col. D. N. McIntosh to Col. John Drew, September 11, 1861, box 43, volume 97, Grant Foreman Collection, Oklahoma Historical Society, Oklahoma City, Oklahoma (hereafter cited as OHS).

3. Samuel Bell Maxey to Matilda Maxey from Fort Towson, February 25, 1864, 3826.965, Samuel Bell Maxey Collection, Gilcrease Institute of American History and Art, Tulsa, Oklahoma.

4. Records of the Osage Agency are held in the National Archives at Fort Worth.

5. Volume 53, Creek Nation Records, OHS.

6. Folder 1 of 3, Claims, box 4-A, (Tahlequah) Civil War, 1861–January 27, 1888, Cherokee Nation Records, OHS.

7. Wiley Britton, *The Union Indian Brigade in the Civil War* (Kansas City, Mo.: Franklin Hudson Publishing Co., 1922); Jason Harris, "A Historiographical Review of the Literature of the Civil War in Indian Territory," *Chronicles of Oklahoma* 89 (Summer 2011): 224; Annie Heloise Abel, *The American Indian in the Civil War, 1862–1865* (Lincoln: University of Nebraska Press, Bison Book edition, 1992); Annie Heloise Abel, *The American Indian and the End of the Confederacy, 1863–1866* (Lincoln: University of Nebraska Press, Bison Book edition, 1993).

8. Colin G. Calloway, *New Worlds For All: Indians, Europeans, and the Remaking of Early America* (Baltimore: Johns Hopkins University Press, 1997);

Richard White, *The Middle Ground: Indians, Empires, and Republics in the Great Lakes Region, 1650–1815 (Cambridge: Cambridge University Press, 1991)*.

9. Elizabeth A. H. Johns, *Storms Brewed in Other Men's Worlds: The Confrontation of Indians, Spanish and French in the Southwest, 1540s–1795* (Norman: University of Oklahoma Press, 1996); Thomas W. Kavanagh, *The Comanches: A History, 1706–1875* (Lincoln: University of Nebraska Press, 1999); David La Vere, *Contrary Neighbors: Southern Plains and Removed Indians in Indian Territory* (Norman: University of Oklahoma Press, 2000).

10. Duane Champagne, *Social Order and Political Change: Constitutional Governments among the Cherokee, the Choctaw, the Chickasaw, and the Creek* (Stanford, Calif.: Stanford University Press, 1992); William G. McLoughlin, *After the Trail of Tears: The Cherokees' Struggle for Sovereignty, 1839–1880* (Chapel Hill: University of North Carolina Press, 1993).

11. Cecile Elkins Carter, *Caddo Indians: Where We Come From* (Norman: University of Oklahoma Press, 1995); Stan Hoig, *Tribal Warfare on the Southern Plains* (Norman: University of Oklahoma Press, 1993); Stan Hoig, *The Peace Chiefs of the Cheyennes* (Norman: University of Oklahoma Press, 1990); Louis F. Burns, *A History of the Osage People* (Tuscaloosa: The University of Alabama Press, 2004).

12. David Wallace Adams, *Education for Extinction: American Indians and the Boarding School Experience, 1875–1928* (Lawrence: University Press of Kansas, 1995); Daniel F. Littlefield Jr. and James W. Parins, *Native American Writing in the Southeast: An Anthology, 1865–1935* (Jackson: University Press of Mississippi, 1995); *The Encyclopedia of North American Indians: Native American History, Culture, and Life from Paleo-Indians to the Present*, ed. Frederick E. Hoxie (Boston: Houghton Mifflin, 1995); Blue Clark, *Indian Tribes of Oklahoma: A Guide* (Norman: University of Oklahoma Press, 2009).

13. Phillip W. Steele and Steve Cottrell, *Civil War in the Ozarks* (Gretna, [La.]: Pelican Publishing Company, 1994); Steve Cottrell, *Civil War in the Indian Territory* (Gretna, La.: Pelican Publishing Company, 1995); David Paul Smith, *Frontier Defense in the Civil War: Texas' Rangers and Rebels* (College Station: Texas A & M Press, 1992).

14. Lela J. McBride, *Opothleyaholo and the Loyal Muskogee: Their Flight to Kansas in the Civil War* (Jefferson, N.C.: McFarland & Company, 2000); Steven L. Warren, *Brilliant Victory: The Second Civil War Battle of Cabin Creek, Indian Territory, September 19, 1864* (Wyandotte, Okla.: Gregath Publishing Company, 2002); Whit Edwards, *The Prairie Was on Fire: Eyewitness Accounts of the Civil War in the Indian Territory* (Oklahoma City: Oklahoma Historical Society, 2001).

15. Amy H. Sturgis, *The Trail of Tears and Indian Removal* (Westport, Conn.: Greenwood Press, 2007); John L. Elder, *Everlasting Fire: Cawokoci's Legacy in the Seminole Struggle Against Western Expansion* (Edmond, Okla.: Medicine Wheel Press, 2004); Clarissa W. Confer, *The Cherokee Nation in the Civil War* (Norman: University of Oklahoma Press, 2007.

16. William Garrett Piston and Richard W. Hatcher III, *Wilson's Creek: The Second Battle of the Civil War and the Men Who Fought It* (Chapel Hill: University of North Carolina Press, 2000); William L. Shea, *Fields of Blood: The Prairie Grove Campaign* (Chapel Hill: University of North Carolina Press, 1992); William L. Shea and Earl J. Hess, *Pea Ridge: Civil War Campaign in the West* (Chapel Hill: University

of North Carolina Press, 1992); Anne J. Bailey, *Invisible Southerners: Ethnicity in the Civil War* (Athens: University of Georgia Press, 2006).

17. Theda Perdue, *Slavery and the Evolution of Cherokee Society, 1540–1866* (Knoxville: University of Tennessee Press, 1979); Daniel F. Littlefield Jr., *Africans and Creeks: From the Colonial Period to the Civil War* (Greenwood, Conn.: Greenwood Press, 1979); Daniel F. Littlefield Jr., *Africans and Seminoles: From Removal to Emancipation* (Westport, Conn.: Greenwood Press, 1977); Dudley Taylor Cornish, *Kansas Negro Regiments in the Civil War* (Topeka: State of Kansas Commission on Civil Rights, 1969); Dudley Taylor Cornish, *The Sable Arm: Black Troops in the Union Army, 1861–1865,* 2nd ed. (Lawrence: University Press of Kansas, 1987).

18. Gary Zellar, *African Creeks: Estelvste and the Creek Nation* (Norman: University of Oklahoma Press, 2007); Kevin Mulroy, *The Seminole Freedmen: A History* (Norman: University of Oklahoma Press, 2007); Celia E. Naylor's *African Cherokees in the Indian Territory: From Chattel to Citizens* (Chapel Hill: University of North Carolina Press, 2008).

19. Mark A. Lause, *Race and Radicalism in the Union Army* (Urbana: University of Chicago Press, 2009); Noah Andre Trudeau, *Like Men of War: Black Troops in the Civil War, 1862–1865* (Boston: Little, Brown and Company, 1998); Gregory J. W. Urwin, "We Cannot Treat Negroes . . . as Prisoners of War," in *Civil War Arkansas: Beyond Battles and Leaders,* ed. Anne J. Bailey and Daniel E. Sutherland (Fayetteville: University of Arkansas Press, 2000).

20. Walter Lee Brown, *A Life of Albert Pike* (Fayetteville: University of Arkansas Press, 1997); Thomas W. Cutrer, *Ben McCulloch and the Frontier Military Tradition* (Chapel Hill: University of North Carolina Press, 1993); David Remley, *Kit Carson: The Life of an American Border Man* (Norman: University of Oklahoma Press, 2011); Tom Dunlay, *Kit Carson and the Indians* (Lincoln: University of Nebraska Press, 2000).

21. Jerome A. Greene, *Washita: The U.S. Army and the Southern Cheyennes, 1867–1869* (Norman: University of Oklahoma Press, 2004); William Y. Chalfant, *Hancock's War: Conflict on the Southern Plains* (Norman: Arthur H. Clark Company, an imprint of the University of Oklahoma Press, 2010); Brad D. Lookingbill, *War Dance at Fort Marion: Plains Indian War Prisoners* (Norman: University of Oklahoma Press, 2006).

22. Thom Hatch, *Black Kettle: The Cheyenne Chief Who Sought Peace But Found War* (Hoboken, N.J.: John Wiley and Sons, 2004); David Fridtjof Halaas and Andrew E. Masich, *Halfbreed: The Remarkable True Story of George Bent—Caught Between the Worlds of the Indian and the White Man* (Cambridge, Mass.: DaCapo Press, 2004); Mark Van de Logt, *War Party in Blue: Pawnee Scouts in the U.S. Army* (Norman: University of Oklahoma Press, 2010).

23. James W. Parins, *Elias Cornelius Boudinot: A Life on the Cherokee Border* (Lincoln: University of Nebraska Press, 2006); Michael Wallis, *The Real Wild West: The 101 Ranch and the Creation of the American West* (New York: St. Martin's Press, 1999); Clyde Ellis, *A Dancing People: Powwow Culture on the Southern Plains* (Lawrence: University of Kansas Press, 2003).

BIBLIOGRAPHY

FEDERAL RECORDS

Annual Reports of the Commissioner of Indian Affairs. Washington, D.C.: Government Printing Office, 1851, 1858, 1862, 1863, 1864, 1865.

Kappler, Charles J., comp. *Indian Affairs: Laws and Treaties.* Washington, D.C.: Government Printing Office, 1904.

Office of Indian Affairs, Letters Received, M234, microfilm, Oklahoma Historical Society, Oklahoma City, Oklahoma.

Report of Lieutenant Colonel G. A. Custer to Major General P. H. Sheridan, in the field on Washita River, November 28, 1868, *Senate Executive Document Number 18*, 40th Congress, 3rd Session.

War of the Rebellion: A Compilation of the Official Records of the Union and Confederate Armies, The. Published under the Direction of the Secretary of War. Series 1, volume 8, part 1; series 1, volume 13, part 1; series 1, volume 22, part 1, 2; series 1, volume 34, part 1, 4; series 1, volume 41, part 1, 3; series 1, volume 42, part 2; series 1, volume 48, part 1, 2; series 4, volume 2, part 1. Washington, D.C.: Government Printing Office, 1880–1901.

ARCHIVES AND RECORDS

Gilcrease Institute of American History and Art, Tulsa, Oklahoma: Grant Foreman Collection, Samuel Bell Maxey Collection.

McFarlin Library, University of Tulsa, Tulsa, Oklahoma: Alice Robertson Collection (Special Collections).

Oklahoma Historical Society, Oklahoma City, Oklahoma: Alice Robertson Papers, Ann Augusta Robertson Moore Papers, Cherokee Nation Records, Choctaw Nation Records, Creek Nation Records, Dallas W. Bowman Collection, Ex-Slave Narrative Collection, Walter Camp Collection (University of Indiana, South Bend), Grant Foreman Collection, Indian Archives, Indian-Pioneer History, Joseph B. Thoburn Collection, Section X Vertical File.

Western History Collections, University of Oklahoma, Norman, Oklahoma: Cherokee Nation Papers (Phillips Collection), Doris Duke Oral History

Collection, Grayson Family Collection, Jay L. Hargett Collection, Indian-Pioneer History, Peter P. Pitchlynn Collection, Stephen Foreman Collection.

Books and Articles

Abel, Annie Heloise. *The American Indian in the Civil War, 1862–1865.* Lincoln: University of Nebraska Press, Bison Book edition, 1992.

———. *The American Indian and the End of the Confederacy, 1863–1866.* Lincoln: University of Nebraska Press, Bison Book edition, 1993.

———. *The American Indian as Slaveholder and Secessionist: An Omitted Chapter in the Diplomatic History of the Southern Confederacy.* Cleveland, Ohio: Arthur H. Clark Company, 1915; reprint edition, Lincoln: University of Nebraska Press, 1992.

Adams, David Wallace. *Education for Extinction: American Indians and the Boarding School Experience, 1875–1928.* Lawrence: University Press of Kansas, 1995.

Alford, Thomas Wildcat. *Civilization and the Story of the Absentee Shawnees.* As told to Florence Drake by Thomas Wildcat Alford. Norman: University of Oklahoma Press, 1936.

Ashcraft, Allan C. "Confederate Troop Conditions in 1864." *Chronicles of Oklahoma* 41, no. 4 (1963): 442–449.

Bailey, Anne J. *Invisible Southerners: Ethnicity in the Civil War.* Athens: University of Georgia Press, 2006.

Baird, W. David, ed. *A Creek Warrior for the Confederacy: The Autobiography of Chief G. W. Grayson.* Norman: University of Oklahoma Press, 1988.

———. *Peter Pitchlynn: Chief of the Choctaws.* Norman: University of Oklahoma Press, 1972.

Baker, T. Lindsay, and Julie P. Baker. *The WPA Oklahoma Slave Narratives.* Norman: University of Oklahoma Press, 1996.

Ballard, Louis W. "Cultural Differences: A Major Theme in Cultural Enrichment." *Indian Historian* 2 (Spring 1969): 4–7.

Barry, Louise, ed. "With the First U.S. Cavalry in Indian Country, 1859–1861—Concluded, Letters to the Daily Times, Leavenworth, III, The Letters, May 3, 1860–April 28, 1861." *Kansas Historical Quarterly* 24, no. 3 (Autumn 1958): 417.

Berthrong, Donald J. *The Cheyenne and Arapaho Ordeal: Reservation and Agency Life in the Indian Territory, 1875–1907.* Norman: University of Oklahoma Press, 1976.

———. "Sauk." *Encyclopedia of North American Indians: Native American History, Culture, and Life from Paleo-Indians to the Present.* Edited by Frederick E. Hoxie. Boston: Houghton Mifflin Company, 1996.

———. *The Southern Cheyenne.* Norman: University of Oklahoma Press, 1963.

Bohlender, Dean A. "The Battle of Poison Spring, Arkansas, April 18, 1864." *Civil*

War Battles in the West. Edited by LeRoy H. Fischer. Manhattan, Kan.: Sunflower Press, 1981.

Bonnifield, Paul. "The Choctaw Nation on the Eve of the Civil War." *The Civil War Era in Indian Territory.* Edited by LeRoy H. Fischer. Los Angeles: Lorrin L. Morrison, Publisher, 1974.

Britton, Wiley. *The Union Indian Brigade in the Civil War.* Kansas City, Mo.: Franklin Hudson Publishing Co., 1922.

Brown, Thomas. "In Pursuit of Justice: The Ponca Indians in Indian Territory, 1877–1905." *Oklahoma's Forgotten Indians.* Edited by Robert E. Smith. Oklahoma City: Oklahoma Historical Society, 1981.

Brown, Walter Lee. *A Life of Albert Pike.* Fayetteville: University of Arkansas Press, 1997.

Burns, Louis F. *A History of the Osage People.* Tuscaloosa: The University of Alabama Press, 2004.

Calloway, Colin G. *New Worlds For All: Indians, Europeans, and the Remaking of Early America.* Baltimore: Johns Hopkins University Press, 1997.

Carter, Cecile Elkins. *Caddo Indians: Where We Come From.* Norman: University of Oklahoma Press, 1995.

Chalfant, William Y. *Hancock's War: Conflict on the Southern Plains.* Norman: Arthur H. Clark Company, an imprint of the University of Oklahoma Press, 2010.

Champagne, Duane. *Social Order and Political Change: Constitutional Governments among the Cherokee, the Choctaw, the Chickasaw, and the Creek.* Stanford, Calif.: Stanford University Press, 1992.

Cheatham, Gary L. "'If the Union Wins, We Won't Have Anything Left': The Rise and Fall of the Southern Cherokees in Kansas." *Kansas History* 30 (Autumn 2007): 154–178.

Clampitt, Brad R. "'An Indian Shall Not Spill an Indian's Blood': The Confederate-Indian Conference at Camp Napoleon, 1865." *Chronicles of Oklahoma* 83, no. 1 (Spring 2005): 33–54.

Clark, Blue. *Indian Tribes of Oklahoma: A Guide.* Norman: University of Oklahoma Press, 2009.

Clifford, Roy A. "The Indian Regiments in the Battle of Pea Ridge." *Chronicles of Oklahoma* 25 (Winter 1947–1948): 314–322.

Colton, Ray C. *The Civil War in the Western Territories: Arizona, Colorado, New Mexico, and Utah.* Norman: University of Oklahoma Press, 1959.

Confer, Clarissa W. *The Cherokee Nation in the Civil War.* Norman: University of Oklahoma Press, 2007.

Conley, Robert J. *The Cherokee Nation: A History.* Albuquerque: University of New Mexico Press, 2005.

Cornish, Dudley Taylor. *Kansas Negro Regiments in the Civil War.* Topeka: State of Kansas Commission on Civil Rights, 1969.

———. *The Sable Arm: Black Troops in the Union Army, 1861–1865.* Lawrence: University Press of Kansas, 1987, second edition.

Cottrell, Steve. *Civil War in the Indian Territory.* Gretna, La.: Pelican Publishing Company, 1995.

Culberson, James. "Two Thousand Choctaws Died During Their Removal." *American Indian* 3, no. 3 (December 1928): 11.

Cutrer, Thomas W. *Ben McCulloch and the Frontier Military Tradition.* Chapel Hill: University of North Carolina Press, 1993.

Dale, Edward Everett, and Gaston Litton. *Cherokee Cavaliers: Forty Years of Cherokee History as Told in the Correspondence of the Ridge-Watie-Boudinot Family.* Norman: University of Oklahoma Press, 1939, paperback edition, 1995.

Daniell, Lewis E. "W. K. Makemson," *Personnel of the Texas State Government, with Sketches of Distinguished Texans, Embracing the Executive and Staff, Heads of the Departments, United States Senators and Representatives, Members of the Twenty-first Legislature.* Austin, Tex.: Smith, Hicks, and Jones, State Printers, 1889.

Debo, Angie. *And Still the Waters Run: The Betrayal of the Five Civilized Tribes.* Princeton, N.J.: Princeton University Press, 1940.

———. *Geronimo: The Man, His Time, His Place.* Norman: University of Oklahoma Press, 1976.

———. *The Rise and Fall of the Choctaw Republic.* Norman: University of Oklahoma Press, 1934, second edition, 1961.

———. *The Road to Disappearance: A History of the Creek Indians.* Norman: University of Oklahoma Press, 1941.

"Diary of Samuel A. Kingman at Indian Treaty in 1865, The." *Kansas Historical Quarterly* 1, no. 5 (November 1932): 442–450.

Dunlay, Tom. *Kit Carson and the Indians.* Lincoln: University of Nebraska Press, 2000.

Ediger, Theodore A., and Vinnie Hoffman. "Some Reminiscences of the Battle of the Washita." *Chronicles of Oklahoma* 33, no. 2 (1955): 137–141.

Edmunds, R. David. *The Shawnee Prophet.* Lincoln: University of Nebraska Press, 1983.

———. "Potawatomi." *Encyclopedia of North American Indians: Native American History, Culture, and Life from Paleo-Indians to the Present.* Edited by Frederick E. Hoxie. Boston: Houghton Mifflin Company, 1996.

Edwards, Whit. *The Prairie Was on Fire: Eyewitness Accounts of the Civil War in the Indian Territory.* Oklahoma City: Oklahoma Historical Society, 2001.

Elder, John L. *Everlasting Fire: Cowakoci's Legacy in the Seminole Struggle Against Western Expansion.* Edmond, Okla.: Medicine Wheel Press, 2004.

Ellis, Clyde. *A Dancing People: Powwow Culture on the Southern Plains.* Lawrence: University of Kansas Press, 2003.

Faulk, Odie B., Kenny A. Franks, and Paul F. Lambert, eds. *Early Military Forts and Posts in Oklahoma.* Oklahoma City: Oklahoma Historical Society, 1978.

Felmly, Bradford K., and John C. Grady. *Suffering to Silence: 29th Texas Cavalry, C.S.A., Regimental History.* Quanah, Tex.: Nortex Press, 1975.

Fischer, LeRoy H. *The Battle of Honey Springs, 1863–1988.* Oklahoma Historical Society, Official Program, Re-enactment, July 16–17, 1988.

Fischer, LeRoy H., and Lary C. Rampp. "Quantrill's Civil War Operations in Indian Territory." *Chronicles of Oklahoma* 46 (Summer 1968): 155–181.

Foreman, Carolyn T. "The Coodey Family of Indian Territory." *Chronicles of Oklahoma* 25 (Winter 1947–1948): 323–341.

———. *Oklahoma Imprints, 1835–1907: A History of Printing in Oklahoma Before Statehood.* Norman: University of Oklahoma Press, 1936.

Foreman, Grant. *Down the Texas Road: Historic Places along Highway 69 through Oklahoma.* Norman: University of Oklahoma Press, 1936.

———. *The Five Civilized Tribes: Cherokee, Chickasaw, Choctaw, Creek, Seminole.* Norman: University of Oklahoma Press, 1934.

———. "Fort Davis." *Chronicles of Oklahoma* 17, no. 2 (June 1939): 147–150.

———. "Reminiscences of Mr. R. P. Vann." *Chronicles of Oklahoma* 11 (June 1933): 833–844.

Foreman, Minta Ross. "Reverend Stephen Foreman, Cherokee Missionary." *Chronicles of Oklahoma* 18, no. 3 (September 1940): 229–244.

Frank, Andrew K. *Creeks & Southerners: Biculturalism on the Early American Frontier.* Lincoln: University of Nebraska Press, 2005.

Franks, Kenny A. *Stand Watie and the Agony of the Cherokee Nation.* Memphis: Memphis State University Press, 1979.

Franzman, Tom. "The Battle of Devil's Backbone Mountain." *Chronicles of Oklahoma* 62 (Winter 1984–1985): 420–428.

Gaines, W. Craig. *The Confederate Cherokees: John Drew's Regiment of Mounted Rifles.* Baton Rouge: Louisiana State University Press, 1989.

Gibson, Arrell M. *The Chickasaws.* Norman: University of Oklahoma Press, 1971.

———. *Kickapoos: Lords of the Middle Border, The.* Norman: University of Oklahoma Press, 1963.

———. *Oklahoma: A History of Five Centuries.* Norman: University of Oklahoma Press, 1965, 1981 edition.

Good, Mary Elizabeth. *Historical Review: Bird Creek Basin from 1800.* N.p.: Corps of Engineers, Tulsa District, 1979.

Grayson, Mrs. G. W. "Prominent Indian Confederates." *Indian Journal* (Eufaula, Oklahoma), May 9, 1914.

Greene, Jerome A. *Washita: The U.S. Army and the Southern Cheyennes, 1867–1869.* Norman: University of Oklahoma Press, 2004.

Halaas, David Fridtjof, and Andrew E. Masich. *Halfbreed: The Remarkable True Story of George Bent—Caught Between the Worlds of the Indian and the White Man.* Cambridge, Mass.: DaCapo Press, 2004.

Hale, Douglas. *The Third Texas Cavalry in the Civil War.* Norman: University of Oklahoma Press, 1993.

Hancock, Marvin J. "The Second Battle of Cabin Creek, 1864." *Chronicles of Oklahoma* 39 (Winter 1961–1962): 414–426.

Harris, Frank H. "Neosho Agency 1838–1871." *Chronicles of Oklahoma* 43, no. 1 (Spring 1965): 35–57.

Harris, Jason. "A Historiographical Review of the Literature of the Civil War in Indian Territory." *Chronicles of Oklahoma* 89 (Summer 2011): 222–235.

Hatch, Thom. *Black Kettle: The Cheyenne Chief Who Sought Peace But Found War.* Hoboken, N.J.: John Wiley and Sons, 2004.

Hauptman, Laurence M. *Between Two Fires: American Indians in the Civil War.* New York: Free Press, 1995.

Hershberger, Mary. "Mobilizing Women, Anticipating Abolition: The Struggle Against Indian Removal in the 1830s." *Journal of American History* 86 (June 1999): 15–40.

Hodges, Bert. "Notes on the History of the Creek Nation and Some of its Leaders." *Chronicles of Oklahoma* 43, no. 1 (Spring 1965): 9–18.

Hoig, Stan. *The Peace Chiefs of the Cheyennes.* Norman: University of Oklahoma Press, 1980, paperback edition, 1990.

———. *Tribal Wars of the Southern Plains.* Norman: University of Oklahoma Press, 1993.

Hood, Fred. "Twilight of the Confederacy in Indian Territory." *Chronicles of Oklahoma* 41 (Winter 1963–1964): 425–441.

Hudson, Charles. *The Southeastern Indians.* Knoxville: University of Tennessee Press, 1976.

Hume, C. Ross. "Historic Sites around Anadarko." *Chronicles of Oklahoma* 16 (December 1938): 410–424.

Hunt, George. "Millie Durgan." *Chronicles of Oklahoma* 15, no. 4 (December 1937): 480–482.

Hurtado, Albert L. "The Modocs and the Jones Family Indian Ring: Quaker Administration of the Quapaw Agency, 1873–1879." *Oklahoma's Forgotten Indians.* Edited by Robert E. Smith. Oklahoma City: Oklahoma Historical Society, 1981.

John, Elizabeth A. H. "Portrait of a Wichita Village, 1808." *Chronicles of Oklahoma* 60 (Winter 1982–83): 412–437.

———. *Storms Brewed in Other Men's Worlds: The Confrontation of Indians, Spanish, and French in the Southwest, 1540–1795.* Norman: University of Oklahoma Press, 1996, paperback edition.

Jones, Douglas C. *The Treaty of Medicine Lodge: The Story of the Great Treaty Council as Told by Eyewitnesses.* Norman: University of Oklahoma Press, 1966.

Josephy, Alvin M., Jr. *The Civil War in the American West.* New York: Alfred A. Knopf, 1991.

"Journal of the General Council of the Indian Territory." *Chronicles of Oklahoma* 3 (April 1925): 32–44.

Kavanagh, Thomas W. *The Comanches: A History, 1706–1875*. Lincoln: University of Nebraska Press, 1999.

Kerby, Robert L. *Kirby Smith's Confederacy: The Trans-Mississippi South, 1863–1865*. New York: Columbia University Press, 1972.

King, Jerlena. "Jackson Lewis of the Confederate Creek Regiment." *Chronicles of Oklahoma* 41, no. 1 (1963): 66–69.

Knight, Wilfred. *Red Fox: Stand Watie and the Confederate Indian Nations during the Civil War Years in Indian Territory*. Glendale, Calif.: Arthur H. Clark Company, 1988.

Lancaster, Jane F. *Removal Aftershock: The Seminoles' Struggle to Survive in the West, 1836–1886*. Knoxville: University of Tennessee Press, 1994.

Lause, Mark A. *Race and Radicalism in the Union Army*. Urbana: University of Chicago Press, 2009.

La Vere, David. *Contrary Neighbors: Southern Plains and Removed Indians in Indian Territory*. Norman: University of Oklahoma Press, 2000.

———. *Life Among the Texas Indians: The WPA Narratives*. College Station: Texas A & M University Press, 1998.

Leckie, William H. *The Military Conquest of the Southern Plains*. Norman: University of Oklahoma Press, 1963.

Littlefield, Daniel F., Jr. *Africans and Creeks: From the Colonial Period to the Civil War*. Greenwood, Conn.: Greenwood Press, 1979.

———. *Africans and Seminoles: From Removal to Emancipation*. Jackson: University Press of Mississippi, 2001.

———. *Chickasaw Freedmen: A People Without a Country, The*. Westport, Conn.: Greenwood Press, 1980.

Littlefield, Daniel F., and James W. Parins. *Native American Writing in the Southeast: An Anthology, 1875–1935*. Jackson: University Press of Mississippi, 1995.

Lookingbill, Brad D. *War Dance at Fort Marion: Plains Indian War Prisoners*. Norman: University of Oklahoma Press, 2006.

Loughlin, Patricia. *Hidden Treasures of the American West: Muriel H. Wright, Angie Debo, and Alice Marriott*. Albuquerque: University of New Mexico Press, 2005.

Mathews, John Joseph. *The Osages: Children of the Middle Waters*. Norman: University of Oklahoma Press, 1961.

Mayhall, Mildred P. *The Kiowas*. Norman: University of Oklahoma Press, 1962.

McBride, Lela J. *Opothleyaholo and the Loyal Muskogee: Their Flight to Kansas in the Civil War*. Jefferson, N.C.: McFarland & Company, Publishers, 2000.

McLoughlin, William G. *After the Trail of Tears: The Cherokees' Struggle for Sovereignty, 1839–1880*. Chapel Hill: University of North Carolina Press, 1993.

McPherson, James M. *Battle Cry of Freedom: The Civil War Era*. New York: Oxford University Press, 1988.

McReynolds, Edwin. C. *The Seminoles*. Norman: University of Oklahoma Press, 1957.

Miner, Craig. *Kansas: The History of the Sunflower State, 1854–2000*. Lawrence: University Press of Kansas, 2002.

Miner, H. Craig, and William E. Unrau. *The End of Indian Kansas: A Study of Cultural Revolution, 1854–1871*. Lawrence: Regents Press of Kansas, 1978.

Morris, John W., Charles R. Goins, and Edwin C. McReynolds. *Historical Atlas of Oklahoma*. Norman: University of Oklahoma Press, 1976, second edition.

Moulton, Gary E. *John Ross, Cherokee Chief*. Athens: University of Georgia Press, 1978.

Mulroy, Kevin. *The Seminole Freedmen: A History*. Norman: University of Oklahoma Press, 2007.

Naylor, Celia E. *African Cherokees in Indian Territory: From Chattel to Citizens*. Chapel Hill: University of North Carolina Press, 2008.

Nieberding, Velma. "Indian Home, 90, Still Stands in Craig Co." *Tulsa (Oklahoma) World*, Sunday supplement, July 8, 1956, p. 36.

Nye, W[ilbur]. S[turtevant]. *Carbine and Lance: The Story of Old Fort Sill*. Norman: University of Oklahoma Press, 1937, 1969 edition.

————. *Plains Indian Raiders: The Final Phases of Warfare from the Arkansas to the Red River*. Norman: University of Oklahoma Press, 1968.

Oates, Stephen B. *Confederate Cavalry West of the River*. Austin: University of Texas Press, 1961.

O'Beirne, H. R., and H. F. O'Beirne. *Leaders and Leading Men of the Indian Territory, with Interesting Biographical Sketches, 1, Choctaws and Chickasaws*. Chicago: American Publishers' Association, 1891.

Papers of Chief John Ross, The. Edited by Gary E. Moulton. 2 vols. Norman: University of Oklahoma Press, 1985.

Parins, James W. *Elias Cornelius Boudinot: A Life on the Cherokee Border*. Lincoln: University of Nebraska Press, 2006.

Perdue, Theda. *Slavery and the Evolution of Cherokee Society, 1540–1866*. Knoxville: University of Tennessee Press, 1979.

Piston, William Garrett, and Richard W. Hatcher III. *Wilson's Creek: The Second Battle of the Civil War and the Men Who Fought It*. Chapel Hill: University of North Carolina Press, 2000.

Rampp, Lary C. "Negro Troop Activity in Indian Territory." *Chronicles of Oklahoma* 47, no. 1 (Spring 1969): 531–559.

Rampp, Lary C., and Donald L. Rampp. *The Civil War in the Indian Territory*. Austin, Tex.: Presidial Press, 1975.

Ream, Robert L. "A Nearly Forgotten Fragment of Local History." *Chronicles of Oklahoma* 4, no. 1 (March 1926): 34–44.

Remley, David. *Kit Carson: The Life of an American Border Man*. Norman: University of Oklahoma Press, 2011.

Richardson, Rupert Norval. *The Comanche Barrier to South Plains Settlement: A Century and a Half of Savage Resistance to the Advancing Frontier.* Glendale, Calif.: Arthur H. Clark Company, 1933.

Richter, Thomas. "The Otoes' Removal to Indian Territory: Or, A Failure to End the 'Idle Pastimes of Their Indian Customs.'" *Oklahoma's Forgotten Indians.* Edited by Robert E. Smith. Oklahoma City: Oklahoma Historical Society, 1981.

Riding In, James. "Geronimo (Goyathlay)." *Encyclopedia of North American Indians: Native American History, Culture, and Life from Paleo-Indians to the Present.* Edited by Frederick E. Hoxie. Boston: Houghton Mifflin Company, 1996.

Roberson, Glen. "The Homeless Peorias." *Oklahoma's Forgotten Indians.* Edited by Robert E. Smith. Oklahoma City: Oklahoma Historical Society, 1981.

Rohrs, Richard C. "Fort Gibson: Forgotten Glory." *Early Military Forts and Posts in Oklahoma.* Edited by Odie B. Faulk, Kenny A. Franks, and Paul F. Lambert, Volume 9, The Oklahoma Series. Oklahoma City: Oklahoma Historical Society, 1978.

Satz, Ronald N. *Tennessee's Indian Peoples: From White Contact to Removal, 1540–1840.* Knoxville: University of Tennessee Press and the Tennessee Historical Commission, 1979, paperback edition.

Schilz, Thomas Frank. "People of the Cross Timbers: A History of the Tonkawa Indians." Unpublished dissertation, Texas Christian University, 1983.

Shea, William L. *Fields of Blood: The Prairie Grove Campaign.* Chapel Hill: University of North Carolina Press, 1992.

Shea, William L., and Earl J. Hess. *Pea Ridge: Civil War Campaign in the West.* Chapel Hill: University of North Carolina Press, 1992.

Slickpoo, Allen. "Nez Perce." *Encyclopedia of North American Indians: Native American History, Culture, and Life from Paleo-Indians to the Present.* Edited by Frederick E. Hoxie. Boston: Houghton Mifflin Company, 1996.

Slover, James Anderson. *Minister to the Cherokees: A Civil War Autobiography.* Edited by Barbara Cloud. Lincoln: University of Nebraska Press, 2001.

Smallwood, James. "Major Stephen Harriman Long, 1820." *Frontier Adventurers: American Exploration in Oklahoma.* Edited by Joseph A. Stout Jr. Oklahoma City: Oklahoma Historical Society, 1976.

Smith, David Paul. *Frontier Defense in the Civil War: Texas' Rangers and Rebels.* College Station: Texas A & M Press, 1992.

Stidham, G. W. "What G. W. Stidham Thinks of Vest's Oklahoma Bill." *Indian Journal* (Eufaula and Muskogee, Creek Nation), January 8, 1880.

Steele, Phillip W., and Steve Cottrell. *Civil War in the Ozarks.* Gretna, [La.]: Pelican Publishing Company, 1994.

Sturgis, Amy H. *The Trail of Tears and Indian Removal.* Westport, Conn.: Greenwood Press, 2007.

Sutherland, Daniel E. "Guerrillas: The Real War in Arkansas." *Civil War Arkansas: Beyond Battles and Leaders.* Edited by Anne J. Bailey and Daniel E. Sutherland. Fayetteville: University of Arkansas Press, 2000.

Szasz, Margaret Connell. "Education." *Encyclopedia of North American Indians.* Edited by Frederick E. Hoxie. Boston: Houghton Mifflin Company, 1996.

Tennant, H. S. "Two Cattle Trails." *Chronicles of Oklahoma* 14, no. 1 (March 1936): 84–121.

To Keep the Drum; To Tend the Fire. Oklahoma City: Mvskoke Publishing Company, 1978, second printing, 1996.

Trafzer, Clifford E. "The Wyandots: From Quebec to Indian Territory." *Oklahoma's Forgotten Indians.* Edited by Robert E. Smith. Oklahoma City: Oklahoma Historical Society, 1981.

Trenholm, Virginia Cole. *The Arapahoes, Our People.* Norman: University of Oklahoma Press, 1970.

Trudeau, Noah Andre. *Like Men of War: Black Troops in the Civil War, 1862–1865.* Boston: Little, Brown and Company, 1998.

Urwin, Gregory J. W. "'We Cannot Treat Negroes . . . as Prisoners of War': Racial Atrocities and Reprisals in Civil War Arkansas." *Civil War Arkansas: Beyond Battles and Leaders.* Edited by Anne J. Bailey and Daniel E. Sutherland. Fayetteville: University of Arkansas Press, 2000.

Utley, Robert M. *The Indian Frontier of the American West 1846–1890.* Albuquerque: University of New Mexico Press, 1984.

Van de Logt, Mark. *War Party in Blue: Pawnee Scouts in the U.S. Army.* Norman: University of Oklahoma Press, 2010.

Wallace, Ernest, and E. Adamson Hoebel. *The Comanches: Lords of the South Plains* Norman: University of Oklahoma Press, 1952.

Wallis, Michael. *The Real Wild West: The 101 Ranch and the Creation of the American West.* New York: St. Martin's Press, 1999.

Warde, Mary Jane. *George Washington Grayson and the Creek Nation, 1843–1920.* Norman: University of Oklahoma Press, 1999.

———. "Now the Wolf Has Come: The Civilian Civil War in the Indian Territory." *Chronicles of Oklahoma* 71, no. 1 (Spring 1993): 64–87.

———. *Washita.* Oklahoma City: Oklahoma Historical Society and Washita Battlefield National Historic Site, National Park Service, 2003, 2005 edition.

Wardell, Morris L. *A Political History of the Cherokee Nation.* Norman: University of Oklahoma Press, 1938.

Warren, Steven L. *Brilliant Victory: The Second Civil War Battle of Cabin Creek, Indian Territory, September 19, 1864.* Wyandotte, Okla.: Gregath Publishing Company, 2002.

Waugh, John C. *Sam Bell Maxey and the Confederate Indians.* Fort Worth: Ryan Place Publishers, 1995.

Wilson, Keith P. *Campfires of Freedom: The Camp Life of Black Soldiers During the Civil War.* Kent, Ohio: Kent State University Press, 2002.

Willson, Walt. "Freedmen in Indian Territory During Reconstruction." *Chronicles of Oklahoma* 49 (Summer 1971): 230–244.

Woodward, Grace Steele. *The Cherokees*. Norman: University of Oklahoma Press, 1963.

Wright, J. Leitch, Jr. *Creeks and Seminoles: The Destruction and Regeneration of the Muscogulge People*. Lincoln: University of Nebraska Press, 1986.

Wright, Muriel H. "History of Fort Cobb, A." *Chronicles of Oklahoma* 34 (Spring 1956): 53–71.

———. "Lieutenant Averell's Ride at the Outbreak of the Civil War." *Chronicles of Oklahoma* 39 (Spring 1961): 2–14.

———. "Notes on the Life of Mrs. Hannah Worcester Hicks Hitchcock and the Park Hill Press." *Chronicles of Oklahoma* 19, no. 4 (December 1941): 348–355.

Wright, Muriel H., and LeRoy H. Fischer. "Civil War Sites in Oklahoma." *Chronicles of Oklahoma* 44 (Summer 1966): 158–215.

Yeary, Mamie, comp. *Reminiscences of the Boys in Gray, 1861–1865*. Dallas: Smith & Lamar, 1912.

Zellar, Gary. *African Creeks: Estelvste and the Creek Nation*. Norman: University of Oklahoma Press, 2007.

Unpublished Materials

"Custer's Oklahoma Fight," unidentified newspaper clipping, 1904, "Battle of the Washita," Section X, Oklahoma Historical Society, Oklahoma City.

Friends of the Oklahoma Historical Society Archives Civil War Collection, 2012.138, Oklahoma Historical Society. Clark, Blue. "Edwards Trading Post." Clark, Blue. "North Fork Town." Clardy, Roberta. "Come Prepared or Not At All." Corbett, Bill. "The Texas Road and the Civil War." Ellis, Clyde. "The 1864 Battle of Adobe Walls." Harmon, Sammie Dennison, and Louis F. Burns. "Hard Rope." Loughlin, Patricia. "The Battle of Historians of Round Mountain." McCormick, Mary F. "John Chupco: A Family Story." Michener, Judith L. "Uncle Wallace and Aunt Minerva Willis." Rea, Bob. "George Bent in the Civil War: Cheyenne Confederate Warrior." Starr, Myra. "War and Schooling." Turner, Al. "Texas and the Civil War." Yellowman, Cheyenne Peace Chief Gordon. "*Hó'nehe, tsex ho'ëhne*, When the Wolf Came: The Cheyenne in the Post–Civil War Era." Welge, William D. "Dallas W. Bowman Lied about His Age." Welge, William D. "Douglas H. Cooper."

Grayson, Georgianna Stidham. Untitled manuscript. Mary Hansard Knight, Okmulgee, Oklahoma.

Jones, Robert Steven. "General James G. Blunt and the Civil War in the Trans-Mississippi West." Master's thesis. Oklahoma State University, Stillwater, 1990.

Schilz, Thomas Frank. "People of the Cross Timbers: A History of the Tonkawa Indians." Dissertation. Texas Christian University, Fort Worth, Texas, 1983.

Trolinger, Patricia Scruggs. "History of the Modoc Tribe of Oklahoma." 2004.

NEWSPAPERS

Indian Journal. Eufaula and Muskogee, Indian Territory. 1878, 1879.

St. Louis Globe-Democrat. St. Louis, Missouri. 1880.

INTERVIEWS

Buffalo Head, Harry. Interview by Irving Peithman, White Eagle, Oklahoma, August 30, 1958, Oklahoma Historical Society, Oklahoma City.

Bull Coming, Kathryn. Interview by Mary Jane Warde, Seiling, Oklahoma vicinity, March 26, 1999. Cheyenne/Washita Project, Oklahoma Historical Society, Oklahoma City.

Burns, Louis F. Interview by Sammie Dennison Harmon and Mary Jane Warde, Pawhuska, Oklahoma, March 31, 2011, Oklahoma Historical Society, Oklahoma City.

Chalepah, Alonzo. Interview by Loretta Fowler, Anadarko, Oklahoma, March 31, 2003. Cheyenne/Washita Project, Oklahoma Historical Society, Oklahoma City.

Cometsevah, Colleen. Interview by Mary Jane Warde, Clinton, Oklahoma, August 20, 1999. Cheyenne/Washita Project, Oklahoma Historical Society, Oklahoma City.

Eagle, Douglas G., Sr. Interview by Mary Jane Warde, White Eagle, Oklahoma, December 13, 2006. Oklahoma Historical Society, Oklahoma City.

Hazous, Sam. Interview by the Hazous family, 1956. Doris Duke Oral History Collection. Western History Collections, University of Oklahoma, Norman.

Heap of Birds, Alfrich. Interview by Mary Jane Warde and Jim Anquoe, Thomas, Oklahoma, vicinity, July 23, 1999. Cheyenne/Washita Project, Oklahoma Historical Society, Oklahoma City.

Jones, Chairman Daniel C. Interview by Mary Jane Warde, White Eagle, Oklahoma, December 13, 2006. Oklahoma Historical Society, Oklahoma City.

Koomsa (Perez), Martha. Interview by Loretta Fowler and Jim Anquoe, Carnegie, Oklahoma, November 25, 2002. Cheyenne/Washita Project, Oklahoma Historical Society, Oklahoma City.

Rhoades, Bill. Interview by Mary Jane Warde, Fort Gibson National Cemetery, September 13, 2011.

Saupitty, Carney, Sr. Interview by Mary Jane Warde, Lawton, Oklahoma, March 12, 1999. Cheyenne/Washita Project, Oklahoma Historical Society, Oklahoma City.

Starr, Moses. Interview by Loretta Fowler, Weatherford, Oklahoma, March 26, 2001. Cheyenne/Washita Project, Oklahoma Historical Society, Oklahoma City.

Turtle, Grover. Interview by Mary Jane Warde and Larry Roman Nose, Watonga, Oklahoma, August 24, 1999. Cheyenne/Washita Project, Oklahoma Historical Society, Oklahoma City.

WEBSITES

"A Place to Call Home." *Texas Beyond History.* http://www.texasbeyondhistory.net/tehas/voices/place.html (accessed April 25, 2011).

Case, Nelson, ed. *History of Labette County, Kansas and Its Representative Citizens.* Chicago: Biographical Publishing Co., 1901, http://skyways.lib.ks.us/genweb/archives/labette/1901/20–26.shtml (accessed January 16, 2013).

Elswick, M. S. Colorado State Archives. "Colorado Volunteers, 1861–1865." http://www.colorado.gov/dpa/doit/archives/civwar/civilwar.html (accessed June 25, 2011).

"First Battle of Newtonia." Missouri Civil War Sesquicentennial. http://mocivilwar 150.com/history/battle/174 (accessed July 12, 2012).

"1st Kansas Volunteer Colored Infantry," Museum of the Kansas National Guard: Historic Units. http://www.kansasguardmuseum.org/1kscvls.html (accessed August 20, 2009).

"Fort Mims State Historic Site, Tensaw, Alabama." http://www.exploresouthern history.com/fortmimsl.html (accessed July 7, 2010).

"James Henry Lane." *Territorial Kansas Online.* http://www.territorialkansas online.org/~imlskto/cgi-bin/index.php?SCREEN=bio_sketches/lane_james (accessed February 16, 2011).

Jones, Trevor M. "Thomas Pegg." *Encyclopedia of Oklahoma History and Culture.* http://digital.library.okstate.edu/encyclopedia/entries/P/PE008.html (accessed November 16, 2010).

Lemon, Holmes Willis. "Chickasaw Horse." *Official Site of the Chickasaw Nation.* http://www/chickasaw.net/history_culture/inter_681.htm (accessed October 2, 2012).

Kansas Historical Society. "Cool Things: First Kansas Colored Infantry Flag." http://www.kshs.org/cool2/coolflg1.htm (accessed August 20, 2009).

Lovegrove, Michael W. "Payne, David Lewis (1836–1884)." *Encyclopedia of Oklahoma History and Culture.* http://www.digital.library.okstate.edu/encyclopedia/entries/p/pa028.html (accessed August 31, 2011).

May, Jon. "Daniel Newman McIntosh." *Encyclopedia of Oklahoma History and Culture.* http://digital.library.okstate.edu/encyclopedia/entries/m/mc030.html (accessed December 8, 2010).

———. "Edwards's Post." *Encyclopedia of Oklahoma History and Culture.* http://digital.library.okstate.edu/encyclopedia/entries/E/ED008.html (accessed September 5, 2012).

———. "Fort McCulloch." *Encyclopedia of Oklahoma History and Culture.* http://digital.library.okstate.edu/encyclopedia/entried/F/FO036.html (accessed February 2, 2011).

———. "Tandy Walker." *Encyclopedia of Oklahoma History and Culture.* http://digital.library.okstate.edu/encyclopedia/entries/W/WA009.html (accessed December 8, 2010).

Museum of the Kansas National Guard. "1st Kansas Volunteer Colored Infantry." http://www.kansasguardmuseum.org/1kscvls.html (accessed August 8, 2009).

McCollum, Timothy James. "Delaware, Western." *Encyclopedia of Oklahoma History and Culture.* http://www.digital.library/okstate.edu/encyclopedia (accessed August 24, 2011).

McClellan, Michael E. "Britton Johnson." Texas State Historical Association, *The Handbook of Texas Online,* http://www.tshaonline.org/handbook/online/articles/fjo07 (accessed April 9, 2011).

Miami, Oklahoma, Visitors Center. "Indian Tribes." http: www.visitmiamiok.com/native/ (accessed July 28, 2011).

National Park Service, "Lava Beds National Monument California." http://www.nps.gov/labe/index.htm (accessed August 24, 2010).

"Only Survivor's Story of Tragedy, The." *Kansas Genealogy.* http://www.kansasgenealogy.com/indians/only_surivior.htm (accessed August 21, 2009).

"Poison Spring, Engagement at." *The Encyclopedia of Arkansas History and Culture.* http://www.encyclopediaofarkansas.net/encyclopedia/entry-detail.aspx?entryID=37 (accessed August 8, 2009).

"Red River War of 1874, The." *Texas Beyond History.* http://www.texasbeyondhistory.net/redriver/ind (accessed August 22, 2011).

Swan, Daniel C. "Native American Church." *The Encyclopedia of Oklahoma History and Culture.* http://www.digital.library/okstate.edu/encyclopedia (accessed September 9, 2011).

Warren, Steven L. "Battle of Middle Boggy." *The Encyclopedia of Oklahoma History and Culture.* http://digital.library.okstate.edu/encyclopedia/entries/M/MI006.html (accessed May 24, 2012).

Westmoreland, Ingrid P. "Albert Pike." *Encyclopedia of Oklahoma History and Culture.* http://digital.library.okstate.edu/encyclopedia/entries/P/PI006.html (accessed December 9, 2010).

INDEX

Barren Fork River, 191
Barton, Seth M., 1st Lt., 51
Bass, Col. Thomas Coke, 170; regiment, 179
Battle Creek, 80, 301
Battles; Achustenalah, 80- 86; Adobe Walls (Texas), 229; Chusto-Talasah, 76–78; Dove Creek (Texas), 230–3; First Cabin Creek, 156–61; Flat Rock Creek, 208–10, 213; Glorieta Pass (New Mexico Territory), 223; Honey Springs, 162–176, 181–2, 189, 202, 224, 226, 270, 272; Horseshoe Bend (Alabama), 11; Jenkins's Ferry (Arkansas), 203; Middle Boggy, 202–3; Newtonia (Missouri), 128–9; Pea Ridge (Elkhorn Tavern, Arkansas), 95–100, 118, 126, 128, 235; Perryville, 187–8 ; Poison Spring (Arkansas), 202–3; Round Mountains (Twin Mounds), 72–3; Second Cabin Creek, 210–217, 227; Soldier Spring, 293; Washita (Washita Massacre), 287–92; Wilson's Creek (Missouri), 58–9
Baxter Springs, Kansas, 105–6, 132, 155, 198, 296
Baylor, John, 45
Bayou Menard, 127
Baze, Jefferson P., 210, 213
Bear, Malucy, 69, 188
Beattie's Prairie, 129
Beauchamp, Pvt. P.G., 85
Beauregard, Gen. P. G. T., 235
Beaver Creek, 287
Beck family, 180
Beecher's Island, Colorado Territory, 286
beef cattle industry, 299, 304; Indian ranchers, 304
Bell, Caroline, 178
Bell, John, 56
Bell, Lt. Col. James M., 58–9, 164, 178, 237
Belmont, Kansas, 121, 139, 205
Bent, George, 58, 235–7, 311
Bent, William, 235, 239, 258
Bentonville, Arkansas, 96
Bertholf, Isaac, family, 176

Bethany, Oklahoma, 244
Big Cabin Creek, 278
Big Foot (Cashesegra, or Tracks Far Away), 27
Big Mountain, 97
Big Mouth, 259–60
Bigdoya, 305–6
Bird Creek, 74–5, 84
bison, 294–5; bison hunters, 283
Black Bear, 236
Black Bear Creek, 295
Blackbear, Eugene, Sr., 236
Black Beaver, 43, 47, 50, 86
Black Beaver Road, 50, 65–6, 84
Black Hawk, 282; Black Hawk War, 282
Black Kettle, 225, 234–6, 259–60, 284, 287–93
Blackburn's Prairie, 208
black soldiers, 131–3, 147–8, 157, 159–61, 210, 283
Bloomfield Academy, 189
Blue River, 126, 160
Blunt, Brig. Gen. James G., 104, 125, 129, 130, 139–40, 154, 160–3, 165–9, 171–2, 174, 181–3, 186,188, 198–9, 226, 247
Blythe, Emma, 217
Board of Indian Commissioners, 294
Boggy Depot, 27, 100, 177, 188, 200, 226, 247, 249
Boley, Oklahoma, 66
Bond, Dr. Thomas Jefferson, 29, 119–20
boomer movement, 303–4
Boone, Agent Albert G., 225, 227
border region , 198
Boston Mountains, 97
Boudinot, Elias, 11, 17, 18, 191
Boudinot, Maj. Elias C., 56, 58, 80, 84, 127, 153, 301–3
Boudinot, William, 301–2
Bourland, James, 224, 226; Bourland Border Regiment, 224
Bowles, Col. John, 168–9
Bowman, Dallas, 119, 169, 171, 174
Bowman, Granville, 119
boys endangered, 196–7, 220
Brazos Reserve, 25, 46–47, 229
Brazos River (Texas), 230
Brewer family, 192

Briartown, 136, 172–3, 184
Bristow, Oklahoma, 115
British-American conflict, 281
Britton, Wiley, 101, 111, 117–8, 129,
    145–6, 155–6, 166
"Brother Jones," 89
Brown, Milton, 249–50
Brown, Samuel W., 66
Brown's Creek, 70
Bruner, Joseph, 75, 78, 82–83, 265
brushmen, 224
Buckner, H. F., 61
Buffalo Creek, 260
Buffalo Head, Harry, 297
Buffalo Hump, 123
Bull Coming, Kathryn Nibbs, 236
Bumpass, 2nd Lt. William P., 118, 440
Burbank, John A., 254
Burnett, John, 19
Burns, Louis F., 67, 216
bushwhackers, 101, 112, 133–4, 146,
    150, 154–5
Butterfield Overland Mail, 30, 32

Cabell, Gen. William L., 154, 156–7,
    160–1, 171, 176–7, 183, 200
Cabin Creek, 27, 107, 156–61, 166, 199,
    207, 211, 215, 218
Cache Creek, 122, 249–50
Caddo County, Oklahoma, 123
Caddo Frontier Guard, 224, 248
Caddo Indians, 5, 6, 24, 25, 43, 46, 54,
    57, 65, 86, 116, 122–4, 138, 223,
    225, 243, 259, 293, 298, 302; chief,
    239; Reserve Caddos, 246; scouts,
    283; Whitebead band, 223
Caddo Jake, 226
Cahokia Indians, 280
calendar histories, 123
California, 299–300
California infantry, 229
California-Oregon border, 296
California Road, 27–8, 42
Camden, Arkansas, 201
Camp Canadian, 215
Camp John Ross, 135
Camp McIntosh, 126
Camp Napoleon meeting, 245–6, 248,
    300; Compact, 246
Camp Supply, 287, 292. See Fort Supply

Camp Weld, 235
Campbell, A. B., 93–94
Campbell, Maj. William T., 108–9;
    Lt. Col., 168, 170
Canada, 281–2, 298
Canadian River, 4, 5, 15, 17, 28, 64, 136,
    171, 173, 175–6, 182, 184, 186, 193,
    197, 203, 218, 227, 229, 247, 249, 292
Candler, William J., 159
Candy Mink Springs (Cherokee
    Nation), 57
Cane Hill, Arkansas, 129
Cantonment Davis. See Fort Davis
Captain, Augustus, 67
captives, 221–2, 261–2
Carleton, Brig. Gen. James H., 227, 229
Carr family, 192
Carruth, E. H., 55, 128
Carson, Col. Kit, 229, 237, 239
Castile, 223
cattle herders, 294
Caving (Cave-in) Banks. See Chusto-
    Talasah
Cedar Creek, 150
Central Plains, 225, 238, 285
Central Superintendency, 238, 254
Chalepah, Alonzo, 4, 292
Chandler Creek, 122
Chapman, Berlin B., 71
Checotah, Oklahoma, 64
Checote, Col. Samuel, 211, 275;
    Muscogee principal chief, 303
Cherokee Advocate, 28, 301–2
Cherokee Brigade, 191
Cherokee Female Seminary, 28–29
Cherokee Indians, 6–7, 11, 13, 87, 124,
    130, 146, 178, 198, 243, 247, 256,
    265; Camp Napoleon Compact,
    246; Civil War violence, 111–5 ;
    factionalism, 35–37, 139, 241, 258,
    272; meeting with Opothle Yahola,
    65; Old Settlers, 13, 18–19; refugees
    in Kansas, 85, 93, 95, 135, 139–40,
    154–5, 205; removal, 17–20;
    resettlement, 25; Ross (Union)
    Cherokees, 137, 139, 146, 210, 237,
    257, 263; Treaty Party, 18, 147
Cherokee Nation, 6, 28, 37, 87, 126–7,
    129–30, 133, 135, 139, 143–5, 148,
    178, 181, 191, 199, 203, 216, 231,

246, 263, 299–300; *Cherokee Nation v. Georgia*, 17; Confederate treaty, 67–8; education, 28–9; freedmen's allotments, 271; Keetoowah Nighthawks, 307; land, 306; Neutral Lands, 37, 56, 139, 277–8; peace agreement, 276–7; population estimates, 264; pro-Confederate exodus, 160, 178; records, 109; secession crisis; 57, 59; slavery ended, 269; Union agitators in, 160; wartime conditions, 195–7.

Cherokee Male Seminary, 29
Cherokee Neutral Lands, 37, 56, 130, 139, 242, 266–7
Cherokee Outlet, 260, 286, 293–5, 297, 303–4, 311; sold, 304
Cherokee Phoenix, 11, 90
Cherokee soldiers, 102, 117–8, 135–6, 148; Confederate-allied, 168, 182, 204, 208, 247; Union-allied, 170
Cherokee Tobacco Case, 301–2
Chestnut, Mary, 54
Chetopa (Kansas), 56, 130, 266, 278
Cheyenne and Arapaho Reservation, 311
Cheyenne and Arapaho Tribes, 236
Cheyenne Indians, 122, 221, 224–5; 233, 235–7, 239, 247, 253, 255, 258–62, 283–95, 300, 308; Chiefs Council of Forty-four, 284; Dog Soldiers, 233, 284; northern Cheyennes, 284; southern Cheyennes, 284; war dance tradition, 309; warrior societies, 284
Cheyenne, Oklahoma, 287
Chicago Times, 303
Chickasaw Indians, 6, 11, 13, 61, 65, 140, 178, 249–50, 256; government, 12; Loyal Chickasaws, 253, 258; refugees, 92–3, 95, 139, 205; removal, 20, 22; resettlement, 25; separation from the Choctaws, 23
Chickasaw Nation, 6, 125, 133, 197, 200, 221, 226, 237, 243, 247, 248–50, 283, 300; Camp Napoleon Compact, 246, 248; Confederate-allied troops raised, 60; declaration of independence, 51; government, 182; lands, 286, 306; population

estimates, 264; refugees in, 181, 189, 192–3, 267; schools, 29; slavery ended, 269
Chickasaw soldiers, 70, 96, 128–9, 135, 162, 164, 171, 248, 250–1
Chikaskia River, 239
Chimney Mountain, 162, 177
Chiricahua Apache Indians, 305–6; reservation, 305
Chisholm, Jesse, 43, 237–9, 258–61; ranch and trading post, 244
Chisholm Trail, 294
Chivington, Col. John M., 223, 235, 238
Choctaws, 23
Choctaw Agency, 89
Choctaw Brigade, 190, 201, 218
Choctaw Indians, 6, 11, 13, 23, 65, 140, 178, 219, 256; constitution, 12; government, 12, 182; refugees, 139; removal, 20–22, 26; resettlement, 25–6
Choctaw Nation, 21, 133, 142, 183, 186–9, 197, 201, 217, 226, 243, 247–9, 300, 311; Camp Napoleon Compact, 246; Confederate alliance, 45, 49; Confederate-allied troops raised, 60; declaration of independence, 51–2; education, 10, 29; lands, 6, 39, 286, 306; politics, 3; population estimates, 264; refugees in, 181, 189, 192–3, 265–6; slavery ended, 269; Union occupation, 175
Choctaw soldiers, 70, 73, 77, 96, 128–9, 135, 162, 164, 171, 202, 208, 218
Choska, 271
Chouteau, Auguste Pierre, 27
Chouteau, L. P., 237
Christianity, 9–10, 119; Christian, 294, 310
Christie, Captain, 138
Chunestotie, 91
Chupco, Jimmie, 265
Chupco, John, 23, 44, 55, 71, 274
Chusto-Talasah (Bird Creek), 74, 89, 91
citizenship, U.S., 9, 283, 301–2
Cimarron Cut-off, 225
Cimarron River, 69, 71, 89, 260, 282, 286
Citizen Potawatomi Indians, 298
Civil War, 87, 100, 102, 120, 152, 217, 221–2, 230, 251, 254; cost, 130;

Indian Territory, 175, 179, 216–7, 221, 238, 252, 258, 263–4, 272, 278, 280–2, 284, 286, 294–9, 309–12; post-war conditions, 263–269, 300–1, 305–7
Clardy, Roberta, 311
Claremore Mound, 215, 237
Clark, 161
Clark, Ben, 287, 290
Clarkson, Col. James J., 103, 107–8
Clarksville, Texas, 214
Clay, Henry, 31, 34, 133
Clear Boggy Creek, 188
Cleveland, Oklahoma, 74
Coahuila (Mexico), 231
Coffey, Col. John T., 104, 107
Coffin, Dr. A. V., 140
Coffin, Supt. of Indian Affairs William G., 106, 140–4, 152–3, 205–7, 241, 243
Coheia (Cowiya, Gopher John, John), 9
Colbert, Benjamin Franklin (Frank), 32
Colbert, Betsy, 31–2, 269–70
Colbert, Buck, 32
Colbert, Gov. Winchester, 189, 201, 248–9
Colbert, Holmes, 31–2, 269
Colbert, Julie, 32
Colbert, Polly, 31–2, 269–70
Colbert, Wash, 249
Colbert's Ferry, 27, 30, 226
Coleman, Isaac, 139
Colley, S. G., 138–9
Colorado, 103, 152, 222–3, 299; Colorado Territory, 122, 150, 225, 233–4, 261, 281; volunteers, 236
Comanche Indians, 4–5, 24, 28, 43, 46–7, 57, 65, 86, 116, 121–3, 138–9, 180, 221–4, 226–7, 236–9, 249–51, 253, 256, 258–9, 261, 283–5, 291–3, 299–300, 302, 311; Camp Napoleon Compact, 246; Chickasaw Nation raid, 249–51; Nokoni, 292–3; Penateka, 121–3, 228, 293; Quahadi, 224, 293; Yamparika, 293
commercial hunters, 294
Committee on the Conduct of the Present War, 101
communication lines, 299
Concharty, 73, 115

Conchate Emathla, 82
Concho River (Texas), 230
Confederacy (Confederate States of America), 3, 41, 94, 96, 100, 129, 140, 217, 223–4, 237, 240, 243–4, 248, 251; agitators, 65; guarantees to the Indian nations, 54, 96, 116, 127, 137, 153–4; Indian Department, 123; representatives to the Grand Council, 245
Confederate-allied Indians, 240–1, 253, 268
Confederate military, 95, 127, 129, 149–50, 177–8
Confederate soldiers, 80–81, 84–5, 122, 134–5, 145, 172, 175, 188, 210, 223, 231, 235, 244
Confederate Trans-Mississippi Department, 199, 244
Confederated Peoria Indians, 280, 300
Congress, 238, 242–3, 300
Conley, Robert J., 102
Constitution, 297
constitutional government, Indian, 29–30
Coodey, Ella, 147–8, 160, 189, 194–5, 216, 311

Coodey's Creek, 161
Coodey, William Shorey, 147
Coody family, 74
Coody's Bluff, 74
Cook, Lt. Horace A. B., 203–4
Cooley, Com. of Indian Affairs, D. N., 252, 256–8, 276
Cooper, Douglas H.; Agent, 43, 53; Brig. Gen., 108, 128, 154; Col., 60–61, 64, 68, 70–73, 75–80, 85–86, 90, 91, 99, 119, 128–9, 145, 160, 164, 171–4, 176, 181, 183, 186, 190, 199–200, 208, 215, 218, 244–5, 247; commander, Indian Territory, 127; Honey Springs battle, 161–3; possible Indian attacks on Kansas, 245–6
Cooweescoowee District, 278
Corinth, Mississippi, 235
Corn Stalk, 287, 290, 292
Cotchochee, 54
Cotton Wood Grove, 245

Durgan, Millie (Saintohoodie), 228–9, 261–2
Duval, George W., 210

Eastern Delaware Indians, 298
Eastern Shawnee tribe, 279, 300; reservation, 279, 296
Eastern Sioux Indians, 251
education, Euro-American, 8–10; federal support for, 29
Echo Harjo, 38, 64
Edwards, Elsie, 16
Edwards, James, 28
Edwards Trading Post (Edwards Store), 28
11th Texas Cavalry, 50
11th U. S. Colored Infantry, 214
Elk Creek (Dirty Creek, Durdy Creek), 34, 161–5, 167, 169–74, 182
Elk Creek (Texas) raid, 227–8, 230, 246, 261–2
Elk Mills, Missouri, 104
Elkhorn Tavern, Arkansas, 96–7
Elliot, Maj. Joel, 291–2
Ellis, Clyde, 309
Ellis, Joe, 65
Elm Spring, 250
Elm Springs, Arkansas, 96, 100
Emancipation Proclamation, 131, 137
Emory, Lt. Col. William H., 47–48, 50–51
Emperor Maxmillian of Mexico, 244
Enid, Oklahoma, 260
Ensworth, Emily, 296–7
Eonahpah (Trailing the Enemy), 288–90
Euchee (Uche, Yuchi) Indians, 43, 72, 130, 132, 139, 205
Euchee soldiers, 72, 101
Eufaula, Oklahoma, 193
Europe, 244; Europeans, 7
Evans, Gov. John, 223, 235; suspicion of Plains Indian-rebel alliance, 233–5
Evans, Maj. A. W., 293

Fairland, Oklahoma, 109, 265
Fall Leaf, Capt., 252, 298
Fall River (Kansas), 92
farming, Indian, 7, 8, 26–7

Farney, Sallie, 15–6
Farnsworth, Agt. F. W., 251–2
federal government, 4, 5, 9, 24, 86, 153, 221, 224, 234, 241, 262; 286, 296–7, 299, 301, 309; agents, 237–8; census, 264; commissioners, 285; excise tax, 301; Indian policy, 309; peace policy, 294
Felihkatubbee, Lewie, 219
Fields, Richard, 67
15th Kansas Cavalry, 121
5th Texas Cavalry Brigade, 208
5th Texas Partisan Rangers, 118, 157, 159, 164–5, 172, 214, 244
54th Massachusetts Infantry, 132
1st Battalion of Seminole Mounted Rifles, 60, 126, 210
1st California Cavalry, 229
1st Cavalry, 47, 49
1st Cherokee Regiment (Confederate-allied), 56, 157, 164, 198, 237, 277
1st Cherokee Mounted Rifles, created, 60, 74; desertion, 75–6, 79; Indian Home Guard (Union), 111
1st Chickasaw Battalion, 126
1st Indian Brigade, 208
1st Indian Home Guard Regiment, 102, 107–8, 129, 131, 133, 157, 167–8, 170, 199
1st Infantry, 48
1st Kansas Battery, 162, 171
1st Kansas Colored Volunteer Infantry Regiment, 131–3, 155–8, 162, 166–9, 171, 179, 201–2, 209–10, 214
1st Missouri Cavalry, 235
1st Nebraska Regiment, 253
1st New Mexico Cavalry, 229
1st Regiment of Choctaw and Chickasaw Mounted Rifles, 60, 72, 77, 99, 119, 126, 162, 169, 200, 202
1st Regiment of Colorado Volunteers, 223
1st Regiment of Creek Mounted Volunteers, 60, 72, 96, 116, 126, 157, 164, 171, 211–2
Fish, Lt. Oliver H., 51
Fitzpatrick, Elizabeth, 228, 261–2
Five Civilized Tribes, 6, 12, 242, 299–300, 302, 304, 306–7; Plains Indian

raids against, 25; purchase of Indian Territory, 23–4;

Flat Rock Creek, 108, 111, 209–10; Flat Rock Ford, 200

Flint District, Cherokee Nation, 114, 133, 146, 180, 270

Florida, 182

Folsom, Capt., 202

Folsom, Christine, 218

Folsom, Col. Sampson, 208, 249

Folsom, David, 8

Folsom, Israel, 3, 36, 40, 218

Folsom, Louisa Nail, 218

foodways, 296

Ford, John S. (Rip), 45–6

Foreman, Maj. John A., 157–8

Foreman, Stephen, 28–9, 90, 137, 149, 183–5, 311; Cherokee government official, 90, 176–7, 185; Pins, 113; pro-Confederate, 91, 108, 112; refugee, 113, 134–7, 175–6, 181, 183–5, 189

Foreman, Susie, 149, 176, 181, 183–5

Foreman, Taylor, 186

Forrester, Lt. Henry, 203

Fort Gibson, Cherokee Nation, 270–1

Fort Gibson National Cemetery, 180

Fort Smith, Arkansas, 30, 138, 145, 156, 177, 182–3, 203–4, 208, 278; federal district court, 301, 303

Fort Smith Council, 272–3, 275, 279; demands presented to the Indian nations, 256–7; Indian delegates, 248, 256–8; lands ceded, 258, 260

forts, 24–5, 51–2, 224–5; Fort Arbuckle, 25, 47–50, 122, 125, 193, 224, 249–50, 283; Fort Bascom, New Mexico Territory, 287, 293; Fort Belknap (Texas), 228; "Fort Blair," 198; Fort Blunt. See Fort Gibson, 145; Fort Chadbourne (Texas), 230; Fort Cobb, 25, 47–48, 86, 106, 122–3, 126, 239, 287, 292–3; Fort Coffee, 24; Fort Davis, 95, 108–9, 126, 129, 133, 136; Fort Dodge, Kansas, 286–7; Fort Gibson, 24, 28, 48, 76, 79, 95, 105,108, 124, 133, 135, 145–8, 154, 156–61, 163, 171, 173–9, 179–83, 186–8, 191, 193, 195–7, 199–200, 203, 205–6, 208, 210, 216, 220, 226–

7; 240, 263–4, 272, 279; Fort Laramie (Wyoming Territory), 261; Fort Larned (Kansas), 138, 227; Fort Leavenworth (Kansas), 50, 103–4; Fort Lyon (Colorado Territory), 235, 287; Fort Marion (Florida), 294, 306; Fort McCulloch, 126; Fort Murray (Texas), 227; Fort Pillow (Tennessee), 132; Fort Riley (Kansas), 252; Fort Scott (Kansas), 49, 55, 95, 105, 106, 111, 128, 139, 145, 154, 160, 198, 210, 212, 227, 267; Fort Sill, 250, 294, 306; Fort Smith (Arkansas), 28, 48–50, 96, 107, 127, 156, 197–8, 200, 203, 208, 214; Fort Supply, 294; Fort Towson, 24, 26; Fort Washita, 25, 47–50, 122, 193, 200, 244, 249–50; Fort Wayne, 24, 129, 144, 250; Fort Wise (Colorado Territory), 126, 180

Fort Worth, Texas, 227

Fos Harjo, 71

Fossett, Capt. Henry, 230–2

Foster, William (Hapetuke), 282

14th Kansas Cavalry, 130, 253

4th Artillery, 285

Fox Indians (Mesquakie), 24, 92, 139, 281–2, 300

freedmen ("free blacks"), 6, 35, 66, 70, 103, 106, 130–1, 179, 269–72; Cherokee, 276–7, 310; Chickasaw, 274; Choctaw, 274; Muscogee, 276, 310–11; rights guaranteed, 256; Seminole, 275, 303

Freedmen's Bureau, 270

Freedom, Oklahoma, 260

freighters, 294

Fremont, John C., 69, 73

French, 281–2; French-British rivalry, 281

frontier militia (Texas), 231

Frozen Rock, 48, 147, 161

furs, 221; fur trade, 281

Gaabohonte (Crow Bonnet), 122

Galveston, Texas, 273

Gano, Brig. Gen. Richard M., 207–16, 218–9, 227; "Gano's Crossing" (Southwest 38th Street, Tulsa, Oklahoma), 215

Garrett, William H., 43
Garvin, Choctaw Gov. Isaac L., 302
Garvin County, 249
General Council of the Indian Nations,
    201
Georgetown, Texas, 165
Georgia, 307
Geronimo (Goyathlay), 305
Gettysburg, Pennsylvania, 160
Gibson, Arrell Morgan, 22, 27, 42, 197
Gibson, Martha, 193–4
Gideon, 196
Gillentine, Capt. N. W., 230–1
Gillett, Capt. L. E. Gillett, 162, 164
Gillpatrick, Dr. Rufus, 147
goldfields, 225
Good, Capt. John J., 82
Goombi, 229
Gordon, Capt. William, 162
grafters, 308
Graham, Thomas, 189
grain production 299
Grand Council, 243, 248, 300; interna-
    tional council, 303, 305
Grand (Neosho) River, 27, 94, 107, 108,
    125, 156, 159, 161–2, 179, 191, 206,
    209, 211, 265, 279
Granby, Missouri, 128
Grant, Gen. Ulysses S., 244, 256, 293
Gratiot Street Military Prison, 235
Grayson, George Washington (Wash;
    Wolf Warrior; Yaha Tustunuggee),
    116–8, 149–50, 166, 173, 186–7,
    203–5, 210–16, 219, 267–8, 275,
    307, 311
Grayson, Georgeanna "Annie"
    Stidham, 52–3, 267, 311
Grayson, James, 186
Grayson, Jennie, 116, 186–7
Grayson, Malone, 187
Grayson, Mary, 31, 271
Grayson, Pilot, 187, 267
Grayson, Sam, 187, 267
Grayson, Watt, 54
Great Lakes, 230, 279, 281
Great Nemaha Reservation, 252
Great Plains, 230, 262, 278
Great Salt Plains, 126
Great Western Trail, 294
Green, Col. Martin E., 58

Green Corn Ceremony, 13
greenbacks, 254
Greeno, Capt. Harris S., 109
Greenwood, A. B., 39
Greenwood, Harris, 249
Gregory, James Roane, 43, 72–3, 115
Greyeyes, 282
Griscom, Sgt. George L., 70, 72–3,
    77, 79
gristmills, 128
Grove, Oklahoma, 100
guardians, 308
guerrillas (irregulars), 129–32, 143;
    guerrilla warfare, 198
Gulager family, 192
Gulf of Mexico, 273; Gulf Coast, 223,
    300
Gurley, O. W., 311
Guthrie, Oklahoma, 311

habeas corpus, 297
Hainai Indians, 223
Halleck Tastanaki (Tustunuggee),
    71, 81
Hancock, Gen. Winfield Scott, 284
Hanks family, 192
Hard Rope (Wehesaki), 67, 150–2,
    287–8
Harlan, Agt. Justin, 144, 154–5, 195,
    206, 263
Harlan, James W., 273
Harlow, Sec. of the Interior William,
    276
Harney, Brig. Gen. W. S., 256
Harris, Lt. Col. J. D., 126
Harrison, Col. Charles, 159
Hart's Spies, 126
Hauptman, Lawrence M., 39
haying, 208, 210, 214
Hazen, Col. William B., 287, 292
Hazous, Sam, 305
Heap of Birds, Alfrich, 289–90
Hebert, Col. Louis, 99
Helena, Arkansas, 160
Henderson, Sen. John B., 285
Hendrix, Annie Eliza, 196–7
Hess, Earl J., 97, 98, 99
Hethuska (War Dance), 297
Hicks, Abijah, 63, 112, 217
Hicks, Charles, 11

Martin, Joseph L. (Joe), 158, 211
Masonry; Indian Masons, 28; Masonic
    Lodges, 28
Massacre Canyon, 295
Massard Prairie, Arkansas, 208
Matthews, Col. A. C., 248
Maxey, Brig. Gen. Samuel Bell, 190,
    199, 208; importance of the Indian
    Territory, 190; refugee responsibil-
    ity, 192–3; relationship with the
    Indian nations, 190
Mayes, Joel B., 58, 198
Mayfield, Huston, 162
McAdoo, Brig. Gen. J. D., 231–3
McAlester, Oklahoma, 301
McAnally, Valentine, 117, 212
McCabe, Edwin P., 311
McCanaless, musician, 195
McClain County, 249
McCormick, Mary F., 23
McCulloch, Brig. Gen. Ben, 53–4, 56–7,
    74, 96–97, 99
McCulloch, Brig. Gen. Henry E., 199
McCusker, Phil, 124
McDaniel family, 74
McGhee family, 278
McIntosh, Col. Daniel N., 15, 53–4, 68,
    72, 76, 78, 96, 99, 116, 126, 135–6,
    138, 148–9, 154, 164, 191, 201, 215
McIntosh, Col. James, 79–84, 86, 90
McIntosh faction, 15, 17, 64
McIntosh family, 83–84, 87, 263
McIntosh, Lt. Col. Chilly, 14–15, 53,
    54, 72, 126, 149, 166–7
McIntosh, Roley, 32
McIntosh, William, 12, 14–15, 149
McIntosh, William (slave), 68, 263
McIntosh place, 174
McLoughlin, William, G., 35–6, 58–9
McPherson, George, family, 264.
    See Mrs. Tom Rattling Gourd
McQuirk, Lt., 82
Medicine Lodge, Kansas, 284, 299
Melton family, 74
Menawa, 14
Mertzon, Texas, 231
Mescalero Apache Indians, 251
Methodists, 136
Mexico, 180, 193, 230–1, 233, 246,
    282, 306

Miami Indians, 253, 255, 280, 296
Miami, Oklahoma, 280
Micco Hutke, 65, 66
Michigan, 280–1
Michigamea Indians, 280
Middle Boggy, 200
Miller Brothers 101 Ranch, 308–9;
    powwow, 309
Miller, Pvt. Henry, 81
"million dollar wagon train," 216.
    See Battles: Second Cabin Creek
minutemen (Texas), 223
missionaries, Christian, 3, 8–10, 13,
    17, 20, 30, 44; Baptist, 10, 29,
    37; Congregationalist, 10, 29;
    Methodist, 10, 20; 29; Moravian,
    10; Presbyterian, 10, 20, 19;
    slavery issue, 35–36
Mississippi River, 235, 281, 300
Missouri, 3, 5, 13, 42, 58, 95, 100, 103,
    107, 128–9, 131, 138, 140, 144–5,
    165, 200, 227, 244–5, 279–81
Missouri cavalry, 128, 202
Missouri River, 295, 297, 300
Missouri State Guard, 58, 103
Missouria Indians, 254, 295, 309
mixed-blood Indians, influence, 8
moral impact of the war, 219–21;
    decline of churches, 220; gambling,
    219; licentiousness, 219; profanity,
    219
Modoc Indians, 296; Modoc Reserve,
    296
Mokohoko, 282
Montana, 297
Moonlight, Capt. Thomas, 105, 106;
    Lt. Col., 171
Mosaio, 289
Mosely settlement, 249–50
Mount Vernon Barracks, Alabama, 306
Mountain View, Oklahoma, 229
Moving Behind, 287–90, 292
Mudeater, Chief Matthew, 281
mules, 212–5, 218, 221, 249
Mulkey, Lt., 231–2
Munahwe, Jackson, 215–6
Murrow, Joseph S., 44, 89, 95, 96, 99,
    100, 134
Muscogee Coweta Town, 116, 149
Muscogee (Muskogee) Indians, 6, 11,

Okmulgee Convention; 299–300; Constitution, 299–300

Oktarharsars Harjo (Sands), 27, 53–4, 64–66, 275

Olathe, Kansas, 198, 298

Old Greer County, 293

Old Northwest, 280

Old Settlers, 13, 18–9, 41, 57

Omaha Indians, 297

Omaha, Nebraska, 297

100th meridian, 294

Opothle Yahola, 14, 27, 35, 53, 54, 64–66, 68–69, 115, 141–2, 153, 241–3, 263, 275, 311; followers, 136, 265; hostility to the McIntosh faction, 241; Kansas, 87; nicknames, 89; refugee in Kansas, 91, 93, 103, 132–3; withdrawal from the Indian Territory, 69–87, 89–90, 179, 181;

Oregon, 297, 299

Oregon Trail, 296

Osage Agency (Kansas), 197

Osage Battalion, 237

Osage County, Kansas, 92, 139, 150

Osage County, Oklahoma, 294

Osage Indians, 4–5, 24, 27, 43, 61, 67, 85, 92, 102, 105, 116, 124, 139, 143, 150–2, 206, 216, 230, 243, 247, 252–3, 256, 258–9, 263, 265, 285, 293–5, 302, 304, 307–8; beheading, 152; Big Hill Osages, 150–1; Big Osages, 67; Black Dog band, 150; Confederate-allied Osage surrender, 248; country, 297; headrights, 308; Kansas reservation, 150, 152, 242; Little Osages, 67; trailers (scouts), 287, 290–1; war dance tradition, 309; "world's richest Indians," 308

Osage Mission, Kansas, 67, 205

Osage River Agency, Kansas, 255

Osage trails, 84–5

Osecola, 23

Otoe Indians, 254, 295, 309

Otoe-Missouria Indians. See Otoe and Missouria

Ottawa County, Oklahoma, 125, 279

Ottawa Indians, 242, 279–81, 299, 302; chief, 283; Ottawa Reservation (Kansas), 139, 242; Ottawa University, 280

Outbreak of 1874, 294. See Red River War

Pacific Coast, 227, 278

Pacific Northwest, 298

Packer, 289

Palmer, Dr., 143

Panola County, Chickasaw Nation, 193

Papequah, 230–1

Park Hill, 28, 57, 63, 67, 108, 109, 144, 181, 191

Park Hill Mission, 113–4

Parker, Col. Eli S., 256

Parker, fed. judge Isaac C., 303

Parker, Quanah, 310

Parker family, 74

Parks, Capt. R. C., 104

Pascofar, 71

Passen, Peter, 63

Patterson, 249

Pawnee Fork, Kansas, 284

Pawnee Indians, 5, 24, 43, 61, 116, 252, 293, 295, 297, 307; Pawnee Nation, 252; war dance tradition, 309

Payne, David L., 303

Payne, Capt. Eugene, 102

Payne County Historical Society, 71

Pea Ridge, Arkansas, 96

peace chief, 225. See Cheyenne Indians

peace policy, 294. See federal government

Pecan, 230–1

Pegg, Maj. Thomas, 41, 60, 67, 75; Acting Principal Chief, Cherokee Nation, 41, 87; 137

Pennington Creek, 249

Pensacola, Oklahoma, 156, 211

Peoria Indians, 253, 255, 280, 296

Perry, Seymour, 34

Perryman, Jacob, 68, 84, 132; Sgt., 1st Indian Home Guard, 201

Perryman, Joseph, 240, 269

Perryman, Mose, 31, 68, 271

Perryman, Patsy, 270

Perryman, Thompson, 240–1

Perryman family, 34, 77, 132, 272

Perryman slaves, 68

Perryville, 27–8, 183–4, 187–8, 199, 226

Petun Indians, 280–1

peyote religion. *See* Native American Church

Phillips, Col. William A., 127, 135–6, 138, 140, 144–7, 154, 160, 197, 200, 207, 243

Piankashaw Indians, 5, 24, 65, 120, 253, 255, 280

Pike, Brig. Gen. Albert, 61, 190, 244; commander, Provisional Army of the Department of Indian Territory, 61, 91, 95–100, 116–8, 125–7; Confederate commissioner, 52–3, 56, 5–58, 67; Pike-McCulloch treaties, 57, 60, 96; 32nd degree Mason, 52; Wichita Agency tribes' treaties, 57–8, 65, 121, 123, 224

Pin Indians, 37, 56, 57–60, 79, 87, 112–4, 128, 147, 186, 191, 196, 211, 213, 247. *See* Keetoowah Society.

Pitchlynn, Capt. William B., 77

Pitchlynn, Peter P., 3, 21, 30, 40, 45, 52, 248

places, sacred, 299

Placido (Hashukana, Can't Kill Him), 46, 123–4

Plains Apache Indians, 5, 24, 122, 221–2, 224–5, 229, 236, 239, 253, 258, 260–1, 285, 287, 292, 302. *See* Apache Tribe of Oklahoma

Plains Indians, 5, 46, 75, 86, 191, 198, 201, 221–2, 233, 237, 239, 241, 247, 249, 283, 286, 295, 300; raiding, 223–4, 251, 283–5, 293, 295; rumored ready to fight for the Confederacy, 237; suspected alliance with the rebel army, 234–5

Platt River, 225, 237–8, 260–1; South Platte River, 225

Pleasant Bluff, 203

Pockmark, Jim, 247; Caddos, 247

Poe, Matilda, 34

Poison Spring, Arkansas, 201

Pomeroy, Samuel, 242

Ponca City, Oklahoma, 260, 297, 308

Ponca Indians, 296–7

Ponca Reservation, 298

Pontotoc County, Chickasaw Nation, 219, 249

Poor Bear, 226, 259

Pope, Maj. Gen. John, 238

Porter, Lt. Pleasant, 209, 213, 269

Possum, 50

Potawatomie (Pottawatomie) Indians, 92, 232, 252–3, 279, 281; Citizen Band, 281; Prairie Band, 281

powwow development, 309–10

Prairie Grove, Arkansas

Presbyterians, 136

Price, Maj. Gen. Sterling, 95–6, 144, 207, 227, 234

Pricked Forehead, 226

Prince, Capt. William E., 49

prisoners killed, incidents of, 198, 202–3, 210. *See* wounded killed, incidents

Proctor, Special Agent A. G., 195–7

Pryor Creek, 214

public land, 301

Puckinachubbe, 249

Pumpkin Ridge, 163–4, 171

Pushmataha, 11

Putuaputiquay (One Who Looks after His Son), 291

Quantrill, Capt. William Clarke, 37, 150, 198–200, 298; Lawrence, Kansas raid, 198

Quapaw Agency, 279, 296–8

Quapaw Creek, 80

Quapaw Indians, 6, 24, 65, 66–7, 93, 103, 139, 253, 256, 258, 279, 300, 302; lands, 125

Quapaw Reservation, 280

Quapaw Tribe of Oklahoma, 309

Quartz Mountain State Park, 293

Quayle, Lt. Col. William, 70, 72, 77

Rabbit Ford, 161

railroads, 238, 273–4, 278, 283, 285, 295, 300–2; Railway Act, 242; railroad lobby, 300; St. Louis and San Francisco Railroad, 303; Union Pacific Railroad, 238

Rainy Mountain Creek, 123

Ramsey, James R., 44, 55

Ransom, George, 239

Rattlesnake Mountains, 163

Rattling Gourd, Mrs. Tom, 264. *See* George McPherson family

Reagan, Col. W. D. Reagan, 244, 246

Scanland, Capt., 164, 172
Scarrel, Joab, 62
Schonmakers, Father John, 67, 150
Schrimpscher family, 192
Schuarte, Lt. Col. Frederick W., 170
Schurz, Sec. of the Interior, Carl, 302
Scott, James, 69–70, 72, 84–5
Scott, Lizzie, 69
Scott, Supt. S. S., 124–5, 127, 192
Scott, Winfield, 15
Scott's Mill, Missouri, 135
Sealy settlement, 249
secession, 3
2nd Arkansas Mounted Riflemen, 80–1
2nd Cavalry, 46
2nd Cherokee Mounted Rifles, 80,
    83–4, 98–9, 164, 178, 211
2nd Colorado Infantry (Cavalry),
    157–8, 167–8
2nd Creek Mounted Volunteers, 63,
    116, 118–9, 149, 154, 164, 166, 171,
    173, 186, 203, 209–12
2nd Indian Home Guard Regiment,
    102–3, 108, 150, 157, 162, 167,
    169–70, 204
2nd Kansas Battery, 157, 160
2nd Kansas Cavalry, 209–10
2nd Kansas Colored Volunteer Infantry
    Regiment, 132, 198–9, 214
Sells, Elijah, 256
Sell's Store, 70
Seminole Indians, 87, 124, 132, 178,
    182, 218, 243, 247, 256, 258, 272,
    298; Camp Napoleon Compact,
    246; Loyal Seminoles, 253, 265;
    meetings with Opothle Yahola, 54,
    65; refugees, 85–6, 93, 95, 139, 205,
    265; removal, 22–3; resettlement,
    23, 25, 27, 43; separation from the
    Muscogees, 6, 8–9, 12, 23; Union
    Seminoles, 170
Seminole Nation, 6, 127, 133, 216, 281,
    300, 311; Confederate-allied, 57;
    division in 1861, 55; education, 29;
    lands, 274, 276, 303, 306; popula-
    tion estimates, 264; Reconstruction
    treaty, 274; slavery ended, 269;
    southern Seminole surrender, 248
Seminole soldiers, 70, 72, 101, 117–8,
    135, 200, 203–4, 208, 211

Senate (U.S.), 226
Seneca Indians, 6, 12, 24, 65, 67, 139–
    40, 146, 159, 253, 256, 258, 279,
    281, 300
Seneca-Cayuga tribe, 279
Seneca-Shawnee Indians, 279
Sepping, Henry, 162
Sequoyah (George Gist, or Guess), 10
Sequoyah, State of, 307
Sergeant Major Creek, 291
Setangia (Sitting Bear), 227
7th Cavalry, 285, 287–8
Seward, William H., 39
Shawnee Agency, 298
Shawnee Indians, 5–6, 24, 28, 46, 65,
    67, 103, 124, 138–9; 143, 197, 242,
    253, 256, 258; Absentee Shawnees,
    120–1; Black Bob Band (Loyal
    Shawnees), 121, 198, 298–9; east-
    ern, 139
Shawnee, Oklahoma, 281, 298
Shawnee Prophet, 10
Shea, William L., 97–9
Shelby, Col. Joseph, 128
Sheppard, Joe, 62, 270–1
Sheppard, Morris, 62, 270–1
Sheppard, W. T., 213
Sheridan, Maj. Gen. Philip, 286, 293
Sherman, Lt. Gen. William T., 286
Shirley brothers, 124
Shirley, John, 47
Shirley, William, 47
Shirley's Trading Post, 57
Shoal Creek, 125
Showetat (George Washington), 57, 223
Simon, Ben, 124
Sims, Col. William B., 74–5, 77
Sinecha, 16
Sioux Indians, 252
6th Kansas Cavalry, 108–9, 160, 162,
    167–8, 170, 188
6th Texas Cavalry, 80–81, 84
Skiatook, Oklahoma, 80
Skiatooka's place, 74
Skullyville, 208
slave codes, 35; codes tightened, 45
slave owners, 35, 179; increasing polit-
    ical power, 35
slavery, abolished, 256; issue, 30–1,
    3–36, 44

slaves, 6–8, 30–1, 218, 264–5; agitation among,160; conditions of, 31–4; emancipation, 130, 137–8; enlistment, 131; Muscogee-Seminole issue, 8–9; Opothle Yahola appeal to, 66; prohibitions against educating, 34; purchase of freedom, 34–5; religion, 34; runaways, 9, 66, 68, 70, 103, 106, 121, 131–3, 178, 218, 264; sale in 1861, 61–2; sent (taken) away, 61, 68, 179; skills of, 34, 132; theft of, 22, 37; threats toward, 35
Slover, James Anderson, 36
Smith, James M. C., 72
Smith, Lt. Gen. Edmund Kirby, 199, 244–5, 248
Smoky Hill River, 122, 225, 233, 236, 284
Society of Friends, 256, 294
Soda Spring, 177
Sodom, 135
Soldier Peak, 293
Soldier Spring, 293
soldiers, Indian; mounted, 61
Sonaki Mikko (Sonukmikko, Billy Bowlegs), Capt., 55, 71, 130, 170.
South Dakota, 297
South Kansas–Texas Regiment, 80
southern states, Indian ties to, 44
sovereignty, 11, 21
Spavinaw Creek, 103, 107
Spears, Captain, 149
Spears, William, 114
Speight's regiment, 232
Spencer Academy, 34
Sperry, Oklahoma, 74
Spillman, Capt. Andrew C., 191–2
Spokogee, 82–3
Spotted Wolf, 226
Spring Frog, 137
Spring River, 107, 125, 297
Springfield, Missouri, 58, 95
St. Louis, 58, 95, 235
Stackpole, Maj., 209
Staked Plains, 227, 293
stampede, the, 175, 181, 188–9
Standard, 214
Standing Bear, 297
Standing-in-Water, 226, 236
Stanton, Edwin, 102

Starr, Myra, 269
Starr, Tom, 62
State of Oklahoma, 221, 310
"states blacks," 310–1
Steele, Brig. Gen. William, 145, 154, 177, 182–3, 186, 188
Stidham, George W., 30, 53, 54, 62, 68, 113, 136, 173–4, 302; family, 267, 269
Stidham Georgeanna (Annie), 267
Stillwater, Oklahoma, 260
Stillwell, Oklahoma, 133, 146
Stith, 1st Lt. Charles H., 212, 214
Stonewall, Oklahoma, 249
stragglers, 224, 227, 233
Strong Bow, 236
Strong City, Oklahoma, 287
Stumbling Bear, 229
Sturgis, Capt. Samuel D., 37, 49–51; Maj., 58; Wilson's Creek, 58
Sugar Creek, 122
Sully, Brig. Gen. Alfred, 286–7
Sulphur, Oklahoma, 222
Summit, Oklahoma, 162
Sundance, 122, 239
surrender of Arkansas, Louisiana, Missouri, and Texas, 245–6
surveyors, 294

Tahlequah, 28, 57, 67, 108–9, 126, 191, 196, 270
Tamaha, Oklahoma, 203
Tamaroa Indians, 280
Tawakoni (Tawaconi) Indians, 25, 46, 54, 139, 142, 302
Tawakoni Jim, 305
Taovaya Indians, 46
taxes, 264
Taylor family, 270
Taylor, Judy, 270
teamsters, 212
Tecumseh, 10, 281
T'ene-badai (Bird-Appearing), 122
Ten Bears, 226, 285, 299
10th Cavalry, 283
10th Illinois Cavalry, 104
10th Kansas Infantry, 107
territorialization, 300
Texas, 3, 28, 42, 45, 48, 52, 57–8, 107, 123, 126, 127, 145, 148, 176, 200–1,

292, 294–5, 298; contractors, 226; military, 227, 235, 258, 279
U. S. Cavalry, 123, 204
U. S. Congress, 94, 302, 307
U. S. Geological Survey, 307
U. S. Highway 81, 294
U.S. House of Representatives, 306
U. S. Senate, 306; Committee on Territories, 302
U. S. Supreme Court, 301–2
Unassigned Lands, 274, 303. *See* Oklahoma
Union army, 281; (federal) forces, 130, 135–6, 148, 150, 160, 172–4, 184–5, 188, 193, 216; *See* Yankees.
Union Indian Brigade, 117, 128, 148, 272
Union Indians, 106, 178, 237, 240, 268
Union Mission, 27
Union scouts, 208–9
United States, 3–4, 132, 134, 137, 152, 236, 238, 241–3, 246–8, 252–3, 284, 295, 298, 300
Union sympathizers, 208
Union veterans, 280
Upper Arkansas Agency, 225, 227
Upshaw, A. M. M., 22
Ute Indians, 287; scouts, 229

Van Buren, Arkansas, 96, 112
Vandiver, Mr., 269
Van Dorn, Maj. Gen. Earl, 46, 95–7, 99–103, 126
Vann, Clarinda, 33
Vann (Van)-Coodey family, 34, 74, 79, 178, 189, 192
Vann, James, 8
Vann, Jim, 32–3
Vann, John Salaule, 147; Mrs. Vann, 147, 189
Vann, Joseph, 70
Vann, Lt. Col. Clement Neeley, 208, 277
Vann, Lucinda, 33
Vann, R. P., 198
Vann, "Rich Joe," 34
Vann, "Young Joe," 34
Verden, Oklahoma, 255
Verdigris River, 79–80, 92, 125, 126, 135, 151, 161, 179, 215, 240, 265, 275
Verner, Joseph, 67

Vicksburg, Mississippi, 160
Vinita, Oklahoma, 301
Virginia, 240, 245
Vore, Maj. Israel G., 189, 244

Waco Indians, 25, 46, 302
Wade, Mrs., 186
Wagoner, Oklahoma, 200–9, 301
Walker family, 278
Walker, George Washington (Tahlakitehi), 56, 130, 266–7, 278
Walker, Lt. Col. Tandy, 60, 128, 162, 164, 171, 191, 201–2; Governor, Choctaw Nation, 60
Walker, Rachel Rogers, 56, 130, 267
Wallace, Pvt. Dixon, 202
Walker, Madam C. J., 311
Walnut Creek (Kansas), 126
Wapanucka Academy, 249
War Bonnet, 226, 234, 236
War Department, 102
Ward, James, 114
Ward, Rochelle Allred, 179–81
Warren, Oklahoma, 292–3
Wars: American Revolution, 102; Green Peach, 301; Nez Perce, 298; Red Stick War, 102; Second Seminole War, 23; War of 1812, 11, 102; World War I, 309; World War II, 309
Washington, 297, 299
Washington, Booker T., 311
Washington, D.C., 226, 278, 289, 300–2, 306
Washita River (Lodge Pole River), 4, 25, 47, 50, 122, 124, 193, 239, 245–6, 249, 287–8, 293, 308
Washita Massacre (Battle of the Washita), 287–92
Watie, Saladin, 192
Watie, Sarah Caroline Bell (Sallie, Sally), 158, 191–2, 199, 247; concern for Saladin Watie, 220–1
Watie, Stand, 17–20; Cherokee Nation principal chief, 248; Civil War period, 36, 56, 59, 60, 79–80, 83–4, 86, 90–1, 96, 98, 100,103–4, 105–7, 109, 111, 126–7, 129–30, 136, 145, 147, 153–4, 157–9, 161, 164, 170–1, 176–8, 181–2, 191–2, 195–9, 203–5, 208–11, 214–6, 218–9, 227, 238,

240, 247–8, 265, 277; government,137, 176, 185; Indian Brigade commander, 248; post-war period, 300–1; regiment of, 148; supporters, 138
Wattles, Lt. Col. Stephen H., 107, 129, 211
Wea Indians, 65, 253, 255, 280, 300
weather, 137. *See* drought
Webber, Charles, 91
Webber's Falls, 59, 62, 100, 133, 145, 147–8, 160, 178, 195, 203
Webster College for Boys, 58
Weer (Weir), Col. William, 104–11, 125
Wells Spring, 249
Wequahoka, 303
Western Delawares, 298
whiskey, 136, 296
White, Charlotte Johnson, 33–4
White Antelope, 225, 234–6
White Bear (Satanta), 229
White Bull, 226
White Eagle, 297
White Shield Creek, 308
White Oak, Arkansas, 201
white settlement, 255
white soldiers in Indian units, 119, 218; surrender, 248
Whitefield, Oklahoma, 208
Whitehorn, Charles, 4
Whitfield, Maj. J. W., 79
Wichita Agency, 25, 47–8, 57, 121, 123–4, 138–9, 142, 223–4, 264; tribes, 258
Wichita Falls, Texas, 228
Wichita Indians, 4–5, 6, 24, 43, 46, 54, 57, 65, 122–4, 129, 256, 259, 284; 293, 295, 298, 305; Wichita Village, 46, 95, 223
Wichita, Kansas, 51, 124, 259
Wichita Mountains, 122, 126, 224, 249–50, 292, 294

Wild Cat, 23
"wild tribes," 152, 205
Williams, Capt. James M., 131–3, 156–7; Col., 156–9, 166, 168, 202, 214
Williams, John, 311
Williams, Loula, 311
Willis, Britt, 34
Willis, Minerva, 34
Willis, Wallace, 34
Willets, Col. Charles, 130, 200
Wilson, John, 283
Wisconsin, 280–1
Wistar, Thomas, 256
Wolf Creek, 287
Woman's Heart, 293
wood cutters, 294
Woodall, Daniel, 196–7
Woodson County, Kansas, 139
Woodward, Oklahoma, 286
Woodward County, Oklahoma, 287
Worcester, Samuel Austin, 63, 112
wounded killed, incidents, 198, 202–3. *See* prisoners killed, incidents
Wright, Muriel H., 71
Wyandot (Wyandotte) Indians, 242, 256, 279–81, 300
Wyandotte, Oklahoma, 265
Wyoming, 297

Yale, Oklahoma, 71
Yankees, 127, 172–3, 213
Yeary, Pvt. James Knox Polk, 214
Yellow Buffalo, 226
Yellow Wolf, 226
Yellowman, Peace Chief Gordon, 284
Young, Col., 82
Young, Col. William C., 123
Young County, Texas, 228
Younger, Cole, 200

Zellar, Gary, 35

MARY JANE WARDE is the author of *Washita* and
George Washington Grayson and the Creek Nation, 1843–1920.